SHAKEN & STIRRED:

THE FEMINISM OF JAMES BOND

SHAKEN & STIRRED:

THE FEMINISM OF JAMES BOND

REVISED EDITION

Robert A. Caplen

The opinions expressed herein are solely those of the author and neither represent nor reflect the views of any other individual or entity. This publication has not been prepared or licensed by, and is not affiliated with any individual or entity that has created, produced, or maintained an affiliation or involvement with the James Bond novels or films.

Library of Congress Control Number:		2012914074
ISBN:	Paperback	0985996102
	Hardback	0985996110
	E-book	0985996129

Join the *Shaken & Stirred*™ discussion—
http://www.bondgirlbook.com
http://www.facebook.com/bondgirlbook
http://www.facebook.com/bondgirlbook2

Contents

In loving memory of Eleanor and Harry

Note to the 2012 Edition

When *Shaken & Stirred: The Feminism of James Bond* was released in October 2010, MGM was teetering on the brink of bankruptcy. The James Bond franchise suspended development and production of its twenty-third film, and it was unclear whether James Bond's license to kill would expire as part of MGM's anticipated demise or simply be renewed after a long hiatus.

Ultimately, MGM averted a financial collapse, and development and production of "Bond 23" resumed without significant delay. *Skyfall*, which stars Daniel Craig in his third mission as Agent Double-O-Seven, is currently scheduled for a November 2012 release in the United States. The timing could not be better, as this year marks the golden anniversary of the first James Bond film, *Dr. No*. Numerous official (and unofficial) celebrations and retrospectives have been planned across the world to commemorate this significant cinematic and cultural milestone. And James Bond recently found himself featured alongside Queen Elizabeth II on the largest world stage: the opening ceremonies for the Games of the XXX Olympiad in London.

Shaken & Stirred: The Feminism of James Bond has received tremendous interest and enthusiastic support during the short period it has been available publicly. I am particularly appreciative of Bruce Scivally, coauthor of *James Bond: The Legacy*, for his comments and suggestions, which are incorporated into this revised edition. I also am grateful to Gloria Hendry and Lois Chiles, two significant contributors to the Bond Girl archetype, for sharing with me their thoughts and impressions about this work.

The *Shaken & Stirred*™ literary series, which will also include a volume entitled *The Post-Feminism of James Bond* that is currently in development, is an independent endeavor with one mission: to explore the impact of the feminist and Women's Liberation movements upon popular culture in a scholarly, but accessible and entertaining, manner. It is my hope that this volume, the first chapter of the Bond Girl's journey, invigorates discussion about Ian Fleming's creation and sheds light upon the evolution of our conceptions about gender equality over the last fifty years.

— Robert A. Caplen
Washington, DC, August 2012

Preface

It's estimated that half the world's population has seen at least one James Bond movie.

—*Playboy*[1]

I still don't understand the appeal of the Bond films, though I respond to them as faithfully as millions of other people.

—Vincent Canby[2]

For nearly half a century, James Bond has maintained a place at the "forefront of popular culture, continuously . . . reflect[ing]—and often anticipat[ing]—changing social attitudes, major developments in world politics, and shifting trends in popular fiction and cinema culture."[3] The cultural saturation is nothing short of a phenomenon[4] of "a rather peculiar kind."[5] Numerous books catalogue the Bond films, both the "official" EON Productions films as well as two "unofficial" installments: *Casino Royale* in 1967 and *Never Say Never Again* in 1983. Former members of the Bond cinematic community have penned tributes, behind-the-scenes reflections, and other works celebrating both the Bond phenomenon and their unique insights into the world's most identifiable secret agent.

A new wave of scholarly critiques of the original Ian Fleming novels has also emerged, and these works share bookshelves with pictorial celebrations of the Bond Girls, encyclopedias chronicling every imaginable gadget from Q Branch, role playing guidebooks, and new editions of Fleming's works. In the realm of multimedia, digital trivia dossiers, numerous video games supported by different platforms, and interactive DVD board games supplement special and ultimate—and now commemorative Blu-Ray—edition DVD movies, which are enhanced with extras and bonus features. Such a wide selection from which the serious Double-O-Seven aficionado can choose begs the question: why another book about Bond?

One answer is simply that there can never be enough of a good thing. The Bond franchise continues to generate interest and intrigue by keeping story lines fresh even after the collapse of the iron curtain, shifts in the global balance of power, and the waxing and waning of social movements. Taken together, the soon-to-be twenty-three "official" and two "unofficial" Bond films represent the second highest-grossing franchise in cinematic history, eclipsed only by the *Star Wars* trilogy and its recently released prequels.[6] Thus, Bond is not, as M rebukes in *GoldenEye*, a so-called "relic of the Cold War."[7] Instead, he continues to stir interest. Or does he?

While the Double-O-Seven aficionado world appears to grow by leaps and bounds, commentators announced in 2005 that there was "a crisis surrounding the world's biggest movie franchise. No one wants to take on the role of James Bond."[8] In fact, the decision by producers not to pursue a fifth film with Pierce Brosnan, thereby rendering the 2002 release of *Die Another Day* his last mission, generated little interest for the role within the acting community.[9] After hanging up his tuxedo, Brosnan remarked that the Bond franchise was "on [its] last legs," an observation that some believed would thrust the series back into same predicaments it encountered following Timothy Dalton's *Licence to Kill* and which precipitated a six-year production hiatus[10] during which "Bond had a near-death experience."[11] In fact, after Daniel Craig signed on to portray Bond for four films in October 2005,[12] *Entertainment Weekly* offered its own recommendations "to freshen the 43-year-old series before it dies another day."[13] Despite well-publicized outrage from Bond fans over the selection of Craig, *Casino Royale*, the twenty-first film in the series that was released in late 2006, employed a backward- and forward-looking story line that invoked the spirit of the original Fleming novel and confirmed that "007 doesn't die, he just regenerates."[14]

A second answer is that little scholarship has been written about the cinematic and literary worlds of Bond. Analyzing the Bond phenomenon beyond the surface may seem somewhat unconventional, or even trite. In fact, James Chapman began his study of the Bond franchise by asking, "Why should we take James Bond seriously?"[15] Other scholars, such as Christoph Lindner, advanced the position that "we can no longer afford not to take James Bond seriously."[16] Notwithstanding Lindner's statement, I personally encountered numerous expressions of incredulity when I embarked upon this endeavor in 2000: to contribute and perhaps help establish, together with a few other works I discovered along the way, a serious field of Bond intellectualism. Despite my and other scholars' efforts, we cannot escape taking a defensive stance to justify why Bond should be accorded appropriate attention. This work is no different, as will be seen, in its efforts to argue why critical studies of Double-O-

Seven are necessary, particularly since I have chosen to write exclusively about the most celebrated, often trivialized, but ultimately academically neglected Bondian subject: the Bond Girl.

The late Albert "Cubby" R. Broccoli, cofounder of EON Productions and longtime producer, wrote, "I often note, with some bemusement, a continuing media usage throughout the world of the phrase 'James Bond Girl' when describing someone of great beauty."[17] Great beauty has, of course, been a central element of the Bond Girl.[18] Heralded for her aesthetics and powers of seduction in countless pictorial celebrations, she is a ubiquitous symbol of glamour and sophistication. *Playboy* has referred to the Bond Girl as "the ultimate creature[] of fantasy,"[19] and the actresses who have depicted her numerous manifestations over the years have been described as "the most ravishing women ever to grace the silver screen."[20] One such celebration, *Bond Girls Are Forever*, was both a film documentary narrated by Maryam d'Abo, who portrayed Kara Milovy in *The Living Daylights*, and a print companion coauthored by d'Abo and John Cork. In both media, *Bond Girls Are Forever* featured interviews with several actresses who reprised the Bond Girl role in an effort to honor the unique sorority to which these women belong.

Long before *Bond Girls Are Forever*, Richard Maibaum, a frequent screenwriter for the franchise, remarked that the Bond Girls "have become fantasy figures arousing powerful emphatic responses in both sexes."[21] Nonetheless, the Bond Girl had been cast for many years primarily as an accessory devoid of either a social or historical context. Her primary focus was to supplement, rather than complement, Bond. Popular culture works about the films idolize her, but academic studies of the films and novels often do little justice in terms of discussing her character development. Instead, these works provide brief references within a broader context.

For example, in their 1987 work *Bond and Beyond: The Political Career of a Popular Hero*, Tony Bennett and Janet Woollacott noted that Bond and the Bond Girl modernized sexuality by representing a "'swinging free' from the constraints of the past."[22] The Bond Girl, they argued, reflected freedom, sexual independence, and a release from "constraints of family, marriage and domesticity."[23] This is certainly true, to an extent, and Bennett and Woollacott qualified their assessment by recognizing that any sexual freedom the Bond Girl exhibited was ultimately defined in male terms.[24] But if the Bond Girl does, in fact, represent a "model of adjustment, a condensation of the attributes of femininity appropriate to the requirements of the . . . norms of male sexuality represented by [James] Bond,"[25] further elaboration is needed.

Tony Bennett and Janet Woollacott touched upon the complexity of Bond Girl portrayals in the franchise. For example, they noted that the "most significant change" associated with the films in the 1970s constituted a narrative shift away from the relationship between Bond and the villain and toward the relationship between Bond and the Bond Girl.[26] Furthermore, they suggested that this shift "clearly constituted a response—in truth, somewhat nervous and uncertain—to the Women's Liberation movement, fictitiously rolling back the advances of feminism to restore an imaginarily more secure phallocentric conception of gender relations."[27] Yet if this narrative shift was clear, Bennett and Woollacott's underlying premise presumed that the Bond Girl began as "'excessively independent,'"[28] a premise that this work challenges. In this regard, *Bond and Beyond* argued that the films of the latter 1970s served as "a 'putting-back-into-place' of women who carry their independence and liberation 'too far' or into 'inappropriate' fields of activity."[29] This work rejects such a contention, which ignores the development of the Bond Girl—and she indeed has one.

Bond and Beyond ultimately centered upon "the figure of Bond,"[30] and I have yet to uncover a work devoted entirely to studying the Bond Girl's development beyond mere pictorials or tributes. For example, Maryam d'Abo and John Cork considered the Bond Girl in the context of a mainstream celebration: "This book is a tribute to one of the lasting icons of feminine strength, beauty and resilience of the past half-century—the James Bond woman. They are at once of a type and yet decidedly individual. And, despite the popular conception, they are anything but subservient to 007."[31] Although Brian Dunbar noted in his critical study of *Goldfinger* that "it is the women who have been the most significant ideological functions," his analysis was limited only to the *Goldfinger* Bond Girls and did not engage in a global consideration of the character throughout the franchise.[32] It is therefore clear that a large void exists, one this work attempts to fill.

Ideologically, were the Bond Girls "harbingers of a new kind of femininity" in that "[t]hey were strong, smart, beautiful, and carried themselves with assurance"?[33] Maryam D'Abo and John Cork certainly contended that the Bond Girl always was the "élite, the alpha-woman."[34] The same belief was advanced by Tony Bennett and Janet Woollacott. Even as early as 1965, Claudine Auger, who portrayed Domino Derval in *Thunderball*, declared that the Bond Girls were the ultimate emancipated women: "They can live without a man doing everything for them because they are independent. They like to decide their future destinies for themselves. They are highly sexual—but only with men worth their loving. They are free, you see, completely free."[35]

But these assessments are not necessarily accurate. This work challenges Claudine Auger's characterization; questions the premises advanced by Tony Bennett, Janet Woollacott, Maryam d'Abo, and John

Cork; and ultimately advances an entirely opposite perspective. Rather than accept the premise that the Bond Girl is a strong, independent character from her inception, this work argues that the Bond Girl must evolve into the character that d'Abo and Cork celebrate as a strong woman. Indeed, the original Bond Girl was never imbued with any characteristics indicative of an independent, liberated woman. Consider, for example, this comment about the literary Bond Girl:

> Honeychile Rider, the heroine of "Doctor No," playfully throws her naked body against Bond as they stew in the villain's luxury spa/prison. "Honey," Bond tells her, "get into that bath before I spank you." She obeys, pouting, "You've got to wash me. I don't know what to do. You've got to show me." Infantilized, stupidly ignorant of the danger of her situation and as horny as hell, Honey epitomizes all that any budding feminist should detest.[36]

This work reveals that a metamorphosis at least a decade overdue—a decade during which producers, writers, and directors remained faithful to a successful formula despite a societal shift toward greater gender equality—finally facilitated a cinematic change in the character and presentation of the Bond Girl.

That change occurred in the mid-1970s when producers needed to update the image and role of the Bond Girl in order to "attempt[] to engage . . . ideas about the independence of women and women's liberation."[37] Ultimately, *The Spy Who Loved Me*, released in 1977, represented the first instance in which a Bond Girl was imbued with substantial credibility. The reconsideration of the Bond Girl that occurred in both *The Spy Who Loved Me* and *Moonraker* reinvigorated and elevated the character from a position of mere accessory to one rightfully revered both aesthetically and substantively. It did not provide an opportunity to put her back into place, as Tony Bennett and Janet Woollacott suggested.

The Bond Girl's evolutionary journey[38] was the consequence—whether willingly or unwittingly—of the necessity to keep up with or catch up to rapidly changing cultural mores. Absent the reconsideration that occurred in 1977, the Bond Girl was on the verge of becoming an anachronistic caricature of her previous self.[39] Ultimately, the Bond Girl experienced a true transformation that facilitated the creation of two new eras of the cinematic Bond that are described in chapter 0013. While this work does not suggest that the Bond films advance or promote feminism, it recognizes that the franchise embarked upon "a significant shift in the terrain of sexual representations"[40] and traces those representations over the course of the past five decades, with specific focus upon the first eleven films.

* * *

Why would one engage in a critical assessment of the Bond Girl? The impetus for this work was twofold. First, my obvious appreciation for both the cinematic and literary worlds of Bond guided me toward analyzing Fleming's creation in a scholarly manner. Second, I wanted to produce an academic piece about the feminist movement that would be accessible to an American male audience. While every student's general introductory course to twentieth-century American history includes a discussion of several social movements—notably the racial, gender, and sexual equality campaigns of the 1960s and 1970s—possessing a cursory knowledge of a subject and having an appreciation for the struggle are quite different matters. Certainly, I gained a rudimentary knowledge of America's ongoing challenges to achieve gender equality. The problem was that I simply lacked a medium through which I could appreciate its impact.

It was not until I had completed most of my undergraduate and graduate studies that I truly "studied" feminism, the Women's Liberation movement, and the campaigns upon which American women embarked in order to elevate their status during the middle and latter parts of the last century. Much to my chagrin, the material seemed difficult to appreciate in a meaningful way. Of course, I cannot speak for all males, but I was not the only observer who recognized that most of my male contemporaries had little, if anything, to contribute to the scholarly discourse that occurred in our classrooms and seminars. I could not say with great resolve that the laudable goal that women's studies courses "should be taken by women and men of all ages, races, and cultures"—and that these courses "look at the meaning and impact of events, ideals and social institutions for women as well as for men"[41]—was fulfilled in my experience. A quick survey of the participation level, let alone the attendance ratio between men and women in the classroom, revealed the great gender disparity I observed when a feminist work was the subject of study and discussion.

What I observed is not unusual or uncommon when men find themselves encountering topics in women's studies. Many male students, through no fault of their own, generally lack the ability to understand—or possess an insouciant attitude toward—feminism. Class compositions of women's studies courses offered at American colleges and universities are taught predominantly by female professors, and male enrollment is typically low.[42] In fact, many post-secondary institutions encourage males to register by attempting to dispel longstanding myths that women's studies courses have reputations for pursuing anti-male agendas. West Virginia University, for example, included the following disclaimer on its

Women's Studies Department Web site:

> Don't let the name mislead you. Women's Studies is not just about women, nor is it about male-bashing or gender wars. Rather, women's studies courses cover a broad range of subjects with sensitivity to gender, race, sexual orientation and class. Women and men are involved in the program both as professors and as students.[43]

While one cannot force a greater number of males to express an interest in women's studies, it is important to realize that current feminist literature and collegiate course offerings may not adequately provide the male student with a frame of reference through which he can appreciate the various and diverse issues addressed by the feminist and Women's Liberation movements. In this respect, I dispute actress Jill St. John's interpretation of the Bond Girl and the Bond franchise as mere entertainment that is "not meant as a social statement or a chronicle of how far women have come in life."[44] Rather, it is crucial to see Bond's world as not merely one relegated to entertainment. In 1966, one critic wrote that she "would be only too happy to believe that Bond movies can serve some constructive purpose."[45] The franchise can, and, in fact, does serve as a portal for lighting a new educational path to understanding and appreciating something significant, substantial, and real.[46]

* * *

The original version of this work was completed and presented before the faculty of the Department of History at Boston University in April 2001. *The World Is Not Enough*, released two years earlier, had become a distant memory. *Die Another Day* was first in production, and Bond was again hovering below the radar. At that time, relatively few academic works focusing upon the cinematic Bond existed. Much, of course, has changed, both in the real and Bondian worlds. With regard to the former, the September 11, 2001 terrorist attacks heralded a new and frightful era of international terrorism with effects we continue to encounter daily. In their aftermath, one scholar questioned whether "single hero movies like James Bond" would even survive.[47]

With regard to the latter, it has been suggested that there are many parallels between the Cold War era and the current global war against terrorism.[48] Despite concerns that "[t]he future of the Bond phenomenon must be in some doubt after the terrorist attacks,"[49] the Bond franchise released its twentieth installment and celebrated its fortieth anniversary with *Die Another Day* in 2002. Bond 20, as it was also dubbed, sparked a renewed interest in Bond scholarship and celebration. In 2003, the

Bloomington campus of Indiana University hosted a symposium that attracted American, British, and Canadian scholars to celebrate the fiftieth anniversary of Fleming's publication of his first Bond novel, *Casino Royale*.[50] Two years later, as noted above, Craig replaced Brosnan, who first assumed the role of Double-O-Seven for *GoldenEye* in 1995 and reprised it in three additional films. Despite concerns that Craig would fail to replicate his predecessor's success, the 2006 release of *Casino Royale* surpassed the opening box office sales of *Die Another Day*.[51] For me personally, my academic interests shifted toward jurisprudence, and consequently, my desire to revise and update the original version of this work was held in abeyance until recently.

This work remains, to the best of my knowledge, the first full-scale critical treatment of the female characters in the Bond franchise. It is unique for its reliance upon the vast literature of popular Bondian cultural and celebratory works and its use of these materials in a scholarly fashion.[52] Of course, it is as much a celebration of both the franchise and the Bond Girl (and her post-feminist manifestations) as it is a critical study and educational tool. Hopefully, this work presents the Bond Girl in an enlightening and entertaining manner as it traces her development from Fleming's mind and pen to the big screen—from the portrayal of Honey Ryder by Ursula Andress in *Dr. No*, the 1962 Bond cinematic debut, to Lois Chiles's performance as Dr. Holly Goodhead in *Moonraker* seventeen years later. It also previews the Bond Girl's significant transformations over the course of the last three decades, beginning with *For Your Eyes Only* in 1981 and continuing through *Quantum of Solace* in 2008, a span of twenty-seven years that I describe as comprising the Post-Feminist Bond Woman and Revisionist Bond Girl eras. The journey of these female characters—together with Miss Moneypenny and M, as portrayed by Dame Judy Dench—is the subject of a future work.

I extend tremendous appreciation to Professor Thomas J. Whalen, without whom the original version of this work would not have come to fruition and whose enthusiasm and encouragement personify the spirit of academic freedom, and to the History Department of Boston University, which provided the environment in which I could develop the original version of this work. Its scholars then acknowledged—and hopefully continue to appreciate—the academic importance of this area of study when few endeavored to explore it. I am also grateful to my family for unwavering support, love, and encouragement.

— Robert A. Caplen
Washington, DC, August 2010

Introduction

It is a mark of James Bond's cultural reach that, for better or worse, a "Bond Girl" has attained a specific meaning in modern parlance, with either positive or negative connotations depending on your point of view (and, perhaps, your gender).

—Ben Macintyre[1]

Fleming gave us beautiful women with whimsical names . . . Cubby Broccoli and Harry Saltzman created what we think of as the Bond girls.

—*Playboy*[2]

[Ursula Andress] did establish . . . the prototype. She is larger than life and a fantasy.

—Jill St. John[3]

"Bond. James Bond." These three words comprise a phrase that is considered the "most famous line uttered in movie history."[4] The name alone conjures up numerous, fantastic images of style, savoir-faire, sexual prowess, displays of derring-do, and "the projection of wish fulfillment."[5] Bond has undoubtedly become one of the most recognizable action heroes in the world and "has placed an indelible stamp on our culture."[6] Indeed, Bond "is arguably the most popular—in the sense of widely known—figure of the post-war period, if not of this century."[7] As early as 1966, a "Heroes of Our Time" list published in *The Times* placed the fictional character fourth behind Sir Winston Churchill, Soviet Premier Nikita Khrushchev, and U.S. President Lyndon B. Johnson.[8] Simply put, the fictional Bond quickly became "one of the twentieth century's most remarkable heroes."[9]

Articles about the Bond novels and films, as well as about the life of Ian Fleming, a former British naval intelligence officer and Double-

O-Seven creator, abound. Biographer John Pearson even penned an authoritative biography of the fictional Bond.[10] Bond's world of fantasy has easily transitioned into our own.[11] In the 1960s, researchers utilized Fleming's novels to test computer programs that identified keywords and sentence structures in order to develop a method for analyzing writings and authenticating authorship.[12] Scottish police employed radar tracking devices similar to those used in *Goldfinger* in an effort to locate stolen vehicles.[13] In 1970, *Time* invoked *Goldfinger* as the possible inspiration behind Whirlpool Corporation's new Trash Masher, a domestic trash compactor that disposed of garbage in a manner similar to automobile junkyards.[14] In 1974, an article in *The Times* described microfilm as a gadget no longer reserved for the likes of Bond.[15] The Royal Navy utilized the image of Commander Bond for recruitment purposes: "Feared by his enemies, adored by the nation, trained by the Navy."[15] Researchers even studied Bond's signature drink, the "shaken, not stirred" vodka martini, to analyze its chemical structure:

> As Mr. Bond is not afflicted by cataracts or cardiovascular disease, an investigation was conducted to determine whether the mode of preparing martinis had an influence on the antioxidant properties . . . . "007's profound state of health may be due, in part, to compliant bartenders" . . . [since] a "shaken, not stirred" example has superior antioxidant powers.[17]

Even the Royal Engineers inquired about developing Bond's underwater breathing apparatus in *Thunderball* for military use.[18] And in 2010, British composer Simon Proctor premiered his "James Bond" piano concerto to audiences in London.[19] As these few examples illustrate, Double-O-Seven has had a greater impact upon our popular culture than one might believe.

Notwithstanding the health benefits of Bond's martini, paying for a piece of his cinematic or literary history could induce cardiac arrest. Collectibles, original film posters, reproductions of gadgetry used in the films, and actual props from the films are in significant demand and fetch steep prices at auction. The bikini worn by Ursula Andress when she, as Honey Ryder, emerged from the ocean in *Dr. No* once sold for approximately $60,000.[20] Signed first edition copies of Fleming's novels have easily eclipsed $3,000 each.[21] These products—together with Bond-trademarked apparel, pajamas, toiletries, sunglasses, toys, and revenues from video rentals and DVD sales—all add fuel to what was presciently termed in 1965 as "the damndest wildfire . . . . of all time—the James Bond Industry."[22] Even then, there was "no joke . . . about the business being done all over the globe by products that bear the 007 label."[23] Just one decade ago, it was estimated that the cinematic "007 juggernaut" yielded approximately $3 billion in sales worldwide, a figure that did not even include television and video revenues.[24]

Despite Bond's intrigue and popularity, Fleming purportedly never intended for his character to evoke such global fervor. Rather, Fleming sought a name that "wouldn't have any . . . romantic overtones, such as Sapperish Peregrine Maltravers . . . . I wanted a really flat, quiet . . . name."[25] When he penned *Casino Royale* in 1953, Fleming

> wanted Bond to be an extremely dull, uninteresting man to whom things happened; I wanted him to be the blunt instrument. One of the bibles of my youth was *Birds of the West Indies*, by James Bond, a well-known ornithologist; and when I was casting about for a name for my protagonist I thought, My God, that's the dullest name I've ever heard, so I appropriated it. Now the dullest name in the world has become an exciting one.[26]

Having borrowed a name for his hero, Fleming wrote the ornithologist's wife, remarking that her husband's name "struck me that this brief, unromantic, Anglo-Saxon and yet very masculine name was just what I needed, and so a second James Bond was born."[27] Unbeknownst to him, Fleming created a legendary fictional icon, although it is entirely possible that Fleming always intended to do so, as discussed below. In return and as an expression of gratitude to the ornithological Bond, Fleming offered his own name "for any purposes you may think fit. Perhaps one day your husband will discover a particularly horrible species of bird which he would like to christen in an insulting fashion by calling it Ian Fleming."[28]

Inevitably, the most fervor generated by Bond centers around the Bond Girl, especially since Bond himself has been described as a "ubiquitous symbol of sexual prowess."[29] Before elaborating about the Bond Girl in her various manifestations, a word about Bond is appropriate. Scholars have recently explored the symbolism behind Bond's masculinity and, more specifically, his reproductive organ. One academic noted that a phallic focus is "partly due to renewed critical and theoretical interest in the cultural representation of masculinity."[30] A recent essay explained:

> Bond's penis is a threat to him—a means of being known and of losing authority, a site of the potentially abject that must instead be objectified as an index of self-control and autotelic satisfaction.
>
> . . . .

> . . . Psychoanalysis holds that the phallus represents power. The phallus itself lacks a universal material sign. The closest signifier is the penis, given male social dominance . . . . The penis fails to live up to this responsibility, however—it is not as powerful as the phallus.[31]

Of course, perhaps the most memorable cinematic phallic scene occurs in *Goldfinger* during which villain Auric Goldfinger straps Bond to a table and displays the power of his laser in an attempt to effect a high-tech castration. In fact, the scene became "the first time a laser [was] used in the plot of a motion picture."[32] Bond's only saving grace was a last-second remark that prompted Goldfinger "to turn off the band of light as it [was] about to reach [Bond's] crotch."[33] *Goldfinger* is also memorable for its introduction of Pussy Galore, "perhaps the most memorable figure in the Bond periphery"[34] and the first manifestation of the modern Bond Girl after whom subsequent leading female characters in the series were modeled.

It is not the symbolism behind Bond's masculinity that is of importance here. Instead, this work analyzes the relationship between Bond and the females with whom he interacts. In 1962, critic Hollis Alpert wrote in the *Saturday Evening Review* that Bond's world was not complete until the beautiful girl "succumbs to Bond's superior style of lovemaking."[35] That same year, *Esquire* described Bond's first and foremost preoccupation as "bedding beautiful women," not eliminating the villain and completing his mission.[36] Indeed, it is general knowledge that Bond "has vanquished more vixens than villains."[37] Countless commentators concurred over the years, buttressing the belief that Bond's "primary concern is the passion of an animal function."[38]

Indeed, Bond would not be Bond without the inextricable link between him and his female protagonist. The relationship between Bond and the Bond Girl has been accentuated at every marketing turn. It was recognized almost immediately that "women were such a basic part of the Bond campaigns."[39] Theatrical previews for *Die Another Day*, for example, featured less Pierce Brosnan and more Halle Berry, with the latter reenacting the ocean emergence scene that Ursula Andress made famous forty years earlier. Timed with the release of *The World Is Not Enough* in 1999, *Vanity Fair* featured a pictorial of several Bond Girl actresses and characterized them as members of a "secret sorority."[40] *TV Guide* organized a similar reunion for and printed interviews with numerous Bond sorority sisters upon whom society, according to one writer, has "been hooked" ever since 1962.[41] And the title of the recent Maryam d'Abo documentary and collaboration with John Cork speaks volumes: *Bond Girls Are Forever*. Certainly, the Bond Girl role has been cast with beauty and sexuality as essential—if not exclusive—components.

Caroline Munro recalled that she appealed to Cubby Broccoli for the role of Naomi in *The Spy Who Loved Me* after he discovered a poster from an advertisement in which she wore a wetsuit and hoisted a knife.[42] Similar casting stories abound and are detailed below. Certainly, producers' fascinations with these leading ladies were apparent, and nowhere is society's infatuation with the Bond Girl better exemplified than in cyberspace, where one search for Bond-related articles yields numerous Web pages specifically devoted to the Bond Girls through pictures, text, or a combination of several multimedia elements.

Internet tributes—together with most books, articles, and documentaries about the fictional character—can be classified as part of what scholar James Chapman termed the Bond fan culture. Taken together, these works are "indicative of their celebratory, anecdotal and uncritical content."[43] Their focus typically centers upon behind-the-scenes production anecdotes, actor-director dynamics, plot summaries of the films, dossiers of the various vehicles Bond drives, descriptions of the form and function of the gadgetry Bond utilizes on his various missions, special effects techniques, pictorials of the women Bond encounters, and the like. While some of these works may be authoritative, they are not intended, as James Chapman noted, to be considered serious studies of the films themselves: "[W]hat they lack in scholarly apparatus they make up for in their lively style and their extensive knowledge of all things 'Bondian.'"[44] Thus, any Bond aficionado intent upon knowing in which film weapons expert Major Boothroyd (later known as Q) introduces "radioactive lint" (*On Her Majesty's Secret Service*) or whether the "Most Famous Car in the World" was, in fact, the Aston Martin DB5 featured in *Goldfinger* has numerous resources available to address such inquiries.[45]

Despite much attention and focus from admirers, few serious Bond film studies exist. As noted earlier, this void is beginning to be filled. The dearth of academic focus upon the films partially resulted from an attitude that Bond should not be taken seriously. Interestingly, Fleming himself advanced that philosophy: "If one has a grain of intelligence it is difficult to go on being serious about a character like James Bond."[46] Fleming publicly maintained that his novels were mere escape literature written for "warm-blooded heterosexuals in railway trains, airplanes, or beds."[47] According to Fleming, his Bond adventures were "not 'engaged.' I have no message for suffering humanity . . . . [I] do not aim at changing people or making them go out and do something."[48]

Directors and producers of the Bond films apparently adopted a similar attitude. During the filming of *GoldenEye* in 1995, for example, coproducer Michael G. Wilson remarked that Bond was merely "escapist entertainment [that] nobody should take . . . seriously."[49] Critics had adopted that viewpoint years earlier, as evidenced by a 1962 *New York*

Times review describing *Dr. No* as "pure, escapist bunk . . . not to be taken seriously."[50] Despite statements to the contrary, Fleming, as will be seen, considered Bond a serious endeavor, carefully modeling his protagonist's fantasy world after his own experiences in the intelligence field during World War II, his own personal desires, and his attitudes about women.

A second explanation as to why the Bond films have been accorded less focus by scholars stems from an ideological schism that developed between cinematic Bond celebrants and so-called Fleming purists, the latter of whom are aficionados of the literary Bond.[51] Maintaining that most cinematic Bond fans are unfamiliar with the novels and merely enjoy the aesthetic and visual pleasure derived from the treatment of the character on screen, the Fleming purists characterize the cinematic Bond as a parody of the original and therefore unworthy of attention. Novelist Ayn Rand, for example, "adored the 007 books" but "was appalled by the films because they were laced with 'the sort of humour intended to undercut Bond's stature, to make him ridiculous.'"[52] Similarly, author Anthony Burgess, who criticized the films for becoming "more and more gimmicky, and less and less psychologically interesting," recommended that filmgoers "get back to the books and admire their quality as literature."[53] Even biographer Andrew Lycett acknowledged that "Bond is now a film-led phenomenon."[54]

The gimmickry, accentuated particularly during the Roger Moore era that spanned eight films from 1973 to 1985, was a deliberate effort by producers to imbue the films with a "sense of humor and lightness" that masked the extreme pessimism and sadomasochistic elements inherent in the original novels.[55] The 2006 version of *Casino Royale*, in a sense, responded to criticism by more accurately reflecting Fleming's original novel of the same title. It has even been suggested that producers are hoping *Skyfall*, the twenty-third installment scheduled for release in late 2012 to coincide with the franchise's golden anniversary, will feature less action sequences in order to attract serious consideration for an Academy Award.[56] Perhaps the franchise is finally addressing the apparent schism between Bond's literary and cinematic worlds.

Only recently have discussions of the Bond films and novels appeared within the same academic work or collection of works. *The James Bond Phenomenon: A Critical Reader* and *Ian Fleming and James Bond: The Cultural Politics of 007*, published in 2003 and 2005, respectively, are two notable examples and are part of a renewed excitement about everything Bondian that has been on the rise since the 1995 release of *GoldenEye*. The increased accessibility of DVD and other digital media may also have prompted a scholastic revitalization that has encouraged academics to accord the same critical attention to the cinematic Bond that his literary counterpart has garnered since the late 1950s. In the early 1980s, one author lamented that the Bond films have "been totally ignored" by scholars and expressed hope that "one day someone will have to produce a scholarly volume on the Bond films that will dissect them in depth and place them in their proper context."[57] In the late 1980s, Tony Bennett and Janet Woollacott wrote that such attention would effectively reverse the "history of critical reaction to the Bond forms [that] has been a history of condemnation: both the novels and the films have been designated unsavoury and harmful or have been disparaged as 'mere escapism.'"[58]

Licence to Thrill: A Cultural History of the James Bond Films, released in 2000, helped forge a new era of cinematic Bond scholarship by relating the franchise to a broader film culture and illustrating how the so-called Bond formula contributed to elevating spy thriller films from B-movie to big-budget motion picture stature. A year later, *The Politics of James Bond: From Fleming's Novels to the Big Screen* traced Fleming's longing for the strong British Empire that dissolved during his lifetime and argued that the cinematic Bond represented an image of British "toughness, sharpness, [and] cleverness" during a period in which American superiority during the Cold War supplanted Great Britain.[59] Conspicuously absent from both works, however, was any substantial attention to the issues of sex and gender. In fact, one criticism of *Licence to Thrill* was its failure to address the cinematic Bond's female counterparts: "The representation of women in the Bond films is a subject worthy of real work—it should be a way to talk about the representation of women in culture generally."[60]

This work focuses almost exclusively upon the representations and various manifestations of the Bond Girl throughout the history of the franchise. Twenty-two Bond films span a period of nearly fifty years in American history and therefore both precede and postdate the modern, "second wave" feminist and Women's Liberation movements. The numerous Bond Girl (a term encompassing the female characters, both minor and major, appearing in the series between 1962 and 1979, and 2002 to present) and Bond Women (a term encompassing the female characters, both minor and major, appearing in the series between 1981 and 1999) characters undergo significant transformations, and a closer examination of this phenomenon is long overdue. Providing a view of the feminist movement and the cultural representations of women in the latter half of the twentieth century through a Bondian lens, this work offers a medium to which readers of all ages can relate and that a wide-ranging audience can enjoy.

Fleming's novels and short stories, all written during the 1950s and 1960s, form the basic models upon which most of the films are based, though only the first two films are "the most faithful to his texts."[61] They warrant examination for the purpose of understanding Fleming's attitudes toward and treatment of—as well as representations of—women. Following Fleming's death in 1964, several authors—notably Kingsley Amis (utilizing the pseudonym Robert Markham), John Gardner, and Raymond Benson—have perpetuated the literary Bond series. Chapter 003 of this work only considers Fleming's works.

As noted earlier, the Bond films are classified in "official" and "unofficial" terms. The twenty-three films that comprise the former category are associated with EON Productions and include *Dr. No* (1962), *From Russia With Love* (1963), *Goldfinger* (1964), *Thunderball* (1965), You Only Live Twice (1967), *On Her Majesty's Secret Service* (1969), *Diamonds Are Forever* (1971), *Live and Let Die* (1973), *The Man With the Golden Gun* (1974), *The Spy Who Loved Me* (1977), *Moonraker* (1979), *For Your Eyes Only* (1981), *Octopussy* (1983), *A View To A Kill* (1985), *The Living Daylights* (1987), *Licence to Kill* (1989), *GoldenEye* (1995), *Tomorrow Never Dies* (1997), *The World Is Not Enough* (1999), *Die Another Day* (2002), *Casino Royale* (2006), *Quantum of Solace* (2008), and *Skyfall* (scheduled for release in 2012).[62] The latter category includes *Casino Royale* (1967), as well as *Never Say Never Again*, a 1983 remake of *Thunderball* starring Sean Connery as Bond. Because these two films are not part of the EON Productions series, they are excluded from consideration.

Shaken & Stirred: The Feminism of James Bond is the first chapter of the Bond Girl's story. It traces her evolution alongside the rise, decline, and legacy of a gender equality movement that inspired American women to challenge their status in society and, in the process, become "shaken and stirred." With a focus upon the unique feminism of James Bond, it is the intent of this work to encourage discourse about feminism generally while enhancing appreciation for the intriguing world of Agent Double-O-Seven.

001

Introducing James Bond: Ian Fleming and His Feminine Mystique

Bond's approach to sex grew directly out of Fleming's own distinctive attitudes to women, which in turn were shaped by the times he lived in, the class he occupied, and his own psychological and sexual preoccupations.

—Ben Macintyre[1]

Your philosophy is splendid in a selfish kind of way,
When your hair was black and curly but not now it is grey,
For you're well over forty and I fear you're getting fat,
You're apt to be forgotten and just an old bad hat.
This dear familiar face is not accustomed to neglect,
And still has the capacity to make other men erect,
So if by chance you meet a pretty Biarritz slut,
Just pause for thought and hesitate before you stuff her up.
And if you need adventure it'll be much as you can do,
To cope with the variety of your ever loving Shrew.

—Anne Fleming[2]

Ian Fleming was a brilliant journalist, a well-respected British naval intelligence officer, and a remarkable literary figure. Yet he seemed to live two lives depending upon the time of day or night.[3] Friends and colleagues recalled a suave personality and charming nature, describing Fleming as an individual imbued with excitement for life. His widow, the former Lady Anne Rothermere, recalled that Fleming persistently tried to "avoid the dull . . . everyday demands of life," instead seeking a lifestyle devoid of boredom.[4] Others remembered the James Bond creator as a strange, puzzling, arrogant, egocentric, "insufferably vain," and "vulgar" individual.[5] John Pearson stressed that Fleming was "exceedingly naughty."[6] Fleming's multifaceted personality was best articulated by Mary Pakenham, a former girlfriend, who recalled that Fleming was "totally unpredictable . . . an enigma."[7] Fleming was very much unlike his brothers, and it became apparent during his youth that he would lead a more unusual life.[8] One particular facet of Fleming's lifestyle was a notorious reputation for playboy tendencies and an accompanying attitude toward women that allegedly verged upon abuse.

Fleming also apparently possessed an affinity for the bizarre in connection with a highly active libido. While in his mid-twenties, Fleming leased what John Pearson described as a "very, very weird" London apartment on Ebury Street in which "only a very unusual character like Ian" would reside.[9] Lacking any windows, the apartment featured grey walls and dark furnishings, all of which were designed "to facilitate seduction."[10] With collections of French pornography prominently displayed, Fleming transformed the apartment into an ideal residence for a bachelor into which a "steady stream of women" flowed.[11] It was also a place where his male friends, a group Fleming termed *Le Cercle gastronomique et des jeux de hasard*, would congregate to play cards and to discuss their recent sexual escapades.

It was likely that these gatherings provided a comfortable environment in which Fleming could vocalize his views about women or adopt those attitudes expressed by others in the group. According to biographers, Fleming's characterizations of women typically involved descriptions of their physical attributes, such as his belief that "busts no longer were the most beautiful feature of a woman's figure but that the buttocks most certainly were."[12] Evidence suggests that Fleming's voracious sexual appetite, which he later affixed to his fictional alter ego,[13] developed in response to his relationship with his mother, whom he believed exhibited oppressive and overbearing behavior toward him throughout his youth.

Fleming was born in 1908 into a highly respected and honorable family. His father, Valentine, was a banker, a member of Parliament, and a high ranking officer in the British Army. Following Valentine's death on the Western Front during World War I, his widow, Evelyn, was left to raise four boys on her own. Apparently ill-equipped to handle this task, Evelyn, it has been suggested, approached childrearing from the viewpoint that she needed to assume complete control of her sons' lives. Impressing upon Fleming and his brothers the notion that their father symbolized virtue and honor, Evelyn expected her sons to follow in the elder Fleming's steps. Accounts suggest that Evelyn required her sons to conclude their nightly prayers with a plea that they grow up to be more like their father.[14]

The loss of his father and his mother's newly defined parental role inhibited Fleming from receiving the nurturing he apparently needed. Fleming's ability to express himself emotionally became stifled, and he later emerged with tastes for sadism, masochism, and a dislike for his mother.[15] Although his older brother Peter apparently posed no objection to his mother's parenting, Fleming considered his mother's behavior overprotective and restrictive. He instead "wanted to do his own thing" and actively sought to free himself from his mother's constraints.[16] Later, Fleming was described as "the sort of man to feel that a too-restricted life was not worth living."[17]

Fleming, like both his father and Peter before him, enrolled at Eton College.[18] Unlike Peter, however, Fleming exhibited little fervor for academics and instead channeled his energies into physical activities, including sports and sex. Fleming continually found himself disciplined (mainly in the form of caning) by the school's headmaster.[19] A family friend, Tina Beal, recalled that Fleming was caned on the morning of an important athletic race.[20] The story became legendary: "[P]oised to win Eton's coveted athletic prize, the *Victor Ludorum*, for the second year in a row[,] . . . [Fleming] asked to be beaten 15 minutes early, then ran the race, with his running shorts still bloodied from the beating, and won the school prize."[21] While some attributed the incident to Fleming's ability to "endure[] the consequences, but still accomplish[] the remarkable,"[22] it also confirmed Fleming's affinity for and proclivity toward masochism.

His athletic prowess was ultimately overshadowed by his sexual desires. Indeed, it has been said of Fleming that he was "tremendously interested in sex" and "studied and pursued the subject, in theory and in practice."[23] In an interview with *The Sunday Times*, Fleming acknowledged that Eton exposed him to "snobbery, sadism, and sexuality . . . the devils in the machine of an Eton education."[24] Fleming frequently violated school policies in order to leave campus and search for young women. Concerned that her son was tarnishing the family name, Evelyn condemned his behavior and believed that Fleming would learn proper discipline through military service. Shortly thereafter, Fleming was transferred to Eton's Army Class Division, and he subsequently enrolled in the academy at Sandhurst. After his arrival at Sandhurst, Fleming again violated the school's evening curfews and proscriptions against sexual activity. When he was discovered in the company of a woman, Fleming's supervising officers grounded him for six months. In what was likely an act of defiance against not only the authorities at Sandhurst but also his mother for her role in facilitating his transfer, Fleming left the academy "under a cloud."[25] Indeed, Evelyn pressured him to resign from Sandhurst rather than face expulsion. Once he left the academy,

Fleming drove to London to "find himself a tart" and, several days later, contracted gonorrhea.[26]

These types of sexual escapades deeply troubled Evelyn, who believed that Fleming's behavior and scandalous conduct discredited and reflected poorly upon the family. As a result, Fleming was branded a black sheep and was chastised for not doing "something respectable" like his brothers, who were garnering admiration from their peers.[27] More significantly, the constant reminder that he would have severely disappointed his father weighed heavily upon Fleming and further damaged his relationship with his mother.

Convinced that her son's conduct resulted either from backwardness or was symptomatic of mental instability, Evelyn was "determined that all her sons should be a credit to her and the family. If they were not, she would rather have nothing to do with them."[28] Distraught over Fleming's idiosyncratic and mischievous behavior, and concerned about what "was to become of [her] difficult, good-looking son," Evelyn enrolled him in an Austrian finishing school and clinic for students with attitudinal problems.[29] The resulting relocation forced Fleming to abruptly end a budding relationship. When he later returned from Europe engaged, Evelyn disapproved, and the subsequent, abrupt end to that relationship solidified within Fleming a deep aversion to both his mother and commitment:

> Deep maternal disapproval finally wrecked his engagement . . . . [Evelyn] made it quite clear what she thought about the girl and the idea of the marriage . . . . There were tears and there were recriminations, but when the girl returned to Geneva Ian Fleming did not travel with her . . . [and] after this he would never dream of marrying anyone.[30]

Since his father's will stipulated that Evelyn reserved the right to alter the division of the Fleming estate, Fleming was aware that eloping would provide his mother with the opportunity to disown and deny him a portion of the family's assets.[31] Highly resentful and out of disrespect, Fleming began referring to Evelyn simply as "M,"[32] a title later bestowed upon Bond's overbearing superior at the Secret Intelligence Service (MI6).

Fleming's contentious relationship with his mother reflects what sociologist Arthur Brittan described as the concept of a childhood "trauma" inflicted upon the male psyche. Incorporating Sigmund Freud's philosophy that a father-son relationship is critical for a young man's development of masculine characteristics, Brittan wrote that a mother who assumes the role of a father figure not only exercises greater power over her son but also impedes his development.[33] A mother-son dynamic such as the one Fleming experienced could force a young male to "struggle to attain an unavoidably elusive 'masculine' identity" due to the dominance of the matriarch.[34] Consequently, "a man's efforts to attain a healthy sex role identity . . . are thwarted by such factors as paternal absence [and] maternal over-protectiveness."[35]

This theory suggests that a mother who raises her son without a father could potentially overpower her child and foster an "insecure male gender identity," which forces the male to "spend the rest of [his] life trying to escape from the consequences of her awesome potency."[36] Such an "escape" may be accompanied by the belief that a female possesses diminished moral equality, leading to a greater likelihood that the male would resent female authority and objectify or exploit women for sexual gratification.[37] Of course, these generalized theories do not account for individual circumstances and cannot be universally applied. Nonetheless, it is apparent that the dynamic Fleming and his mother shared greatly shaped and molded his attitudes toward females. It is only natural that Bond, Fleming's archetype of the charismatic, charming, "handsome debonair" hero would reflect his creator's background and views about relationships.[38]

* * *

Fleming exhibited an "arrogant and supercilious" attitude during his young adulthood, and he displayed a "moody" disposition toward women.[39] Fleming himself once remarked that he was "going to be quite bloody-minded about women" and get from them what he desired "without any scruples."[40] Indeed, Fleming apparently "made little effort to hide the fact that he found women inferior" and later expressed such views to Alan Schneider, his counterpart at the U.S. Office of Naval Intelligence: "Women were not worth that much emotion . . . [and were present to satisfy] continual interest in sex without any sense of shame or guilt . . . . [Women] were like pets, like dogs, men were the only real human beings."[41]

Fleming wrote in his notebooks that "men want a woman whom they can turn on and off like a light switch," adding, "Women have their uses for the relief of tension. The only time people are not alone is just after making love. Then the warmth and languor and gratitude turn them into happy animals. But soon the mind starts to work again and they become again lonely human beings."[42] Other writings evinced Fleming's belief that women were "animals to be petted, bought presents for, made a fuss of—but not to be accepted as real human beings at all" because they were ultimately just objects of sexual desire.[43]

Interestingly, the women with whom Fleming interacted apparently ignored his beliefs or chauvinistic behavior. Ralph Arnold, one of Fleming's close friends, recalled that Fleming "was irresistible to women" and that "there were always enough . . . women to go around."[44] Despite an abundance of women in his life, Fleming never offered any of his partners anything beyond a physical relationship. Instead, he "could never hope to understand [women], but if he was lucky he felt he might occasionally shoot one down."[45] One former girlfriend recalled that she knew no man who "had sex so much on the brain as Ian."[46] In fact, Fleming was "almost obsessively interested in the subject," behavior that was considered "very unusual . . . to find in an Englishman."[47]

While Fleming often boasted about his conquests, he nonetheless always maintained a certain amount of distance, continually refrained from commitment, and preferred to view women as illusions in order to ensure that he would not give away anything of himself. As one friend recalled, Fleming's attitude toward women was extremely complex: "He was so obsessed with [women], he made such an issue over sex, that he always made me think of the man who denounces the demon rum because he feels guilty for wanting to get drunk. His exasperation came because he couldn't take them or leave them alone."[48] Another close friend remarked that, despite his ability to attract members of the opposite sex, Fleming's attitude made him a "very poor lover."[49]

Fleming recalled that "what happens is that, as with drugs, [I] need a stronger shot each time, and women are just women. The consumption of one woman is the consumption of all. You can't double the dose."[50] Indeed, his commentary in *The Man With the Golden Gun* about Bond was semiautobiographical: Bond "knew, deep down, that love from Mary Goodnight, or from any other woman, was not enough for him. It would be like taking 'a room with a view.'"[51] Nevertheless, Fleming understood that "you won't have a lover if you don't love."[52] At the same time, Fleming would remark that "as long as a woman's flesh is clean and healthy, what does it matter what shape [and who] she is?"[53] Detaching himself from the women he was dating or with whom he was sleeping, Fleming "remained safe from love and all its uncomfortable complexities . . . he could maintain his mystery."[54] Sexual relations devoid of an emotional component also enabled Fleming to reaffirm his self-confidence and assurance: "Sex . . . means showing that [you are] capable [of] freedom . . . powerful, masterful, in control."[55] Certainly, the control Fleming possessed over his sexual experiences stood in sharp contrast to the lack of control he felt during his youth.

The frequency of Fleming's sexual encounters did not facilitate either satisfaction or happiness. Instead, they made him even more restless.[56]

Fear of sexual boredom, coupled with an inability to derive satisfaction, contributed further to Fleming's inability to exhibit emotion toward women.[57] In his first Bond novel, *Casino Royale*, Fleming described his protagonist in semiautobiographical terms:

> With most women his manner was a mixture of taciturnity and passion. The lengthy approaches to a seduction bored him almost as much as the subsequent mess of disentanglement. He found something grisly in the inevitability of the pattern of each affair. The conventional parabola—sentiment, the touch of the hand, the kiss, the passionate kiss, the feel of the body, the climax in bed, then more bed, then less bed, then the boredom, the tears and the final bitterness—was to him shameful and hypocritical.[58]

Fleming never placed responsibility for these feelings and any sexual shortcomings that he may have experienced upon himself. "Technique in bed," he recalled, "is important, but alone it is the scornful coupling that makes . . . affairs . . . so distasteful."[59] Later, Fleming maintained that "some women respond to the whip, some to the kiss. Most of them like a mixture of both," and a woman always "likes the door to be forced."[60]

Regardless of a particular woman's sexual preferences, evidence suggests that Fleming did not hold the women with whom he engaged in sexual relations in high regard. In his opinion, English women were "absolutely filthy."[61] By contrast, Fleming believed that American women were overly preoccupied with cleanliness and would, as he wrote in a short story, "gargle . . . with TCP [after kissing as if they] had a cold."[62] Nationality aside, a woman's physique, too, provided little consolation to Fleming. He described an affair with a dancer as "very unsatisfactory" because she claimed to be too tired after her performances.[63] Similarly, Fleming found that models and actresses failed to provide fulfillment because they were usually too "frightened of getting bruised or bent."[64] He also became involved with a plus-sized woman, whom he dubbed a "galloping bedstead."[65] But she, too, apparently provided no satisfaction. Ultimately, Fleming concluded that older women were the best lovers because "they always think they may be doing it for the last time."[66]

Although his sexual partners and the act of intercourse itself seemed somewhat distasteful to him, Fleming was not deterred. Accounts indicate that Fleming approached women with condescension, usually offering a snide remark to initiate conversation and then proceeding to discuss either himself or sex. The routine worked well. Lisl Popper, one of Fleming's romantic interests in Austria, recalled that she "was delighted" by Fleming and "never left [him]."[67] During his stay on Ebury Street, Fleming refined his seduction technique to a formula involving candles, dinner and drinks with Viennese waltz music on his gramophone in the background, and conspicuously placed collections of erotica, which included pictorials of women engaging in sadomasochistic sexual acts.

Fleming's knowledge of sexual fetishes and practices is apparent from the following quote, taken from a story he penned shortly before his death in 1964:

> James Bond smiled at the thought of her and wondered what they would do together . . . . And that bar, again still undiscovered, which . . . was the rendezvous for sadists and masochists of both sexes. The uniform was black leather jackets and leather gloves. If you were a sadist, you wore the gloves under the left shoulder strap. For the masochists, it was the right . . . . [I]t would be fun to go and have a look.[68]

Fleming's pictorial displays of women "strapped to beds, pressed against shower doors, or posed as passively waiting for their men to come and take control" were designed to arouse and pique his companion's interest.[69] Free from the "usual English prudery and reticence about sex," Fleming brought an uninhibited side out of the women with whom he was involved, one of whom described his seduction routine as "always exciting."[70]

Whatever his methods, Fleming found himself frequently escorting a guest into the bedroom. The empowerment he derived from these encounters, however, was not limited to the confines of his apartment. In public settings, Fleming often directly broached the subject of sex and reportedly solicited relations within a period of thirty minutes after meeting a woman he desired.

Fleming's numerous sexual conquests ran the gamut. In addition to the women described above, he was romantically involved with a Rumanian countess, a tomboy daughter of a businessman, the underage daughter of a naval officer, an art connoisseur, a former American showgirl, and the daughter of a British colonel, to name a few.[71] Fleming even conducted a secret affair with Christine Granville, a married Polish spy with whom he reportedly used code names and secret messages in order to conceal their relationship.[72] Fleming dated many of these women simultaneously, an art he refined during his tenure at the finishing school in Austria, where, at one point, he divided his time among three women. As a former girlfriend recalled, Fleming was "totally amoral in sex" and "quite ruthless about girls."[73]

One particular girlfriend is worth mentioning. Fleming entered into a serious relationship with Muriel Wright, the woman that biographer Andrew Lycett claimed was the model for "the original Bond girl."[74]

Nicknamed Mu, Wright was entirely devoted to Fleming and became his "cowering slave," while Fleming treated her with disrespect before he "ruthlessly discarded" her.[75] Author Ben Macintyre noted, "Ian enjoyed showing Mu off to his friends . . . . But he undoubtedly treated her very badly. Even though they were unofficially 'engaged', Fleming was consistently and relentlessly unfaithful to her, and, unlike some of his lovers, she minded."[76]

Muriel Wright nevertheless exhibited the traits of Fleming's ideal woman: she was "undemanding, helpful[,] . . . seem[ed] to want to please, to make one happy."[77] She adored him, a trait that ultimately proved fatal: "Adoration bored [Fleming]. Bored with a woman, no one could be more elusive, more cold, if necessary more brutal, than Ian Fleming. The kindness which was an undoubted part of his character did not extend to the women who loved him."[78] As long as Fleming's women satisfied his sexual appetite and remained relatively quiet, he seemed relatively content: "When women's minds started to work they lost that animal capacity for giving the happiness and relief which [I] needed from them."[79]

Although her adoration of Fleming may have been fatal, Muriel Wright's ultimate demise was quite tragic. In March 1944, Wright, who returned home one evening after delivering to Fleming his weekly package of cigarettes, was killed in her sleep during an air raid.[80] One of Fleming's former colleagues later recalled that "the trouble with Ian is that you have to get yourself killed before he feels anything."[81] Following Wright's death, Fleming began an affair with Anne O'Neill that continued during the course of her short-lived marriage to Esmond Rothermere.

Fleming confessed that Anne was the first woman with whom he actually spent an entire night, as opposed to leaving before sunrise.[82] Well past the age of forty, Fleming learned that Anne was pregnant with his child. Aware that bringing a child into the world would "change his life more radically than anything he had done before," he felt obligated to marry Anne.[83] She later recalled that Fleming "entered marriage with characteristic gloom and foreboding. He told me, 'I can promise you nothing. I have not an admirable character. I have no money. I have no title. Marriage will be entirely what you can make it.'"[84] Unable to promise Anne that he would preserve his fidelity to her, Fleming "was consistently and almost immediately unfaithful" to his wife.[85] Nevertheless, Fleming's marriage, ironically, provided him with a unique opportunity that would ultimately fulfill his mother's desire that he bring honor to the family.

002

Justifying James Bond: Taking 007 and Ian Fleming Seriously

Ian Fleming could find only contempt for anyone who tried to read anything into Bond.

—*Time*[1]

To me, the James Bond films are fun, and to take them too seriously would spoil the whole game.

—John Brosnan[2]

Somehow Bond movies seem to sail above all realities without actually denying them. Neither do the films argue with critics who charge them with being callous, violent or chauvinist. They neutralize criticism as often as not by being too witty and good-humored to be taken too seriously.

—Vincent Canby[3]

Playboy *and Bond defined the male mystique for the latter half of the 20th century.*

—*Playboy*[4]

Ian Fleming began typing his first James Bond novel, *Casino Royale*, in January 1952.[5] He publicly maintained that he began writing for his own personal pleasure,[6] an endeavor "born as a counterirritant or antibody to my hysterical alarm at getting married at the age of forty-three."[7] According to Andrew Lycett, Fleming "peddled this line so consistently" that his wife became highly agitated by what she perceived was an insulting statement.[8] Fleming refused to diverge from the story and instead elaborated upon and embellished it. He recounted that the prospect of marriage terrified him to such a degree that he began writing to "anesthetize [his] nerves . . . [he] sat down, rolled a piece of paper into [his] battered portable [typewriter], and began."[9] Marriage, according to Fleming, substantially "trapped" him because it was "the last thing he wanted to do . . . and then he was caught" unexpectedly.[10]

Fleming was troubled by the responsibilities that accompanied marriage and the necessity of settling down. Apparently, nuptials were "too much for him to deal with."[11] As John Pearson elaborated, because Fleming refused

> to accept that a mistress could also have a mind, [Fleming] remained safe from love and all its uncomfortable complexities and safe from being found out . . . . [H]e made it quite clear that he never intended to [marry] if he could possibly help it. His idea of the only possible wife was a woman who was "double-jointed, and who knew when to keep quiet and make sauce bearnaise."[12]

Fleming ascribed his aversion to marriage to Bond, who opines in *Diamonds Are Forever*: "I'm not sure I'd want to [marry]. She'd get me handing round canapés in an L-shaped drawing room. And there'd be all those ghastly 'Yes you did No I didn't' rows that seem to go with marriage. It wouldn't last. I'd get claustrophobia and run out on her."[13] Moreover, Fleming realized that his marriage would require childrearing, which Fleming similarly disfavored: "The main danger of breeding is that you may double the strengths but you may also double the weaknesses."[14] In short, Fleming "never really wanted to be involved in anything which would tie him down [and] inhibit his freedom,"[15] and it is "tempting to see shades of Fleming's turbulent marriage in Bond's attitude to women."[16]

Like much of Fleming's life, distinctions between fact and myth are continually blurred. The inability to discern fact from fiction stems, in part, from the accidental destruction of Fleming's private papers by his secretary. While Fleming steadfastly maintained that marriage provided him with the impetus to write, he had, in fact, been interested in penning a novel as early as 1933, the year in which his brother Peter published a story entitled *Brazilian Adventure*. Peter subsequently enjoyed a successful literary career, which further solidified Fleming's inferiority complex. A family friend recalled that people would ask if Peter's younger brother was as much a success as Peter or "up to it," to which the answer would invariably be "No, not really."[17] Fleming subsequently abandoned writing: "[M]y brother Peter's the writer in the family and he's really terribly good at it."[18]

One year prior to Fleming's marriage, Peter published *The Sixth Column*, which served as "a stern reminder" to Fleming that he "wanted to write serious . . . novels, and was determined not to let his brother steal a march on him again . . . . "[19] He turned to his typewriter. Usurping the name Moneypenny from *The Sett*, one of Peter's unfinished novels, Fleming bestowed it upon M's secretary, a character later immortalized on film by actress Lois Maxwell. The budding sibling rivalry—or at least a rivalry from Fleming's perspective—continued even after Fleming's Bond novels became popular. Indeed, Fleming eventually removed a comment from an introduction to one of his Bond novels about how "Peter Fleming's books have won distinguished literary acclaim."[20]

Given Fleming's experience within the British intelligence community during World War II, a book about espionage or a "spy novel to end all spy novels" seemed appropriate.[21] Allen Dulles, former director of the CIA, recalled that Fleming's desire to write a spy novel merely reflected a broader trend during the late 1940s and early 1950s: "Great governments have gone into the spy business[,] . . . large organizations have been built up and they are engaged in a kind of conflict that seems to intrigue people[, and] this generation seems attuned to spy stories."[22] Notwithstanding any trends, Fleming had the requisite institutional knowledge. He was "[s]upremely equipped[,] . . . trained in diplomacy, later a Moscow correspondent for Reuters[,] . . . [and] an officer in British Naval Intelligence," whose "expertise accrued to him like dividends. In time he turned it over to Bond."[23] More importantly, Fleming "knew the requisite ingredients for a dish to set before [the public]—money, sex and snobbishness, beaten into a fine rich batter, with plenty of violence to make it rise in the pan."[24]

Although a fear of marriage and a desire to gain respect within his own family may have factored into Fleming's decision to begin writing, they were not the sole reasons. Fleming's wife was one of London's well-known socialites and frequently entertained a circle of literary friends at their residence. Fleming detested these occasions:

> What happens if I attend a dinner party in my own house is that all the interesting men are placed by Annie at her end of the table and I get stuck at the bottom of the table with the less interesting wives who are craning their necks to hear what Annie and the interesting men are saying instead of listening to my stammer.[25]

Indeed, Fleming recognized that becoming an important novelist would facilitate his acceptance into Anne's social group, which included such notables as Somerset Maugham and Malcolm Muggeridge.

On a more practical level, Fleming faced the reality that he needed an income in order to provide for his unborn child, and he believed that writing would solve his monetary concerns. Commenting upon what he viewed as meager sales profits from the first printing of *Casino Royale*, Fleming requested higher royalties from his publisher: "In order to free myself to write more books for you I simply must earn more money from them."[26] In 1964, *Time* reported that Fleming "had been born with everything except money. The creation of James Bond made up for that lack. It returned him an estimated million dollars a year . . . . "[27] Fleming never concealed his financial motivation, explaining during a lecture at Oxford University that "if you decide to become a professional writer[,] you must . . . decide whether you wish to write for fame or money. I write, unashamedly, for the latter."[28] In short, Bond enabled Fleming "to gain a fortune."[29]

While prestige and money seemed important, Bond ultimately held a much deeper significance for Fleming, who needed constant excitement in his life: "He felt society owed him an interesting life and he went about to get it. In many ways it was through Bond that he achieved it."[30] It has been said that Fleming created Bond as the vehicle through which the author, "the ultimate bachelor [who] lived a lifestyle of adventure and intrigue," could "live this life forever."[31] Perpetuating his bachelor lifestyle through Bond seemed to be a vicarious compromise with or reconciliation of the fact that marriage would change Fleming's lifestyle. Thus, Fleming, himself a fundamental "hero worshipper," created Bond as his own personal savior, a character that could forever pursue Fleming's passions for women, golf, fast cars, gambling, and skin diving even if Fleming himself could no longer do so.[32]

Not surprisingly, Fleming noted that the most admirable trait Bond exhibited was the character's "efficiency and his way with blondes," perhaps a reference to the fact that Fleming married a brunette.[33] For the middle-aged, married Fleming, Bond enabled him to "play out these feelings in his books [through] James Bond's pleasures."[34] John Pearson observed that Bond is "the man who would always succeed where Fleming failed."[35] Indeed, Bond

> was not a spy—he was a man of action; and although he suffered from almost all the weaknesses Fleming pretended to despise in himself—his fear, his materialism, his drinking and womanizing—he could always turn these weaknesses to good account and always win: the ideal . . . figure for Fleming.[36]

Fleming himself remarked that Bond was his "pillow fantasy, and fantasy isn't real life by definition."[37] It was, according to Fleming, "very much the Walter Mitty syndrome . . . the author's feverish dreams of what he might have been—bang, bang, bang, kiss, kiss . . . [i]t's what you would expect of an adolescent mind, which I happen to possess."[38]

One of Fleming's great strengths was the way in which he breathed life "into his dream, of seeing [himself] through the eyes of James Bond."[39] According to John Pearson, Fleming's

> real gift as a reporter lay in his ability to see certain dangerous or exotic or exciting situations through the eyes of James Bond . . . . [He] was doing what he could do best—describing his own sensations, isolated in a world of novelty and beauty . . . just as the hero of his books is always alone, and if he had later changed the "I" to "Bond" . . . for Bond was a mask which this anxious romantic would slip on when he wanted to elaborate one of his private fantasies or put his delinquent schoolboy's view of the world into a form which was immune both to ridicule and criticism.[40]

Indeed, it is apparent that "James Bond is a projection of what Ian Fleming would like to have been."[41]

While Fleming may very well have been realizing his own fantasies vicariously through Bond, one colleague suggested that the "marked resemblance between Fleming and Bond" was more profound in that Fleming daydreamed that he was Bond and spoke "as if Bond really exists."[42] Malcolm Muggeridge agreed: "Fleming really was Bond, who truly represented all his hopes and dreams . . . money, sex, and snobbishness . . . . "[43] Fleming's stepson, Lord O'Neill, always viewed Bond as the embodiment of Fleming,[44] and John Pearson wrote that "James Bond is . . . Fleming's dream of a self that might have been—a tougher, stronger, more effective . . . character than the real Fleming."[45] Of course, Pearson's assessment can be discounted since he authored biographies of both Fleming and the fictional Bond.

John Pearson, Malcolm Muggeridge, and Lord O'Neill were not the only individuals who recognized the Fleming-as-Bond and Bond-as-Fleming dichotomy. Cubby Broccoli reportedly—and frequently—confused Fleming with Bond, utilizing the terms "'in the spirit of Ian Fleming' and 'in the spirit of James Bond' interchangeably."[46] Many traits shared by both Fleming and his fictional alter ego have been succinctly summarized:

> The biography of Fleming and that of James Bond have many points in common, the writer projected a good deal of himself in his character. Fleming had been a Commander in the Navy, liked blue suits, preferred shoes without laces, and wore only moccasins, like Bond. Fleming, like Bond, had been a member of Naval Intelligence, the Navy's Secret Service . . . . Fleming was a keen player of golf, smoked every day sixty cigarettes . . . , spoke French

> and German: like Bond . . . Fleming, as a young reporter, had often attended motor racing at Le Mans and, like Bond, had a passion for cars[.] . . . Fleming . . . tried to use his special ability as a gambler to win . . . money from some members of the German espionage group [during the war] but he lost everything . . . : James Bond was to take posthumous revenge . . . by winning everything from Le Chiffre at the baccarat table of the Casino of Royale-les-Eaux . . . . Fleming had made underwater dives with Commander [Jacques] Cousteau: Bond was a subaquatic expert. Fleming had even allowed Bond to use his special recipe for Martini: three measures of Gordon's gin, one of vodka, and a half-measure of Kina Lillet.
>
> Ian Fleming, the author, was a gentleman. James Bond, the character, is also a gentleman.[47]

Although it is true that an author writes about what he or she knows,[48] it is apparent that "everything about James Bond [had] distinct resemblances between him and his creator."[49] Yet Fleming refused to acknowledge a personal connection to Double-O-Seven: "Bond is a highly romanticized version of *anybody*, but certainly not I, and I certainly couldn't keep up with him."[50]

* * *

Numerous newspaper and magazine articles have traced Fleming's real-life inspirations in order to uncover similarities between Bond and the author. One journalist suggested that Fleming lifted Bond from Duckworth Drew, William Le Queux's secret agent: "There can be no doubt that Fleming knew of Drew when he sat down to plot Bond's . . . adventures."[51] As early as 1964, *Time* reported that Bond was not only a fictional image of the author but also a "composite of commando and intelligence types Fleming knew."[52] Since the debut of the cinematic Bond, articles with titles such as "Will the real James Bond please stand up?" have been abundant.[53] Andrew Lycett identified four former Fleming colleagues—Merlin Minshall, Michael Mason, and Commanders Wilfred Dunderdale and Alexander Glen—as individuals whose personalities and characteristics Fleming coalesced into the fictional Bond.

But much disagreement persists. While Fleming may have borrowed traits from people with whom he associated, many believe that Fleming was "the central figure" of Bond.[54] John Pearson, for one, cited the connection between M and Fleming's mother as a prime example:

> Fleming often called his mother M. There seem to be distinct parallels between the demanding old autocrat in Universal Export bestowing on James Bond his grudging praise, his terrifying blame, and the way Mrs. Val[entine] Fleming tended to treat her son Ian . . . . [H]is mother was certainly one of the few people he was frightened of, and her sternness toward him, her unexplained demand, and her remorseless insistence on success find a curious and constant echo in the way M. handles that hard-ridden, hard-killing agent, 007.[55]

Bond's sarcastic complaint to Tiffany Case in *Diamonds Are Forever* highlights this connection: "I'm almost married already. To a man. Name begins with M. I'd have to divorce him before I tried marrying a woman."[56] It is entirely plausible that Fleming's bitterness over his broken engagement and the role his mother played in facilitating its demise underscores Bond's remark.[57]

Other connections are also apparent. Major Boothroyd, the weapons expert in Fleming's novels, was inspired, in part, by writer and weapons connoisseur Geoffrey Boothroyd, who corresponded with Fleming and offered suggestions to improve Bond's fictional weapons arsenal. Weapons and gadget expert Q, also named Major Boothroyd on film and portrayed by actor Desmond Llewelyn, was also modeled after Charles Fraser-Smith, a wartime colleague who reportedly invented highly sophisticated spy equipment and accessories. Bond's CIA counterpart, Felix Leiter, was based upon two of Fleming's close friends.[58]

Bond's name, as mentioned above, held particular meaning for Fleming. But what about the ubiquitous number Double-O-Seven? The origin of "007" can be traced to the German diplomatic code 0070 used to send the Zimmerman telegram during World War I. Fleming was privy to this information, having been assigned to the naval intelligence department that first broke the code.[59]

And what about all of the interesting names of each literary Bond Girl? From Vesper Lynd in *Casino Royale* to Kissy Suzuki in *You Only Live Twice*, each name of Bond's "eager bedmates . . . embod[ies] most of Fleming's own . . . view[s] of female[s] . . . formed during [his] hit-and-run affairs . . . ."[60] All of these connections between Bond's fictional world and Fleming's own personal experiences support the contention that Bond was simply "Fleming's mouthpiece."[61] As John Pearson noted, Bond was "a mouthpiece for the man who inhabits him, a dummy for him to hang his clothes on . . . from the very first page Fleming seems bent on exploiting material drawn from his own mind and memory."[62]

* * *

That Bond served as Fleming's "mouthpiece" begs the question: "Why should we take James Bond seriously?"[63] A sufficient answer is difficult to ascertain, and Fleming himself did not make the task any easier. Of course, Fleming actively promoted the notion that Bond should not be taken seriously, dismissing his novels, as noted above, as works "written for warm-blooded heterosexuals in railway trains, airplanes, or beds."[64] Novelist Kingsley Amis wrote that Fleming failed to understand the simple maxim that "people take you at your own valuation," and Fleming's own comments that his books "tremble on the brink of corn" contributed to an atmosphere in which others did not take his work seriously.[65]

But what Fleming may have said or written ran quite contrary to his actions. Though he once said that "if one has a grain of intelligence it is difficult to go on being serious about a character like James Bond," Fleming treated Bond as a very serious endeavor.[66] In fact, he wrote that his Bond novels were specifically designed for "the total stimulation of the reader all the way through, even to his taste buds."[67] Therefore, one must dismiss Fleming's contention that he only sought to cater to warm-blooded heterosexuals.

Just as the reader "must not be unable to stop reading," Fleming developed a highly elaborate method to which he would adhere when he produced each Bond novel.[68] He preferred to write from his vacation retreat in Jamaica, a low, modern house he named GoldenEye that was built facing the Caribbean Sea.[69] Fleming committed himself to writing for an average of four hours each day, which approximated two thousand words. He also "made no corrections until the book was finished" so as to not distract himself[70] from the "rough idea of where he was going, but he never looked back . . . [and] only tried to keep the narrative driving straight ahead."[71]

The attention and serious manner with which Fleming approached the Bond novels is apparent: "It's no good writing for the muse, I find. I must regard it as office work, and bloody well get on with it."[72] Two separate accounts shed light into the elaborate routine to which Fleming strictly adhered.[73] According to John Cork and Bruce Scivally,

> [a]fter a morning swim on the reef, he had a breakfast of scrambled eggs and Blue Mountain coffee . . . . At nine, he then went to one of his carefully selected locations to write . . . . In the early years, Fleming often wrote in the main living room, but later, when he had a more difficult time exiling houseguests, he would take his typewriter into the bedroom. Eventually, he had his living room desk installed

> in a small building on the edge of his property so he could escape all household distractions.[74]

Andrew Lycett presented a similar, albeit slightly different version:

> Every morning [after breakfast] he made his way across the small veranda into the main living-room. He shut the big doors, closed the jalousies, and opened his big roll-top desk. For . . . hours he pounded the keys of his twenty-year-old Imperial portable typewriter. At noon he emerged[,] . . . he slept for an hour, and then . . . he returned . . . . Ian was a man of routine, and that writing regiment, now established, continued for the next dozen years, whenever he was at GoldenEye.[75]

For the "accumulation of . . . fine points of detail," Fleming "always carried a pad with him 'for jotting down the things one sees as one goes along. For the rest of it [he] use[d] a research service in London.'"[76]

Kingsley Amis wrote that the Bond novels contain an extensive amount "of efficiency, of pace, of craftsmanlike attention to detail."[77] Fleming preferred precision, using exact names for objects whenever possible, noting that attention to detail and minutae "excite[d] and interest[ed]" him.[78] It also made for effective writing: "The more we have of this kind of detailed stuff laid down around a character, the more interested we are in him."[79] He also enlisted the aid of friends to read drafts, make stylistic suggestions, and help verify details or identify factual errors.[80] Other aspects of Fleming's writing, such as settling upon the name "Blofeld" for his arch-villain, required little research: Fleming perused a membership directory list at the Boodles club until the name "Henry Blofeld" piqued his interest.

Even the typewriter Fleming utilized was carefully selected. Sampling several typewriters until he found one to his liking, Fleming settled upon a German portable model. To celebrate the completion of *Casino Royale* and his new status as a novelist, Fleming replaced the portable with a custom Royal typewriter plated entirely in gold.

The seriousness Fleming accorded to crafting Bond's fictitious world translated to his efforts to promote his novels. Unlike most authors, Fleming himself solicited favorable reviews, usually with the enticement of a personally inscribed copy: "'I have sent copies around to all our friends asking them to give it a hand in America.'"[81] He even lobbied Somerset Maugham to provide this favorable review of *Casino Royale*: "[This is] the first of what I trust will be truly the first of a great many books . . . it goes with a swing from the first page to the last and is really thrilling all through . . . you really managed to get the tension to the highest possible pitch."[82]

Looking to establish an American market for Bond, Fleming contacted three of the largest publishing houses—Doubleday, W.W. Norton & Company, and Alfred A. Knopf, Inc.—to print *Casino Royale*. All three, citing the novel's implausibility and emphasis upon violence, rejected it. Scribner's ultimately published the work, and Fleming networked extensively with contacts in New York to promote the book. It sold so poorly that it was renamed *You Asked For It* when it appeared in paperback in the United States.[83] Fleming left no sector of advertising, ranging from radio and television spots to magazine and newspaper articles, uncovered. Later, he solicited the assistance of a friend to write the introduction to his omnibus *Gilt-Edged Bonds*, which praised Fleming for his ability to "capture[] the imagination of a generation with his stories of adventure and intrigue."[84]

By contrast, unsolicited reviews were mixed. Some praised Fleming for being "intensely observant, acutely literate [who] can turn a cliché into a silk purse with astute alchemy. No question."[85] Others were less laudable. It was, however, clear from a review of *Thunderball* in *The Times* that Fleming was well-attuned to his critics: "Mr. Fleming has been reading his reviews . . . [*Thunderball*] is a highly polished performance, with an ingenious plot . . . and plenty of excitement."[86] A 1954 review of *Live and Let Die*, Fleming's second Bond novel, praised the book as "an ingenious affair, full of recondite knowledge and horrific spills and thrills."[87] *Goldfinger* was "backed up by [Fleming's] sound writing and . . . sophisticated mind."[88] One review in *The Sunday Times Literary Supplement* praised Fleming as "the most interesting recent recruit among thriller-writers."[89] With *On Her Majesty's Secret Service*, considered "one of the most engaging Bond novels,"[90] *The Times* declared that it was "an indisputable fact that Mr. Fleming is a most compelling storyteller."[91]

But all that glittered was not gold. *From Russia, With Love*, attacked as a crude attempt to produce a spy thriller during the Cold War, was characterized as leaving the reader "uneasily hovering between fact and fiction."[92] A review published in the *New Statesman* characterized *Dr. No* as "the nastiest book" the critic ever read and a work that was "badly written to the point of incoherence."[93] A review of *The Spy Who Loved Me* in The Times noted that the book "lack[ed] . . . careful construction and must be written off as a disappointment."[94] One critic degraded Fleming's entire Bond series: "[T]hey just aren't writing bad books like they used to."[95] Despite Fleming's travels to Japan in 1962 to research *You Only Live Twice* and the fact that it became an immediate bestseller upon its release in 1964,[96] the novel was described by critics as a work representing the extent to which Bond was "a symbol of our collective frivolity."[97] *Time* reprinted Malcolm Muggeridge's critique of Fleming's Bond:

British novelist Ian Fleming works in his study at GoldenEye, 1964.
(Express/Stringer/Hulton Archive/Getty Images)

> While admitting that Bond's "instant appeal to attractive women, his dash and daring and smartness combined with toughness, make him every inch a hero of our time," [Muggeridge] also notes that "insofar as one can focus on so shadowy and unreal a character, he is utterly despicable: obsequious to his superiors, pretentious in his tastes, callous and brutal in his ways, with strong undertones of sadism, and an unspeakable cad in his relations with women, toward whom sexual appetite represents the only approach."[98]

Regardless of critical acclaim or disdain, Fleming believed that quantity outweighed quality, and he vowed to "write another book quickly before the critics have had a chance to savage the first."[99]

The volume of material Fleming produced began Bond's ascent into the realm of ubiquity. Beginning in 1957, the *Daily Express* began a serialized comic strip version of *Casino Royale* that ran for 139 days.[100] Two years later, *Playboy* discovered the Bond novels and began serializing them in an attempt to "aestheticise them."[101] Scene depictions accompanied the *Playboy* serializations and were supplemented with interviews of and articles by Fleming. Hugh Hefner remarked that the contemporary edge inherent in Fleming's novels appealed to his readers and that a "marriage" between Bond and *Playboy* "was a natural."[102] Indeed, "[f]rom the outset, *Playboy* and the movie Bond were linked in the public eye. We both liked gadgets and girls. A Bond movie was '*Playboy* magazine with a gun.'"[103] Hefner later added, "What my life was all about, in the Playboy mansion, was connected to James Bond. At one point I said, 'We both love the gadgets, we both love the girls. He's the only one that has the license to kill. But I have a better license.'"[104]

* * *

The year 1961 "was shaping up to be . . . a very interesting year for 007."[105] *Life* published a list of President John F. Kennedy's ten favorite books. Ranked ninth was Fleming's *From Russia, With Love*.[106] Kennedy's interest in Bond "gave Fleming's books a great life, and Ian well knew it."[107] Allen Dulles had, in fact, been introduced to Fleming's novels by Jacqueline Kennedy, who reportedly gave him a copy of *From Russia, With Love* with an accompanying note: "Here is a book you should have."[108] Fleming's new publisher, Signet, exploited the presidential endorsement. One advertisement, which depicted the White House with a light shining from one window, was captioned, "You can bet on it he's reading one of these Ian Fleming thrillers."[109]

The following year, *Time* reported that Fleming was President Kennedy's favorite mystery writer,[110] and Kennedy later requested a private screening of *Dr. No* in the White House cinema. Kennedy was reportedly reading a Bond novel the night before he was assassinated.[111] In fact, reports surfaced that Lee Harvey Oswald was also reading a Fleming novel the night before Kennedy's assassination,[112] supposedly corroborated by a *New York Times* report less than a week later that Oswald "checked out a number of science-fiction books and Ian Fleming spy mysteries" from the library during the summer of 1963.[113]

The presidential connection was not lost upon Fleming, who "could not help but enjoy the fact that the most important man on the planet also happened to be a James Bond fan."[114] Indeed, Fleming remarked that it was "'very nice to know that a President . . . enjoy[s] my books. It's also very good for sales.'"[115] He opined that the president enjoyed his novels because of their combination of physical violence, effort, and triumph, all of which he said reflected President Kennedy's PT-boat experiences.[116] At the same time, Fleming recognized that "*many* politicians seem to like my books[,] . . . perhaps because politicians like solutions, with everything properly tied up at the end."[117]

Although President Kennedy enjoyed Fleming's novels, it is also apparent that the president attributed a greater significance to them—and, in turn, to their creator—than one might think. During a dinner in March 1960, Kennedy solicited Fleming's advice on how the United States could depose Fidel Castro in Cuba. Fleming "described how he would use 'ridicule' to force Castro out of office. Since the Cubans only cared about money, religion, and sex[,] . . . fake dollar bills should be dropped on the island to destabilize the currency, as well as leaflets declaring Castro to be impotent."[118] During another, more famous exchange between Fleming and Kennedy, Fleming shared his belief that "Americans should drop leaflets from the air, informing the Cuban people that their beards were a natural receptacle for radioactivity and would lead to their long-term impotence."[119] While Fleming may have made these remarks with tongue firmly implanted in cheek, historians have considered his discussions with Kennedy as examples that "underscore how out of touch JFK was with the reality of clandestine operation, while his obsession with the fantasy world of espionage conjured by Fleming accounts for his inexplicable romance with the CIA."[120] Columnist Vincent Canby observed:

> Whether accurately or not, the first films made from the Bond novels came to characterize a number of aspects of the Kennedy Administration with its reputation for glamour, wit and sophistication, and its real-life drama and melodrama. Indeed, the President himself could be seen as a kind of Bond figure, and the 1962 Cuban missile crisis as a real-life Bond situation.[121]

To placate the president, the CIA "encouraged Kennedy's James Bond fantasy"[122] as Kennedy sought to emulate much of Bond's fictional world in the actual practice of espionage.[123] Nevertheless, it is clear that Kennedy, like Fleming, took Bond seriously, even if Kennedy's efforts to translate Bond's fiction into reality were flawed.

* * *

Contrary to what Fleming claimed, Bond was not simply a creation designed to divert his mind from marriage. Fleming's self-deprecation obfuscates the seriousness of his endeavor, and it is apparent that reasons abound as to why Bond should be taken seriously. Fleming certainly did, and others, including an American president, have as well. In 1964, *Time* noted that Bond, "though thoroughly amoral, nevertheless served the public good—a combination that proved irresistible to an age dedicated to affluence and to being with it."[124] Indeed, as early as 1959, *Playboy* identified Bond as an endeavor serious enough to warrant an alliance. Nearly fifty years later, it is perplexing to retain an equivocal attitude about Bond when it is clear that the fictional character should be accorded but one type of consideration: serious. Very serious.

003

The James Bond Novels: Women in Print

[Ian Fleming's] proper place in literature . . . is with those demi-giants of an earlier day: Jules Verne, Rider Haggard, Conan Doyle. Ian Fleming has set his stamp on the story of action and intrigue, bringing to it a sense of our time, a power and a flair that will win him readers . . . .

—Kingsley Amis[1]

Bond is cruel and sensuous. He uses people, especially women. He's vaguely on the side of right, which legalises all kinds of revolting standards. But Fleming did create a myth in Bond.

—Nick Webb[2]

[T]he Fleming novels do something the films cannot possibly do: They put us inside Bond's body. We're . . . in the driver's seat with Bond, with his aching head and multiple scars, his stomach tightening with the ants of fear, his job on the line because of some recent failure and part of his mind on a woman he'd be better off leaving alone. Fleming lets us in, and the movies do not.

—Emily Jenkins[3]

[T]he fat man who sits with a blonde woman. At the table by the cassa. She is from Vienna. Her name is Lisl Baum. A luxus whore.

—Kristatos, to James Bond in "Risico"[4]

Ian Fleming completed twelve James Bond novels and two collections of short stories: *Casino Royale* (1953), *Live and Let Die* (1954), *Moonraker* (1955), *Diamonds Are Forever* (1956), *From Russia, With Love* (1957), *Dr. No* (1958), *Goldfinger* (1959), *For Your Eyes Only* (collection of short stories, 1960), *Thunderball* (1961), *The Spy Who Loved Me* (1962), *On Her Majesty's Secret Service* (1963), *You Only Live Twice* (1964), *The Man With the Golden Gun* (1965), and *Octopussy and The Living Daylights* (collection of short stories, 1966). According to Allen Dulles, no other author "would have the audacity to try to bring Bond back" following Fleming's death.[5] History, as noted previously, has proven otherwise.[6]

In his seminal study of the Bond novels, novelist and scholar Umberto Eco defined the structure of Fleming's novels as a sequence of "oppositions" or "limited number[s] of permutations and reactions" that drive the narrative.[7] Others elaborated upon Eco's assessment, arguing that the structure of each Bond novel is replete with

> "sexism and imperialism . . . inscribed within the very form of the Bond novels . . . . As the relations between Bond and the villain and between Bond and the girl develop and move toward their resolution, a series of collateral ideological tensions is thus simultaneously worked through and resolved. It is in this way that the Bond novels achieve their 'ideological effect' . . . of placing women back in position beneath men."[8]

The appearance of the Bond Girl figures prominently within the plot.

Tony Bennett and Janet Woollacott divided a typical Bond novel into nine distinct episodes. In the first episode, Bond is assigned a task by M. In the second episode, Bond is introduced to either the villain or the villain in a vicarious form. Thereafter, the third episode features Bond giving a "first check to the villain, or the villain giv[ing] a first check to Bond."[9] During the fourth episode, the Bond Girl presents herself. In the fifth episode, Bond either "possesses 'the girl' or begins her seduction."[10] During the sixth episode, Bond and the Bond Girl, "either simultaneously or at different moments," are captured by the villain.[11] In the seventh episode, the villain tortures Bond and, in some cases, the Bond Girl.[12] The eighth episode finds Bond defeating the villain, either by killing him or his representatives, or assisting with their killing. Finally, during the ninth episode, a convalescing Bond "possesses 'the girl,' whom he then loses; she either leaves him or is killed by the villain."[13] It is from this general structure that the cinematic Bond Girl has emerged.

Maryam d'Abo and John Cork characterized the cinematic Bond Girl as

> independent, defiant, and probably dangerous. She has broken away from the location of her birth, venturing fearlessly into the wider world. She is searching for something, a sense of exhilaration, adventure, risk. The odds are that somewhere she took a wrong turn, met the wrong man and endured the wrong personal tragedy. Now, she has found herself in one of life's dark cul-de-sacs.[14]

Are these attributes derived from the novels? Umberto Eco identified at least five specific character traits of the literary Bond Girl. Although she is both beautiful and good, the Bond Girl nonetheless becomes "frigid and unhappy by severe trials suffered in adolescence."[15] Her experiences condition her to the service of the villain, and it is Bond who causes her to "appreciate[] human nature in all its richness."[16] Bond possesses her, but he ultimately loses her.[17] According to one critic, "the Bond Girl is inside the plot rather than sitting on the sidelines."[18]

But the Bond Girl is also on the outside, literally. Early cover artwork and designs for the novels, which were created by Sam Peffer, reflected the prominent role that the Bond Girl possessed in the books. In fact, the cover for the Pan Books edition of *Live and Let Die* featured an illustration of Solitaire "show[ing] little of the confidence and sexual self-assurance that Fleming instilled in the women of his novels."[19] Thus, within the literary context, the Bond Girl served both as a character essential to the narrative structure and as a marketing tool.[20]

One particular irony in Fleming's writing was his failure to "adhere to the conventional trajectory of spy fiction" in terms of gender.[21] Whereas women were typically "outsiders" or in "subservient positions" functioning "as peripheral romantic interest[s]" in other novels, Fleming portrayed his women as "enabling mechanism[s]."[22] Most notably, "the British Secret Service depends upon its female infrastructure: women carry the files, operate the decoders, oversee the paperwork, screen the appointments, and supply the canteen services which keep the institution running. Headquarters hums with efficient women."[23] This observation may suggest that Fleming imbued his female characters with admirable, strong traits, particularly since one scholar classified Fleming's women as "not simple sexpots, but ruling-class goddesses."[24] Yet Fleming ensured that the roles he created for his female characters were wholly subordinate: men "had an excuse for fragmentary affairs . . . for the women, an affair outside the Service automatically made you a 'security risk' and . . . you had a choice of resignation from the Service . . . or of perpetual concubinage to your King and country."[25]

A tension, nonetheless, is inherent in Fleming's female characters. Although they are relegated to virtual second-class citizens, the Bond Girls are essential components of the plot, aiding Bond throughout his various missions. As Christine Bold noted, women "are equally indispensable on the front lines of international spying":[26]

> Bond frequently depends on women to guide him through the enemy territory of his exotic locations: Honeychile Rider, who knows the Jamaican tides and island terrain . . . . Kissy Suzuki, who steers Bond to and rescues him from Blofeld's Garden of Death . . . . Tiffany Case, who skillfully false-deals him the winning cards at the Spang brothers' Las Vegas casino . . . . As often as Bond snatches women from the jaws of death, they repay the compliment: Pussy Galore thwarts the arch-villain's plans and saves the lives of not only Bond but the entire population of Fort Knox . . . . Domino Vitale fires the fatal spear in Emilio Largo, SPECTRE agent, just as he is about to shoot Bond.[27]

Yet at the same time, women were distractions: "It was time to clear the silly bitch out of [Bond's] mind and concentrate on the job."[28]

How did Fleming reconcile the Bond Girl's effective assistance and integral role with her inherent inferiority? In many ways, he did not at all. For example, in *For Your Eyes Only*, Bond scolds Judy Havelock: "'Don't be a silly bitch . . . . This is man's work.'"[29] Perhaps Fleming's focus upon the Bond Girl's physique and the notion that a woman's body was created for Bond's ultimate pleasure undermines whatever other constructive, admirable attributes she possesses.

To that end, it is interesting to note that Fleming utilized the term "girl" throughout his writings: "It is no secret that Fleming's fiction ritually works to objectify and infantilise its 'girls', as these sexually mature women are routinely named."[30] Moreover, it has been described as "a cardinal rule of Fleming's fiction that women who serve—and service—the British espionage forces are buxom, slim, long-legged, lightly tanned—and, more often than not, they wear their long, glossy hair curved into the nape of the neck."[31] Indeed, the Bond Girl's physical appearance was a prominent element in Fleming's fiction.

Umberto Eco determined that the Bond Girl's aesthetic appearance was her primary attribute—"the girl is beautiful and good"[32]—and Fleming detailed his heroines' physical features with great precision. Blondes, preferred over brunettes and redheads, constitute a majority of the literary Bond Girls. In *Dr. No*, Fleming wrote of Honeychile Rider that her hair "was ash blonde. It was cut to the shoulders and hung there . . . . [T]he naked girl with the strands of fair hair, reminded Bond of . . . Botticelli's Venus."[33] Mary Goodnight possesses a "golden bell of hair [that] fell back to embrace her neck."[34] Mary Ann Russell, the heroine of *From A View To A Kill*, has pale skin that reminds Bond of velvet, and her "blonde hair was silk—to the roots."[35] In *The Book of Bond, or Every Man His Own 007*, Kingsley Amis, writing under the pseudonym William Tanner, reassured non-blondes that they could remain desirable: "If you aren't [blonde] by nature, don't color your hair artificially unless you're prepared to give hourly attention to the roots . . . . [D]ark-brown, blue-black and black hair is also permissible."[36]

Beyond hair color, blue or grey eyes, a small nose, full lips, and short, unpainted fingernails are also typical features Fleming bestowed upon the Bond Girl. In *Live and Let Die*, Solitaire's "eyes were blue, alight and disdainful,"[37] her hair is "blue-black," and she possesses a "sensual mouth which held a hint of cruelty."[38] Tatiana Romanova, who appears in *From Russia, With Love*, is "a very beautiful girl" who possesses "fine dark brown silken hair," "soft pale skin," "eyes of the deepest blue," a wide mouth, and "full and finely etched" lips.[39] Mary Goodnight has "wide-apart blue eyes, now ablaze with the moon . . . ."[40]

Vesper Lynd in *Casino Royale* is adorned in a "skirt [that] was closely pleated and flowed down from a narrow, but not a thin, waist."[41] Her eyes, like those of Solitaire, Mary Goodnight, and Tatiana Romanova, are "wide apart and deep blue," while her skin is "lightly sun-tanned and bore no trace of makeup except on her mouth which was wide and sensual."[42] Tiffany Case, the heroine of *Diamonds Are Forever*, enjoys the following introduction:

> She was sitting half naked, astride a chair in front of the dressing table, gazing across the back of the chair into the triple mirror. Her bare arms were folded along the tall back of the chair and her chin was resting on her arms. Her spine was arched and there was arrogance in the set of her head and shoulders. The thin black strap of her brassiere across the naked white back, the tight black lace pants and the angled thrust of her legs whipped at Bond's senses.[43]

These types of descriptions were systematically employed by Fleming. For example, Gala Brand, who appears in *Moonraker*, possesses a "strapping body . . . incredibly erotic in the tight emphasis of the clinging brassiere and pants . . . [with] a soft flat stomach descending to the mystery of her tightly closed thighs."[44] Mary Goodnight wears a short-skirted pink frock that is "all tight against the bosom and the hips" with buttons down the back.[45]

While Fleming privately stated that he preferred a female's posterior, which he felt was a woman's most alluring attribute, he nevertheless painstakingly described his Bond Girl's bosom. Fleming's focus upon the breasts prompted one author to satirically suggest that Fleming possessed an apparent obsession: "[The Bond Girl] has fine, jutting, splendid, faultless, exquisite, perfectly molded, beautiful, unrestrained, perfect, firm, proud, hilly, perky, thrusting, out-thrown, unashamed, swelling, full, luscious, . . . delicious, hard . . . protuberances."[46]

The characterizations were virtually endless. Any shortcomings Gala Brand possesses are overcome by "the swell of her breasts, which were as splendid as Bond had guessed from the measurements on her record sheet."[47] Vesper Lynd is described as wearing a dress that is "lasciviously tight across her fine breasts."[48] Honeychile Rider is imbued with "beautiful firm breasts . . . [that] jutted towards [Bond] without concealment."[49] In *Goldfinger*, Jill Masterton's breasts "thrust against the black silk of [her] brassiere,"[50] and Bond quickly notices Dominetta Vitale's "high-riding and deeply V-ed" breasts in *Thunderball*.[51] Fleming described Solitaire's firm bosom in a seduction scene: "He freed his right hand and put it between their bodies, feeling her hard breasts . . . he slipped it down her back until it came to the cleft at the base of her spine."[52] Of course, none of these women's assets rivals those of Tatiana Romanova, whose breasts Fleming described as simply "faultless."[53] In sum, "[f]ine breasts, splendid breasts, faultless breasts, beautiful firm breasts, thrusting breasts, high-riding and deeply V-ed breasts [we]re very important" in Fleming's Bond mythology.[54]

Physical assets formed the cornerstone of Fleming's writing. In a brief moment of clarity, Bond contemplates marriage to Contessa Teresa di Vicenzo in *On Her Majesty's Secret Service*, but his reasons for doing so are misplaced: "Hell! I'll never find another girl like this one. She's got everything I've ever looked for in a woman . . . . She seems to love me. She'd let me go on with my life."[55] Of her many attributes, Teresa di Vicenzo's coital performance is Bond's first and foremost concern: "She's beautiful, *in bed* and out."[56] But bedroom prowess requires optimal physical conditioning, and Fleming cautioned that too much exercise ultimately detracted from a woman's feminine quality. Tatiana Romanova's posterior, for example, is "so hardened with exercise that it had lost the smooth downward feminine sweep, and now . . . it jutted like a man's."[57] *Elle* sought to justify Fleming's focus upon the body by suggesting that "the main point of the message between the Bond girl and her man is . . . commit[ment] to the body and to movements."[58]

Fleming's commitment to the bodies of his Bond Girls diverted attention away from his shortcoming in the area of character development. In a chapter entitled "Beautiful Firm Breasts," Amis explored how Fleming introduced his literary Bond Girl, noting a consistency in presentation that varied little between each book. The Bond Girl's skin, for example, is often suntanned, her eyes are almost always blue, her height is approximately five foot seven inches or taller, and although her frame is not thin, she is very physically fit. Fleming "evolved something approaching a formula for the presentation of Bond's fair quarry. Its most noticeable feature is that . . . the given girl appears in the first place . . . *she* is going to turn up."[59] The attributes of these female characters are summarized in Appendix B.

* * *

The Bond Girl's physical characteristics aside, Fleming imbued Bond with a contemptuous attitude toward women. Indeed, Bond reflects many of Fleming's attitudes about raw sexual prowess, and the spy's first and foremost concern is the "passion of an animal function."[60] In *On Her Majesty's Secret Service*, Teresa di Vicenzo herself commands Bond to "'[d]o anything you like[,] . . . [b]e rough with me. Treat me like the lowest whore in creation.'"[61] Bond's physical attraction to Dominetta Vitale in *Thunderball* is intense as he schemes to steal her from her current love interest:

> [She is a] sensual girl—a beautiful Arab mare who would only allow herself to be ridden by a horseman with steel thighs and velvet hands, and then only with curb and saw-bit—and then only when he had broken her to bridle and saddle . . . for the moment another man was in the saddle. He would first have to be unhorsed.[62]

It is clear that the horseman-saddle image represents both pure animalistic sexual function and a necessity for the male to assume a dominant role over the female, though Fleming did not go so far as to describe Dominetta Vitale in the same manner as Teresa di Vicenzo.

The distinction between pure physicality and domination, however, was blurred by sadistic, and even masochistic, tendencies. In *Thunderball*, Bond's excitement over Dominetta Vitale is described as follows: "She had a gay, to-hell-with-you-face that . . . would become animal in passion. In bed she would fight and bite and then suddenly melt into hot surrender."[63] Judy Havelock's face is "wild and rather animal, with a wide sensuous mouth . . . . "[64] In *Casino Royale*, Bond sees "luck as a woman, to be . . . brutally ravaged, never pandered."[65] Later, Vesper Lynd's capture receives a graphic description: "Apart from her legs, which were naked to the hips, Vesper *was only a parcel*. Her long black velvet skirt had been lifted over her arms and head and tied above her head with a piece of rope."[66]

As the foregoing passage from *Casino Royale* indicates, Fleming prominently incorporated images of physical abuse into his novels. Bound and naked, Honeychile Rider is left to be devoured by crabs in *Dr. No*, while Vivienne Michel is severely beaten and raped in *The Spy Who Loved Me*. In *Live and Let Die*, plans are devised to drag Solitaire behind the villain's yacht, leaving her corpse to sharks. A beaten Gala Brand is left to a fiery demise from a rocket's exhaust in *Moonraker*. In *From Russia, With Love*, a deadly fight between two gypsy women is vividly detailed, creating a scene that was masterfully replicated on film:

> The girls tore apart and backed away like cats, their shining bodies glinting through the last rags of their shifts and blood showing on the exposed breasts of the big girl . . . her right foot lashed out in a furious *coup de savate* that made a slap like a pistol shot. The big girl gave a wounded cry and clutched at herself . . . [the] other foot kicked up to the stomach and she threw herself in after it.[67]

Regardless of whether his descriptions were meant to arouse or to fascinate, Fleming never emboldened his female characters. Instead, he induced pity for and encouraged negative responses to them from his readers.

Fleming also addressed the very sensitive subject of rape. *The Spy Who Loved Me*, which "ha[d] nothing to do with spying but everything to do with the co-option of the female reader,"[68] is narrated from the perspective of Vivienne Michel, a twenty-three year-old woman who "confirms all the sexist and racist stereotypes of the earlier Bond novels; her stories confirm that women do define themselves by their bodies, they are child-like naifs who need the guidance and protection of a man . . . . Above all, [she] underwrites Bond's sexual dominance over women."[69] In a chapter entitled "Bimbo," Vivienne Michel reflects:

> All women love semi-rape. They love to be taken. It was his sweet brutality against my bruised body that had made his act of love so piercingly wonderful . . . .
>
> . . . .
>
> . . . Brave, strong, ruthless with women—these were the qualities that went with his calling . . . .
>
> . . . [H]e was as I had thought him to be. Yes, this was a man to love.[70]

Similarly, in *Casino Royale*, Bond is intrigued by the thought of conquering Vesper Lynd because each time would "have the sweet tang of rape. Loving her physically would each time be a thrilling voyage . . . . Bond awoke in his own room at dawn and for a time he lay and stroked his memories."[71] The observation that all "sorts of sexual wish fulfillment do abound in the Bond chronicles" included the recognition that Fleming sought to depict both the romantic and the sadistic conquest.[72]

Fleming's descriptions of the Bond Girl's previous life experiences were also wrought with blatant sexism. Indeed, the Bond Girl represents a departure from the ideals of femininity "as specified by patriarchal ideology."[73] Typically, she "took a wrong turn" or "endured the wrong personal tragedy" at some point in her life.[74] Fleming reflected this "wrong turn" in several ways. For example, Dominetta Vitale is orphaned and raised without a father figure, factors that contribute to her sense of misplacement. Both Tiffany Case and Pussy Galore survive childhood rapes. While they share a similar traumatic experience, their responses are quite different. Pussy Galore embraces lesbianism, while Tiffany Case practices celibacy. Rejecting Bond's advances, Tiffany Case explains, "In case you're interested, I've never what you'd call 'slept with a man' in my life."[75]

In order to right the so-called "wrong turn" that plagues these and other female characters, Bond is assigned the task of effectuating a readjustment. Bennett and Woollacott commented upon this phenomenon: "In . . . responding to the challenge posed by 'the girl,' putting her back into place beneath him (both literally and metaphorically), Bond functions as an agent of the patriarchal order."[76] Indeed, Bond ultimately succeeds at awakening Tiffany Case's sexual desires.

The case of Tilly Masterton in *Goldfinger* is noteworthy. Fleming described her as a "reserved" young woman who, unlike the so-called properly aligned female who would melt in the presence of the masculine Bond, "responded with cool politeness" toward him.[77] She is "described in much the same manner as all the other generically beautiful women in the Bond books, except for a certain amount of emphasis on 'something faintly mannish and open-air about the whole of her behaviour and appearance.'"[78] Her relationship with Pussy Galore is "adoringly" close, with Tilly Masterton believing that Pussy Galore is "divine,"[79] and since the latter "gets the girls she wants," Bond concludes that the former is a lesbian.[80] Fleming offered the following critique, which extended beyond commentary related to sexual preference:

> Tilly Masterton was one of those girls whose hormones had got mixed up. [Bond] knew the type well and thought they and their male counterparts were a direct consequence of giving votes to women and

> 'sex equality'. As a result of fifty years of emancipation, feminine qualities were dying out or being transferred to the males. Pansies of both sexes were everywhere, not yet completely homosexual, but confused . . . a herd of unhappy sexual misfits.[81]

Since Tilly Masterton cannot "place herself correctly to Bond as woman to man," she is of no value and, accordingly, is slated for death.[82] Indeed, other scholars have similarly noted this reality within Fleming's works.[83]

While Bond fails to reposition Tilly Masterton's sexuality and save her life, he succeeds in realigning Pussy Galore. Throughout *Goldfinger*, Pussy Galore is presented as "vulgar[,] but lower-class in a way entirely foreign to representations of the American South."[84] The leader of a lesbian crime syndicate and an associate of the villain Auric Goldfinger, Pussy Galore ultimately permits "good to triumph over evil in the end."[85] But her awakening requires the intervention of Bond, who employs considerable charm. Once she succumbs to Bond, Pussy Galore "ceases to be one with her name (in order to assume it as object rather than subject) that she switches sides . . . . James Bond and heterosexuality are able to carry the day."[86] At the conclusion of *Goldfinger*, Pussy Galore and Bond engage in the following colloquy:

> "They told me you only liked women."
> "I never met a man before."
> "All you need is a course of T.L.C."
> "What's T.L.C.?"
> "Short for Tender Loving Care treatment. It's what they write on most papers when a waif gets brought in to a children's clinic."
> "I'd like that."
> She looked at the passionate, rather cruel mouth waiting above hers . . . she looked into the fiercely slitted grey eyes.
> "When's it going to start?"
> Bond's right hand came slowly up the firm, muscled thighs, over the flat soft plain of the stomach to the right breast, its point was hard with desire. He said softly, "Now." His mouth came ruthlessly down on hers.[87]

Unlike Tilly Masterton, who is "killed by the wrong sort of man because she places her faith in women," Pussy Galore is permitted to live because she is "converted by the right sort of man. She not only lives, but lives to tell the tale of how it was that she had come to make her initial mistake."[88] That mistake, of course, is a sexual attraction toward women. Moreover, it is perplexing that the "right sort of man" to facilitate her so-called reawakening possesses a cruel, ruthless mouth and fiercely slitted eyes, a predator about to devour his prey.

Fleming's sexual realignment of those Bond Girls who fail to conform to the traditional role prescribed for women was buttressed by a writing style that undermined the female characters. Many publications reprint the first sentence of *Casino Royale* to celebrate the beginning of the Bond legacy, but all virtually ignore the last sentence of the novel: "The bitch is dead now."[89] The 2006 cinematic version of *Casino Royale* effectively incorporates this quote, though a female M, portrayed by Dame Judy Dench, quickly reminds Bond that this characterization of Vesper Lynd is inappropriate.[90] In addition to the term "bitch," Fleming also included "'[w]hore, 'tart,' [and] 'prostitute' [as] words Bond used about women."[91] Although the following example is wrought with a stylistic flaw, Fleming's intent is not lost upon the reader, for Bond always seems eager to conquer a female. After all, a woman is always ripe for a conquest: "As a woman, he wanted to sleep with her."[92] And on the rare occasion wherein Bond does not pursue a woman, he complains:

> What the hell do they want to send me a woman for? . . . And then there was this pest of a girl. He sighed. Women were for recreation. On the job, they got in the way and fogged things up with sex and hurt feelings and all the emotional baggage they carried around.[93]

In short, Fleming presented the Bond Girl as a female who merely served as a vessel through which Bond could enjoy physical gratification. She is ultimately a "defenseless child of nature, a wanderer[,] . . . an orphan, a waif[,] . . . purely and simply sex object[]."[94]

Finally, a few passages that indicate the degree to which Bond holds contempt for his female love interests are telling. Indeed, it seems as though every facet of a female falls victim to scrutiny. For example, Dominetta Vitale is criticized for her inability to drive like a woman. Fleming, through his fictional mouthpiece, opined about women generally:

> Women are often meticulous and safe drivers, but they are very seldom first-class. In general Bond regarded them as a mild hazard and he always gave them plenty of road and was ready for the unpredictable. Four women in a car he regarded as the highest danger potential, and two women as nearly as lethal. Women together cannot keep silent in a car, and when women talk they have to look into each other's faces. They have to see the other person's expression . . . [they] distract each other's attention from the road ahead.[95]

When Vesper Lynd is captured by the enemy, Bond reflects, "These blithering women who thought they could do a man's work. Why the hell couldn't they stay at home and mind their pots and pans and stick to their frocks and gossip and leave men's work to the men . . . the silly bitch."[96] In *Diamonds Are Forever*, Tiffany Case chastises Bond for treating her poorly, stating, "You really don't treat a girl right," and implores him to "look at the way that nice man treats his girl."[97] Bond's terse response is wholly dismissive: "He's past the age of consent . . . he must be sixty. Up to forty, girls cost nothing. After that you have to pay money, or tell a story . . . . I'm not forty yet."[98]

* * *

Fleming's Bond novels present neither strong nor capable female characters. Instead, the narrative reaffirms, in no uncertain terms, sexual stereotypes that convey the author's ideal gender dynamic: subordination.[99] Yet author Furio Columbo wrote that the Bond Girl is "very similar to the girl that many of us can find close to our own home shores. Only she is more free, more adventurous, more desperate, completely uprooted from her normal context (fantasy becomes dream) and is quite at the mercy of [man's] wishes."[100] Was Columbo accurate in his assessment?

While it may be true that the Bond Girl desires to live a free and adventurous life, it seems that only her exotic travels and adventures with Bond depart substantially from anything many women in America encountered. Fleming's novels explicitly reflect a desire to keep women within a sphere of domesticity. In fact, many characterized women's lives in terms of confinement to the roles of housewives within a rigid, patriarchal society. As the decade of the 1960s unfolded, American women began to both question and challenge the traditional and prevalent gender role defined for them, a role that Fleming perpetuated in his Bond novels and was advanced by countless others. Before considering the cinematic version of Fleming's Bond Girl, it is instructive to trace the portrayal of women on screen prior to 1962, the year in which audiences were first introduced to *Dr. No*.

004

Before the Bond Girl: Women on Film

We are encouraged to worship men in life, love, bed, war and politics but we are only encouraged to worship girls on film.

—Julie Burchill[1]

[Film] . . . really reinforced masculine dominions. It was as if females, once their sexual freedom had become commonplace, no longer concerned anybody as people.

—Marjorie Rosen[2]

"[E]very society has formed a set of conclusions and prescriptions for . . . behavior on sex differences."[3] American popular culture played an influential role in defining, presenting, and perpetuating gender stereotypes throughout the twentieth century. Feminists have argued that the television and print media "bombarded girls and women with powerful normative signals which embody and perpetuate female subordination and inferiority."[4] Nowhere were these signals more pronounced than in American cinema.

Professor Marjorie Rosen asserted that "films have been a mirror held up to society's porous face. They therefore reflect the changing societal image of women—which, until recently, has not been taken seriously enough."[5] Although film may have subjugated women, cinema also empowered them: "The film industry maneuvered to keep women in their place; and yet these very myths . . . catapulted women into spheres of power beyond the wildest dreams of most of their sex."[6] Like the women who have been portrayed before and alongside the Bond Girls, the Bond Girls' transformation reflects the changing images of women and their societal roles. To place the Bond Girl in proper context, this chapter briefly examines how Hollywood depicted female characters prior to 1962.

The images of actresses, wrote film critic and author Molly Haskell, "stay with us" because they produced "moments in which their uniqueness made [them] stereotypes."[7] The first such stereotype was that of the vamp (or the femme fatale), which was made famous by actress Theda Bara. The vamp was beautiful, extremely bold and daring, and also predatory: she was "a person of a malignant and loathsome character" who ruthlessly took advantage of others.[8] The vamp, which possessed a remarkable ability to manipulate, quickly became an extremely popular character. Bara herself found instant acclaim when she instructed her man to "Kiss me, my fool" in the 1915 film *A Fool There Was*. She later reprised the role of the vamp in such films as *The Serpent* (1916), *The Vixen* (1916), and *The She-Devil* (1918), all of which, as their titles suggest, capitalized upon images of predatory women. In essence, the vamp "made helplessness, which previously and ever since has been the desirable norm for girls on film, look insipid and uninspiring."[9] The popularity of the vamp enabled Bara to star in forty films between 1915 and 1918.

The image of a predatory woman seemed contrary to the image of a more reserved, demure woman that was widely accepted in American popular culture during the World War I era. According to Marjorie Rosen, the vamp represented pure escapist entertainment:

> She was sex, blatant and overt and so far removed from reality that she could not possibly be a threat to audiences newly probing their own sexuality . . . she was unnatural; therefore, she was safe. The movie-going public could ogle without feeling guilt and discomfort—and most of all, without feeling desire. For there was no confusing Theda Bara with the girl next door. Not even with the *bad* girl next door.[10]

The vamp, therefore, was purely hyperbolic, giving audiences a glimpse of an implausible, sexually aggressive, and assertive female as an escape from the realities of warfare.

Due, in part, to the vamp's exaggerated attributes, the actresses who portrayed vamp characters garnered poor reputations and were eventually typecasted. In her biography, *Memoirs of a Star*, actress Pola Negri described her experience:

> I had gained recognition in America playing [the role of a vamp]. I did not feel that my first role in this country should be of another woman devoid of morals . . . . I wanted to play interesting roles with some

> depth and instead found myself . . . cast as a clothes horse wearing a series of lavish gowns and an exotic make-up . . . . Hollywood thought of me only in terms of playing "vamps."[11]

By the early 1920s, the image of the vamp quickly became outdated, and vamp actresses soon found themselves without work.

One can speculate that the execution of convicted spy Mata Hari, whose name became synonymous with that of a femme fatal, signified the death of the vamp. Hollywood studios began replacing the vamp with images of flappers and cute good girls—girls who harbored the desires of bad girls but to a much lesser degree than the vamp. In her demise, the vamp left a lasting legacy: women were quickly emerging as on-screen sexual objects. The vamp became the foundation for sex to forever blanket the American cinematic landscape.

Shortly after the vamp yielded to the flapper, an additional role emerged: the mysterious vixen, which was best exemplified through the performances of Marlene Deitrich, Greta Garbo, Jean Harlow, and Mae West. These women can be considered the first Hollywood "sex goddesses." Garbo and Dietrich brought an enigmatic element to the role of the sex goddess, with Garbo usually accepting roles in which her characters sought eternal love. Garbo projected "the perfect metaphor for the Hollywood film": sex transformed and spiritualized.[12] Unlike the vamp, the sex goddess was neither predatory nor actively seeking a man. Rather, her male counterparts were drawn to the sex goddess's fragility. He actively pursued *her*. While she initially declined her suitor's overtures, she ultimately succumbed, believing that love would ultimately triumph.

Director Josef von Sternberg wrote that "it is the nature of a woman to be passive, receptive, dependent on male aggression, and capable of enduring pain . . . . [S]he is not normally outraged by being manipulated."[13] These beliefs were overtly fused into film either through explicit dialogue or visual depiction. The former is exemplified by the following statement from the 1936 film *A Woman Rebels*:

> As women, the first thing of importance is to be content to be inferior to men, inferior in mental power in the same proportion that she is inferior in physical strength. A really sensible woman feels her dependence. She is conscious of her inferiority and therefore grateful for support.[14]

Hollywood found its spokeswoman in Greta Garbo, whose characters fused emotional suffering with feminine weakness and submission. In short, "Garbo appeal[ed] to men and adherents of male supremacy."[15]

At the same time, writers and producers during the 1930s sought to empower their female characters. But the manner in which they believed their films empowered women actually degraded either other female characters or the female protagonist herself. Harlow, for example, rose to stardom by portraying characters who alienated their female counterparts through their carefree attitudes, abilities to be emotionally available, and preparedness to give of themselves. At the same time, however, these characters were often misled and were susceptible to abuse from men. Despite these character shortcomings, Harlow herself represented the archetype of the beautiful blonde bombshell, garnering acclaim for starring in films such as *Red Dust* (1932), *Bombshell* (1933), and *Reckless* (1935).

Harlow's character in the 1936 film *Wife vs. Secretary* epitomized the "divide and conquer" theme that Hollywood promoted during this period. Portraying an innocent secretary, Harlow accidentally triggers a sequence of events that arouse the suspicions of her supervisor's wife. The wife, who appears "evil-minded" and "bitchy," is juxtaposed alongside Harlow's character, who emerges as a symbol of purity, and the film was paradigmatic of how "women become scapegoats for men who refuse to . . . accept responsibility" for their actions and decisions.[16]

Similarly, the characters Mae West portrayed succeeded in alienating their on-screen female counterparts, although West utilized a slightly different approach. Whereas Harlow's characters were plausible, West's were hyperbolic and outrageous. With an amazing ability for one-liners such as "I used to be Snow White, but I drifted," West reversed sexual stereotypes in her films and made it difficult for female audiences to identify with her characters.[17]

Unlike any of her predecessors, Mae West dominated both the plot and the male characters appearing in her films. She seduced merely for her own pleasure. Despite her many masculine qualities and personal insecurities about her own femininity, West became an object of sexual desire in her own right. While certainly bold and daring for her era, West remained successful because she refused to take herself seriously. Ultimately, male audiences accepted her because they accorded her similar treatment:

> Men could laugh good-naturedly at her audacity; it wasn't threatening because Mae was not a potential conquest—she was one of the boys, and her banter borrowed from and elevated locker room sass . . . . [N]ever before and never since has a women been so thoroughly in control of her destiny.[18]

Though she may have controlled her own destiny, West was nonetheless confined by her generation's attitudes about sex. In 1928, she garnered national notoriety after she wrote, produced, and starred in a play entitled *Sex*, and was subsequently incarcerated for obscenity. A year later, another West play, *Drag*, was banned on Broadway for its homosexual themes. West's ultimate legacy suggests that, by bending the definition of sex and femininity, she actually reinforced the myth of male supremacy. In so doing, West perpetuated the sex goddess role, which remained a constant in American cinema throughout the 1930s.

America's entry into World War II in 1941 resulted in the mobilization of approximately eleven million men. Consequently, women became responsible for perpetuating the war economy. As one commentator noted in 1943, "the balance of power rests in women's hands. Literally."[19] That same year, Norman Rockwell's "Rosie the Riveter" graced the cover of the *Saturday Evening Post* and became a ubiquitous symbol of the American workingwoman's "patriotic gesture" to her country.[20] The wartime transformation had a significant impact upon women: "The need for women to take the places of absent men increased the incidence and acceptability of women in public places. Women had more money to spend and enjoyed greater freedom of movement, congregation and opportunity to meet other women."[21]

This wartime transformation also necessitated an adjustment in the manner in which women were portrayed on film. Movies of the 1940s that featured various "Rosie the Riveter" characters were dubbed "women's pictures" for their depiction of women's lives against the backdrop of their jobs. The shift likely reflected the composition of the viewing public. With most men enlisted or fighting abroad, the majority of filmgoers became women. Rather than display a genuine interest in addressing issues women faced, Hollywood studios were attuned to their wartime demographic and catered to their target audience.

A 1943 advertisement for the Women's Army Corps, which called upon women to join the war effort, is representative of the manner in which women were recruited into various sectors of the wartime economy:

> Women! Men are dying on the battlelines. Can you *live* with yourself on the sidelines . . . when YOU can help shorten the war . . . by joining the WAC? By joining the WAC, YOU—an American woman—can send more strength to our Armies abroad by releasing a man for combat. You can hurry the day of victory—and help bring more of our fighting men home alive.[22]

Hollywood explored and exploited this new female role. Indeed, many female characters were portrayed as hardworking patriots. In 1943, Ann

Sothern starred as an aircraft worker in *Swing Shift Maisie*. A year later, Claudette Colbert portrayed a welder in *Since You Went Away*, and Lucille Ball's character worked in a military defense plant in the 1944 film *Meet the People*. Other films brought women to the warfront as brave nurses attending to wounded soldiers. Hollywood also explored the world of the female professional. Rosalind Russell starred in several films in which she depicted the "ideal" workingwoman, including *Design for Scandal* (1941), *This Thing Called Love* (1941), *What a Woman!* (1943), and *She Wouldn't Say Yes* (1945).

Regardless of the setting, women were rarely depicted in the home tending to the hearth during this period. Films of the wartime era helped reinforce changes in gender roles while also incorporating propaganda. "Manlessness" was addressed by presenting images of women who lost a husband or son. Despite their loss, these women were not precluded from leading productive lives. To temper the solemnity of war, Hollywood also produced several career comedies. *Woman of the Year*, a 1941 film starring Katherine Hepburn, depicted a female character who marries but lacks any concept of domestic responsibility. Thoroughly "unable to turn on the gas or perk coffee [and] separate eggs through a strainer,"[23] Hepburn's character is removed from a domestic setting and instead focuses upon her career as a political journalist competing for recognition alongside her male counterparts.

The female characters portrayed in these wartime "career woman" films were strong. They exuded confidence, demonstrated capability, contributed to society, and were highly patriotic. In essence, they were anomalies, convenient characters devised to perpetuate the motion picture industry during a period of crisis and vehicles through which to promote the American war effort. Following the Allied victory, Hollywood took an abrupt about-face turn and quickly adopted a substantially different message for working American women: go home.

As early as 1943, the *New York Times* forecasted that women would ultimately return to the domestic sphere once the war concluded:

> Most [women]—whether they will admit it or not—want only to marry, have a home and children and a man to do their worrying (and sometimes their thinking) for them. Some marry wanting children and can't give them. Some simply want a life of ease—with a marriage license.[24]

With the return of millions of war veterans, women were forced to vacate their wartime positions so that men could reoccupy and resume their prewar civilian jobs. As Marjorie Rosen noted, the expulsion of women from the workplace was designed to reassure men that their places in society were firmly implanted.[25] Those women who ultimately remained in their postwar positions did so at their own peril. Indeed, they received significantly reduced salaries as employers hoped to use fiscal persuasion as a method of encouraging women to leave. By 1947, over three million women either vacated or were removed from their wartime positions.

Following the war, Hollywood studios reverted to projecting the stereotypical ideal woman, who was either an object of sexual affection and desire or an insignificant character whose primary concern revolved around finding a husband. Those women who rejected the belief that they should return to the domestic sphere—so-called "ambitious women"—were portrayed as evil seductresses or emotionless wives in the films of the late 1940s.[26] The theme of marriage, which had swept across television networks with situation comedies such as *Leave It to Beaver*, *Father Knows Best*, and *The Donna Reed Show*, now permeated the big screen.

Indeed, many of the films produced during the 1950s centered upon the theme of marriage. The women in *Three Coins in the Fountain* (1954), *Gentlemen Marry Brunettes* (1955), *Gentlemen Prefer Blondes* (1953), *How to Marry a Millionaire* (1953), *Seven Brides for Seven Brothers* (1954), and *A Woman's World* (1954) all actively seek husbands. Of course, marriage required the planning of a wedding ceremony, which was the main focus of a series of films devoted exclusively to the occasion itself: *Father of the Bride* (1950), *The Catered Affair* (1956), and *High Society* (1956). The ideal marriage succeeded, in part, because the woman possessed the characteristics befitting an ideal wife, and films such as *The Glenn Miller Story* (1954) and *Strategic Air Command* (1955) explored those themes. Hollywood, of course, portrayed these marriages as romantic and requiring little effort, and many of these films were replete with happy endings. In so doing, Hollywood presented a false notion that marriage would ultimately and completely satisfy a woman while defining her role in life as a wife, mother, and keeper of the home.

But Hollywood also depicted conflicting images of how a woman could make her marriage succeed. Film historian Jeanine Basinger summarized what women in the 1950s gleaned from contemporary film:

1. Marriage fails when you don't have enough money, and marriage fails when you have too much money. (Problem established: money)

2. Marriage fails when you have children and pay too much attention to them, and marriage fails when you have children and don't pay enough attention to them. (Problem established: children)

3. Marriage fails when you get dull and frumpy and lose your attractiveness to the opposite sex, and marriage fails when you get glamorous and well dressed and become too attractive to the opposite sex . . . . (Problem established: infidelity)

. . . .

5. Marriage fails if you don't work to help out with economic problems, and marriage fails when you go to work and make money of your own. Marriage fails if you have a career, and marriage fails when you don't have a career. Marriage fails if you are too independent, and marriage fails if you're not independent enough. (Problem established: career conflicts and independence)[27]

Accordingly, cinema utilized marriage as an opportunity to subtly influence the way women behaved while simultaneously cautioning them about the consequences of pursuing actions or possessing beliefs that diverged from the domestic lifestyle.

* * *

Marriage was only one thematic element during the 1950s. The decade also gave rise to the emergence of sex without sex. Marjorie Rosen characterized the decade as one defined by "mammary madness."[28] Hollywood's emphasis upon femininity, including flattering skirts, strapless gowns, and hourglass figures, brought a new level of sex appeal to cinema. At the same time, the strict censorship provisions of the Hollywood Code rapidly yielded, permitting studios greater freedom, particularly with regard to sexual liberties. While the idea of sexual freedom began to gain acceptance, producers and studios nonetheless hesitated to venture into uncharted territory. Studios began producing films in which female characters lacked depth and substance but ultimately compensated for these shortcomings by possessing physical attributes.

No actress embodied sex appeal in the late 1950s and early 1960s like Marilyn Monroe. In *Some Like It Hot* (1959) and *Let's Make Love* (1960), Monroe captivated audiences as a beautiful blonde whose figure overshadowed her intellectual shortcomings. Other actresses, namely Sheree North, Jayne Mansfield, Anita Ekberg, and Diana Dors, portrayed similar characters. In *The Girl Can't Help It* (1957), Mansfield's character attempts to coalesce the worlds of marriage and "sex pot," as evidenced by one scene in which she seductively holds a milk bottle to her chest while remarking that she "just want[s] to be a wife, have kids . . . [but] no one thinks I'm equipped for motherhood."[29] The films of the 1950s attempted to restore the image of traditional womanhood, but a new approach was emphasized: a woman's physical attributes became primary eye candy. More importantly, any emotional desires the female character might have possessed were quelled by the ideal that utopia ultimately existed in matrimony and at home.

The films of the 1950s also promoted the bad girl / good girl dynamic, which would also be explored in films during the following decade. Whereas Marilyn Monroe exemplified the bad girl, Hepburn, Doris Day, and Debbie Reynolds represented the good girl, a respectable woman for whom marriage was appropriate. Conversely, the bad girl had an unacceptable preoccupation with sex and was unfit for matrimony or any type of relationship in which fidelity was expected.

Within a decade, the so-called bad girl began shedding her derogatory characterizations as the notion that a woman could be physically satisfied without the constraints of marriage slowly garnered greater acceptance. Professor Susan J. Douglas offered her own interpretation of what became known as "the double standard":

> In the early 1960s, the voices of the schoolmarm, the priest, the advice columnist, and Mom insisted, "Nice girls don't." But another voice began to whisper, "Oh yes they do—and they like it, too." We saw these girls . . . [and] we could try on different roles, from starlets who said yes to starlets who said no to those who said, "Maybe, but I'm just not sure yet." And as we saw on the big screen that it was sometimes possible *not* to get punished for having sex with your boyfriend, some of us began to wonder.[30]

Consequently, the cinematic image of the 1960s woman developed into that of a new, young, *single* female whose desire for sex "becomes not simply an appetite or a matter of individual taste, but the supreme, defining quality of the self . . . . [W]ill she or won't she becomes the unspoken question."[31]

The approval of the birth control pill by the Food and Drug Administration in 1960 facilitated this transformation, and journalist Gloria Steinem, writing in *Esquire* in 1962, opined that these cultural changes required movie studios to adjust accordingly: "Hollywood . . . can no longer build plots on . . . fainting heroines and expect to be believed."[32] One of the first responses to these changes from Hollywood was *Breakfast at Tiffany's* (1961), which starred Audrey Hepburn as Holly Golightly. Wide-eyed and small-breasted, Holly's character was a significant departure from the 1950s female lead. She earns her living as a pseudo-escort, parties frequently, indulges in alcohol and cigarettes, and is anything but an innocent virgin.[33] Independent and abhorring marriage, or even the thought of relying upon a man, Holly stands in sharp contrast to the obedient, subservient archetype of femininity that pervaded the previous decade of film.

Holly introduced a milieu into which the Bond Girl became a prominent figure. Like Holly, the Bond Girl *appears* as a seemingly sexually liberated woman who is self-sufficient and not dependent upon a male. Tony Bennett and Janet Woollacott argued that these elements enabled American women to derive pleasure in the Bond films since the Bond Girl character "represented a certain 'liberated' sexuality in comparisons with other representations of female sexuality."[34] As a form of fantasy, the Bond Girl supposedly offered women escapist entertainment and vicarious freedom from the confinement they may have encountered in their regular, everyday lives. However, the Bond Girl did not provide total escapism because her "liberation," Bennett and Woollacott argued, was "organized around a male notion of sexual freedom."[35] Even Sean Connery agreed: "There isn't a girl-next-door in the entire lot. And I suppose that's what appeals most to the men in the audience about Bond's playmates. They are so utterly unreal, the kind of women you meet only in your fantasies and your dreams."[36]

* * *

The Bond Girl began her cinematic journey during an era in which Hollywood embraced a woman's freer sexuality. Of course, the Bond Girl did, to some degree, follow this charted path, and "*Dr. No* was one of the first films to fully embrace sex as a libidinous sport."[37] While a sexually liberated, leading female character may suggest that Hollywood came full circle in its portrayal of women, the Bond Girl ultimately represented a longing toward a greater subordinate role for women and a rejection of progress toward sexual equality. Her initial appearance in *Dr. No* introduced an archetype that was reinforced, perpetuated, and ultimately refined for approximately fifteen years. Later, the Bond Girl encountered a wholesale reconsideration after it became apparent that her representation was no longer identifiable to audiences in an era replete with rapid social change. The Bond Girl's beginnings, what she represented, what she reflected, how she was portrayed, what she was a reaction against, what she eventually became, and where she is going today are charted throughout the remainder of this work.

005

Introducing an Archetype: *Dr. No* and *From Russia With Love*

The Bond films . . . occupy a significant place in cinema history in that they mark the transition of the spy thriller from the netherland of the B-movie to the glossy, big-budget world of the A-feature.

—James Chapman[1]

I avoid porn . . . that's for home movies. Bond is sadism for the family. You'd have to be kinky to find our films erotic.

—Harry Saltzman[2]

Satyriasis is psychiatrically defined as "excessively great sexual desire in the male." Our James Bond is afflicted by it, in a nice sort of way.

—Richard Maibaum[3]

In order to present James Bond and the Bond Girl to large, cinematic audiences, adaptations of Ian Fleming's novels were necessary. For years, Fleming pursued numerous avenues to promote Bond and indicated an interest in bringing the spy to both television and motion pictures. In a letter to his publisher, Jonathan Cape, Fleming wrote that he was "praying that something may be forthcoming from one of the reprint societies, or the films, to offset my meager returns on what has turned out to be a successful book."[4] More importantly, Fleming presciently observed, "I have an idea that one of these days the film and television rights of James Bond and his adventures may be worth quite a lot of money, and I hope you agree that there's no point in throwing them away."[5]

Intent upon bringing Bond to television, Fleming actively sought assistance from friends and close associates in Hollywood: "If you get a chance of putting in a word with the TV tycoons for *Casino* [*Royale*]," he wrote, "I shall be grateful."[6] In 1954, Fleming sold the rights for *Casino Royale* to the Columbia Broadcasting System (CBS). On the October 21, 1954 broadcast of *Climax Mystery Theater*, William Lundigan presented the first live-action treatment of Bond starring American actor Barry Nelson.[7] That television adaptation went "unnoticed and was soon forgotten."[8]

Also in 1954, Fleming reportedly began negotiations with CBS and the National Broadcasting Company in an attempt to create a television pilot. These efforts proved unsuccessful. Four years later, CBS once again expressed an interest in creating a television series about Bond, and Fleming wrote and submitted plots for six episodes. Ultimately, the project was abandoned.

Initial efforts to create Bond films also fared poorly. Hungarian producer Sir Alexander Korda expressed an interest in *Live and Let Die*, but he later withdrew. Through a personal friend, Fleming was introduced to Irish director, writer, and producer Kevin McClory, with whom Fleming hoped to create the first Bond film.[9] McClory, along with Ivar Bryce, completed a screenplay entitled *James Bond, Secret Agent*.[10] Fleming later used this plot as the basis for *Thunderball*, sparking litigation over the intellectual property rights.[11] Although McClory's efforts to enjoin the release of the novel before it reached bookstores were unsuccessful,[12] the resulting legal entanglements delayed further discussions of any cinematic adaptation. Discouraged, Fleming sold the screen rights for *Casino Royale* to Russian director Gregory Ratoff for a mere $6,000. A cinematic version of *Casino Royale* would not be produced and released until 1967. Nearly four decades later, EON Productions released its own version of *Casino Royale* starring Daniel Craig.

During the mid-1950s, American producer Cubby Broccoli expressed an interest in the Bond novels. His colleague at the time, Irving Allen, began negotiating with Fleming, even though Allen was quite apprehensive about the endeavor.[13] Fully aware of the restrictions imposed upon filmmakers' displays of sexual images, Allen rejected the idea that his and Broccoli's company should produce a Bond film. In fact, Allen declared that "the books were not even good enough for television."[14] Screenwriter Richard Maibaum recalled:

> Cubby gave me two of the James Bond books . . . I read them and liked them enormously. Cubby was very excited, too, but Irving Allen didn't share his enthusiasm. So Cubby put them aside . . . with the censorship of pictures that existed then, you couldn't even have the minimal sex and violence that we eventually put into the pictures.[15]

Broccoli also was unsuccessful in encouraging Columbia Pictures to pick up the rights to future Bond films.

Broccoli was not the only producer interested in Bond. David Picker, a United Artists executive, thought Alfred Hitchcock should produce a Bond film, but those efforts never materialized.[16] In 1960, Canadian film producer Harry Saltzman approached Fleming, and the two began negotiating for an option on all of the Bond novels with the exception of *Casino Royale*. Saltzman's company, however, lacked the financial resources, and the option fell through. A year later, Broccoli learned of Saltzman's interest in bringing Bond to the big screen, and Broccoli and Saltzman agreed to establish a partnership in order to secure the rights and pitch the idea to executives.

Together, Broccoli and Saltzman formed two companies: EON Productions to produce the films and Danjaq to manage the films' copyrights. They simultaneously approached United Artists and Columbia Pictures, with the latter agreeing to provide EON Productions with financial backing for one film that starred a well-established lead actor. Broccoli and Saltzman rejected these conditions, believing that the success of a Bond feature rested upon making a series of films starring a relatively unknown actor. In June 1961, the producers met with David Picker at United Artists, and an agreement was reached within an hour.[17] "To everyone's surprise," United Artists agreed to provide full financial backing to Broccoli and Saltzman:[18] the first Double-O-Seven film would be produced for slightly less than $1 million.[19] Fleming's dream of seeing Bond on film would be realized, and his financial concerns were allayed: he would receive $100,000 for each film and a percentage of the profit.[20]

* * *

Before they even assembled a production team that would eventually include Richard Maibaum, scriptwriter and producer Terence Young, and art director Ken Adam, Broccoli and Saltzman searched for a lead actor to portray Bond. The problem that producers encountered in 2005 was nothing new as no actor seemed interested in the part when it was first advertised. A 1961 press release indicated that producers were "having trouble casting James Bond for their upcoming series of feature films."[21] The criteria included a male actor between the ages of twenty-eight and thirty-five, who was at least six-feet tall, possessed "blue eyes, dark hair, rugged features—particularly a determined chin—and a British accent."[22] Actors Michael Craig, Roger Moore, Patrick McGoohan, and Bob Simmons were leading candidates. Peter Anthony, a professional male model, satisfied the prerequisites, but the producers turned him away due to his inability to "cope with such a demanding part as Bond at first try."[23]

Saltzman eventually stumbled upon Scottish actor Sean Connery who, according to Broccoli, "had [the] balls" for the role.[24] Saltzman elaborated: "As he left the office, we all went to the window and watched him cross the street. What impressed me was that a man of his size and frame could move in such a supple way."[25] Fleming, however, complicated matters by actively supporting actors David Niven and Roger Moore as his choices. Fleming articulated his opposition to casting Connery by continually referencing Connery's work as a truck driver: Fleming "was not sure if a working-class Scotsman had the social graces to play his hero."[26]

In fact, Connery's accent and his lack of polish were valid reasons not to cast him. Nonetheless, producers selected him as the obvious choice, and "Connery's working-class exterior made Bond a hero who was harder to label as a snob."[27] As described by Terence Young, Connery was "a darn good actor" who "had a sexual quality."[28] He was offered a seven-year contract. Fleming, fully aware that he did not have the authority to choose the leading actor, withdrew from the debate and remarked that he was "staying away from all this side of the business."[29]

As John Cork and Bruce Scivally recounted, Fleming's concerns were noted and addressed. Terence Young worked with Connery to acclimate him to the type of role he would be portraying, even requesting that Connery sleep in his suits so that he would feel comfortable moving in them.[30] To teach Connery how to order fine wine, Young invited him to luxurious restaurants. Connery frequented clubs in order to learn cards and casino etiquette. Even Fleming worked with Connery, assisting with his accent, educating him in espionage, and instilling in him the vision of Bond.[31] Ultimately, Young remarked that the three ingredients for Bond were "Sean Connery, Sean Connery, and Sean Connery."[32]

Broccoli and Saltzman cast British actor Bernard Lee and Canadian actress Lois Maxwell as M and Miss Moneypenny, respectively. Lee was chosen for his perfect realization of "the prototypical father-figure."[33] Maxwell earned her role after Fleming remarked that she was "exactly the woman" he envisioned for Miss Moneypenny: "a tall, distinguished-looking woman with the most kissable lips in the world."[34] Both the roles of M and Miss Moneypenny were "given enough attention to establish a relationship which could be repeated for each successive film."[35] Lee starred as M in the first eleven films, while Maxwell appeared as Miss Moneypenny in the first fourteen.

***Dr. No*[36]**

The first Bond film, which was released in 1962, was referred to as "the headiest box office concoction of sex and sadism ever brewed."[37] In a review for *New Republic*, Stanley Kauffmann remarked that *Dr. No* was "most notable for its numerous attractive girls."[38] In fact, Richard Maibaum deliberately created new characters, including Sylvia Trench and Miss Taro, when he adapted the screenplay from the Fleming novel. Doing so "increased the sex quotient . . . . Bond needed to be an irresistible image of masculinity, an idealized male sex symbol, who, unlike clean-cut American heroes, never flinched when faced with the prospect of a sexual liaison."[39] British actress Eunice Gayson earned the part of Sylvia Trench primarily due to her fulsome proportions.[40] Technically, Sylvia is the first Bond Girl to appear on film, although she is a relatively minor character.

The casting of the primary Bond Girl, Honey Ryder, has an interesting history. International film star Julie Christie originally auditioned for the part. Despite her renowned acting skills, Broccoli chose not to cast her because she had "no tits."[41] Swiss actress Ursula Andress submitted a photograph of herself in a wet black T-shirt that ultimately caught Broccoli's attention: "'We picked her picture out of a pile of rejects. She was dripping wet, and she looked beautiful.'"[42] Thereafter, he reportedly remarked to Saltzman that "this is the girl."[43]

Andress was offered the part even before directors met her in person,[44] and Broccoli was pleasantly surprised when he did meet her: "'When I got to Jamaica for the filming, there was this beautiful creature, and I thought she was great, and I knew then that she was the type of girl we should use for future leading ladies . . . .'"[45] Terence Young recalled that "Ursula had . . . that virginal, sexy quality, that innocent quality. Cubby [Broccoli] was right. We needed a girl with tits."[46] The *New York Times* even noted that Andress's figure made her a bikini manufacturer's "dream girl."[47] Directors also seemed impressed by the fact that Andress often did not wear a bra on the set: "As she danced, those wonderful breasts were just swaying."[48]

United Artists was also intent upon marketing Andress as their "new starlet." Former glamour model and photographer Bunny Yeager, who had previously photographed Bettie Page, was invited to Jamaica to photograph Ursula Andress.[49] Later, Andress, like many actresses who portrayed Bond Girls, appeared nude in numerous *Playboy* pictorials.

Eunice Gayson, Ursula Andress, and a third actress, Zena Marshall, constituted the "flock of beautiful, half-clad girls all saying come-hither" in *Dr. No*.[50] One additional character is worth mentioning. The film features an unidentified, overly zealous female photographer who follows

Bond. Although a considerably minor role (and one not discussed further here), Terence Young was drawn to Marguerite Lewars, an airline ticketing agent working in Jamaica. Lewars was asked to read for the part of Miss Taro, but she declined, refusing to participate in a scene that required her to be "wrapped in a towel, lying on a bed, kissing a strange man."[51] Instead, she read for and earned the role of the photographer. Not surprisingly, Lewars was the reigning Miss Jamaica at the time. Indeed, directors believed that she and her sister were "the two most beautiful girls in Jamaica."[52]

* * *

Bond films begin with the now-famous gun barrel scene,[53] which is "the most recognizable trademark in cinema history."[54] The gun barrel scene is followed by a short teaser or pre-title sequence, which precedes the equally famous title sequences that are known for "silhouettes of all these girls with the hair and the long legs and the beautiful bodies."[55] Roger Moore once remarked that "[i]f anything was going to get censored on Bond, it was the titles."[56] But *Dr. No* neither follows this progression nor contains provocative scenes of naked females. Instead, the gun barrel scene is followed by the title sequence, and the film begins thereafter.

The first Bond title sequence begins with the famous *James Bond Theme*, which was composed by Monty Norman. As the theme unfolds, a dark screen is awash with colorful, pulsating dots synchronized to the rhythm. This theme quickly and seamlessly flows into a calypso rhythm amid "a brilliant jumble of color . . . as silhouettes of dancing women move in time to [the] beat."[57] The title sequence, while relatively undeveloped compared to subsequent versions, set the standard for those that followed with its focus upon "elegance, wit and sex."[58] Unlike later iterations of the title sequence, the *Dr. No* installment is relatively devoid of sexual overtones. Dancing silhouettes conceal any defined bodily features other than fully clothed attire, and silhouettes of male dancers join in the festivities.[59] Despite only presenting colorful silhouettes of undulating, clothed figures in the title sequence, Maryam d'Abo and John Cork argued that *Dr. No*'s key ingredient was still sex. Indeed, the film's poster art similarly established a precedent for evoking images of sex as graphic artist Mitchell Hooks presented Bond alongside four voluptuous and scantily clad women.[60]

* * *

Dr. No opens "with Bond being seduced by one woman"[61] and introduces the spy to the audience in an elegant casino setting that permits him to take chances, both in terms of cards and women.[62] The Le Cercle casino scene finds Bond engaging in a game of baccarat with Sylvia Trench, a character created solely to "increase the number of sexual partners for Bond."[63] Substantiating scholar Laura Mulvey's argument that "cinematic codes create a gaze, a world and an object, thereby producing an illusion cut to the measure of desire [in] a woman's to-be-looked-at-ness," Sylvia's role in the film is purely functional, as evidenced by her static and underdeveloped character.[64] She exudes sexuality in the way in which she carries herself at the baccarat table and in the way she appears.

Indeed, the audience is introduced to her when the camera pans upward from the baccarat table, revealing her chest before her face comes into view.[65] While every player at the table is adorned in either a tuxedo or black attire, Sylvia wears a bright red dress with one shoulder exposed. Her hair is pulled back, revealing her entire neck. Her lipstick matches her dress color, and her nails, coated with red polish, are finely manicured.

Sylvia's skills at baccarat are lacking, and she turns to a gentleman at her left to coolly and nonchalantly state that she "needs another thousand."[66] It is therefore quite possible that she is enjoying herself on someone else's account. Nevertheless, Sylvia remains determined to best Bond, even though her physical attraction to him is blatantly apparent from both her dialogue and her mannerisms. With respect to the former, Bond remarks that it "looks like you're out to get me," to which Sylvia replies, "It's an idea at that."[67] With respect to the latter, Sylvia alights from the table at the same time Bond announces that he must leave. Either aggressively staking her claim to him or so overcome by his essence that she cannot help but be drawn toward Bond, Sylvia resumes a dialogue replete with innuendo:

> *Sylvia*: Too bad you have to go—just as things were getting interesting.
> *Bond*: Yes. Tell me, Miss Trench, do you play any other games?
> *Sylvia* (*expressing a sly look on her face*): Golf, amongst other things.[68]

Bond invites her to dinner the following day. Sylvia, licking her lips, responds that his offer "sounds tempting."[69] In an effort to play hard to get, Sylvia asks Bond if she can decide in the morning. Bond's conduct toward Sylvia in this scene appears dismissive. Preoccupied, Bond coldly presents her with his business card and leaves.

It is then up to Sylvia to pursue Bond, which she proceeds to do aptly. As he exits, focus is placed upon Sylvia looking out toward the camera as

Swiss actress Ursula Andress poses on the set of *Dr. No*, 1962.
(John Kobal Foundation/Hulton Archive/Getty Images)

she watches Bond, her eyes shifting down briefly to the business card in her left hand and immediately back up toward Bond's direction. Despite Bond's offer for dinner the next day, Sylvia lacks the ability (or desire) to wait. Instead, she sneaks into Bond's hotel suite, disrobes, replaces her red dress with one of his pajama tops, and begins practicing her golf putt.

Upon his return later that evening, Bond discovers Sylvia, although the audience initially sees only her legs, which are nearest to the camera with Bond farthest away from the viewer. Initially, it is unclear to whom these legs belong. When asked how she entered his quarters, Sylvia replies with what is essentially a non-answer: "I decided to accept your offer."[70] Her response prompts Bond to remind her that the invitation was for "tomorrow afternoon."[71] A sexually charged dialogue ensues, replete with subtle sexually suggestive conduct:

> *Bond*: Tell me, do you always dress this way for golf?
> *Sylvia*: I changed into something more comfortable. (*raising the golf club and touching it seductively*) Oh, I hope I did the right thing.
> *Bond*: Oh, you did the right thing, but you picked the wrong moment. I have to leave immediately.
> *Sylvia* (*approaching Bond*): Oh, that's too bad. Just as things were getting interesting again. (*kissing Bond and wrapping her arms around his neck*) When did you say you have to leave?
> *Bond*: Immediately. (*embracing again*) Almost immediately.[72]

Interestingly, the scene depicts Bond's fists clenched, although his right fist is holding on to the golf club he takes away from Sylvia. His left hand in a fist suggests that he is being bound by Sylvia, that her enhanced sexual prowess is somewhat unnatural or too forward. After all, it is she who pursues him and enters his suite. Bond's conquest of her would reassert his authority over her and "restore" the natural balance of their dynamic. Alternatively, his clenched left fist indicates complete detachment, a disinterest in or unwillingness to embrace her fully.

Assume that Sylvia represents a "certain 'liberated' sexuality in comparison with other representations of female sexuality in contemporary . . . American films."[73] In *Dr. No*, she is portrayed as a predatory woman determined to acquire Bond and to seek out what she desires. She appears to succeed. In some respects, these attributes might make Sylvia a Bondian equivalent of Holly Golightly. But this conclusion is negated by what is actually perceived by the audience, who knows nothing about Sylvia beyond these few scenes. It would be inaccurate to believe that Sylvia's sexual prowess, standing alone, thrusts her into the category of a liberated and strong woman. Indeed, Sylvia never appears again in *Dr. No*. Her brief reemergence in *From Russia With Love* depicts an archetype that is in direct opposition to a liberated and strong female. As discussed below, she appears needy, immature, and entirely disposable.

The character of Sylvia was initially envisioned to reemerge in several Bond films, as evidenced by her brief appearance in *From Russia With Love*. Eunice Gayson recalled that Terence Young wanted the character to appear at the beginning of a series of six Bond films. Each time, Sylvia and Bond "are just about to get to it and he's always bleeped away."[74] The sixth film was supposed to finally give Sylvia an opportunity to succeed in her pursuit of Bond.[75] This idea was ultimately scrapped after *From Russia With Love*.

Sylvia offers a puzzling ideological challenge to the female audience. Tony Bennett and Janet Woollacott wrote that the women in the early Bond films "offered an image of women freed from domesticity and allowed sexual desire without either marriage or punishment . . . ."[76] They suggested that this liberated female sexuality was portrayed only in terms of Bond's sexual freedom, and one may assume that it is he who derives the greater pleasure from his encounters. Yet the Sylvia-Bond dynamic presented in *Dr. No* suggests that Bond, while quite capable of conquering Sylvia, nevertheless does so slightly unwillingly. Indeed, one might say that Bond is doing *her* a favor and that she enjoys the fruits of his labor while he acts solely for Queen and country.

* * *

When an overly assertive female character such as Sylvia appears in the films, she is seen as anomalous, particularly when juxtaposed alongside an extremely traditional and submissive counterpart. The character of Miss Taro, "developed to provide another sexual encounter for Bond," is one such example.[77] Portrayed by Zena Marshall, Miss Taro serves as a secretary to Pleydell-Smith, the chief secretary of the colonial government in Jamaica. She also works for the villain, Dr. Julius No. Marshall recalled how Terence Young envisioned the character of Miss Taro: "She's Chinese, but you don't really play her Chinese, you play her more international, mid-Atlantic . . . . [She's] a woman men dream about, but who doesn't really exist."[78] Unlike Sylvia, who actively pursues Bond, Miss Taro is subjected to his advances and persistent attempts at seduction.

Bond is introduced to Miss Taro when he meets with Pleydell-Smith at the Government House in Kingston. Summoned by Pleydell-Smith to bring into the office all files pertaining to Dr. No, Miss Taro emerges at the door and states that the files cannot be found. The cinematography

James Bond (Sean Connery) presents his business card to Sylvia Trench (Eunice Gayson) in *Dr. No*.
(MGM Studios/Hulton Archive/Getty Images)

employed for her introduction to the audience is, like her character role, exactly opposite of that used in the Sylvia-Bond miniature golf scene. With Bond in the foreground sitting in a chair, Miss Taro appears in full in the background. Bond cocks his head to view her behind him. Although his head movement is slight, it is apparent that he is eyeing her figure, beginning with her legs and moving upward toward her chest and face.

Bond next encounters Miss Taro when he discovers her kneeling before a door leading to Pleydell-Smith's office. She quickly appears preoccupied looking for the missing files, though her antics do not escape Bond, who sternly states as he hovers over her, "That's a naughty little habit, listening at keyholes."[79] His tone, while constantly firm, warms somewhat as he initiates a seduction:

> *Bond*: I'd just hate to think you're going to spend the whole afternoon looking for these things.
> *Miss Taro* (*pausing to respond while thumbing through the file in her hand*): No. I have the afternoon off.
> *Bond* (*responding quickly*): Now there's a coincidence, so have I. Why don't you show me around the island?
> *Miss Taro* (*ceasing review of a file, closing it, and turning around to face him*): What should I say to an invitation from a strange gentleman?
> *Bond*: You should say "yes."
> *Miss Taro* (*shaking her head*): I should say "maybe."
> *Bond* (*mocking her response*): Three o'clock. My hotel. Maybe?
> *Miss Taro* (*drawing her head downward while lifting her eyes toward him*): Yes, maybe.
> *Bond*: Good.[80]

Miss Taro then watches through a set of blinds as Bond leaves the Government House.

Miss Taro's next on-screen appearance occurs when Bond telephones her at her mountain apartment. She appears in a white robe and in the process of undressing. As the phone rings, she climbs over the bed to answer it, sprawling her body across the sheets. She picks up the receiver, reclines on her stomach, and lifts her right leg into the air to reveal her calf and metallic-colored high-heeled shoes. Like Sylvia, Miss Taro wears bright red lipstick and nail polish. As she convinces Bond to "collect" her at her apartment, where it is "nice and cool," Miss Taro rolls over onto her back, her chest stretching toward the ceiling.[81]

Despite her cooing, Miss Taro never expects to actually see Bond. Instead, her overture is merely a "ruse to lure him into an assassin's trap."[82] Miss Taro is therefore entirely surprised when Bond, having successfully thwarted the enemy, arrives at her apartment. Of course, she claims that her surprise stems from the fact that she "didn't expect [Bond] here so soon" as she emerges still wet from a shower,[83] a moment author Steven Jay Rubin described as "one of the film's highest points."[84]

While Miss Taro attempts to excuse herself to dress, Bond pulls her to him using the towel that is draped around her neck. "Don't go to any trouble on my account," Bond responds.[85] She withdraws, causing Bond to respond with a quick double entendre: "Forgive me, I thought I was invited up here to admire the view."[86] A telephone call from her (male) superiors interrupts this conversation, and Miss Taro is seen expressing disbelief as to why Bond appeared in the first instance. She is instructed to detain Bond, though she does not respond affirmatively to this directive. Instead, Miss Taro states that she will "try" to keep him for a couple of hours.[87]

At the conclusion of her telephone call, Bond enters the room and resumes his seduction undeterred:

> *Bond* (*sitting down next to her on the bed and referencing her hair*): It's rather beautiful . . . .
> *Miss Taro*: Thank you.
> *Bond*: Tell me, do you always wear it up?
> *Miss Taro*: Don't you like it that way?
> *Bond* (*positioning his hands behind her to remove the towel from her body*): Yes, very much. With your, sort of, face, it's wonderful.
> *Miss Taro* (*grabbing her chest to prevent the towel from falling*): What's going on behind my back?
> *Bond* (*removing his hands*): Nothing. Look, no hands![88]

Bond embraces Miss Taro, they fall into bed together, and the scene fades to evening shortly after Bond has concluded his second sexual conquest. Interestingly, this particular scene was filmed several times in order to keep Marshall "covered up for the more prudish" markets.[89]

With evening bringing the sound of crickets chirping in the background, Bond declares to Miss Taro that he is hungry and wants to "go out to eat."[90] In true submissive form (and an effort to carry out her superiors' instructions to detain him), Miss Taro offers to prepare him a Chinese meal at the apartment because, by her own admission, she likes cooking. Miss Taro further justifies her preference by noting that it is more fun to remain alone, reinforcing Bond's philosophy that "he only intends to stay if she sleeps with him."[91] Ultimately, Miss Taro returns to the bed, where Bond once again embraces her while conspicuously detaching himself from the conquest by checking his wristwatch. Miss

Taro's only request: that Bond be careful because her nail polish is wet.[92]

Zena Marshall recalled that the role of Miss Taro required her to "be this attractive little siren, and at the same time I was the spy, a bad woman."[93] As the bad woman, Miss Taro is even more expendable than Sylvia. Indeed, Bond's on-screen encounter with Miss Taro serves another effect. Duping her into believing that they are traveling to dinner by taxi, Bond places Miss Taro into an unmarked police car and instructs the other passenger, the police superintendant, to book her and to "be careful of her nail varnish."[94] In response, Miss Taro spits in Bond's face. Maryam D'Abo and John Cork described the scene's effect:

> The scene is a twist on a long history of *femme fatales* and fallen women who lure men into traps with the promise of easy sex. Invariably, the man is at the woman's mercy. In James Bond's universe, it is Bond who seizes control, coldly manipulating the situation so that it is the villainess who finds herself played. Audiences in 1962 had never seen anything like this.[95]

Miss Taro represents not only an objectified woman who easily submits to Bond but also a mechanism through which he can manipulate and, to some degree, humiliate a female.[96] Her failure to detain Bond renders her incapable of carrying out orders, and the ease with which Bond outsmarts her exacerbates the extent to which she is entirely out of her element in a world of espionage presumably reserved for men.

* * *

The primary Bond Girl in *Dr. No* is Honey Ryder, referred to as "the prettiest and the nakedest of Bond's innumerable pliant girls."[97] Her first appearance on the beach of Crab Key has been described as one of the most memorable scenes in cinematic history: "Her entrance . . . is a special moment. The camera catches her emerging from the sea onto the beach dressed in a skimpy white bikini."[98] In an article entitled "No, No, A Thousand Times No," *Time* suggested that Ursula Andress "fill[ed] a wet bikini as if she were going downwind behind twin spinnakers."[99] Another *Time* article described the same scene: Honey was "a skin diver who seems to wear her air tanks in front."[100] Andress's entrance "and the way that she just walked out of the Caribbean in a clinging white bikini" was forever ingrained in the audience's mind, particularly since she "has remained, indelibly, the series' image of sweet female sexuality."[101] Maryam D'Abo and John Cork aptly summarized the scene:

> She walks casually on to a beach in her white bikini, a belt with a sheathed diving knife resting against her hip. She tosses her shells and mask on the sand, softly singing a calypso tune, unselfconscious of her natural beauty and unaware that Bond is watching her. When Bond lets his presence be known, it is Honey who takes charge. She stands defiantly, shoulders back, ready to fight. "Stay where you are," she commands.[102]

Awoken by her seductive voice, Bond is immediately struck by her beauty, and the effect Honey has upon him is apparent in his various radiant facial expressions. When Honey asks Bond whether he is also looking for seashells, he simply replies, "No, I'm just looking."[103]

Besides simply looking exotic, Honey, unlike Sylvia and Miss Taro, seems assertive, resourceful, and competent at first glance. Bond, slowly approaching her, states that he promises that he will not steal her seashells. An overly confident Honey responds, "I promise you that you won't either," and draws a knife to maintain her distance.[104] Authors Gary Giblin and Lisa Neyhouse maintained that Honey is truly an independent woman: "She is a capable, self-sufficient, determined young woman [who] doesn't need James Bond . . . to take care of her."[105] This sentiment was echoed by Maryam d'Abo and John and Cork, who wrote, "[S]he is certainly strong enough and smart enough to be part of Bond's world."[106] Indeed, Honey's character strengths include the fact that she (1) has taught herself the complete encyclopedia through the letter *T* (and boasts that she even knows more than Bond), (2) seems to support herself financially by selling seashells, (3) exacts revenge against a rapist by placing a black widow spider into her assailant's mosquito net, and (4) possesses some knowledge of Crab Key, the latter quality serving to protect her and Bond temporarily from Dr. No's henchmen. Recognizing these apparent attributes, *The New Yorker* sarcastically questioned, "What won't they think of next?"[107]

Notwithstanding these skills, Honey's on-screen interaction undermines her entire character and any independent attributes she possesses. Despite her strong-willed entrance from the ocean, she appears increasingly more tentative around Bond, even twirling her hair with her fingers in a childlike fashion. Held in captivity along with Bond, she struggles to perform the simplest of tasks by having difficulty buttoning her blouse. She demonstrates a childlike fascination with the beauty of Dr. No's aquarium as if seeing the underwater world for the first time. Given that she makes a profession out of diving for seashells, Honey's reaction to the aquarium is peculiar. Indeed, producers deliberately sought to accentuate Honey's childish nature and "sexually charged innocence"[108] by having Ursula Andress's "flat" Swedish accent dubbed

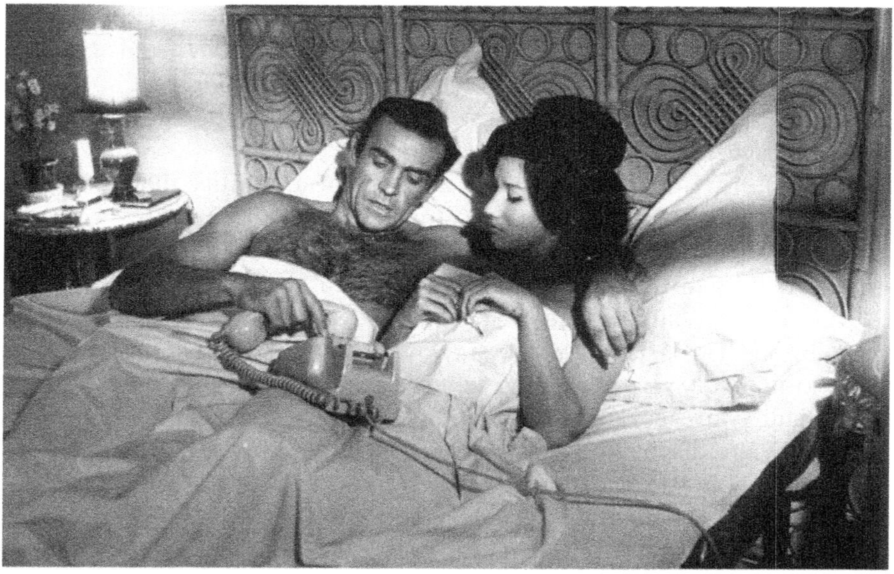

Miss Taro (Zena Marshall) finds a way to detain James Bond (Sean Connery) in *Dr. No*.

(George Konig/Rex USA)

over by British actress Monica van der Zyl, whose "girlish English" was better suited for the part.[109]

Despite her professed worldliness, Honey confesses that she "never met a detective before"[110] and is easily duped into believing that a mysterious dragon roams Crab Key. She even claims to have seen an object that has "two great glaring eyes, short tail and pointed wings, breathing fire."[111] In fact, when Bond tries to explain to her (and to Quarrel, his assistant) that there is no such thing as a dragon, Honey asks, "How do you know there aren't?"[112] She remains convinced that tire tracks she observes are actually dragon tracks, even though the so-called dragon is, in reality, a tractor covered with metal sheeting and fitted with a flame thrower.[113]

Ultimately, Bond views Honey as more of a liability than an asset. Comments such as "What are we going to do with her now," confirm this belief.[114] In fact, the "filmmakers . . . allow . . . the heroine to be captured and tied up to await the hero's appearance in the final reel."[115] Every indication suggests that Bond does not want Honey entangled in his mission. He instructs her to stay away, but she persistently remains close to his side. Earlier, Bond advises Honey to leave the island, but she defiantly refuses, stating she would leave when she decides to leave. When they are discovered by Dr. No's henchmen, the "girl" is instructed to remain where she is standing, while Bond is instructed to approach his captors. Interestingly, only Bond is handcuffed, and only he is instructed to accompany them. It is apparent that even Dr. No's henchmen have no interest in detaining Honey. When they walk away with Bond, Honey follows, prompting a confrontation. The scene ends with her continuing to follow Bond, who is now being dragged on the ground.

This conduct stands in stark contrast to Maryam d'Abo and John Cork's assessment that "Honey is another innocent caught up in Bond's adventure."[116] It is not accurate that she "does not need Bond to save her."[117] Rather, it appears that Bond must save her from herself. Honey has only herself to blame for the entanglements in which she finds herself, and it is her stubbornness and need to be beside Bond that result in her imprisonment. Bond even appears to arrange for her release with Dr. No, but it is she who refuses:

> *Bond*: There's no point in involving the girl at this stage. She has nothing to do with us. Let her go free, she'll promise not to talk.
>
> *Honey*: No I won't. I'm staying with you.
>
> *Bond*: I don't want you here.
>
> *Dr. No*: I agree. This is no place for the girl. Take her away.
>
> *Honey*: No! No![118]

Honey Ryder (Ursula Andress) discovers James Bond on Crab Key in *Dr. No.*
(Everett Collection/Rex USA)

Again, Honey is referred to by both Bond and Dr. No as a "girl," not a woman. Ultimately, she finds herself bound to a sloping floor and left to drown as the water level rises. Bond rescues her, and she rewards him in their escape boat.

The film concludes with Honey and Bond in their boat on the open sea. Stranded without fuel, Honey asks—somewhat helplessly—what they will do, to which Bond responds, "We can swim or . . . ."[119] When Honey responds with "Or what," Bond, sitting on the floor of the boat while she is in a seat, instructs her to "come here."[120] She obliges without objection, and the scene fades. Although Maryam d'Abo and John Cork observed that "Honey's stance beside Bond when they are found—like a captain at the prow of a ship—shows her continued strength and independence,[121] Honey does nothing other than stand with hands upon her hips. Incidentally, although this scene concludes the film, it was the first that Sean Connery and Ursula Andress filmed together, making it entirely possible that Andress had not settled into the role during early filming.[122]

On the escape boat, Honey caresses Bond and suggestively descends from the seat where they both were reclining to the floor of the boat. Bond slowly releases the rope that is towing their boat. Honey observes his conduct and, again, expresses no opposition. Instead, she continues to embrace him as the boat is left to drift. Thus, *Dr. No* establishes the following reality: "Bond saves the girl; the girl sleep with him: it is a simple contract."[123]

* * *

Dr. No depicts Bond's conquest of three women. Each character lacks the sophistication, interest, or development that elevates them above positions of sexual objects. Although Honey certainly outlasts Sylvia and Miss Taro in duration on screen, she offers little more than her female counterparts. Instead, Honey remains active in the plot to build anticipation that Bond might have a chance to seduce her at the conclusion of the mission.

Contrary to the belief that the Bond Girls of *Dr. No* represented a new breed of femininity to be admired, *Dr. No* laid a foundation for introducing the Bond Girl as a symbol of the opposite of female independence and self-sufficiency. The "ideal" Bond Girl is an amalgamation of Sylvia, Miss Taro, and Honey: beautiful, sexy, good or evil, detrimental, devious or innocent, and expendable. Add to the calculus that producers used voiceover actors for both Sylvia and Honey, and one emerges with the impression that the Bond Girl is even denied her own voice. As a result, she "is, literally, reduced to the level of an object only to be looked at."[124]

Following *Dr. No*'s success, producers instinctively understood "what aspects of Fleming [the audience] enjoyed, and, more importantly, how they wanted his stories treated."[125] How they would capture the essence of the Bond Girl in subsequent films would, in part, define the success of the franchise.

From Russia With Love

Released in 1963, *From Russia With Love* was the first Bond film to introduce the trademark sexually suggestive title sequences that "totally fetishise[]" women.[126] As the orchestral theme song begins, the figure of an exotically attired belly dancer appears undulating against a dark background. The film title and credits ebb and flow seductively across various moving portions of her body, including her arms, stomach, back, thighs, and buttocks. Of note is the juxtaposition of Bond's license number "007," which appears for the first time in the credits across the dancer's wide-eyed face and then her shaking bosom.

Once the film begins and the audience is introduced to the crime syndicate SPECTRE and its plot for world domination,[127] the focus shifts to Bond, who is enjoying a picnic in a boat on the banks of a river with Sylvia, again portrayed by Eunice Gayson. The two engage in playful conversation and embrace before they are interrupted by the sound of a beeper. Excusing himself, Bond gets out of the boat, explaining that he has to make a phone call. Sylvia complains, "But we haven't eaten yet. I'm starving."[128] Her tone is nothing short of whiny. Instead of taking something to eat for herself, Sylvia follows Bond to his car, where he has removed a telephone from the dashboard and has called headquarters to speak with Miss Moneypenny. Sylvia, once again, is wearing bright red lipstick and nail polish; however, she is now adorned in a two-piece bikini with a floral design. Her stomach is fully exposed, revealing an athletic figure. Impetuous, she begins to cause trouble while Bond is on the telephone.

Bond explains to Miss Moneypenny that he is "reviewing an old case," much to Sylvia's annoyance.[129] She questions, "So I'm an old case now, am I?"[130] Bond finally instructs Sylvia to be quiet, and he informs Miss Moneypenny that he is on his way. Sylvia, however, pulls the receiver out of Bond's hand, defiantly exclaiming that "he is not on his way!"[131] Bond yanks the receiver out of her hand and verbally scolds her for such childish conduct: "Sylvia! Behave."[132]

Sylvia, however, refuses to comply. While Bond promises her that they will "do this again" sometime soon, an unconvinced Sylvia responds, "Do what? Last time you said that you went off to Jamaica."[133] Complaining that she has not seen Bond for six months, Sylvia begins unbuttoning Bond's shirt, behavior that prompts him to forcefully smack her hand. At first, Bond informs Miss Moneypenny that he will report in an hour, but after Miss Moneypenny remarks that his "old case sounds interesting," Bond modifies his response: "Make that an hour and a half."[134]

This power play between Bond and Sylvia suggests that the latter has prevailed, seducing the former in order for him to submit to her wishes. Indeed, Sylvia acts as though she is the victor: she unbuttons Bond's shirt, turns her head approvingly, bites her lip while she silently claps her hands together, and displays a smile on her face. Moreover, as Bond inquires "about that lunch," Sylvia releases a seductive girlish laugh.[135] Though she may have her moment with Bond, Sylvia also gives off the appearance of a spoiled child whose only leverage is to begin a tantrum. Her success at detaining Bond is undermined by her childish demeanor. She deliberately interferes with Bond's telephone conversation and manages to agitate Bond to the point where he must physically strike her into submission. Although she appears sexually aggressive, Sylvia's conduct is unbecoming, and she must be tamed due to her lack of self-restraint. The only discipline Sylvia seems to understand is sexual in nature.

Not surprisingly, Eunice Gayson's voice was once again dubbed, but this time producers believed that her own natural voice "was thought too prim" for the scene.[136] This Sylvia, six months removed from her prior manifestation in *Dr. No* when the story line resumes, exemplifies the "girl with a pretty face and a large bust [who] automatically drools as soon as she hears [Bond's] name."[137] Her role in *From Russia With Love*, as before, is purely functional. She not only serves as an additional sexual conquest for Bond; she establishes continuity between the two films in the manner Terence Young envisioned. Sylvia, as noted above, never resurfaces again in the franchise.

* * *

Producers interviewed over two hundred actresses for the role of Tatiana Romanova, the film's primary Bond Girl, and advertised their search for "a voluptuous, young Greta Garbo."[138] Ultimately, they selected Italian actress and former Valentino model Daniela Bianchi after Terence Young viewed her photograph.[139] A runner-up in the 1960 Miss Universe pageant who won the title of "Miss Photogenic," Bianchi was also a former Miss Rome.[140]

"[G]loriously beautiful,"[141] Daniela Bianchi added an "exotic beauty" to the cast[142] and was immediately introduced to the press before a single scene had been filmed.[143] Nevertheless, producers found fault with

Bianchi's voice, which was dubbed throughout the film, and the shape of her legs. During a scene in which Bond and Kerim Bey, his contact at Station T Turkey, use a periscope to spy upon a meeting in the Russian Consulate, Tatiana enters the room. Only her legs, which *Time* described as "two important Soviet secrets,"[144] are visible through the lens:

> *Bond*: Wait a minute. A girl has just come in.
> *Kerim Bey*: Probably Romanova. She's the only one who's allowed to. How does she look to you?
> *Bond*: Well from this angle, things are shaping up nicely. I'd like to see her in the flesh. Yes . . . .[145]

The legs did not belong to Bianchi. A body double was used for the scene, and publicity photos taken during her bedroom scene with Sean Connery deliberately concealed her legs as well. Yet *Playboy* seemed unaffected by Bianchi's legs, which were prominently displayed in multiple pictorials.

The plot of *From Russia With Love* centers around the triviality of female emotion and the ease with which a woman can be manipulated by others. In fact, *From Russia With Love* was one of the first Bond films in which "[t]he theme of women trapped in oppressive, suffocating situations" became commonplace.[146] To summarize, SPECTRE devises an elaborate scheme through which to acquire a Lektor decoding device and murder Bond by utilizing the services of Tatiana, an unsuspecting Soviet cipher clerk and corporal of State Security who believes she is working for the Soviets. Tatiana possesses no characteristics befitting a cunning spy. Rather, she has an "engaging, optimistic smile" and bright features.[147] A former ballet dancer, it is immediately apparent that Tatiana's physical appearance is of primary importance both for the success of the mission and for her superior, Colonel Rosa Klebb.

Diametrically opposite Tatiana's glowing appearance is Klebb, who was portrayed by actress Lotta Lenya. Klebb was "the perfect visualization of Fleming's toad-like lesbian"[148] and has been characterized as the "anti-Bond woman," a character who is "unattractive, severe, and nearly sexless until she reveals a potentially predatory lesbian desire."[149] Seemingly attracted to Tatiana, Klebb orders her to remove her jacket. Observing her figure, Klebb informs Tatiana that she is a "fine looking girl."[150] Klebb's apparent lesbianism was necessarily toned down for the film adaptation of the novel. Nevertheless, the scene contains "risqué undertones for the time,"[151] and the audience observes how Klebb casually places her hand on Tatiana's knee only to subsequently remove it after noticing Tatiana's negative reaction. Author Raymond Benson noted that the casting of Lenya as Klebb accentuated the character's "toad-like" and "perverse" qualities since Lenya's acting ability enabled viewers to observe with great clarity the juxtaposition of an unattractive and "evil" lesbian with an innocent, yet naïve, beautiful heroine.[152]

The following exchange between the two women further highlights their differences:

> *Klebb* (*reading Tatiana's file with thick, black framed glasses*): I see you trained for the ballet.
> *Tatiana* (*nodding*): But I grew an inch over the regulation height, and so . . . .
> *Klebb* (*interrupting*): And then you have had then three lovers?
> *Tatiana* (*expressing sharp disapproval*): What is the purpose of such an intimate question?
> *Klebb* (*cracking a whip against the desk*): You're not here to ask questions! You forget to whom you're speaking?
> *Tatiana* (*pausing, then nostalgically recalling*): I was in love.
> *Klebb*: And if you were not in love?
> *Tatiana*: I suppose that would depend on the man.
> *Klebb*: Sensible answer. (*rising from the desk, approaching Tatiana, and presenting a photograph of Bond*) This man for instance?
> *Tatiana*: I cannot tell. Perhaps if he was kind . . . toward me.[153]

Klebb then unveils the purpose of the mission and Tatiana's role in its execution: "I have selected you for a most important assignment. Its purpose is to give false information to the enemy. If you complete it successfully, you will be promoted. From now on, you will do anything [Bond] says."[154] Tatiana's refusal would result in her immediate death. Caressing Tatiana's shoulders and face, Klebb informs Tatiana that she is fortunate to have been selected for this mission, a duty Klebb terms a "labor of love."[155]

Left with no alternative, Tatiana obeys Klebb's orders, claims that she has fallen in love with Bond. She requests that Bond rendezvous with her in Istanbul and expresses her desire to defect to Great Britain. In other words, the film centers around "a libidinous Russian cipher clerk . . . who has somehow heard of Bond's charms, informs the British Secret Service that for one night with him she'll do anything—like turn over the latest Soviet cipher machine."[156]

Back in London, M and Bond discuss the absurdity of Tatiana's claims of affection, with M considering it "ridiculous" and Bond describing it as simply "crazy."[157] Nevertheless, both ultimately rationalize that such craziness is typical of women who easily "fall in love with pictures of film stars."[158] Thus, within the first twenty minutes of the film, the audience discovers that Tatiana is merely an attractive pawn caught up in events that are beyond her knowledge and comprehension. Chosen for her beauty by SPECTRE, the crime syndicate exploits Tatiana based upon the assumption that Bond, unable to resist an attractive woman, will place himself in a precarious and compromising position that will facilitate his demise.

Of course, the exploitation is not merely limited to SPECTRE. M informs Bond that a brand new Lektor decoding device is the bait, and Bond notes that the CIA had been seeking a Lektor for years. According to M, MI6 has sought one as well. M, who advises Bond that Tatiana would turn over the Lektor provided that Bond personally retrieve her from Istanbul and deliver her and the machine back to England, assigns Bond to the mission: "If there's any chance of us getting a Lektor, we simply must look into it."[159] While Bond expresses some hesitation, asking what happens if he does not "come up to expectations" in the flesh, M simply instructs him to "just see that you do."[160]

As is apparent, both sides—SPECTRE and MI6—have no regard for Tatiana. She is but a mechanism. For the former, she is the conduit through which SPECTRE can compromise and kill Bond. For the latter, she is an empty vessel who will transport a highly valuable decoding device back to England. Interestingly, although Tatiana promises to deliver the Lektor to Bond, her only real task on this mission is to rendezvous with him. Indeed, her usefulness during and success with the mission are defined solely in terms of how convincingly she can feign falling in love with Bond. It therefore goes without saying that Tatiana's mission, to which she is forcefully conscripted, reduces her to an object of desire, a woman who is *required* to sacrifice herself and submit completely to another man's will, both physically and emotionally, in order to effectuate the purposes of others.

Bond, of course, offers little objection to Tatiana's apparent willingness to do as he wishes. Kerim Bey offers his own insight about the circumstances:

> *Bond*: She'll do anything I say.
> *Kerim Bey* (*laughing*): Anything? My dear James, you're not using this. (*patting his temple*) It all sounds too easy to me. We don't even know if she's telling the truth.
> *Bond*: Well, I intend to find out.
> *Kerim Bey*: Where, in the hotel?[161]

Bond indicates to Kerim Bey that his focus upon the mission is rivaled only by his desire to conquer Tatiana, regardless of her intentions:

Italian actress Daniela Bianchi poses on the set of *From Russia With Love*, 1962.
(United Artists/Archive Photos/Getty Images)

> *Kerim Bey*: My friend, she's got you dangling.
> *Bond*: That doesn't matter. All I want is that Lektor.
> *Kerim Bey* (*smiling*): All? Are you sure that's all you want?
> *Bond* (*raising his eyebrows and smiling*): Well . . . .[162]

As the scene fades from view, both laugh, knowing fully well that Bond, given a carte blanche opportunity by Tatiana herself to utilize her as he wishes, will likely not balk.

* * *

Before considering Tatiana in detail, other female characters appearing in the film warrant brief consideration. Although Maryam d'Abo and John Cork suggested that "there is really only one Bond Girl" in *From Russia With Love*,[163] three additional women enhance an already sexually-charged plot.

The first is Kerim's Girl, as the credits identify her. Her name, or lack thereof, certainly defines the importance of her character: a pure object. Portrayed by actress Nadja Regin, Kerim's Girl makes her first appearance sprawled across a bed in Kerim Bey's office. Wearing bright red lipstick and nail polish, she is dressed in a tight peach-colored dress. She seductively lies on her back with her head closest to the camera, a position that provides a direct view downward toward her chest, and erotically places her necklace in her mouth as she attempts to coo Kerim Bey to her. When she receives no response, she turns over onto her stomach and arches her back to accentuate her bosom. Disinterested, Kerim Bey ignores her, and she continues to slither seductively and impatiently in an attempt to get his attention. Dissatisfied by his failure to respond, she rises, approaches Kerim Bey, and begins massaging his shoulders. Kerim Bay remains dismissive, answering her question of whether he is happy to see her with a mundane, sarcastic response that he is "overjoyed."[164] Persistent, she asks whether she no longer pleases him, and Kerim Bay commands her to "be still."[165] Yet she disobeys and ultimately convinces him to go "back to the salt mines."[166] Moments later, a bomb explodes in the office. When Bond later arrives, Kerim Bey explains what happened: he was relaxing, and, after the bomb detonated, "the girl," to whom he refers in a condescending tone, "left in hysterics."[167] Bond lightens the mood: "Was your technique too violent?"[168]

Violent technique best characterizes the gypsy fight scene described earlier in the novel. When Kerim Bey and Bond arrive at the gypsy camp, which constitutes a portion of the film adding "visual spice,"[169] the former explains to the latter that "two girls in love with the same man have threatened to kill each other. It must be settled the gypsy way."[170]

As a prelude to the ensuing fight, a belly dancer entertains the crowd. Producers focused particular attention upon her moving torso as she "writhes sinuously about the camp" in response to the shouts and catcalls from the male observers.[171] The camera also captures several of Bond's facial reactions as a beaming smile is revealed. Drawn to Bond's table, the belly dancer offers him a personal performance, perhaps the perfect balance for the forthcoming sadistic clash between the two women competing for the same man.

Actresses Martine Beswick and Aliza Gur performed the roles of dueling gypsies Zora and Vida, respectively. Although they portrayed minor characters, both actresses were cast on the basis of their appearances. Beswick, who later appeared in *Thunderball*, was a former Miss Jamaica who began her career as a fashion model. Gur, a former Miss Israel, competed against and resided with Daniela Bianchi during the 1960 Miss Universe pageant.[172]

The gypsy fight scene has been described as a catfight between "two voluptuous vixens in a clawing, strangling, pseudo-judo battle of wills."[173] Initially clothed in skirts and traditional head coverings, the women shed their attire, expose their bare thighs, and engage in battle wearing low-cut tops that emphasize their breasts. Aliza Gur recalled that Terence Young insisted that "more legs fly[] in the air,"[174] evidence that producers wanted to capture as much skin on film as possible. After all, the scene was choreographed to be "both thrilling and erotic."[175]

The fight sequence "was considered quite shocking for its time."[176] Ending prematurely when the gypsy camp is attacked, Bond, in a rare act of clarity, later pleads that the gypsy elders "stop the girl fight" entirely.[177] For his efforts, Bond is assigned the task of deciding which woman is entitled to marry the man they both desire. Bond is then visited in his quarters by Kerim Bey, who is escorted by Zora and Vida. He reminds Bond that the gypsy elder "said for you to decide. So decide."[178] Bond replies, "Might take some time."[179]

Bond thoroughly contemplates a decision as night turns to morning, but the audience must speculate as to his ultimate recommendation. He and the two women emerge in the morning quite satisfied, with both women eager to serve him breakfast, and Bond neither protests nor passes upon the opportunity to be serviced by two very "willing ladies."[180] Indeed, Zora and Vida enable Bond to increase the number of sexual conquests during his mission while requiring absolutely no character development.

* * *

Most of *From Russia With Love* focuses upon Bond's interactions with Tatiana. Gary Giblin and Lisa Neyhouse argued that Tatiana, a former

Soviet Army officer, represents a strong, liberated woman who, like Bond being "sent out to pimp for England," uses her body in order to succeed on a mission.[181] This description, however, is wholly insufficient, mainly because it ignores Tatiana's on-screen behavior. Whatever attributes Tatiana possesses that might be construed as off-camera strengths are, in fact, severely undermined by her on-camera demeanor. The most prominent trait that undercuts her character is a pervasive sense of girlish naiveté.

Bond is first introduced to Tatiana after he hears her sneak into his hotel suite and observes her naked figure scurrying into his bed through a curtain, a scene described simply as "daring" for its time.[182] This image, in fact, was "right at the edge of acceptability" for audiences in 1963.[183] The bedroom scene, however, was imbued with tremendous humor during filming. Daniela Bianchi recalled, "I was very concerned about keeping the sheet tight around me, because underneath I was dressed in a body stocking. Sean [Connery], naturally, did everything he could to complicate things."[184]

While Tatiana's unequivocal desire to climb into the bed of a stranger wearing only black stockings and a black choker around her neck may attest to her self-assurance, sensuality, and willingness for sexual exploration, the twinkle in her eyes and expressions on her face are more adolescent. Tatiana's juvenile quality is not lost upon Bond, who, wearing only a blue towel and pointing his gun, "properly" introduces himself by shaking her hand. Although billed as a Soviet Army officer, Tatiana asks Bond to "[b]e careful. Guns upset me."[185]

After examining Tatiana, Bond notes that he, too, is a "bit upset."[186] Bond describes Tatiana as "one of the most beautiful girls" he has seen, and she obligingly smiles but self-consciously protests that her mouth is too big. Maryam D'Abo and John Cork best described what happens next:

> James Bond looks at her mouth, shown glistening in close-up, and utters a double entendre that made those who understood it in 1963 nearly choke on their popcorn. "No, it's the right size. For me, that is." The music comes in, Bond kisses Tatiana, and the audience knows that we need not worry about the awkward morality of the relationship.[187]

Thus, within a few moments of their introduction, Bond and Tatiana have consummated their preordained, faux relationship. Yet unbeknownst to either of them, Klebb and SPECTRE agents record their tryst on film from behind a double-sided mirror, adding a voyeuristic element to the film. Later, the audience learns how the film of this encounter plays into SPECTRE's grand design.

Tatiana Romanova (Daniela Bianchi) prepares for James Bond's return to his hotel suite in *From Russia With Love*.
(Everett Collection/Rex USA)

One critic's observation that Bond's women, "upon rising from the nearest bed[,] look . . . supremely satisfied" is quite apt with respect to Tatiana.[188] Appearing to have discovered the essence of her femininity for the first time, Tatiana is consumed by a desire to engage in intercourse with Bond. Of course, Tatiana informs Klebb that she has had lovers in the past, but her fascination with Bond is not lost upon the audience. Bond, on the other hand, is more focused upon extracting useful information from her and deriving any physical gratification for himself when needed. The following dialogue is indicative of Tatiana's fixation:

> *Bond*: About the machine.
> *Tatiana*: That's all you are interested in, not me.
> *Bond*: Business first.
> *Tatiana*: I know, once you have got what you want.
> *Bond*: I haven't got it yet. But if you tell me about the machine, well, afterwards, we won't always be working on the company's time.
> *Tatiana*: All right. What do you want to know?
> *Bond*: Talk into this. (*pointing to the recording device that looks like a camera*) Answer my questions quietly, but clearly. How large is the machine?
> *Tatiana*: Like, like a typewriter.
> *Bond*: Weight?
> *Tatiana*: About 10 kilos. In a brown case, brown like your eyes.
> *Bond*: Keep it technical. Self-calibrating or manual?
> *Tatiana*: Both . . . . (*expressing disinterest in technicalities*) James, couldn't we?
> *Bond* (*dismissing her tangent*): Not now. Talk into the camera. How many keys?
> *Tatiana*: Symbol or code keys?
> *Bond*: Both.[189]

The recording of this conversation is transmitted back to London.

In the next scene, M sits in his office with six male government officials and Miss Moneypenny as they listen to the recorded conversation between Bond and Tatiana. As the recorded dialogue becomes even more suggestive, Miss Moneypenny registers immediate visual responses of shock and curiosity. The dialogue continues:

> *Tatiana*: The mechanism is, oh James. James, will you make love to me all the time in England?
> *Bond* (*expressing disinterest and in a brash tone*): Day and night. Go on about the mechanism.
> *Tatiana*: Oh, yes, the mechanism . . . . Tell me the truth? Am I as exciting as all of those Western girls?

> *Bond*: Oh, once when I was with M in Tokyo, we had an interesting experience . . . .[190]

M abruptly stops the recording and dismisses Miss Moneypenny, indicating that she should not be privy to conversations that are better suited for the men. She nonetheless continues to listen from the speaker at her desk, where the audience hears further evidence of Tatiana's immaturity:

> *Tatiana*: James, come closer. I want to whisper something.
> *Bond*: Go on with what you're telling me. (*pausing briefly*) No, not that! The mechanism![191]

Thus, behind Tatiana's supposed façade as a Soviet cipher clerk and corporal of State Security lies a young woman with an inability to focus or control her physical desires.

Although all of these actions could be perceived as merely following orders, it seems that Tatiana is trying too hard; her feigned love for Bond is forced and implausible. While Tatiana is not a "traditional spy,"[192] her espionage skills seem quite ineffective. Indeed, it quickly becomes apparent that Tatiana's interest in completing her mission has been supplanted by her true love for Bond.

Tatiana's immaturity is further highlighted by her conduct on the Orient Express train. After Bond provides her with a falsified passport identifying her as "Caroline Summerset," Tatiana expresses approval of her alias and silently mouths it to herself repeatedly. Her approval turns to protest when she learns that the fake Summersets have no children: "Not even one little boy," she asks Bond in an annoyed tone.[193] To ensure her comprehension, Bond replies in the negative in Russian, prompting Tatiana to once again mouth the alias as if awed by it.

When Bond instructs Tatiana to lock their cabin door, Tatiana responds obediently with a quick, firm, and obsequious "okay."[194] At another point during their journey, Bond directs Tatiana to answer the cabin door because she is nearest. She willingly obliges without protest or comment: "Oh, all right."[195] In order to appease her displeasure with the fact that she has "nothing to wear" to uphold the appearance of their faux marriage, Bond presents Tatiana with an elegant nightgown and a suitcase full of clothing.[196] A mesmerized Tatiana is nearly speechless. She holds the gown to her body and spins around, forecasting the brief modeling performance she gives later. Author John Brosnan observed that these scenes demonstrate that Tatiana is "more than willing to play the part of the new bride all the way" than fulfill her obligations as a Soviet spy.[197]

Next, Tatiana is seen gazing at herself in the mirror. She takes a section of her hair, pulls it across her face between her mouth and nose to form a mustache, and begins making humorous facial expressions. She hardly seems to comprehend the gravity—or exhibit any cognizance—of the drama unfolding around her. Rather, her primary and sole concern is making love to Bond.

Bond, on the other hand, utilizes Tatiana's submissive, seemingly adolescent traits to his advantage, and his treatment of her is quite abusive. With unfettered authority over her, his character devolves at times into that of a scornful parent disciplining a child rather than a man interacting with a female colleague or lover. After Tatiana protests that she would rather stay with him in bed (and engage in further lovemaking) than dress for the restaurant car, Bond holds her upper arms and responds, "Just do as I say."[198] Tatiana replies, "Yes, James," and Bond smacks her posterior as he walks past her.[199]

Although Tatiana knows nothing of SPECTRE's plot to assassinate Kerim Bey on the train, any trustworthiness Bond may have attributed to her is "shattered"[200] following his death. Demanding that Tatiana disclose the truth, Bond grabs her by the arms, lifts her from the seat, and pulls her toward him:

> *Bond*: Kerim's dead.
>
> *Tatiana*: Dead?
>
> *Bond*: I want the truth.
>
> *Tatiana*: James, you're hurting me!
>
> *Bond* (*shaking her*): I'll do worse than that if you don't tell me. You're doing this under orders, I know. What are they?
>
> *Tatiana*: I don't know what you mean.
>
> *Bond*: Liar. (*slapping her across the face, which sends her body falling backwards upon the seat*)
>
> *Tatiana*: Even if you kill me, I can say nothing. I did not know that anything like Kerim's death would happen. But, when we get to England, I'll tell you.
>
> *Bond*: Go on. Tanya, maybe they didn't let you in on all of it, but whatever you do know, tell me.
>
> *Tatiana* (*crying*): I know I love you, James. I love you.
>
> *Bond*: Just tell me.
>
> *Tatiana*: I love you, I love you, it's true.
>
> *Bond* (*displaying the extent to which he is not convinced*): Sure.[201]

Bond then pushes Tatiana's weakened body back onto the seat as if he discards her.

The scene produced mixed responses. Maryam d'Abo and John Cork noted that the "genius of this scene is that the violence weakens Bond . . . he himself is unable to ignore his emotions for her."[202] But Bond's actions suggest otherwise, as it is he who pushes Tatiana's head back into her lap and walks away, leaving her to sulk by herself. By contrast, Richard Maibaum recalled the reasons for Bond's reaction: "He thought she was involved in the death of his friend . . . he reacted like a . . . normal human being."[203] The scene ultimately reaffirms that Bond's emotional allegiance, if he has one, lies with Kerim Bey and the mission, not with Tatiana.

Tatiana was and remains expendable following this interaction between her and Bond, and Bond continues to treat her as such. He tacitly watches Donald "Red" Grant, a SPECTRE assassin, lace her wine with a poison that induces her collapse and later warns her that if she cannot bring herself to move, he will leave her behind. He implores her to "Come on, or I'll leave you here," but Tatiana pleads that Bond stay with her.[204] Bond must grab her and force her to accompany him; otherwise, Bond would not hesitate to abandon her.

At the conclusion of the film, Tatiana successfully kills Klebb, thereby saving Bond from Klebb's menacing poison-tipped shoe. Producer Barbara Broccoli described her impression of Tatiana: "I don't consider her a victim. She was exploited by her vicious, manipulative boss but in the end she gets out of the situation and heroically saves Bond's life."[205] Tatiana reflects that Klebb was a "horrible woman" as she stands behind a seated Bond and caresses his shoulder with the gun still in her hand.[206] Realizing that the gun is in her hand, which causes him to register a highly uncomfortable look on his face, Bond, now thoroughly annoyed, takes it from her. Although grateful for disarming Klebb, Bond nevertheless appears disgusted by Tatiana's recklessness. Indeed, while Tatiana previously remarked that guns upset her, it is Bond who seems considerably unnerved when one finds its way into her hands.

Bond's reaction is justified as Tatiana initially struggles with the weapon, seemingly representing her mixed feelings about killing Klebb. In essence, her conduct reflects the extent to which her professed love for Bond is, in fact, a ruse. If she truly loved Bond, then Tatiana would have acted upon instinct and would not have hesitated to discharge the gun.

Lost upon Tatiana is the fact that, while she saves her own life and avoids the wrath of Klebb, it is Bond who emerges victorious. Bond possesses the Lektor, has eliminated "Red" Grant, and outmaneuvers SPECTRE. Tatiana presumably returns to Russia free from Klebb's wrath. At the same time, the depth of the SPECTRE plot is beyond Tatiana's comprehension, and her status as a pawn is exacerbated at the conclusion of the film when Bond destroys the film of them in bed together. She still has no idea what transpired.

Several film critics "simply and unequivocally declared the picture to be very good fun,"[207] including Shana Alexander, who wrote that *From Russia With Love* was "outrageously funny."[208] Yet watching women fight each other with the intent to kill and observing a man physically abusing a woman left much to be desired for others. One critic found the film "quite distasteful" and added that *From Russia With Love* "may not be a harmful movie [but] there almost literally can be no such thing as a harmless movie."[209] Others blamed Fleming for even imagining scenes such as the gypsy fight, arguing that "blood-and-sex . . . fantasy is . . . after a certain age—say, sixteen—unacceptable."[210]

* * *

Dr. No and *From Russia With Love* set the standard for developing the Bond Girl archetype in subsequent adventures: "Bond-girl was lust discreetly personified: a combination of playmate, girl Friday and sphinx."[211] Honey Ryder and Tatiana Romanova, while beautiful, are relatively functionless. Their characters are, for the most part, undeveloped, one-dimensional, and unsophisticated. Like other Bond Girls who would later appear in the franchise, Honey and Tatiana "were essentially characterless. They invited sexual interest, gratified sexual desire, and made themselves useful"[212] in terms of facilitating or reaffirming male sexual prowess. Others, of course, disagree. Professor Camille Paglia argued that Bond's seduction of the Bond Girls actually "honour[s] them" because he is not "the kind of lounge lizard who draws women back to his bachelor pad in so many of those movies of the late Fifties and Sixties."[213]

Regardless, the Bond Girls of *Dr. No* and *From Russia With Love* lack the independence necessary to warrant their being dubbed strong characters, and Bond's conduct toward them is reprehensible. These characters' weaknesses are accentuated in order to enhance Bond's masculinity and his strengths. As a result, the Bond Girl seems fit for sacrifice. While Honey Ryder gathered seashells and Tatiana Romanova convinced herself that she loves Bond, American women, as the 1960s unfolded, began to confront new, real, and important viewpoints that challenged preconceived notions about their place in society.

006

A Mystique of Femininity: Marriage, Conformity, and a New Voice

Women aren't brought up to think well enough to talk. It's a revelation for a man to find a woman he can really talk to. I began to realize a while back that many of my best friends were men.

—Betty Friedan[1]

In every country of the world, with one exception, women are banished whenever men sit down to talk. The exception is the United States. Here we let women enter into the conversation. It is the worst mistake man has made . . . . Separation of the sexes is rigidly enforced elsewhere for the good reason that women historically have shown themselves to be incapable of conversing in a civilized, rational manner.

—George Sumner Albee[2]

Girls get dumber and dumber as they get older and older. We all know that. We have all always *known that.*

—Vivian Gornick[3]

In 1949, an article dubiously titled "Women are Intellectually Inferior" appeared in *The American Mercury*. The author suggested that women were foreclosed from possessing and demonstrating genius on account of genetics: "The female, with two X-chromosomes, has a good chance of having the unfavorable recessive genes . . . . [T]here are, in fact[,] . . . undesirable characteristics on the X-chromosome."[4] According to that author, "[e]ven the small number of outstanding women exhibit gifts which cannot compare with those of the giants of masculine genius."[5] Wholly unscientific and unsubstantiated, these statements nevertheless reflected and reinforced a common postwar notion that women belonged within the home. In the midst of a social and economic reconversion from wartime production to civilian normalcy, a movement rapidly emerged that focused upon reaffirming women's sphere of domesticity.

During this era, men typically pursued women more for their potential reproductive and child-rearing capabilities than for intellectual prowess. Images of marriage became virtually ubiquitous. Author Elaine Tyler May observed that "everywhere they turned, young women found instructions on 'how to catch a husband' or 'how to snare a male.'"[6] Marriage, of course, represented conformity, and the complacency into which American society fell during the 1950s served as a convenient diversion from postwar complexities. According to Betty Friedan, the repercussions women experienced due to society's willingness to return to a prewar mindset were severe:

> Women went home again just as men shrugged off the bomb, forgot the concentration camps, condoned corruption . . . . [I]t was easier, safer, to think about love and sex than about communism[,] . . . it was easier to look for Freudian sexual roots in man's behavior, his ideas, and his wars . . . . [T]hey were a kind of personal retreat . . . . [W]e [women] lowered our eyes from the horizon, and steadily contemplated our own navels . . . [and our] personal commitment [became] a catch-all commitment to "home" and "family."[7]

By 1962, Dr. George Gallup and Evan Hill identified the "composite woman" in America as "a full-time housewife and mother [who] is not employed outside the home."[8]

Throughout the 1950s, the sooner a woman found a husband and walked down the aisle, the better off she—and society in general—became. Young women increasingly were engaged while still enrolled in secondary school, and marriage before the bride reached her twentieth birthday became a common trend. In response, many high schools began employing marriage counselors. Many of those women who graduated from high school without a husband enrolled in colleges and universities, but their matriculation was intended more for the purpose of immersing themselves into a new environment where they could find a husband than for furthering their own intellectual development. In a 1961 speech honoring students at State University College in Cortland, New York, sociology professor Rozanne M. Brooks remarked:

> While it is true that the female college student is welcomed on the campus today—that welcome is likely to be reserved and in some cases merely pragmatic. Often her motives are questioned and her scholarly intent is looked upon with suspicion . . . . Now, I am not prepared to argue that American women students do not husband-hunt while in college; they do[,] . . . they are encouraged to do so . . . [and] I can't think of a better place for . . . young women to look . . . . I'll [even] wager that every one of the young women being honored tonight is interested in finding a husband. At least she is, if she hasn't already found one.[9]

Friedan sarcastically referred to the "new degree" these women earned in colleges and universities across the country as the "Ph.T," or "Putting Husband Through."[10]

In order to accommodate the rising marriage rate of its students, universities began constructing dormitories for married couples. Once married, approximately 60 percent of women ultimately abandoned their studies to devote themselves to their family responsibilities as housewives. A 1962 article in *The Yale Review* suggested that "many young women—if not the majority—seem to be incapable of dealing with future long-range intellectual interests . . . . [Instead,] the mother's job in training children and shaping the life of her family should draw on all a woman's resources."[11] Former Radcliffe College president Mary I. Bunting noted the irony inherent in an educational structure that enticed women to enter institutions of higher learning but encouraged them to emerge as housewives: "We don't think it matters what women do with their education. Why, we don't even care if they learn to be good mothers. If we really cared, we would have developed good college courses to prepare them for motherhood."[12] As a result, Betty Coed, as she was dubbed, represented "the greatest waste in America" because an educated woman became "mired in mere motherhood and fail[ed] to keep up with the degree she earned before she was married."[13]

Was Betty Coed wasting away at home? Women simply were neither expected nor encouraged to offer significant contributions to society through the knowledge they acquired in college. Rather, a woman's supposed "greatest fulfillment" was the management of domestic affairs and the rearing of children.[14] "Woman's place is in the home" became a catchall phrase, suggesting that "only men possess[ed] the appropriate equipment to cope with the professions and other occupations entailing high level responsibility."[15] In 1963, the president of Chatham College published an article in *Saturday Review* wherein he posed a blunt question: "What's the use of educating women?"[16] Female domesticity, the author argued, was not only healthy, it reflected the high level of importance Americans placed upon parenthood. "We do a great disservice to American women," he wrote, "by dismissing their role as wives and mothers as unfortunate dissipations of time and talent. The educated woman who becomes a wife and mother has an enormously important job to do. If done well, it cannot help but engage every aspect of her education."[17]

Many educators did not stop there. In fact, some argued that an aura of "self-pity" debilitated women, preventing them from recognizing and accepting that fulfilling the housewife expectation was actually a form of equality. An educated woman bore the solemn responsibility to "develop for herself and transmit to her family a social conscience."[18] Only through her role as a housewife could a woman "find true happiness [and] return to her real and joyful self. She must relearn that surrender to her biological destiny is . . . a wonderful privileged condition."[19]

Naturally, the positions of housewife and homemaker were touted as the most admirable careers to which a woman could aspire. The housewife was portrayed as a veritable heroine in women's magazine fiction and lauded across university campuses. In an address to the 1955 graduating class of Smith College, politician and diplomat Adlai Stevenson emphasized the importance of America's housewife, which, he explained, constituted the best way a woman could be involved in social and political discourse. Nowhere was such involvement best exemplified, according to Stevenson, than in "the living room with a baby in your lap or in the kitchen with a can opener in your hand . . . . I think there is much you can do about our crisis in the humble role of housewife. I could wish you no better vocation than that."[20]

A 1961 editorial in *Life* forecasted the potential unrest that was brewing in American living rooms and kitchens: "Most US women call themselves 'housewives,' and the country is incalculably in their debt. But the term also covers a great pool of idleness and futility."[21] Yet a Gallup poll conducted the following year suggested that many women surveyed actually embraced this domestic role.

One respondent indicated that she was "'[her] own boss. If I don't want to do the dishes or the laundry right now, I can do them later. My only deadline is when my husband comes home. I'm much more free than when I was single . . . . [A] married woman has it made.'"[22] A second respondent preferred her domestic role since it relieved her from worrying about issues that seemed far removed from her personally: "I let my husband take care of the big things such as who's going to be secretary of the UN and whether we'll get to the moon first. I take care of the little things such as what club we'll join."[23]

Friedan cautioned that some women "who don't have the discipline" to resist the trend toward domesticity would ultimately "be no more alive than their green stamps."[24] Yet a third Gallup respondent admitted that she was perfectly content serving in a subordinate capacity within her marriage, even going so far as to rationalize that doing so was necessary: "A woman needs a master-slave relationship[,] whether it's husband and wife, or boss-secretary. This shows she's needed and useful. Women who ask for equality fight nature. They wouldn't be happy if they had it. It's simply biological."[25] The poll suggested that women had embraced the concept that "being subordinate to men is a part of being feminine" without objection or hesitation and that, by doing so, women "need[ed] . . . a husband to lean on."[26]

These respondents exemplified the precise situation Simone de Beauvoir described ten years earlier in her influential work, *The Second Sex*:

> [W]oman has always been man's dependent, if not his slave; the two sexes have never shared the world in equality. And even today woman is heavily handicapped . . . . [A]lmost nowhere is her legal status the same as man's, and frequently it is much to her disadvantage . . . . [A]t the present time[,] . . . it is still a world that belongs to men—they have no doubt of it at all and women have scarcely any . . . . [W]oman may fail to lay claim to the status of subject because she lacks definite resources, because she feels the necessary bond that ties her to man regardless of reciprocity, and because she is often very well pleased with her role as the *Other* . . . .
>
> . . . .
>
> Yes, women on the whole *are* today inferior to men; that is, their situation affords them fewer possibilities. The question is: should that state of affairs continue?
>
> Many men hope that it will continue[.][27]

One man who permitted these apparent gender inequities to continue, whether knowingly or unwittingly, was John F. Kennedy, who engaged in what has been termed "benign neglect" of female constituents after his victorious presidential campaign in 1960. Each female that Kennedy appointed in his administration filled minor or insignificant positions.[28] As a result, Kennedy's New Frontier program was criticized as one that "for women [appeared that] the New Frontiers are the old frontiers."[29]

Only after intense lobbying did the Kennedy administration conduct a reexamination: "President Kennedy has found it necessary to order Federal departments and agencies not to practice discrimination against women in government career service."[30] Esther Peterson, a former member of Kennedy's campaign staff, the director of the Women's Bureau, and the highest-ranking female in Kennedy's administration, successfully persuaded the president to create a Commission on the Status of Women, which was established by executive order in December 1961.

According to one scholar, Kennedy's decision to establish the commission was merely diversionary. The commission was not the product of an administration that desired to address women's issues. Rather, it "obviat[ed] . . . further responsibility for women's concerns . . . . Kennedy apparently felt no need to pursue other means of recognizing women voters."[31] In fact, the executive order's preamble seemingly undermined the commission's purpose:

> Whereas a Governmental Commission should be charged with the responsibility for developing recommendations for overcoming discriminations in government and private employment on the basis of sex and for developing recommendations for services *which will enable women to continue their roles as wives and mothers* while making a maximum contribution to the world around them.[32]

Kennedy appointed Peterson, who was considered "an expert . . . on problems of women," the executive vice chairperson of the newly established commission.[33] Although described as "the one political woman who had Kennedy's ear," Peterson never encouraged the president to increase the number of female appointments within his administration.[34] And if she did, those requests fell upon deaf ears.

The Commission on the Status of Women was divided into seven subcommittees: education, federal employment, home and community, protective labor legislation, private employment, social insurance and taxes, and civil and political rights. The civil and political rights subcommittee brought the Equal Rights Amendment (ERA) onto its agenda. In 1963, the commission delivered its official report, *American Women*, to President Kennedy. The report included recommendations such as expanding educational opportunities for homemakers, reforming Social Security to provide greater benefits for widows and dependents of households headed by single women, revising federal hiring statutes to eliminate discriminatory practices, and enacting an equal pay act that had been proposed decades earlier but had never become law.

None of the committee's recommendations sought to "alter the long-standing cultural assumption that a woman's 'biology determined her social destiny,'" to dispel the notion that "a woman's place was in the home," and to refute that her "primary obligation" was her husband and children.[35] Rather, *American Women* suggested that "[w]idening the choices for women beyond their doorstep does not imply neglect of their education for responsibilities in the home. Modern family life is demanding, and most of the time and attention given to it comes from women."[36] Thus, the report accepted the sphere of domesticity as a *fait accompli* and left it intact and unchallenged.

But not all women embraced the sphere of domesticity to which they were being relegated. A significant percentage of American women entered the work force despite encountering significant obstacles that eventually forced many to forego prospects of a career. One substantial hurdle facing female employees concerned disproportionate compensation between men and women for performance of the same tasks.[37] Although the Equal Pay Act was enacted in 1963 and represented the commission's most successful recommendation, the law ultimately achieved little to eliminate the disparity between male and female wages. In fact, the clause "equal pay for equal work" in the original legislation was modified to "equal pay for comparable work" in the final bill.[38]

American Women was perceived by advocates of women's rights as being "buried in bureaucratic file drawers . . . . [A]ll the talk, and the reports, and the Commission . . . were only examples of tokenism."[39] The frustration many women experienced was headlined in a front-page *New York Times* article in 1963, which noted a recommendation from *American Women* that women would need to "sue for Equal Rights."[40]

Yet not a single lawsuit seeking equal gender rights was filed during the two years the commission convened. Nevertheless, the two-year period afforded women the opportunity to become more vocal and to express discontent over the societal roles to which they had been relegated. Men also joined the campaign, but in limited numbers. Sentiment began to mount that "women may have been 'emancipated' when the Nineteenth Amendment gave them the vote in 1920[, but] in the middle of the twentieth century . . . women [we]re still far from emancipated."[41]

While the commission was "the first time so broad a study of discrimination against women ha[d] been undertaken,"[42] it became apparent that any effort to achieve tangible results would require a different approach. During this period, Friedan began formulating her ideas for "a real movement on the part of women themselves to change society."[43] In the *Saturday Evening Post*, one columnist noted that women should no longer accept the generalized conceptions that they were weak or submissive, eventually observing that a battle of the sexes was becoming "fiercer than ever."[44] Quoting Aeschylus, who believed that "it is thy place, woman, to hold thy peace and keep within doors," the article called upon women "to find ways of challenging men."[45]

In 1960, journalist Marion K. Sanders lamented that "three-quarters of all American wives still toil only in their homes—and have no acceptable alternative."[46] Therefore, the first challenge women could present was actually utilizing their college degrees and entering the professional world, thereby dispelling the myth that they "contribute little" to society and reversing the stereotype that they were relegated to "rear-guard[s]" of history.[47] While another commentator suggested that married women were "not happy" with their positions in the home,[48] Sanders elaborated, describing housewives as "a discontented class" who had been continually subjected to "a cult" of domesticity perpetuated by a popular culture that quelled any protest.[49]

Women were advised to resist "wallow[ing] in the soupy Eden of daytime TV or the women's magazines" and to assume an active role in advancing themselves.[50] Of course, doing so required considerable motivation and discipline, particularly in light of a unified campaign to preserve the *status quo*. After all, it became increasingly clear that "whoever controlled women consumers controlled American money."[51]

To that end, American women became the targets of a burgeoning magazine industry that was committed to perpetuating the homemaker as an ideal. *Ladies Home Journal*, *McCalls*, and *Good Housekeeping*, known as "the big three," competed directly with numerous other publications—notably *Everywoman's Family Circle*, *Vogue*, *Glamour*, *Harper's Bazaar*, *Mademoiselle*, *Redbook*, *Cosmopolitan*, *Ingenue*, and *Seventeen*—to attract readers while peddling similar messages.[52] Despite this saturation, voices emerged encouraging women to cease trading in their college degrees for "mothballs" and to "enter a profession and to stick with it even if this involves postponing motherhood."[53] Failure to do so, women were warned, would have disastrous consequences: "We are doomed to a permanent scarcity so long as the peculiar and often irrational pressures of our society impel the majority of American women to limit their labors to their own four walls."[54]

A 1962 article in *Esquire* suggested that "one of the rights a woman should have is the right not to avail herself of her rights."[55] According to this article, women lacked equal standing with men because women, unlike men, "assume[d] their own equality . . . [but] they will not accept the full challenge of emancipation [and] tend to settle for far less."[56] In support of the contention that women merely acquiesced to their circumstances without question or resistance, willingly allowing themselves to enter a "great pool of idleness and futility," the article recalled the story of a woman who wholly abandoned a career in civil engineering in exchange for a domestic home life.[57] She, like many women, trained "all the faculties of [her] mind," but voluntarily resigned herself to "grovel[] scarcely above the animal kingdom and inspire[] only a vapid tenderness."[58] Women apparently accepted the fact that "there has never been a female Shakespeare, a female Mozart, or a female Einstein" and, as such, had become their own Achilles' heel, undermining their own ability to elevate or change their status:[59]

> A woman [who] had a chance at a "career" felt obliged to seize it[,] . . . [yet] guilt assailed her if she failed to do so; she was letting down her sex and confessing her own weakness . . . . [A] sense of self-pity . . . is another underlying cause . . . for the frantic rush to the cave and the exclamations of delight [since] women's main ambition today is to acquire and hold a mate . . . . [W]ork outside the home . . . holds no attraction in itself, unless it is subservient to the demands of an individual household.[60]

Undermining their own efforts, nevertheless, played into another stereotype attributed to women: victimization. According to one commentator, woman was "unique, as far as victims go, in that she has been trained to be ill at ease admitting it. Her trouble is that she is doing comparatively well as a victim—making a buck, running a family . . . ."[61] These views, of course, encountered substantial criticism.

Perhaps one of the strongest and most recognized voices of opposition was Friedan, who promoted the idea that a "woman is first of all a person, not a mommy, not a sex object, not an unpaid dishwasher—that she needn't choose between house and career but [could] have both." She published *The Feminine Mystique*, one of the most influential works of the modern feminist movement, in 1963. Considered "in popular lore to be the spark that ignited second-wave feminism," *The Feminine Mystique* began without mincing words:[62]

> Something is very wrong with the way American women are trying to live their lives today . . . . [T]he problems and satisfaction of their lives, and mine, and the way our education has contributed to them, simply did not fit the image of the modern American woman as she was written about in women's magazines, studied and analyzed in classrooms and clinics, praised and damned in a ceaseless barrage of words ever since the end of World War Two. There was a strange discrepancy between the reality of our lives as women and the image to which we were trying to conform, the image that I came to call the feminine mystique.[63]

Friedan observed that the beginning of the feminist movement involved "having to turn new corners: coming to dead ends, looking in vain for blueprints or answers from books and authorities" in order to realize that the lives women had been leading required something more.[64] According to Friedan, the focus upon elevating the individual that had been prevalent both before and following World War II had suddenly shifted toward a different objective: "fulfillment with the role of housewife and motherhood."[65] The shift was merely part of a larger movement that sought to accentuate and glorify femininity. Indeed, it was during this period that anthropologist Margaret Mead's work emphasized the unique sexual and biological responsibilities that women possessed.

But Friedan protested these developments, criticizing the movement that sought to teach women "adjustment within the world of home and children."[66] Her objections were directed at Mead and others who promoted the concept that only "neurotic, unfeminine, unhappy women" sought societal advancement, whereas truly feminine women supposedly "d[id] not want careers, higher education, political rights—the independence and the opportunities that the old-fashioned feminists fought for."[67] Friedan argued that

> [t]he vision the mystique took from Margaret Mead was of a world where women . . . will earn the same respect accorded men for their creative achievements—as if possession of uterus and breasts bestows on women a glory that men can never know . . . . [Her] eloquent pages made a great many American women envy the serene femininity of the bare-breasted Samoan[,] . . . breasts unfettered by civilization's brassieres, and brains undisturbed by pallid man-made knowledge of the goals of human progress.[68]

Conforming to Mead's prescriptions inherently confined women, Friedan asserted, because the "feminine mystique prevented women from realizing their full human potential by locking them into domestic prisons."[69] The degree of disdain Friedan possessed for the positions into which she believed society constrained women was strikingly evident in her characterization of the home as a woman's "comfortable concentration camp."[70]

Friedan's rhetoric, nevertheless, was undermined in several ways. She herself admitted that "the new mystique is much more difficult for the modern woman to question than the old prejudices, partly because the mystique is broadcast by the very agents of education and social science that are supposed to be the chief enemies of prejudice . . . ."[71] One such "old prejudice" was rooted in Freud's concepts of sexuality and the notion that anatomy and nature "determined woman's destiny."[72] Although Freud's writings had been reanalyzed and reinterpreted by American psychoanalysts and social scientists throughout the 1940s, most of his theories about femininity remained relatively unchallenged. Women had been "exposed to his dogma, as it was accepted unquestioningly in that era and taught by psychologists and sociologists, and in those ubiquitous courses on 'Marriage and the Family' which sprang up in every college."[73] In fact, Freud's blatant sexism was prevalent in his work—in passages such as "[T]he . . . girl is as a rule less aggressive[,] . . . less self-sufficient; she seems to have a greater need for affection . . . and therefore to be more dependent and docile"—and his personal and private correspondence.[74]

Freud's writings suggested the existence of a sexual hierarchy in which women were inherently subordinate to men:

> Women are different beings . . . from men . . . . It is really a stillborn thought to send women into the struggle for existence exactly as men . . . . It is possible that changes in upbringing may suppress all a woman's tender attributes, needful of protection . . . , and that she can then earn a livelihood like men . . . . [I]n such an event one would not be justified in mourning the passing away of the most delightful thing the world can offer us—our ideal of womanhood.[75]

As to the question of female emancipation in the late nineteenth century, Freud expressed adamant opposition. Women who gained total freedom, he posited, contributed to the destabilization of society because all "reforming action in law and education would break down."[76] Furthermore, according to Freud, "[n]ature ha[d] determined woman's destiny through beauty, charm, and sweetness. Law and custom have much to give women that has been withheld from them, but the position of women will surely be what it is: in youth an adored darling and in mature years a loved wife."[77]

Freud's portrayals of women and an apparent failure on the part of scholars to challenge his views concerned Friedan, who wrote that Freud promoted the vision of women as "strange, inferior, less-than-human species. He saw them as childlike dolls, who existed in terms only of man's love, to love man and serve his needs."[78] Disappointed that scholars like Mead trained under—and were therefore influenced by—the Freudian model, Friedan embarked upon her own campaign to deconstruct and to question Freud's views of women.[79] Although she initially argued that a woman's supposed penis envy suggested not a "refusal to accept her sexual deformity" but instead reflected Freud's misconception that a woman's "wish to be equal is neurotic,"[80] Friedan, in retrospect, conceded that her reinterpretations of Freud were "blasphemous" at the time.[81]

But Freud was not the root of the problem. In fact, Betty Friedan wrote that "the identity crisis for women" resulted not from Freudian notions of femininity but rather from women's own attempts to discover themselves through "the dull routine of housework."[82] American women,

Betty Friedan addresses a conference in New York, 1971.
(Associated Press)

Friedan resolved, must "begin to take [their] li[ves] seriously" and actively prevent the feminine mystique from "burying millions of women alive."[83] By breaking out of the "housewife trap and truly find[ing] fulfillment as wives and mothers—by fulfilling their own unique possibilities as separate human beings," women could, Friedan believed, spark their own political and social movement that could facilitate much-needed and long-overdue change.[84] Friedan noted that there was "so much unnecessary martyrdom . . . it wouldn't be better to have a lot of . . . dreary virtuous housewives [who soon] won't call themselves housewives."[85]

As expected, criticism of *The Feminine Mystique* abounded. Betty Friedan's work was characterized as a "virtually fact-free vision."[86] Others dismissed *The Feminine Mystique* as a "rabble-rousing" work that demonstrated the extent to which issues about gender were permeated by "a strange aura of frivolity":[87]

> The problem that Mrs. Friedan doesn't face is, how free can anyone be to define his or her own personality? In the past, circumstances defined it very strictly for women (housework had to be done: therefore housework was "feminine"); now . . . the woman who says no, I will define myself my own way, is likely to become frozen in an attitude—of classical femininity or aggressive efficiency . . . .
>
> . . . [S]ociety's definitions can be almost as binding as nature's . . . .[88]

Others accentuated Friedan's radical past in an effort to undermine the work as a "watered-down" interpretation of Marxism that focused solely upon middle-class women.[89] Author Daniel Horowitz noted one particular irony in Friedan's writing: Friedan was plagued with uncertainty because she herself, as a suburban housewife during the 1950s, succumbed to the feminine mystique. Indeed, Friedan was "trapped by one of the comic conventions [she is] out to destroy—the convention of the female preacher."[90] As such, Friedan's attempt to identify with the mainstream was apparently unsuccessful because it constituted a "reinvention" that was designed to make her premise work.[91]

Betty Friedan also was criticized by women, many of whom attacked her narrow focus and apparent failure to consider ethnicity and socioeconomic factors. Others resented having their roles as housewives presented as a waste of productivity. For example, one columnist complained that *The Feminine Mystique*, which was written by the "high priestess of the Salvation Through Job gospel," was nothing but a "shrill, humorless polemic, packed with data from . . . psychiatrists, anthropologists[,] . . . Feminologists, and interviews with women who are as gabby as they are unhappy."[92] But one writer debunked any notion of female productivity, suggesting instead that "woman may try to catch up, but she just doesn't have the footwork."[93] Moreover, women allegedly suffered from identity complexes that inhibited them from advancing their cause for equality: "When she is practical[,] . . . she lacks romance[;] . . . when she rejects romance[,] . . . she's frigid; when she argues in her defense[,] . . . she's manipulative[;] . . . when she turns bitter and feels sorry for herself, she is the 'Jewish Mother.'"[94]

Despite these and other remonstrations, Betty Friedan was not ignored, and the importance of *The Feminine Mystique* could not be overstated. While other works, such as Helen Gurley Brown's *Sex and the Single Girl*, appeared in the early 1960s, *The Feminine Mystique* "became the opening salvo in the most far-reaching social revolution of the century."[95] Scientific studies fully shattered the absurd conjectures about a woman's genetic inferiority: "No IQ tests yet devised show that either men or women are innately brighter. . . ."[96] Indeed, many studies revealed quite the opposite: female intellectual superiority was demonstrated in "linguistic abilities [and] psychologically, [where] women get higher marks than men."[97]

Studies aside, the 1960s began with recommendations like the following one that appeared in *Harper's Magazine*:

> With her A.B. in hand, tomorrow's college graduate should be encouraged to enter a profession . . . . The delusion that every woman must be a chambermaid, cook, and nurse—in addition to any other work she may do—is archaic . . . . Women, like men, should give their highest skills to a society which badly needs them.[98]

As the decade unfolded, American women became increasingly vocal about their status, seeking media through which to express their discontent and reinvent themselves. Coinciding with a strengthening civil rights movement, an increase in the number of women earning college degrees, and a burgeoning female workforce coping with sexual harassment and discrimination, *The Feminine Mystique* added fuel to a fomenting conflagration waiting to engulf American politics and culture.

* * *

During a time of racial and social turbulence, the James Bond franchise provided audiences with an element of escapist entertainment. But it did much more, representing one medium through which to preserve traditional gender politics and views about the appropriate role for women.[99] The Bond Girl, it turned out, became part of a first line of defense against an impending gender crisis that was brewing on the homefront.

007

Reinforcing an Archetype: *Goldfinger* and *Thunderball*

[Sean] Connery quickly perfected the technique that is the essence of screen sex appeal: the art of being highly suggestive while preserving all the cinematic decencies. . . . Connery-Bond turned the business of physical lovemaking into a verbal game.

—Andrew Rissik[1]

That's the first time I've tasted women. They're rather good.

—James Bond[2]

In Agent 007's world, almost every woman is a 10, *from the hotel attendant to the villain's girlfriend to the car rental girl to the female assassin, from the sexpots to the psychopaths.*

—*Playboy*[3]

[Pussy Galore] was a wonderful character to play . . . . It's much more fun to play a bitch or a toughie or something other than a goodie-two shoes.

—Honor Blackman[4]

The success of *From Russia With Love* enabled Cubby Broccoli and Harry Saltzman to firmly and permanently establish James Bond within the United States market. Although their first two Bond films were well received by audiences, Broccoli and Saltzman endeavored "to create the biggest Bond yet."[5] Consequently, their next Bond film would be the result of a "conscious effort" to appeal to American audiences,[6] especially since the majority of the plot in *Goldfinger* takes place in Miami and at Fort Knox, Kentucky.

In fact, "it was not until the release of *Goldfinger* that United Artists decided to give Bond a full-scale American promotional campaign,"[7] and *Goldfinger*, with its "predominantly American" setting replete with a "conspiracy . . . directed against America,"[8] quickly became "the first of the Bond films to be classified as a box-office blockbuster."[9] *Goldfinger* opened to "immense publicity and record-breaking takings."[10] As one writer noted, the film "was so popular that many theaters stayed open twenty-four hours a day to accommodate the crowds . . . . [It] rewrote the record book from its first day in release."[11] In 1965, *Time* noted that *Goldfinger*'s box office sales were "astonishing," particularly after the film sparked increased ticket sales for a double showing of *Dr. No* and *From Russia With Love* that rivaled the earnings those films generated during their initial, individual releases.[12]

Goldfinger ultimately became the fastest-grossing film of all time.[13] One year later, *Thunderball*, a film described as firmly implanting "James Bond's place in popular culture,"[14] did what seemed virtually impossible: it eclipsed *Goldfinger* in box office sales.[15] In fact, *Thunderball* was the highest grossing film of 1966.[16] Together, the two films have been described as Hollywood's "first blockbusters."[17]

Goldfinger

Goldfinger represents "the peak of the series"[18] as well as its "turning point" in terms of popular appeal.[19] Part of the film's success, of course, stems from its portrayal of women. Replete with "several off-color quips [which] shove[d] it into [the] adults only"[20] realm, *Goldfinger* offered audiences "the most alluring gallery of women ever seen in the series . . . [by] introducing its female characters in outrageous fashion."[21] As one television promotional advertisement announced, *Goldfinger* gave audiences a mixture of "business with *girls* and thrills, *girls* and fun, *girls* and danger."[22]

Most memorable, of course, is the ubiquitous image of Jill Masterson's golden girl, memorialized on film by Shirley Eaton. Prior to *Goldfinger*'s release, one critic had already noted the visual impact of Eaton's character: "You must have seen by now . . . the girl painted from head to toe in gold."[23] Indeed, Eaton's golden girl has been characterized as "one of the decade's most memorable, erotic images."[24] The original film posters exploited the eroticism associated with the figure of a naked woman glistening in gold in a marketing campaign intended to "drive all teenagers into hormonal overdrive" and fill theaters.[25] Model and actress Margaret Nolan, who portrayed the part of Dink, Bond's masseuse at the Fontainebleau Hotel in Miami Beach, modeled for the poster art[26] and was described as one of the film's "many attractions."[27]

The posters, however, merely teased and foreshadowed the portrayals awaiting the Bond Girls in the film. Producers wasted no time introducing female characters in *Goldfinger*, bringing them into view in the pre-title sequence, which was designed specifically to "satisfy . . . Cubby [Broccoli's] generous quota of pretty ladies."[28] *Goldfinger* begins with a "mini-movie"[29] in which Bond infiltrates a Mexican opium laboratory hidden within an oil storage tank. After he carefully sets explosives, Bond walks to a nearby club where he watches Bonita, a beautiful tarantella dancer and double agent, perform.[30] The explosives Bond planted detonate in the background, and the ensuing conflagration engulfs the laboratory. As the crowd scatters following the explosion, Bonita, seemingly furious that her performance was interrupted, returns to her dressing room. Bond remarks that he has "unfinished business to attend to" as he dangles a set of keys to Bonita's dressing room.[31] Of course, the "unfinished business" is Bonita, who was portrayed by Nadja Regin, the actress who performed the role of Kerim's Girl, the cooing mistress in *From Russia With Love*. One author suggested that Bonita "lures [Bond] to her bedroom,"[32] though it is not apparent that Bond is walking into a trap.

In the next scene, Bonita soaps herself in a bathtub, which is located at the corner of the room. Both the initial expression on her face as Bond enters the room and the close-up image of her suggest that she feels cornered. As the camera switches to Bond, a wider angle reveals the remainder of the room, which gives the illusion that Bond can maneuver about freely. The contrast is telling, juxtaposing the predator (Bond) in complete control over his surroundings alongside the prey (Bonita) that is clearly trapped.

Bond tosses a towel toward Bonita, who rises from the bathtub, and the two embrace. Bonita, like Tatiana Romanova before her, is unnerved by Bond's gun. She implores, "Why do you always wear that thing," reaffirming to the audience that there is a history between them and that Bond, in fact, does have so-called unfinished business to which to attend.[33] His reply that he has a "slight inferiority complex" induces a smile on her face, and the two resume their embrace.[34] Bond's firm, authoritative grip on Bonita's upper arms is not unlike that which he employs in *From Russia With Love*.

Bonita's brief role in *Goldfinger* is not merely sexual. It is functional insofar as she serves both as a sword and a shield for Bond. Bond notices the reflection of an assassin while he gazes into her opened eyes, shifting the audience's attention away from a sexual conquest and toward emphasizing *his* resourcefulness. After all, it is an ingenious Bond who adeptly utilizes a woman's anatomical features to his competitive advantage. Rather than move Bonita aside to protect her from the ensuing attack, Bond instead swings her around and throws her directly in front of the assassin. The result, of course, is that Bonita, and not Bond, is struck.

John Brosnan noted that Bond "swings her round just as the attacker whirls his club and *she catches the full impact*."[35] Similarly, John Cork and Bruce Scivally wrote that Bond "whirls [Bonita] around so that the bandit smashes her with the wooden cosh."[36] After disposing of his assailant, Bond regains his composure, gathers his belongings, and, without hesitation, exits, leaving Bonita on the floor to moan in pain and appear dazed. A disposable object, Bonita has served her usefulness and, like a weapon used during battle, can simply be discarded or left behind once the aggression ceases. It is not lost upon the audience that Bond makes no effort to assist her and simply dismisses the circumstances as "positively shocking,"[37] which refers to the assassin's electrocution and not the fate that befalls Bonita.

* * *

The main image displayed throughout *Goldfinger*'s title sequence is that of the golden girl, particularly since the color gold "seems to pervade every scene, giving it a distinctive motif that the other films have lacked."[38] Eaton claimed that she was shocked to discover that producers opted to use a second actress, upon whom the directors "practice[d] painting the gold paint" for the sequence because, unlike Eaton, that actress possessed "big boobs, [a] big bum, [and was] a totally different type of woman."[39] Nolan, who posed for the film's poster art, was the actress featured in the title sequence.[40]

Superimposed over the buxom golden girl body are images foreshadowing the plot of the film, as well as brief sequences from *Dr. No* and *From Russia With Love*. These images gloss seductively over numerous portions of the golden girl's body, beginning with her hand and face, and progressing to her mouth, shoulders, chest, arms, thighs, and calves. A profile view of the golden girl's midriff is in view when Pussy Galore is introduced during the title credits. In fact, producers superimposed Sylvia Trench's golf-playing scene from *Dr. No* over the golden girl's chest, depicting the proverbial hole in one as the golf ball's trajectory traces her cleavage.

As these scenes project across the golden girl's body, recording artist Shirley Bassey performs the film's title song, which instantly became a success and reached number one on the charts within two months after the soundtrack album was released.[41] While the song evokes the grandeur of gold, careful attention to the words suggests a pedantic, condescending tone that cautions young, pretty, and impressionable women about their susceptibility to a man's charms. It begins by characterizing Auric Goldfinger as the creator of a "web of sin" into which a naïve, young, "pretty girl" is enticed to enter.[42] The lyrics caution: being lured by Goldfinger is the "kiss of death" because his heart, while made of gold, is nonetheless an empty, cold heart.[43] Indeed, the lyrics peddle a message that women easily succumb to the glamour of a façade and are incapable of seeing beneath the surface to uncover an underlying truth. More fundamentally, the lyrics suggest that a man can easily lead a "girl" into believing he loves her by showering her with glittery possessions, actions that veil his true intention to exploit her sexually.[44] One film critic found the entire title sequence, together with the title song, wholly distasteful: "The title song, in which Shirley Bassey insists that Goldfinger loves only gold while the titles appear beside scenes superimposed on gilded girls, is even worse."[45] Nevertheless, the cautionary advice offered to the unworldly "pretty girl," ironically, is presented against the backdrop of Nolan's fulsome figure, which is anything but adolescent.

* * *

Goldfinger begins with Bond lounging at the Fontainebleau Hotel, where he is receiving a massage from a blonde masseuse named Dink. The first dialogue the audience hears is Dink asking Bond, "How's this?"[46] Bond's response, "It's nice," leaves much to the audience's imagination since neither Dink nor Bond is in view.[47] Finally, the spectacle comes into focus, and the audience, together with Felix Leiter, discovers Bond as he lies on his stomach while Dink, who is wearing a blue one-piece bathing suit, services him. Eager to attend to Bond, Dink continues to keep her hands on Bond, even as he turns around and sits up to greet Felix. Indeed, the close-up of Dink places her chest at the middle of the screen, enabling the audience to fully absorb her physical assets. As Bond rises to greet his CIA counterpart, Dink obligingly follows, her entire body now displayed, though neither Bond nor Felix indicates an interest in speaking with her. The dialogue attributed to Dink is anemic, at best:

> *Dink*: How's this?
>
> *Bond*: It's nice, very nice.
>
> *Dink*: Just here?
>
> *Bond*: No, a little lower, darling.

> *Leiter* (*seeing Bond receiving a massage*): I thought I'd find you in good hands.
> *Bond*: Felix! Felix, how are you? Dink, meet Felix Leiter.
> *Dink* (*complying*): Hello.
> *Bond*: Felix, say hello to Dink.
> *Leiter*: Hi, Dink.
> *Bond*: Dink, say good-bye to Felix.
> *Dink* (*turning to Bond, not understanding*): Hmm?
> *Bond*: Man talk.[48]

This constitutes the totality of Dink's dialogue.

It is interesting to note that Bond does not inform Dink that he needs to attend to business matters with Felix. Rather, he deliberately characterizes the subject in terms of gender, which has the exclusionary effect of relegating Dink to the realm of the unfit to overhear the conversation. It also reaffirms her subordinate role. In fact, Bond could have employed any other reasonable term to suggest or indicate the confidential nature of the conversation in which he and Felix are about to engage. Then again, the expectation of privacy while discussing top-secret matters at a crowded hotel pool is ultimately questionable.

Having established that Dink is not welcome in the "man talk" conversation, Bond facilitates an exit for her that is literally more striking than her introduction. After informing a confused Dink that her usefulness has essentially expired, Bond places his hands on Dink's arms, turns her around to push her away, and spanks her on the buttocks. Dink falls out of view and is never seen again, a true testament to her superfluity. Yet Dink is visually significant because she enables Bond to firmly reinforce his masculinity in the film, an essential element given the challenge he later encounters from Pussy Galore's apparent lesbianism. Despite her brief presence, the character of Dink brought considerable fame to Nolan, who graced the pages of *Playboy* shortly after *Goldfinger*'s release.

It is also interesting to note how Bond successfully pries a hotel room key from a female attendant. Stopping the unnamed attendant in the hallway, he grabs a chain from her waist that holds Goldfinger's room key and pulls the key toward the door, effectively dragging the attendant with it. By the time she verbally protests, Bond already has the key practically in the door lock, and her only remark is a meager one: "That's Mister Goldfinger's suite."[49] She holds on to the key as Bond enters, staring blankly at the door as it closes before her. Without a word, she walks away dumbfounded as if nothing occurred. For the third time in the film's short introductory minutes, Bond has easily and effectively asserted himself over a woman he encounters.

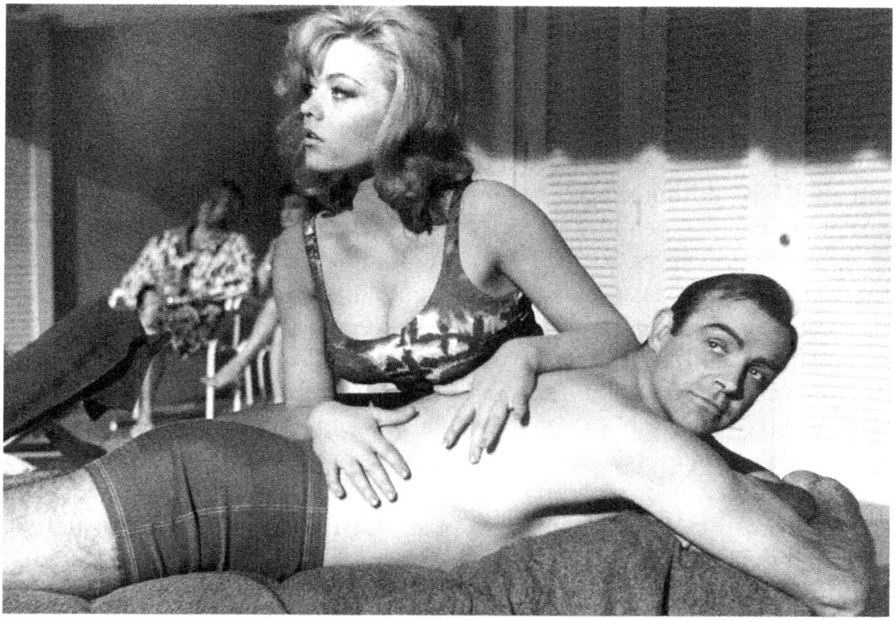

Dink (Margaret Nolan) ensures that James Bond (Sean Connery) is in good hands in *Goldfinger*.

(Everett Collection/Rex USA)

* * *

Once inside Goldfinger's hotel suite, Bond discovers Jill. To Eaton's dismay, but like Eunice Gayson, Ursula Andress, and Daniela Bianchi before her, producers dubbed her voice in order to achieve a more "prissy" tone.[50] Jill is first seen reclining on a chaise lounge wearing a black bikini, her right leg lifted in the air (a similar position in which the audience finds Miss Taro as she answers the phone on her bed in *Dr. No*). The scene has been described as "sexily prone."[51] Much of the background around Jill is white, save for some greenery in the top corner of the screen and a blue towel covering the chaise lounge. The blue focuses the audience upon Jill, who is strategically positioned to "aid[] and abet[]" Goldfinger by using binoculars to see his opponent's playing card hand and by speaking into an audio receiver to tell Goldfinger which cards his opponent holds.[52] The camera angle focuses closely upon the binoculars, which has the effect of accentuating Jill's chest.

Bond approaches Jill and turns off the receiver, prompting Jill to spin around. Startled and angered, Jill exclaims, "Who are you," to which Bond gives his signature response.[53] When the camera returns to the suite balcony, the previously startled Jill is now sprawled on the chaise lounge, this time on her back with her chest pronounced. Bond leans his body over hers in order to gaze into the binoculars and encounters no protest from Jill. Thus, Bond quickly and easily exhibits an authoritative presence over her. She is completely subdued by him, both physically and metaphorically, and submissively responds to his interrogation:

> *Bond*: What's *your* name?
> *Jill*: Jill.
> *Bond* (*persisting*): Jill who?
> *Jill*: Jill Masterson.
> *Bond:* Tell me, Jill, why does he [cheat at cards]?
> *Jill*: He likes to win.
> *Bond*: Why do you do it?
> *Jill*: He pays me.
> *Bond*: Is that all he pays you for?
> *Jill*: And for being seen with him.
> *Bond*: Just seen?
> *Jill*: Just seen.
> *Bond* (*appearing satisfied with her response*): I'm so glad. You're much too (*pausing as he quickly gazes at her chest*) nice to be mixed up in anything like this, you know.[54]

This dialogue highlights Jill's purely functional role: a paid escort who does as she is told for remuneration. She neither acknowledges her culpability in facilitating Goldfinger's fraud nor expresses any remorse for doing so. Furthermore, she expresses no displeasure over receiving compensation for whatever services Goldfinger demands from her. Jill's malleability is fully established in this scene, and it is apparent that she will do virtually anything a man wants if the price is sufficiently high.

While Jill presumably exercises free will to choose her employer, the opposite, in fact, appears true. Once Bond assumes control over Goldfinger's card-playing fate and compels him to begin losing, it appears as though Jill has been emancipated. A smile forms across her face for the first time. Almost immediately, Jill is intrigued by Bond, who takes full advantage of the effect he has over her, hastening a seduction:

> *Jill*: I'm beginning to like you, Mister Bond.
> *Bond*: Oh, call me James.
> *Jill*: More than anyone I've met in a long time, James.
> *Bond*: Yes. What are we going to do about it?
> *Jill (lighting up with excitement)*: Yes, what?
> *Bond*: I'll tell you at dinner.
> *Jill*: Where?
> *Bond*: Well, I know the best place in town.[55]

As the scene fades, Bond lifts the back of the chaise lounge toward him, thereby raising Jill closer to him in order for them to embrace. Of note is the fact that Bond's position does not change. Indeed, he does not move at all. Rather, it is Jill's body that is raised so that their lips unite. Her face indicates that she is in awe of Bond and "the way he smiles."[56] As scholar Elisabeth Ladenson noted, Jill's sudden captivation is inherent in the fact that she "loses no time in switching sides."[57]

These subtleties reveal an interesting dichotomy within Jill's character. She seems beholden to Goldfinger, who, in turn, relies upon her eavesdropping. Maryam d'Abo and John Cork suggested that Jill is "serving unhappily" as Goldfinger's "paid companion,"[58] though it is apparent that nothing precludes her from leaving his employ. In fact, within a matter of moments, she develops a strong liking toward Bond beyond anything she has experienced with anyone else, and suddenly a cloud is lifted. Interestingly, Bond offers her nothing except, perhaps, a brief respite from Goldfinger. But Jill's rapid ability to succumb to Bond's charm is diametrically opposite the semi-assertive position she possesses with Goldfinger. After all, Goldfinger assigns her the important task of informing him of his opponent's cards and presumably trusts her to give an accurate accounting. In essence, by permitting Bond to

Jill Masterson (Shirley Eaton) begins to like James Bond (Sean Connery) in *Goldfinger*.
(Rex USA)

extricate her from Goldfinger, Jill actually becomes more dependent and a weaker character. Unfortunately, Jill cannot serve two masters, and her demise is imminent because her loyalties have shifted toward Bond. M, however, reminds audiences that Bond merely "borrowed" Goldfinger's girlfriend.[59]

In the next scene, Bond and Jill are in bed together, with the "best place in town" revealed as Bond's hotel suite. In the background, a portable radio broadcasts the daily news that "[a]t the White House this afternoon, the President announced that he was entirely satisfied . . . ."[60] Bond, still embracing Jill, reaches over and switches off the radio, adding, "That makes two of us."[61] Jill also seems wholly satisfied, but her satisfaction is irrelevant. In fact, she seems somewhat restless and craves more attention from Bond. As Bond sits up to speak to Felix on the telephone, Jill rises as well and begins placing her golden locks of hair around Bond's ear in an effort to distract him. Eaton recalled the scene: "I'm playful as well as sensuous, and while he is talking on the phone, I edge over the bed and tickle his ear with my hair. I improvised that, it was all my idea. Somebody said to me the other day: 'That's one of the sexiest things I've ever seen on the screen.'"[62]

The scene is reminiscent of the beginning of *From Russia With Love*, where Bond and Sylvia are picnicking together. In both cases, Bond is on the telephone and is being distracted by impetuous, sexually aggressive women. Whereas Bond characterizes Sylvia as an "old case" to Miss Moneypenny,[63] he informs Felix that he is unable to meet because "something big's come up,"[64] a reference more about his physical condition than about Jill. In fact, Sylvia warrants some form of reference, albeit an unflattering one, from Bond in his conversation with Miss Moneypenny. Jill, however, is not extended the same treatment. Nevertheless, Bond's conduct toward both women is virtually identical. Although he does not smack Jill, Bond responds to her interruptions by taking his entire hand, placing it over her face, and pushing her backwards onto the bed. She falls with a tremendous grin across her face, just as Sylvia smiles in triumph.

His conversation with Felix concluded, Bond gazes back at Jill, who is lying seductively on the bed with her lips slowly parted in an inviting manner. Bond approaches her, she wraps her arms around him, and a bigger smile is displayed across her face. Yet Bond is not concerned. Instead of embracing her, he reaches toward the edge of the bed for a bottle of wine, which has lost its chill. A disappointed Jill implores why they need another bottle of wine, to which Bond responds, in a manly, authoritative tone: "My dear girl, there are some things that just aren't done, such as drinking Dom Pérignon '53 above a temperature of thirty-eight degrees Fahrenheit."[65] He ultimately never returns to the bed,

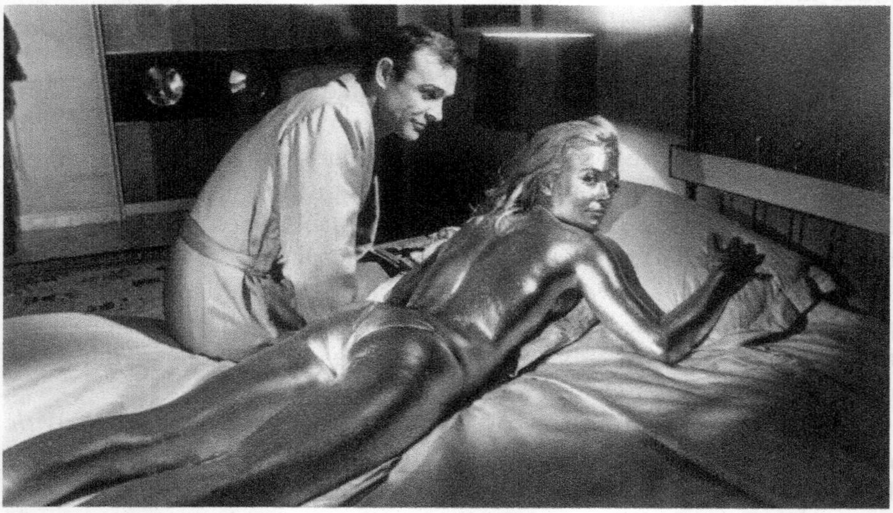

British actress Shirley Eaton and Scottish actor Sean Connery pose on the set of *Goldfinger*, 1964.
(Keystone/Stringer/Hulton Archive/Getty Images)

having been struck unconscious from behind by Oddjob, Goldfinger's servant and chauffeur.

Once he regains his composure, Bond stumbles back into the bedroom and discovers Jill strewn naked across the bed painted entirely in gold, the apparent victim of skin asphyxiation. D'Abo and Cork claimed that Jill is "the first 'good girl' in the Bond films that James Bond cannot save."[66] But this description ultimately fails to account for her participation in Goldfinger's fraud. In essence, all that Jill may glitter is not, in fact, pure gold.

Of the famous scene, Shirley Eaton explained, "Once I was painted, I felt terribly hot and uncomfortable, because it seals the skin. It looked sexy—but it didn't feel sexy."[67] While the scene was sexy, it was also disturbing due to its "tones of necrophilia" and the fact that Bond, captivated by the "erotic spectacle," stares at her lifeless golden body.[68] In fact, Bond himself appears shocked and unnerved, and M later reminds Bond that he is on an assignment and not pursuing a personal vendetta: "If you can't treat it as such, coldly and objectively, Double-O-Eight can replace you."[69] Bond places his hand upon her skin and looks at her entire body, then promptly telephones Felix. As John Cork and Bruce Scivally noted, Broccoli and Saltzman "understood that audiences would be both shocked and attracted by the image of a nude, glittering corpse."[70] Felix offers a light moment by asking whether the dead girl is Dink, but she offers a golden touch of a different variety.

Shirley Eaton recounted how she was cast, which suggests that producers sought a woman who exuded pure sex appeal for this scene:

> My closest girlfriend knew Harry Saltzman . . . [and] he said to her, "I can't find anybody sexy enough for the part of Jill Masterson," and she told him: "I know . . . Shirley Eaton. And when I have my parties all I can say to you is that when Shirley dances every man in the room has an erection." And it was sort of true . . . . [T]he main thing he wanted to know was would I be painted naked in gold paint? I had never been photographed naked in my life, but I do have a sense of fun. I . . . said: "If it's done tastefully, why not?" I wanted to be in *Goldfinger*, even though the role was the smallest I'd played.[71]

These few minutes on screen gave Eaton the distinction of becoming one of the most photographed actresses of the 1960s.

But not all reviews of Jill's "lily-like body [covered] from head to toe" were glowing.[72] As suggested above, the scene has been described as "both eerie and surreal," and verging on perversion, particularly since Bond subsequently learns that cabaret dancers avoid death by leaving a small section of skin bare at the base of the spine in order to allow the skin to breathe.[73] In an effort to "quieten critics," Broccoli and Saltzman permitted the press on the set, thereby enabling "[h]undreds of photos of the event" to be taken.[74] As a result, Shirley Eaton achieved "screen immortality"[75] for the part and forever "bronzed" the image of the Bond Girl as a beautiful sex object to be fetishized by audiences.

* * *

Bond also encounters Jill's sister, Tilly Masterson, who embarks upon a personal mission to avenge Jill's death. Tilly was portrayed by British fashion model Tania Mallet, who, despite having no acting experience,[76]was previously considered for the role of Tatiana in *From Russia With Love*.[77] Tilly immediately piques Bond's interest when he observes her passing in a vehicle on a Swiss highway. But in a rare moment of clarity, Bond admonishes himself to maintain discipline. Alas, he ultimately succumbs to his own temptations, though he also seeks a bit of revenge himself. Tilly, in a previous effort to assassinate Goldfinger, accidentally misfires and practically kills Bond. Thereafter, Bond follows her, passes her alongside the road, and prevents her from passing. Finally, Bond motions for her to pass. In the meantime, he engages a device on his Aston Martin that punctures two of Tilly's tires. Consequently, her car veers off the road and crashes into a ditch.

Understandably, Tilly is shaken and unnerved from the ordeal. Bond, running over to the car, ingratiates himself by assuming the role of the strategically placed hero coming to her aid: "Are you all right? Here, let me help you. You know you're lucky to be alive."[78] Bond adds that he has never seen a double blowout of tires before, which, he opines, might be a "defect of some sort."[79] This manufactured damsel-in-distress incident is unsettling, particularly given the fact that Bond intentionally causes an accident that could have seriously injured or killed Tilly. But these repercussions are wholly lost upon Bond, who is more concerned with utilizing Tilly for information and seducing her: "I'm so glad it's on the car and not you. You don't look like the kind of girl who should be ditched."[80]

Tilly, however, is unimpressed with Bond. Their subsequent conversation is terse, with Bond attempting to catch Tilly in a lie about the contents of the case that contains her rifle. Ultimately, Bond leaves Tilly by herself at a gas station. Indeed, Tilly's attention is focused elsewhere: "she is single-mindedly intent on payback."[81]

Bond later encounters Tilly, this time outside Goldfinger's factory in the darkness of night, as she again attempts to assassinate Goldfinger. When Bond sneaks up behind and grabs her, he inadvertently triggers Goldfinger's silent alarms. As she winces in pain from Bond's grasp, Tilly acknowledges her intent to kill Goldfinger on account of Jill's demise. Bond asks, "If you wanted to kill him, why did you shoot at me?"[82] Tilly, still struggling to free herself from Bond's grasp, explains, "I didn't, I was shooting at him."[83] Bond's response is imbued with condescension: "Well, you're a lousy shot."[84]

During their attempt to escape Goldfinger's henchmen, Bond utilizes additional features built into his Aston Martin, much to Tilly's delight. Indeed, she smiles widely when Bond releases a smokescreen, and she has a fascinated look on her face throughout the entire car chase that ensues. Ultimately, Tilly follows Bond's instruction to run into the woods, though she remains well within range of Oddjob, whose perfect aim unites his bowler hat lined with a metal razor disk with Tilly's body. She is instantly killed. Tilly's failure to kill Goldfinger facilitates Bond's capture and ultimately subjects him to an unpleasant encounter with Goldfinger's laser.

Tilly is the perfect embodiment of weakness. Blinded by her hatred of Goldfinger, she focuses upon vengeance to the exclusion of anything else. While her situation may evoke sympathy, Tilly lacks the skill to effectuate the outcome she seeks. Indeed, her inability to properly discharge a firearm indicates that she is reckless, refusing to take the time to learn how to utilize the weapon and instead acting solely upon passion and without rationale. She descends upon a path to perdition without thinking about any consequences and unwittingly delivers Bond to Goldfinger. More significantly, by crossing paths with Bond in the first place, Tilly interferes with and ultimately compromises his mission. She is quickly forgotten following her untimely demise.

* * *

If anything brought *Goldfinger* into the "adult realm," it was the one Bond Girl characterized as "highly susceptible to male influence":[85] Pussy Galore. Fleming lifted the name from a madame working in Sarasota, New York, during the 1950s.[86] Her on-screen persona was brought to life by Honor Blackman, who achieved recognition in her own right for her role on *The Avengers* television series and whose "blonde hair and buxom femininity" ensured her the part in *Goldfinger*.[87] Blackman recalled that she was the "hottest thing in England at that time," and because she performed judo on *The Avengers* and the role of Pussy Galore required her to do the same, her casting "was just a sidestep."[88] Her character's name created such interest in the film that "people [were] walking out of theaters all over the world talking about YOUR name."[89]

Indeed, "filmmakers . . . had to decide how to deal with the risqué name" of Pussy Galore.[90] Studio executives were understandably "nervous" and considered changing the name to Kitty Galore.[91] Blackman, however, recalled that the name was simply "tongue in cheek" and was not something about which to worry.[92] EON Productions ensured that Fleming's original character name would be retained when it leaked the name to the press during production. Author Graham Rye offered one account of how the name was retained:

> At the time of the film's release, there was an uproar over the name . . . and the film-makers were unable to get it past the American censors. Then *Goldfinger* opened in London and Honor was presented to Prince Philip. The next day the newspapers ran a picture of him headlined "Pussy and the Prince." That was the clincher. The American censor gave the film the all-clear.[93]

Retaining the name Pussy Galore in the film generated immense publicity and firmly established the series as a cultural phenomenon both within the Bond context and beyond.

With regard to the character's legacy within the Bond context, Pussy Galore set a precedent forever plaguing subsequent Bond Girls, who have been assigned deliberately outrageous, "patently sexual" names.[94] Audiences

> delighted in the device and soon writers were trying to outdo themselves dreaming up not-so-vaguely-sexual names for characters. Certainly for the Bond producers, the reaction to the name Pussy Galore inspired the same kind of response, with future Bond women including Plenty O'Toole, Holly Goodhead, Bibi Dahl, Octopussy, Jenny Flex and Xenia Onatopp.[95]

Outside the Bond context, the "name as sex joke began a tradition."[96] Indeed, satires abound throughout popular culture, both in print and on film. In its March 1974 spoof of the film, for example, *Mad* sarcastically referred to the infamous Bond Girl as "Tushy Galore."[97] More recently, the Austin Powers trilogy gave Pussy Galore a modern update with several similarly named female counterparts, including Alotta Fagina,[98] Felicity Shagwell, Robin Swallows, Ivana Humpalot,[99] Foxxy Cleopatra, Fook Mi, and Fook Yu.[100]

As the name bluntly implies but the film attempts to tone down, Pussy Galore is a lesbian.[101] Nevertheless, she "incarnates everything that male heterosexuality seems to demand of representations of female homosexuality."[102] Her ability to remain immune to Bond's charm is ultimately short-lived as her convictions wither throughout the film.

Pussy Galore's introduction to Bond and the audience is classic and memorable. Bond, regaining consciousness aboard Goldfinger's private jet and attempting to familiarize himself with uncertain surroundings after being shot with a tranquilizer gun, finds himself face-to-face with a beautiful blonde woman gazing and smiling down upon him. Disoriented, Bond questions, "Who are you?"[103] The response is terse: "My name is Pussy Galore."[104] Bond smirks and responds, "I must be dreaming."[105]

* * *

Before elaborating upon Pussy Galore, it is interesting to note that the same scene that introduces her unique character juxtaposes her alongside an obsequious flight attendant named Mei Lei, who is assigned the tasks of preparing Bond a drink and spying on him. Unlike Pussy Galore, who is dressed in a black suit with a gold blouse underneath, Mei Lei wears a tight gold top that covers her bosom and arms but exposes her midriff. A long gold-and-white skirt completes the ensemble. As she walks away, Bond admires her buttocks. Bond then enters the lavatory, and Pussy Galore instructs her copilot to have Mei Lei "keep an eye on him."[106]

Mei Lei fails at this simple task, becoming completely outwitted by Bond. Bond quickly discovers each peephole in the lavatory, much to Mei Lei's surprise and shock. In essence, Mei Lei is merely an aesthetic and substantive foil for the seemingly strong, "mannish" Pussy Galore.[107] She serves as a vehicle through which Bond appears resourceful and assertive, even as Pussy Galore challenges both of these attributes, as well as Bond's masculinity.

* * *

Bond, of course, is not dreaming when he encounters Pussy Galore. Employed by Goldfinger as his personal pilot, she represents the first Bond Girl who *initially* appears competent. One author described Pussy Galore as "a reflection of the more liberated and self-sufficient women of the Sixties."[108] Was she? On the one hand, the audience observes her as "cocky, confident and capable; she flies planes, brandishes guns, excels at judo, runs her own business and deals with the world . . . on her own terms."[109] On the other hand, Pussy Galore simply serves a functional role for her male employer in order to receive a financial payout from Goldfinger's ill-fated Operation Grand Slam: "Why else would I be in it, Mister Goldfinger?"[110] At the same time, she operates an all-female aerial stunt show named Pussy Galore's Flying Circus, presumably exhibiting some business acumen. Yet pervasively undermining whatever positive attributes she may possess is an undercurrent suggesting that Pussy Galore is different from the other Bond Girls.

Pussy Galore (Honor Blackman) awaits the arrival of her crew of female pilots, known as Pussy Galore's Flying Circus, in *Goldfinger*.

(Everett Collection/Rex USA)

Pussy Galore appears bold and assertive and refuses to succumb to Bond's suggestive dialogue. Indeed, she refuses to extend any latitude to Bond. For example, after she informs Bond that she is Goldfinger's personal pilot, Bond inquires as to how personal, a similar question to which he subjects Jill before he effectively seduces her. Pussy Galore, however, is impenetrable, responding in a terse, annoyed tone, "I'm a damn good pilot. Period."[111] Then, in an effort to recover and obtain some reaction from Pussy Galore, Bond toasts to Goldfinger's Operation Grand Slam; however, she continues her work unaffected. Finally, an annoyed Pussy Galore instructs Bond to "turn off the charm, I'm immune."[112]

These attributes, of course, are foreign to previous female characters in the series, and therefore Bond must increase his efforts to assert his masculinity and somehow break through Pussy Galore's icy exterior. His first attempt occurs aboard Goldfinger's jet as he informs Pussy Galore that firing a bullet at him at such a close range would pierce the fuselage and send them both "into outer space together."[113] Such a detailed explanation is provided in response to Pussy Galore's ultimatum that Bond can either cooperate or not. After listening to Bond ramble about his knowledge of ballistics, Pussy Galore simply responds that his apparent decision to cooperate is "very sensible," and it is she who has the final word.[114] Raising a gun to his cheek, she asks rhetorically, "You like close shaves, don't you?"[115]

Bond is not impressed with Pussy Galore. Rather, his challenge is to overcome her cold demeanor through humor, sarcasm, and innuendo. He notes that she is a "woman of many parts," utilizing the term *woman* rather than girl.[116] Such a statement represents a conscious acknowledgment by Bond that he is encountering a different type of female than those to whom he is accustomed. Indeed, each female character heretofore presented in the series is simply referred to as a *girl*. But "girl" is not an apt description for Pussy Galore, and Bond realizes it, as Pussy Galore "has more to offer as a character than the bland personalities of the usual Bond Starlets."[117]

Use of the term *woman* also suggests that Pussy Galore's status as a Bond Girl, up until this point in the film, is misplaced. In order to be classified as a Bond Girl, Pussy Galore must, of course, be a *girl*. Yet by Bond's own account, Pussy Galore is clearly a *woman*. The woman-girl dichotomy is visible throughout the remainder of the film as Bond persistently endeavors to chisel away at Pussy Galore's rigidity in order to transform her from an independent, assertive, lesbian woman employed by the villain into a dependent, passive, heterosexual girl who has Bond to thank for liberating her from the villain's grasp.

This mission to transform Pussy Galore initially backfires against Bond. As he attempts to suggest that the two have bourbon since they are "both off duty," Bond is instead brought before an awaiting Oddjob:

> *Bond* (*referencing the decapitation of Tilly*): Manners, Oddjob. I thought you always took your hat off to a lady. (*turning to Pussy Galore*) You know he kills *little girls* like you.
> *Pussy Galore*: Little boys, too.[118]

Whatever personal triumph Bond may experience by referring to Pussy Galore as a "little girl" is short-lived. As his facial expression suggests, Bond's reduction to a "little boy" characterization is unsettling and heightens the unique sexual imbalance that *Goldfinger* presents.

Gary Giblin and Lisa Neyhouse suggested that Bond is "'impotent' in contrast to the character of Pussy Galore," the latter of whom seems equally as capable as Bond himself.[119] For example, Pussy Galore discovers Bond spying upon Goldfinger. Rather than wait for Bond to discover her, Pussy Galore stealthily sneaks up behind him, grabs on to his legs, and literally pulls them out from under him. She then proceeds to throw him against the wall. A stunned Bond asks, "Pussy, who taught you judo?"[120] An additional witticism that they "must have a few fast falls together sometime"[121] leaves her unimpressed, but the remark nonetheless serves as another attempt by Bond to reassert himself as the dominant male character. This is not the first fall Bond experiences with Pussy Galore.

The film also offers a contradictory portrayal of Pussy Galore, endeavoring to establish her as its strongest lead female while simultaneously attempting to undermine her character's credibility. For example, Bond admires the aerial display of the Flying Circus, noting that they are "talented chaps," a suggestion that the pilots are men.[122] Interestingly, Pussy Galore does not correct him. Rather, she responds, "They should be. I trained them."[123] The audience discovers that the Flying Circus is composed of five buxom blonde pilots, one of whom emerges from her cockpit displaying an accentuated figure while a sultry soundtrack plays. These "pulchritudinous female pilots," it is presumed, also prefer the female persuasion[124] and are wholly devoted to Pussy Galore, to whom they run in synchronization after landing and affectionately address as their "Skipper."[125] Their presence exacerbates the tension between Pussy Galore's "flawed" sexuality—namely, her lack of interest in Bond—and the nearly flawless appearances of the members of her Flying Circus, who, like Pussy Galore, are also objects of desire for heterosexual men.

Despite her apparent independence and imperviousness, Pussy Galore's character begins to display significant cracks. After Bond is caught spying by Pussy Galore and is escorted outside to Goldfinger, the villain questions why Bond is not resting in his prison cell. Bond responds: "Well, they are delightful, but it's much too nice to stay indoors. I ran into Miss Galore, and she suggested that we join you."[126] Pussy Galore, however, is not amused by Bond's fabrication, but her only response is to cock her head quizzically toward Bond. She registers a similar puzzled expression after Goldfinger curiously reacts to information that Bond heard his entire debriefing about Operation Grand Slam.

Pussy Galore also understands that she works for Goldfinger and is not, by any stretch of the imagination, an equal in his operation. She addresses him as "Mister Goldfinger" and permits him to stroke her hand, albeit briefly.[127] In fact, Pussy Galore is assigned the task of performing the dirtiest of Goldfinger's work. Goldfinger informs his financiers that he possesses Delta 9, "an invisible nerve gas which disperses fifteen minutes after inducing complete unconsciousness for twenty-four hours."[128] He adds, "Tomorrow at dawn, the Flying Circus of my personal pilot, Miss Pussy Galore, will spray it into the atmosphere"[129] in and around Fort Knox, thereby enabling him to enter the gold repository. Thus, Pussy Galore has the dubious distinction of being tasked with gassing the United States military in order to facilitate Goldfinger's penetration of Fort Knox. This, of course, is not the only demand Goldfinger places upon his employee. In an effort to give the appearance that Bond is "as happy as possible,"[130] Goldfinger *suggests* that Pussy Galore change into something more comfortable. It is clear that the suggestion is, in fact, a directive.[131] Indeed, Goldfinger laughs as she leaves, realizing he is about to perform a coup d'etat.

Pussy Galore emerges in a low-cut lavender top neatly tucked into her pants with her bosom highly prominent. Even Goldfinger notes that she looks "very chic" and instructs her to "entertain Mister Bond *for me*," once again an emphasis upon the subordinate role she plays.[132] Pussy Galore complies but, by doing so, gives Bond the opportunity to shift her status away from a "woman" and toward a "girl." Indeed, in these scenes Pussy Galore's femininity ultimately overshadows her henchwoman / lesbian traits, and it is at this point in the film that her sexual realignment takes flight:

> *Pussy Galore*: Well, how about it handsome? (*taking her arm and wrapping it around his*) Don't you think it's time we got to know each other socially?
> *Bond* (*expressing bewilderment*): Well, the new Miss Galore. Where do you hide your gold knuckles in this outfit?

Pussy Galore: Oh, I never carry weapons after business hours.
Bond: Eh? So you're off duty?
Pussy Galore: I'm completely defenseless.
Bond (*gazing down quickly at her chest*): So am I.[133]

Of course, the suddenly social version of Pussy Galore is simply an act designed to give Felix the impression that Bond is not being held captive by Goldfinger. It succeeds. Observing Bond and Pussy Galore hand in hand, Felix says, "That's my James," and concludes that "Double-O-Seven seems to have the situation well in hand . . . . [L]et's get back to the hotel."[134] Although Felix does not have the benefit of knowing the dynamic between Pussy Galore and Bond, his comment is a harbinger for things to come.

During their walk together, it is Bond who controls the conversation as well as the direction they are headed. He reminds Pussy Galore that Goldfinger is "quite mad," a comment that tones down the lightheartedness she feigns.[135] A curious Bond essentially lures Pussy Galore into an open stable and, in doing so, places *her* in a defensive position for the first time. It is clear that her authority over Bond is evaporating, particularly since Bond again—but without retort—refers to Pussy Galore as a *girl* rather than a woman:

Bond: You're quite a girl, Pussy.
Pussy Galore (protesting that they are inside the barn): I'm strictly the outdoors type.
Bond: I'd like to think you're not in all of this caper.
Pussy Galore: Skip it, I'm not interested, let's go.[136]

Semantics now give way to physical action and domination. As she turns to walk out of the stable, Bond grabs on to her arm, whirling her around and into his arms. He asks, "What would it take for you to see things my way," but Pussy Galore responds, "A lot more than you've got."[137] A persistent Bond inquires as to how she knows, but she does not want to know. Bond is not winning the battle of wits, but the tide is changing.

Instead, Bond again grabs her, causing her to spin around as he draws her into him. He asks, "Isn't it customary to grant a condemned man his last request?"[138] The verbal tit-for-tat ceases and the physical tension between her and Bond explodes. Pussy Galore flips Bond into the hay. Bond is now on the ground while Pussy Galore stands over him demanding that he get up. Bond responds in kind, tripping Pussy Galore and prompting her to fall onto the hay. Bond rises and now towers over Pussy Galore. He extends his hand to help her rise, and she unsuccessfully attempts to flip and throw him back into the hay. Instead, Pussy Galore is overpowered by Bond's strength and finds herself flipped. Bond approaches her, sits down in the hay himself, and, with a smile, remarks, "Now, let's both play."[139] He then proceeds to pounce atop her. Though she initially mounts considerable resistance, it is futile. Her arms, which are stretched out in an effort to oppose Bond's advance, ultimately wrap around Bond as they kiss, thereby indicating her eventual, forced consent. The audience is left to presume that the two consummate their newfound dynamic following a most "violent seduction."[140]

The stable scene represents "the central confrontation in the movie"[141] and serves an "ideological role" since "Bond needs to seduce [her] in order to 'reposition' [her] on the side of right."[142] Blackman recalled that any explicit reference to Pussy Galore's lesbianism was omitted from the film: "I'm glad they didn't, because it would have seemed so ridiculous that she would change overnight just because James Bond took her to bed."[143] Yet this is exactly what happens: "Pussy Galore [is] a Lesbian converted to happy heterosexuality by the strong male emanations (and judo holds) of our hero."[144] Or, as Blackman herself described it, Pussy Galore "starts out as a lesbian . . . and then, of course, Bond changes her mind, which is kind of an odd way to be a lesbian anyway . . . ."[145]

While Tony Bennett and Janet Woollacott maintained that Pussy Galore requires no sexual repositioning,[146] her repositioning is, in fact, threefold. First, it reaffirms that Bond's masculinity prevails. Bond's ability to emerge as "the strong man, the all-powerful one who triumphs over evil incarnate" is ultimately preserved.[147] Second, it signals that heterosexuality is a natural instinct and suggests that homosexual tendencies are unnatural *preferences* that cannot coexist in Bond's heterosexual world. If Pussy Galore is to survive, then she must be reformed. Thus, she forgoes her apparent lesbian tendencies, opting to replace them with more acceptable, heterosexual desires, in order to be with the hero and to engage in her own self-preservation. Third, her sexual reawakening and repositioning is an extension of the basic metaphor that good triumphs over evil. Pussy Galore's rendezvous with Bond in the stable signals her complete defection from Goldfinger toward an allegiance to Bond.

Gary Giblin and Lisa Neyhouse argued that what is described here as the third effect does a "dramatic disservice" to the vitality of Pussy Galore's character.[148] While she and her Flying Circus are hired to release the Delta 9 nerve gas over Fort Knox, Pussy Galore ultimately switches the nerve gas at the last minute. The audience, however, does not realize this yet, as her conversion is "a relatively understated affair,"[149] and it is quite possible that none of the Flying Circus pilots is aware either. In fact, the only suggestion that something is amiss with Pussy Galore is that she has traded in her black-and-gold attire for a white suit with

Pussy Galore (Honor Blackman) flips James Bond (Sean Connery) in a stable in *Goldfinger* . . .
(George Elam/Daily Mail/Rex/Rex USA)

golden blouse, which she wears while piloting Goldfinger's helicopter upon arrival at Fort Knox. Perhaps this wardrobe change represents a symbolic cleansing and reformation.

Indeed, once the crisis is averted, Felix informs Bond that Pussy Galore "helped us switch the gas in the canisters. By the way, what made her call Washington?"[150] Bond, thoroughly surprised, opines, "I must have appealed to her maternal instincts."[151] Certainly Bond never compels Pussy Galore to switch the nerve gas and turn against Goldfinger. Nevertheless, his courtship of her, which is consummated in the stable, facilitates both his conquest of Pussy Galore and Goldfinger's demise: *Goldfinger* highlights that "Bond can only defeat the villain *through* his sexual possession of the girl."[152] The audience is ultimately "led to believe that [Pussy Galore] informs the CIA of Goldfinger's conspiracy as a consequence of the passionate kiss which ends the mock battle in which she and Bond engage in Goldfinger's stables."[153]

At the conclusion of the film, Pussy Galore is piloting the plane on which Bond and Goldfinger spar. It is curious that she even engages in this action, particularly since she has essentially chosen Bond over Goldfinger's villainy. Indeed, it can be inferred that Pussy Galore aids Goldfinger in commandeering a presidential jet, as Maryam d'Abo and John Cork noted: "It is reasonable to ask why by the end she hasn't ditched Goldfinger or turned him over to the authorities, but no one ever does."[154] Perhaps she simply is not the independent woman she appears to be earlier in the film. Nevertheless, as she struggles to handle the plane after the cabin is depressurized, it is Bond who suggests that the two eject after Pussy Galore registers several looks of desperation and helplessness. Her pilot skills, therefore, are called into question in this scene, and the audience is left with an impression that Pussy Galore's hard exterior is merely a thin, fugacious façade waiting to be dissolved by Bond so that her true self can be exposed.

Despite Pussy Galore's physical strength and adeptness at judo, Bond pulls her to the ground to prevent her from signaling a rescue plane that is surveying the area: "Oh no, you don't. This is no time to be rescued."[155] Indeed, like Jill before her, Pussy Galore's smile is beaming, and she offers no objection to Bond's embrace as the rescue plane passes them by. Thus, while Pussy Galore initially is presented as an assertive and capable female lead, these attributes are built over an incredibly shaky foundation. She is, at first, anomalous within the Bond mythology as a *woman* with homosexual tendencies. Moreover, because Pussy Galore is a veritable puppet to Goldfinger, any notion that she is a liberated female is entirely false. On this point, Maryam d'Abo and John Cork disagreed, suggesting that Pussy Galore possesses autonomy and self-confidence: "[s]he can fight, make love, seduce, and scheme right alongside 007."[156]

. . . but James Bond (Sean Connery) returns the favor, flipping Pussy Galore (Honor Blackman) into the hay in *Goldfinger.*

(Keystone/Stringer/Hulton Archive/Getty Images)

Yet Pussy Galore fights *for* Goldfinger, makes love to Bond because *he* overpowers her, and engages in a *passive* seduction with Bond that prompts him to double his efforts toward conquest. The fact that she switches the Delta 9 nerve gas is likely a selfish act, the result of not "intend[ing] to be part of the mass murder of tens of thousands,"[157] a fact she probably ignored at the time Goldfinger hired her. These attributes do not represent a character who engages in free will. Rather, Pussy Galore *reacts* to circumstances that are imposed upon her by men. Not a single action she takes in the film is based upon her own independence.

Ultimately, Pussy Galore is, in many ways, not unlike Tatiana, Jill, or Honey Ryder. Instead, "[h]er goal, apparently, is to become Honey Ryder,"[158] as she informs Goldfinger that she wishes to retire to Jamaica and get back to nature once she receives her payout from Operation Grand Slam. She is, like her predecessors, subservient and passive. Her single unique quality is the rougher exterior she exhibits, a trait that must be shed if she is to survive in Bond's world. Although Pussy Galore embarks upon a circuitous journey throughout *Goldfinger*, her conversion defines for her a fate that is no different than the leading Bond Girls of the previous two films. Her successor in *Thunderball*, Dominique "Domino" Derval, follows in her footsteps and endures a similar realignment.

Thunderball

Goldfinger has been praised as the best film in the series. Following the frenzy surrounding its Christmas 1965 release,[159] *Thunderball* succumbed to harsh criticism, even as the film firmly established Bond's reputation for "ruthless sexuality."[160] While Broccoli and Saltzman sought to produce a film that was bigger than before,[161] a 1966 cover feature of the film in *Life* described *Thunderball* as "a titillating but careless representation of a succession of physical sensations."[162] One critic described the film as "bigger, more expensive, more elaborate, and longer than the others in the series—but not better" and noted that the "thin" plot was merely "decorated by some pretty girls."[163] The so-called thin plot, another critic wrote, had been thinned out "almost to a vanishing point," thereby requiring that the sex and violence be "correspondingly stepped up."[164] *Time* stated that the script "hasn't a morsel of genuine wit,"[165] and many described *Thunderball* as "*too* epic: over-long and slow."[166] For one commentator writing in *The New Yorker*, the film was devoid of anything particularly interesting, was "violent and valueless, and the only discernible goal [was] . . . looking rich and sexually desirable."[167] Most recently, *Thunderball* was described as "poorly edited," with Connery characterized as "look[ing] bored,"[168] observations likely stemming from the film's "fractious production."[169] But even in 1966, critics suggested that Bond himself, as well as "[t]he very premise of the picture[,] [wa]s a bore."[170]

Not all critiques of *Thunderball* were negative. *The New Yorker*'s Brendan Gill wrote that the film outranked the previous Bond installments in quality.[171] Moreover, he did not observe the ennui that others attributed to Connery: "*Thunderball* owes a great deal to how immensely accomplished Sean Connery has become in the role of James Bond."[172] Indeed, it was "rare" for a sequel such as *Thunderball* to surpass its original, *Dr. No*, even after four years.[173]

Brendan Gill's assessment was not anomalous. In fact, *Thunderball* was described as the "most spectacular" of the Bond films at the time,[174] and Saltzman offered his own optimistic view: "What we've done is to create a modern mythology. Every guy wants to be Bond, and every girl wants to be chased by him."[175] *Thunderball* became the "most successful Bond film of the '60s"[176] and remains one of the most popular films in the series.[177]

* * *

Given the global appeal of *Goldfinger*'s explosive opening, producers made every effort to ensure that the pre-title sequence of *Thunderball* had "all the right ingredients" to rival its predecessor.[178] In fact, the pre-title sequence underscores *Thunderball*'s extreme violence. It begins with Bond attending a funeral when his attention focuses upon the apparent widow of the deceased. The woman with Bond, a French station liaison, asks if there is anything her organization can do to further assist him, to which he responds after quickly lowering his head to examine her figure, "Later perhaps."[179] The widow, whose face is obscured by a veil, opens the car door to a limousine and is driven away to a large mansion. Bond notices a peculiarity in the widow's conduct and decides to follow the limousine. He arrives at the mansion and awaits her arrival.

The widow is quite surprised to see Bond when she enters the room. In this scene, the camera completely blackens out her face, making it wholly indiscernible. As Bond approaches, he remarks, "Madame, I've come to offer my sincere condolences."[180] Immediately thereafter, Bond unleashes an uppercut to the widow's face. The audience soon discovers that the widow is actually a male villain dressed in disguise. Bond, of course, already knew this: "My dear Colonel Bouvar, I don't think you should've opened that car door by yourself."[181] Notwithstanding the ultimate revelation, the lasting impression of the scene is that of Bond striking what appears to be a woman directly in the face. Of the scene, one critic wrote, "We know that Bond has a rough way with women but this is ridiculous!"[182] After an elaborate fight scene in which Bond disposes of this villain, *Thunderball*'s title sequence, replete with the franchise's trademark imagery, commences.

* * *

Depicting black silhouettes of curvaceous women swimming seductively, performing flips, and slithering across the screen, *Thunderball*'s title sequence has been described as "the first of the heavily symbolic cod-Freudian sequences" for which Maurice Binder achieved acclaim.[183] It incorporated live-action sequences that featured photographed nude models and became the benchmark for subsequent Bond films that employed "slow-motion, colorful lighting, rippling bubbies, and the silhouettes of shapely female bodies."[184] Depicted together with the sexy undulating women are frogmen carrying and shooting harpoon guns to invoke the film's aquatic theme. The frogmen and mermaid imagery creates a man's "underwater sex fantasy" in which the women are "hunted down."[185] Indeed, the swimming female silhouettes appear as if they are being chased by the mermen throughout the sequence. At one point, two female images appear to converge in such a manner suggestive of a brief Sapphic kiss before diverging. Binder's title sequences have been described as creating a shorter movie within a movie,[186] but one critic was unimpressed, suggesting that *Thunderball*'s lavish visual sequence accompanied by the powerfully effective title song had lost its originality: "[E]ven subaqueous sex cannot keep the formula entirely fresh."[187] But subaqueous sex drew audiences, as *Time* anticipatorily revealed in 1965: "There will even be underwater sex . . . ."[188]

Adding to the suggestive visual representations is the voice of Welsh recording artist Tom Jones, who performed the eponymously titled theme song.[189] Only one year removed from his release of "It's Not Unusual," the iconic singer helped place both the *Thunderball* soundtrack and its title song high on the music charts.[190] The lyrics, which invoke Bond's prowess and success, boast that he gets "any woman he wants" and express his willingness to break hearts without regret.[191] Thus, the song suggests that Bond, the archetypal playboy, is a man who naturally commands attention and respect. Rather than caution women like Bassey's "Goldfinger," "Thunderball" celebrates Bond's adeptness at female conquest.

Indeed, Bond is unabashed in exhibiting his professed understanding of women and ability for sexual conquest in *Thunderball*. For example, while he visits SPECTRE villain Emilio Largo, Bond gazes back at Largo's mistress, Domino, an action that prompts Largo to turn around and accidentally point the barrel of a gun at Bond. Bond simply swats the gun down and takes it away from Largo. After a brief examination of the weapon, Bond states that it "looks more fitting for a woman."[192] Largo then inquires as to whether Bond knows much about firearms. In response, Bond quips, "No. I know a little about women."[293]

* * *

The audience first discovers Bond convalescing at the Shrublands health clinic, where he is recovering from injuries sustained during his pre-title sequence battle with Colonel Bouvar. There, he meets a blonde nurse named Patricia Fearing, who was portrayed by British actress Molly Peters. Peters, a former brunette pin-up model, had never been on a sound stage prior to auditioning for the part.[194] Her casting added a "combination of naïvete and sensuality" to Patricia's character.[195]

Maryam d'Abo and John Cork described Patricia as an osteopath, a "smart, strong, and . . . trained professional in a then-innovative field of alternative medicine (not merely a nurse as she is often described)."[196] Yet Patricia exhibits no characteristics that would place her beyond the realm of a nurse. Certainly, she is not a physician, and her attire—first a light blue-colored blouse and skirt and then a white ensemble—suggests that she is a nurse. In fact, she later reveals that she reports to a superior, a *physician* named Dr. Wain. It is apparent that she can read an X-ray image and operate a machine, but that is the extent of her training that the audience observes.

As Patricia examines an X-ray of Bond's back, Bond stands behind her and suggestively places his right hand over her right shoulder. He asks, "Do I seem healthy," to which Patricia responds, "Too healthy," as she removes his arm from her shoulder.[197] Patricia attempts to maintain a semblance of professionalism while Bond peppers the dialogue with sexual overtones. After she asks him to hold his arms above his head, Bond lowers them over her head, enveloping her as he kisses her. She struggles to break free from this unwanted behavior, stumbling back: "Behave yourself, Mister Bond. Oh, I can see there's only one place to keep you quiet."[198] She ultimately presents a motorized traction table utilized to stretch the spine. The contraption nearly kills him.

Patricia straps Bond onto the traction table and remarks that it is the first time she has felt safe all day. At this point, the scene reveals Bond's refusal to acknowledge a woman's discomfort over his advances and innuendo, which he continues to exhibit; emphasizes his raw sexual tendencies; and incorporates elements of bondage. After all, the only way that Patricia feels safe is with Bond bound to a table, his arms and legs outstretched and constrained. After she activates the machine, Patricia leaves, stating that she will "look in to see how you're doing in

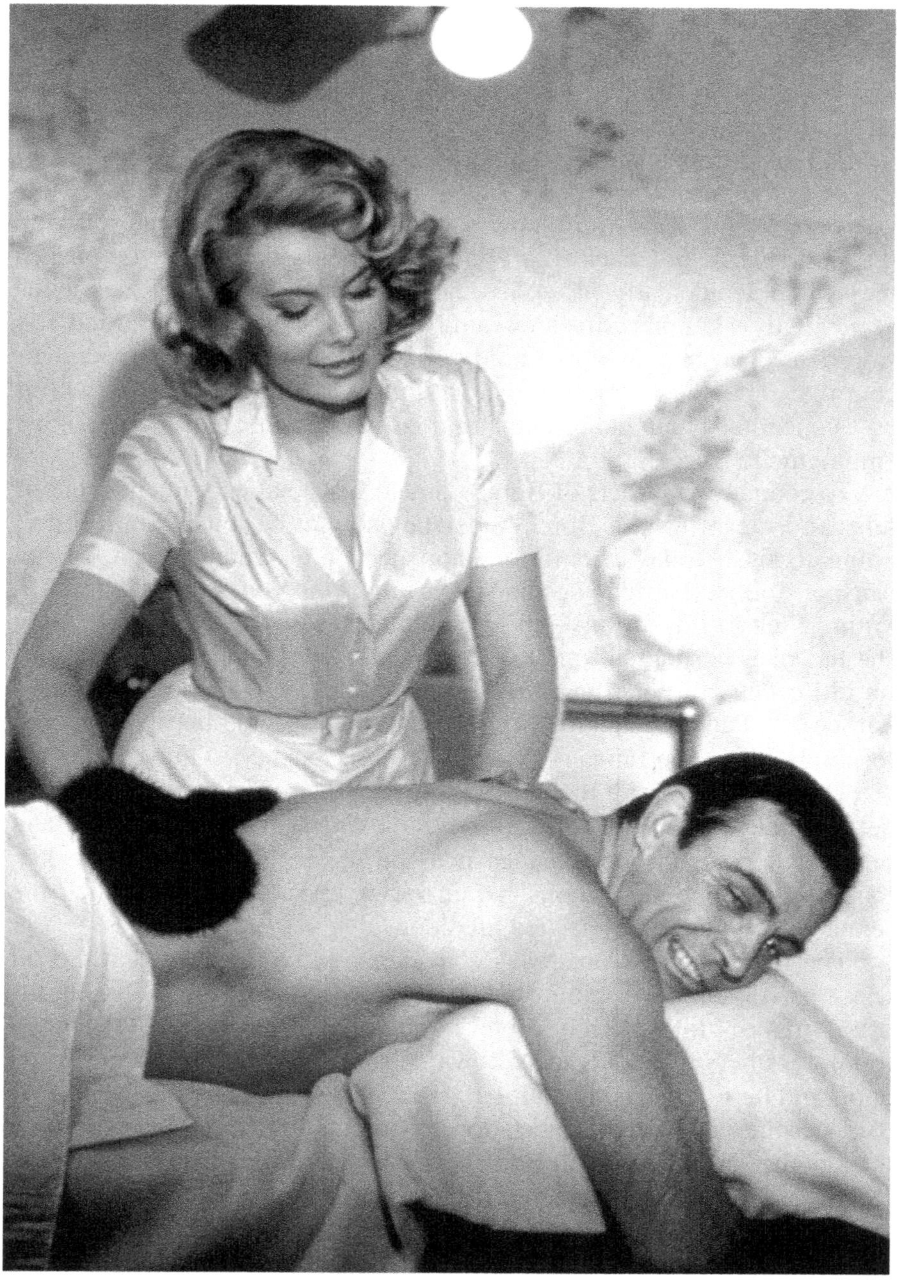

Patricia Fearing (Molly Peters) nurses James Bond (Sean Connery) back to health in *Thunderball*.
(Everett Collection/Rex USA)

fifteen minutes."[199] Her departure, however, is a substantial mistake and indicative of her inexperience. Five minutes later, Bond is attacked by Count Lippe, who switches the machine to its highest power setting in an effort to kill Bond.

Patricia ultimately arrives to turn off the machine. Unaware of Count Lippe's infiltration, she states, "You could've been killed. Oh, you poor dear, I can't think how it could've happened. I can tell you, it's a miracle I came back when I did. I can only think that you pushed the switch accidentally."[200] Why she believes Bond pushes the switch accidentally when his arms are bound at the wrist is curious, particularly since it is clear that he would not have been able to reach the machine's controls. This fact, of course, is lost upon a distraught Patricia, who is now concerned about her errant judgment and possible termination of her employment.

To counter the effects of Bond's ordeal, Patricia recommends that he relax in a steam room. Bond, understandably, is furious: "Somebody's going to wish today had never happened."[201] Acutely aware of her irresponsibility, Patricia becomes fearful: "Oh, you wouldn't tell Dr. Wain. Please, I'd lose my job."[202] Whatever authority Patricia thought she has over her patient quickly evaporates, and Bond seizes upon this turn of events, responding, "Well, . . . I suppose my silence could have a price."[203] Patricia, shaking her head and then waving her index finger, responds, "You don't mean—" as Bond interrupts her: "Oh, yes."[204]

The two wind up in the steam room together. The translucent glass permits the audience to see Bond removing Patricia's clothing and pressing her naked body against it as he places his hands beside her. Essentially, Bond blackmails her in order to successfully realize the sexual encounter he has desired all along.

The steam room scene "was considered so provocative that the set was cleared" during filming.[205] *Playboy* cited it as one of the highlights of the film.[206] Interestingly, Bond never forces Patricia into the stream room. Rather, as he advances toward her, *she* opens the steam room door, and he follows her in with a grin across his face. Thus, it is clear that, despite her verbal protestations, Patricia simply resigns herself to the fact that she must permit Bond to possess her sexually. In this regard, she is hardly a strong character. Her failure to remain with Bond while the machine is in operation and the ordeal that follows places her in a compromising position, and she must weigh the lesser of two apparently unpleasant options: facing the truth with Dr. Wain and potentially losing her job or giving herself up sexually to Bond in exchange for his silence. As this is Bond's world, the weak Patricia succumbs to the latter choice. Interestingly, following this encounter, Patricia no longer refers to Bond as "Mister Bond." Instead, she now addresses him as "James."

But Bond is not quite finished receiving payment for his silence. In a subsequent, equally provocative scene, a naked Patricia lies face-down on a bed while Bond wears a mink glove to massage her back. *Newsweek* observed that "Bond himself has little to do but . . . rub a lady's back with a mink glove (O, decadence!)."[207] The camera concentrates upon her facial expressions, which vacillate between erotic and animalistic. Bond explains that the mink "reduces the tensions," though Patricia disagrees: "Not mine."[208] An airplane flies overhead, prompting Patricia to complain that the noise is "enough to drive you mad," though she concedes as she moans that Bond's mink glove is a more plausible explanation for her mounting frustration.[209] When Bond closes the window, he observes curious activity outside, decides to get dressed and investigate, and makes up an excuse that he desires some exercise. His sudden shift in behavior prompts Patricia to respond, "You must be joking."[210]

Bond essentially walks out on her, leaving her naked in bed, thoroughly aroused, and in a virtual state of *coitus interruptus*. She expresses her displeasure during a subsequent fire alarm, sarcastically asking Bond if he has had enough exercise for one evening. To Patricia's delight, Bond suggests that he has not, and it is assumed that they resume their sexual activities shortly thereafter.

Bond leaves the clinic the next morning and is escorted to his vehicle by Patricia. She no longer seems angry that Bond departs in the midst of a mink seduction and reveals the extent to which she seems infatuated with him. By contrast, Bond reveals the extent to which he is wholly apathetic and disinterested:

> *Patricia*: You will write, or telephone at the very least?
> *Bond*: Oh, day by day. But I'm truly sorry to have to dash off like this, but there's been a bit of a flap at the office.
> *Patricia*: What kind of work do you do anyway?
> *Bond*: Oh, I travel. A sort of licensed troubleshooter . . . . Keep in touch.
> *Patricia*: Anytime, James, any place.
> *Bond*: Another time. (*stating in a disinterested tone*) Another place.[211]

There is, of course, no other time or place. Patricia is never seen again, having served her function as a pure sexual conquest and a reminder of Bond's potency, vigor, and ability to take advantage of situations to reap sexual benefits.

While Maryam d'Abo and John Cork claimed that Patricia is "the only professional whom Bond deals with at the clinic,"[212] Patricia's interactions with Bond are, in fact, highly unprofessional. The audience, of course, knows the reasons behind her willingness to be sexually involved with a patient, but the predicament she creates for herself does not justify her subsequent actions to gain Bond's silence. As such, the film presents an image of Patricia as a highly incapable character whose redeeming qualities or medical expertise are overshadowed by her complete willingness to let Bond have his way with her on his terms.

* * *

Complementing Patricia's submissive character is Paula Caplan. Paula was portrayed by Martine Beswick, who previously appeared as the gypsy Zora in *From Russia With Love*. For this role, producers required that Beswick sunbathe herself for two weeks prior to filming so that she would look the part of an "island girl."[213] Although she is supposed to work with Bond, Paula is anything but his equal, must cater to each of his demands, and essentially works *for* Bond rather than *with* him. Adding insult to injury is Bond's demeanor toward her, which is both condescending and dismissive. Interestingly, his relationship with her is strictly platonic, despite her apparent desire to change those circumstances.

Paula is with Bond on a small boat when he first encounters Domino. He instructs Paula to "tell London I've made contact with the girl."[214] Paula, however, notes that she will inform London that Bond has "seen the girl," sarcastically quipping that he really has not made contact with her.[215] Bond has a better idea to make contact. As his and Paula's boat appears to stall, Bond removes a plug, requests that Domino take him to Coral Harbour, and leaves Paula in the "service boat."[216] It is clear that Paula's halfhearted hand gesture in response to Bond is indicative of annoyance that he has deserted her. As Bond leaves with Domino, Paula tosses him a shirt. She is left behind in the stalled boat, which is completely idle. Bond neither cares nor is concerned about Paula's return to shore.

Later, Paula and Pinder, whom Bond describes as "our man here,"[217] meet Bond and Felix downtown. Bond immediately reprimands Paula for being late. He also neglects to introduce her to Felix. An oversight, perhaps? To the contrary, Bond makes a point to introduce Pinder to Felix. When Felix inquires, "Who's the girl, James," Bond simply responds that she is his "assistant."[218] In fact, when Bond, Pinder, Paula, Felix, and Q are all together at their makeshift headquarters, Paula is observed engaging in the most important of espionage activities: hanging up clothing.

When she next appears on screen, Paula is lounging in Bond's hotel suite wearing a tight blue dress. Fiona Volpe, who is discussed below, enters with a key in hand. Both are surprised to see each other. Their apparent rivalry for Bond's affection, however staged by Fiona, is nevertheless a fitting commentary about Bond:

> *Fiona*: Oh, hello.
> *Paula* (*standing up, surprised*): Oh, hello.
> *Fiona*: Our Mister Bond must have a very high opinion of himself.
> *Paula*: Opinion?
> *Fiona*: Yes. He has a date with me too. (*displaying the room key*)
> *Paula* (*registering a confused look but hearing a knock at the door*): Excuse me.[219]

Paula leaves the room to answer the door. Before she does so, however, she fixes her dress and glances at herself in the mirror, ultimately believing that Bond has arrived. But when she opens the door, Paula is overpowered by two of Largo's henchmen. She is ultimately bound to the bed and becomes a kidnapping victim.

Bond learns of Paula's disappearance from Felix and leaves to investigate. Paula, however, is uncooperative with Largo's interrogators and apparently "won't talk."[220] Bond is ultimately too late to rescue her, as Paula kills herself by ingesting a cyanide pill. When Bond finally discovers her lifeless body, he registers no real reaction.

Bond's inability to rescue Paula is indicative of the fact that they possess absolutely no on-screen chemistry. Bond never attempts to seduce her, and Paula is essentially useless to him both as a sexual object and a so-called colleague. Paula's short-lived appearance merely adds to the film's overall visual stimulation and reflects the extent to which a lack of sexual chemistry between Bond and a female is aberrational. In essence, a lack of sexual tension between Paula and Bond foreshadows her demise.

* * *

Fiona, of course, is responsible for Paula's death. Portrayed by Luciana Paluzzi, who originally auditioned for the role of Domino but was told she was better suited to portray the "bad girl," Fiona has become "one of the most memorable female roles in the entire series."[221] Steven Jay Rubin wrote that Fiona is "the perfect example of the type of woman the producers liked to cast as a ruthless villain in the early 007 thrillers—European, large-breasted, and very sexy."[222] Her ruthlessness is apparent in her adeptness at killing. Indeed, she is part of SPECTRE's execution branch, "repeatedly uses her perfect body and voracious sexual appetite to seduce and then murder her male prey,"[223] and ultimately vows to kill Bond herself.

Paula Caplan (Martine Beswick) and James Bond (Sean Connery) make contact with Domino Derval in *Thunderball*.
(Everett Collection/Rex USA)

In her first on-screen scene, Fiona embraces Major François Derval in bed. When the phone rings, she answers that she is Derval's "social secretary."[224] Her tight, light blue-colored dress accentuates her bosom, and it becomes immediately apparent that she is willing to "us[e] her feminine charms" to her advantage.[225] As Major Derval is called away to duty, he asks if she will be back when he returns. Her response is noncommittal, which prompts him to declare that he may not be in the mood for sexual exploits later. Clearly, *his* sexual desires take precedence over hers, and it is he who sets the schedule for their lovemaking. But the audience soon discovers that Fiona has the upper hand in this scene. Instead, she challenges Derval's contention that he may not be in the mood: "Do you want to bet?"[226] He responds that she "knows your François," once again attributing her desires to his prowess, but she quickly corrects him: "I know me."[227]

Fiona orchestrates Derval's death, and he is replaced with a double, Angelo Palazzi, who has undergone plastic surgery to fill Derval's place and perform an integral role in SPECTRE's mission. Nevertheless, despite the image that she is a woman of authority, Fiona is undermined by Palazzi's demand of a greater payment for his services than that to which he and SPECTRE initially agreed. Left with no viable response to Palazzi's demand, Fiona acquiesces, though she lacks the authority to modify the terms of the agreement. As Palazzi leaves, he reminds her, "The rest of my money, just have it ready."[228] All Fiona can do is nod, and she bears the burden of informing Ernst Stavo Blofeld, the leader of SPECTRE, of this new monetary arrangement into which she has been blackmailed.[229]

Fiona is unaccustomed to having the tables turned on her. She typically issues, rather than takes, orders. Having successfully plotted Derval's murder, she ensures that her directives are carried out flawlessly by her male associates, all of whom work under her direction. The architect of Paula's abduction, Fiona even chastises her male accomplices for failing to quiet Paula's screams sooner: "Don't let her make so much noise. Use the chloroform."[230] But her specialty appears to be murder. In another scene, Fiona, who is riding a motorcycle, launches a missile at a car that is shooting at Bond. The driver, Count Lippe, is immediately killed. It is later revealed that Blofeld instructs Fiona to kill Count Lippe because Lippe is responsible for hiring the greedy Palazzi.

Bond first encounters Fiona while hitchhiking. He asks for a ride and inquires as to how far she intends to drive. Her response, which is preceded by a devious smile, is essentially a non sequitur: "You better fasten your safety belt."[231] They formally introduce themselves to each other as Fiona drives in excess of one hundred miles per hour. During the course of this unnerving ride, Bond discovers that Fiona is a SPECTRE agent. When Fiona delivers Bond to the hotel where they both are apparently staying, Bond is visibly shaken:

> *Fiona*: You look pale, Mister Bond. I hope I didn't frighten you.
> *Bond*: Well, you see I've always been a nervous passenger.
> *Fiona*: Some men just don't like to be driven.
> *Bond*: No, some men just don't like to be taken for a ride.[232]

It is clear from this sparring that Bond will have a difficult task of overcoming Fiona.

Fiona is next seen shooting clay pigeons with Largo, apparently discussing the fact that Bond is spying on their operation. She chastises Largo for wanting Bond dead "because he tries to make love to your . . . woman."[233] Largo corrects her, stating that Bond is an enemy of SPECTRE and, for that reason, should be killed. Fiona, however, continues to critique Largo: "If Bond had died last night as a result of your hastiness, his government would have known for certain the bombs are here. When the time is right, he will be killed."[234] She then declares, "I shall kill him."[235] In essence, Fiona removes Largo from the equation, endeavoring to accomplish the feat of killing Bond herself, even though it is Largo who ultimately wants him dead.

As these descriptions demonstrate, Fiona's character represents a substantial departure from the females portrayed in the series to date. She is aggressive, dangerous, and adept at utilizing her sexuality as a weapon. Of course, it must be remembered that Fiona is the archetypal female villain. Thus, like Pussy Galore, whose homosexuality is considered unnatural, so too is Fiona's hyper-heterosexuality, which the audience soon discovers.

Bond returns to his hotel suite and hears the sound of splashing water. He cautiously enters the bathroom and discovers Fiona bathing herself in the bathtub. Partaking in her own game of seduction, Fiona seems surprised to see Bond, even though she is in *his* bathtub in *his* hotel suite. Bond, however, is quite pleased to observe her naked and seemingly vulnerable. He "naturally takes advantage of this subtle seduction ploy":[236]

> *Fiona*: Aren't you in the wrong room, Mister Bond?
> *Bond*: Not from where I'm standing.
> *Fiona*: Since you are here, would you mind giving me something to put on?[237]

Bond complies with Fiona's request by approaching the bathtub and offering her a pair of *slippers*.

Fiona Volpe (Luciana Paluzzi) informs Emilio Largo that she will kill James Bond in *Thunderball*.

(Pierluigi Praturlon/Rex USA)

Bond sits down in a chair directly facing the bathtub and takes in the view before him as if preparing for a performance. Fiona is not impressed. Glaring back at Bond, and in a somewhat annoyed manner, she drops the slippers to the floor. She then removes the towel from her head, unleashes her fiery red hair, and uses the towel to cover herself as she stands up. She expresses pleasure at seeing Bond again, while Bond shares a similar sentiment. The expression on his face suggests that he is quite distracted by the virtually naked body standing before him. Consequently, his responses are akin to those delivered by an automaton. Interestingly, Fiona, rather than Bond, suggests that Bond remove his clothing under the absurd pretense that he will catch cold.

The next scene is replete with sheer eroticism and sexual energy, and it is perhaps the most provocative heretofore displayed in the series. As the tension Bond and Fiona display earlier in the film culminates, they now "seem barely able to contain the sexual sparks before sleeping together."[238] The camera faces Bond and Fiona post-coitus in bed, but it is positioned behind the intertwining design of the bed's brass headboard. The angle creates an effect that both are caged in, as if to suggest that their raw sexual prowess requires containment. Fiona is atop Bond in the bed, endeavoring to have a second round with him. Bond, however, indicates that they must stop because he has a meeting with Largo at the Junkanoo, a Bahamian street parade. Fiona's response indicates her frustration: "Questions, questions. All I get is questions."[239] She reminds Bond that the music will go on for hours:

> *Fiona*: But the music is going to go on all night anyhow, enough to drive you wild.
> *Bond* (*resting his head on his hand, somewhat disinterested*): Yeah?
> *Fiona*: Do you like wild things, Mister Bond, James Bond? (*proceeding to bite his shoulder*)
> *Bond* (*grimacing from her bite and gently pushing her down on the bed*): Wild? You should be locked up in a cage.
> *Fiona* (*grabbing onto the headboard as they kiss*): This bed feels like a cage. All these bars. Do you think I'll be . . . safe?[240]

Her hands quickly collapse on the bed as her voice rises in pitch, clearly an insinuation that Bond has once again driven her to a sexual peak, a climax that is aptly represented by the Junkanoo celebration that immediately follows.

Fiona gets what she wants insofar as the sexual encounter is extended. There is no indication, of course, that Bond protests against additional extracurricular activity. When they are dressing to leave for the Junkanoo, Fiona, who displays animalistic tendencies in bed, nevertheless places the blame entirely to Bond: "You made a shocking mess out of my hair, you sadistic brute."[241]

Once Bond and Fiona have slept together, they then endeavor to kill each other. As *Esquire* noted, Fiona "is the only girl Bond beds who still wants to kill him after *la petit mort*."[242] Fiona seems to outsmart Bond, at least initially, as she effectively corners him with her male associates and holds him at gunpoint. Bond, however, quickly begins to reassert himself over her, all the while recognizing that she has a gun pointed in his direction: "Not that it matters, but [the gun] was under the pillow all the time."[243] In essence, Bond seeks to reposition Fiona, whom he knows is a SPECTRE associate, by sleeping with her, as he does with Pussy Galore. But unlike Pussy Galore, Fiona is inherently evil and is not merely an accessory to the villain's scheme. Rather, Fiona is an integral part of SPECTRE's mission and, as such, cannot be persuaded to join Bond's cause.

Nevertheless, Bond does not pass up a sexual encounter, even if the attempt to realign Fiona is futile. In fact, he refers to Fiona as a "girl," a clear and conscious attempt at ideological conquest in the absence of success at repositioning through sex. As the two continue to verbally spar, it is clear that Fiona tenuously remains in control despite Bond's ability to unnerve her:

> *Fiona*: Vanity, Mister Bond, is something you know so much about. (*beginning to walk away*)
> *Bond*: My dear girl, don't flatter yourself. What I did this evening was for king and country. You don't think it gave me any pleasure, do you?
> *Fiona* (*stopping, turning around, slamming the door beside her, and regaining her composure*): But of course. I forgot your ego, Mister Bond. (*approaching him*) James Bond, who only has to make love to a woman and she starts to hear heavenly choirs singing. She repents and immediately returns to the side of right and virtue. But not this one. (*straightening his tie*) What a blow it must have been, you having a failure.
> *Bond*: Well, can't win them all.[244]

Fiona's passion and anger are contrasted by Bond's complete calm demeanor. His dry, disassociated sarcasm ultimately undermines her entirely. While she certainly distinguishes herself from Pussy Galore, it is apparent that Fiona is significantly wounded by Bond's remarks. In an effort to display her evaporating authority, Fiona instructs her male associates to get their getaway car and directs Bond's exit from the hotel.

Fiona Volpe (Luciana Paluzzi) and James Bond (Sean Connery) maneuver around the brass headboard "cage" in *Thunderball*.

(Associated Press)

But Bond orchestrates a clever escape, much to Fiona's surprise. In fact, she initially seems more concerned about smoking a cigarette than stopping Bond from running away. She attempts to recover from the embarrassment by issuing further orders to her henchmen. Nevertheless, Bond causes her considerable bewilderment as she is unable to find him in the midst of the ongoing Junkanoo.

Fiona ultimately discovers Bond at the Kiss Kiss Club. Feigning dancing together, she reminds him that "it's no good trying to escape."[245] But Bond has successfully usurped authority away from Fiona. Indeed, her prior directives and orders have dissolved into mere recommendations. "*Why don't you* come with us quietly," she asks him, rather than commanding him.[246] Bond, of course, declines. John Brosnan aptly described what ensues:

> [Bond] spots a couple of [Fiona's men] on the edge of the dance floor but he doesn't see the one who has hidden behind a backdrop near the band. As the bongo drummer . . . approaches a climax in his playing, the SPECTRE man prepares to fire. But at the last moment Bond, noticing that Fiona is looking expectantly over his shoulder, spins her round, at the precise instant the gun is fired . . . . Fiona receives the bullet meant for Bond and dies in his arms.[247]

Fiona's demise is reminiscent of the way in which Bond utilizes Bonita as a human shield in *Goldfinger*. While Bond notes in *Goldfinger* that the violence is shocking, he reveals a much more lighthearted demeanor after Fiona's death, placing her on a chair and remarking, with a bit of a laugh to the couple sitting next to her, "Mind if my friend sits this one out? She's just dead."[248] This statement, one critic wrote, was simply a "sick joke,"[249] but it is indicative of the fate that befalls a woman who resists Bond.

Must Fiona die? Absolutely. As James Chapman observed, Fiona represents the "first instance in the Bond films of a woman whose allegiance proves stronger than Bond's sex appeal."[250] As Bond's world depends upon the premise that any female who cannot resist him is unnatural, any aberration must be excised. In one respect, Fiona can be considered the first so-called sexually liberated woman in the series. But female sexuality is subordinate to Bond's sexuality, and a hypersexual woman simply cannot coexist with him in his world: "Fiona's refusal to be repositioned seems . . . a more progressive and independent character trait for a Bond girl, [and] the film reasserts its sexist code by quickly killing her off."[251]

But James Chapman's characterization goes too far. Fiona's progressivism is restricted to the coital realm. Her raw, animalistic sexual desire does represent a substantial departure from previous Bond Girls and, although they may be groundbreaking attributes, they are nevertheless out of place for the Bond Girl archetype the franchise developed. Outside the sexual realm, Fiona is simply a foil for Pussy Galore. Peeling back a façade of independence reveals the real truth: she is a subordinate employee of both Largo and Blofeld, and, as such, is answerable to higher, more powerful male authorities. Even her fiery red hair, which accompanies her daredevil persona, takes her outside the realm of Fleming's ideal Bond Girl, which he vividly described in his novels.

* * *

Domino is the complete opposite of Fiona in that she is simply "a vulnerable plaything."[252] Unlike Fiona, who is unbreakable until she is forever silenced, Largo's mistress "switches allegiance fast" when she encounters Bond.[253] Consequently, Domino, like Pussy Galore before her, is permitted to live.

An "absurd number of actresses vied for the part" of Domino.[254] Notables such as Faye Dunaway and Raquel Welch auditioned for the role,[255] which was considered "the most complex and demanding of any female lead yet in a Bond film."[256] Claudine Auger ultimately was cast. In its 1965 pictorial of Auger, *Esquire* displayed her in quite revealing attire, noting that "she had the savvy to test for the part in this costume of her own devising. It may have influenced the producers a mite, as it no doubt influences you, reader, and you're not even casting a movie."[257] A French model and actress whose tall and curvaceous figure "helped her win the title of Miss France at the tender age of 15,"[258] Auger possessed the "perfect balance of innocence and sex appeal."[259] Her *Esquire* pictorial was so sexually suggestive that one caption strongly advised men to channel their energies elsewhere: "Put this magazine down, go to the kitchen and give your wife the best kiss she's had in a year. Then finish her off."[260] Curiously, while "twenty-five percent of the screen time takes place underwater,"[261] Auger was cast with the producers' full knowledge that she was an inexperienced swimmer.[262] Her aesthetics, clearly, were more important than anything else, especially since a stunt double was used for filming underwater scenes.[263]

Like *Esquire* readers, Bond has a similar reaction when he views Domino's photograph in the official dossier, and he requests that M reassign him to Nassau, in part, so that he will have an opportunity to meet her. Even Miss Moneypenny is suspect of Bond's request for reassignment when she views the photograph: "Smashing figure. I don't suppose that has anything to do with your request?"[264] Indeed, Miss Moneypenny's agitation over Bond's departure in pursuit of another woman prompts her to sarcastically ask how he would even recognize Domino, to which he responds, "I couldn't miss. She has two moles on the left thigh."[265]

The scene shifts to the Bahamas, where Bond observes Domino snorkeling off a reef. To his delight, Bond seizes an opportunity to reprise his role of a hero who aids a woman in distress: her flipper becomes trapped between coral. Bond lodges it free, and they both return to the surface together. Almost immediately after coming up for air, Bond commences an authoritative and persistent seduction:

> *Domino*: Thank you, Mister . . .
> *Bond*: James Bond. I arrived soon after you went down. I've been admiring your form.
> *Domino*: Have you now? Your name's James Bond, and you've been admiring my form?
> *Bond*: Most girls just paddle around. You swim like a man.
> *Domino*: So do you.
> *Bond*: Well, I've had quite a bit of practice. Do you come here often?
> *Domino*: Whenever I'm bored. Practically every day.
> *Bond*: What else do you do and where?
> *Domino*: You don't waste time, do you?
> *Bond*: No.
> *Domino* (*handing him a star fish, as a token of her appreciation*): For effort.
> *Bond*: Oh, thank you. I'll wear it so you'll know me next time. (*watching Domino climb onto the boat, then staring at her thigh, pleased with himself that he identified her on account off her two moles*) I was right. Couldn't miss.
> *Domino*: I'm not with you.
> *Bond*: Oh you soon will be.[266]

Bond's approach is arrogant, but his persistence is translated into action. As noted above, Bond requests and secures a ride on Domino's boat, leaving Paula behind. The pretext for his request is that Bond has a very important appointment. Yet as soon as he and Domino arrive ashore, Bond proposes that the two lunch by the pool. Domino's question, "How about your urgent appointment," receives neither an acknowledgment nor a response from Bond, and the two are next seen doing exactly as Bond suggested: dining by the pool.[267]

As they lunch poolside, Bond again subjects Domino to an interrogation, and she remains perplexed by Bond's persistent inquiry: "Don't you ever stop asking questions?"[268] The conversation halts when she observes an employee of her "guardian" staring at her from across the

French actress Claudine Auger poses on the set of *Thunderball*, 1965.
(Everett Collection/Rex USA)

pool.[269] This, of course, prompts Bond to inquire further, but he turns the questioning into an opportunity to continue injecting innuendo:

> *Bond*: Your guardian has you watched?
> *Domino*: He likes to know where I am.
> *Bond*: I don't blame him.[270]

Thus, it is apparent that Domino's activities and actions are carefully monitored and controlled by her mysterious guardian, Largo.

When she observes Largo's yacht arriving ashore, Domino abruptly excuses herself. Bond, of course, is surprised, but he remains undeterred to see her again:

> *Bond*: You're not going too soon?
> *Domino*: I'm afraid so. (*pointing to the yacht with a head motion*) My guardian's yacht.
> *Bond*: Oh, really?
> *Domino*: He'll be expecting me. (*offering a handshake*)
> *Bond*: May I come with you? I'd love to meet your guardian.
> *Domino*: Oh, no. (*turning to walk away*)
> *Bond*: Will I see you again?
> *Domino*: It's a small island.
> *Bond*: Perhaps we can have dinner.
> *Domino*: No.
> *Bond*: My dear, uncooperative Domino . . .
> *Domino* (*interrupting*): How do you know that? (*turning toward Bond and stopping*) How do you know my friends call me Domino?
> *Bond*: It's on the bracelet on your ankle.
> *Domino*: So, what sharp little eyes you've got. (*walking away*)
> *Bond* (*smirking to himself after she leaves*): Wait till you get to my teeth.[271]

Just as he ordains that he and Domino have lunch by the pool, so, too, does Bond ensure that he and Domino partake in the supposedly forbidden dinner. It is therefore apparent that Domino disobeys Largo because Bond compels her to do so, not because she actually wants or chooses to do so. From the moment he meets Domino, Bond is in complete control, gleaning the information he seeks, initiating his seduction, and influencing her actions.

During a casino scene, Domino is perched next to Largo, gazing at Bond across the *chemin de fer* table like a statue. In essence, she functions as a prop, much in the same way that Goldfinger desires to be seen with Jill. Largo's losing streak is interrupted by Domino, who reminds him that he promised to buy her a drink. Largo refuses: "Soon, my dear. I want to get my money back first."[272] But Bond offers to purchase a drink for Domino, and the two walk away together. What is supposed to be a drink, however, ultimately turns into dinner. Once again, Bond has effectuated the outcome he desires, and he again presses Domino for information. This time, Domino reveals the nature of her relationship with Largo:

> *Bond*: I understand you're Mister Largo's niece.
> *Domino*: It sounds better than, what would you say? Mistress? Kept woman?
> *Bond*: I wouldn't say that. So where did you meet him?
> *Domino*: In Capri. I was there with my brother, François. Strange, I found Emilio attractive . . . then.[273]

It is apparent that Domino not only feels trapped by Largo, but she herself acknowledges her unfortunate circumstances by referring to herself as a kept woman. Her conversation with Bond seems like a breath of fresh air for her, and she is immediately forthcoming about Largo and her brother. It is also apparent that she feels free in his arms when they are dancing, stating that Bond holds her in a manner that is quite unlike Largo.

Largo ultimately interrupts their tryst, but it is clear that Bond intends to see her again. Unlike before, Domino is now quite willing:

> *Bond*: How long are you staying on here in Nassau?
> *Domino*: We are going the day after tomorrow.
> *Bond*: As I said, we haven't got very much time.
> *Domino* (*noticing Largo*): Emilio wants to leave.
> *Bond*: Are you sleeping aboard tonight?
> Domino (*pulling away from Bond and beginning to walk back to their table*): I hope you'd not be so obvious.
> *Bond*: Well, when one has little time, one sort of has to be obvious.
> *Domino*: You know where you can find me.[274]

Once Domino is back in Largo's grasp, Largo commands her to disclose the substance of her conversation with Bond, and she complies with his order. As their boat departs, Domino gazes back toward Bond, suggesting that their brief encounter is, indeed, a brief respite from her captivity.

Bond next sees Domino swimming in one of Largo's pools. She finds herself struggling to reach a towel, and Bond offers his assistance. Throughout the film, Domino is portrayed as in need of something or incapable of accomplishing anything on her own. Her considerable beauty is tarnished by an inherent incapacity and lack of individuality. In

James Bond (Sean Connery), Domino Derval (Claudine Auger), and Emilio Largo (Adolfo Celi) raise the stakes at a casino in *Thunderball*.

(MacGregor/Stringer/Hulton Archive/Getty Images)

many respects, she appears to audiences as "an actual bimbo."[275] In fact, she appears primarily in "breathtaking bikinis and bathing suits."[276] After she emerges from the pool, both Largo and Bond observe her applying makeup. She notices their gazes, giggles, and excuses herself to change. Curiously, she replaces her bathing suit with an even smaller bikini. Again, Domino's aesthetic purpose cannot be overstated.

Later, Domino and Bond engage in aquatic relations behind a reef. When the two emerge from the water, Bond kisses her and expresses hope that they "didn't frighten the fish."[277] She, however, steps on a poisonous sea egg spine, which requires Bond to assume, yet again, the task of acting as her savior. He commands her to sit down and turn over while he bites down on her foot and extracts a spine. She then confesses that, with the exception of her brother, Bond is the only man to make her cry.

Although she implies that Largo has not brought her to tears, it is apparent that he subjects her to considerable abuse. In fact, she appears to harbor severe insecurities, believing that as soon as Bond intends to discuss something serious with her, it is his way of telling her that he no longer desires her:

> *Bond*: Domino I have to tell you something.
> *Domino* (*shifting her facial expression to one of resignation*): Oh, I'm sorry, James. I'm sorry to embarrass you, speaking of love. I know . . .
> *Bond* (*interrupting*): I must hurt you again.
> *Domino* (*anticipating what he is about to tell her*): You're going away. "So sorry, my dear, but it's all over."
> *Bond*: No, it's about your brother.[278]

She begins to tear as she realizes that her brother is dead. But when Bond states that he needs her assistance, she has a remarkable epiphany: "Of course. That's why you make love to me."[279] Ultimately, she is correct. Bond implores her to trust him, but she is dismissive of his request for her aid. Finally, in order to get Domino to understand, Bond resorts to physical dominance, forcefully grabbing her arm: "Look, Largo had your brother murdered, or it was on his orders."[280]

Bond explains that he requires Domino's assistance to ascertain where nuclear bombs will be loaded onto Largo's yacht. He cautions her that this task will be both dangerous and difficult. Of course, Bond cares little for what fate would befall Domino in the event that she, once again, finds herself incapable and is caught spying. She simply responds, asking rhetorically, "What can he do to me that he hasn't already done,"[281] and agrees to assist.

Bond has effectively destroyed Domino's allegiance to Largo, an endeavor he commences early in the film but solidifies with his sexual conquest. Once he consummates their affair, Bond effectively substitutes himself as Domino's guardian. Domino makes clear to Bond that she is "doing this for my brother for what he did to him. But promise me one thing, you will kill Largo for me, whatever happens."[282]

Suddenly, and quite curiously, Domino remembers what she believes is an important detail and conveys it to Bond. It is unclear what precisely jogs her memory. What is clear, however, is that, notwithstanding her noble declaration that she wishes to avenge her brother's death, Domino is ultimately not assisting Bond on account of her own free will.

Bond's willingness to place Domino in physical danger without reflection or reservation further illustrates her purpose as a functional object. He gives her a Geiger counter to detect the presence of radiation and instructs her on its use. But Bond does nothing to assist her in avoiding Largo's suspicions of her treachery. Disobeying Largo's instructions that she remain in her cabin aboard the yacht, Domino takes the Geiger counter and begins walking about the yacht. An extremely agitated Largo discovers her:

> *Largo*: I told you to stay in your cabin.
> *Domino*: It's stuffy in there. I want a breath of air.
> *Largo* (*placing his hand against the wall to prevent her from moving*): My dear, did you not hear me? (*looking at the device in her hand*) Where did you get that?
> *Domino*: I bought it this morning.
> *Largo*: Let me see.[283]

Largo reaches for the device and knocks it out of her hand. He then firmly grabs on to Domino's hair when she bends down to pick it up, causing her to wince. Pulling her to her feet by her hair, Largo accuses Domino of receiving the "little toy" from Bond,[284] throws her into the cabin and onto the bed, and declares, "There is no escape for you. Like your friend, you've been a little too clever. And now you are caught!"[285]

The cinematography in the next scene heightens Largo's sinister and sadistic tendencies. He appears in dark profile with a mirror above the bed reflecting an image of Domino, who is restlessly squirming with her wrists and ankles bound. The scene remains dark as Largo coldly states, "You've given me much pleasure, Domino. But in return, unless you tell me how much Bond knows, I'll be forced to cause you great pain."[286] He holds ice in one hand and a cigar in the other, informing her that he will apply both "scientifically and slowly" to maximize her torture.[287] Although she screams from the pain, Domino's torture is short-lived as

Largo is interrupted by his physicist. As he leaves, Largo cautions her, "Do not live in hope, my dear. There is no one to rescue you."[288]

Indeed, Bond never rescues Domino from her captivity, which indicates her importance to him. Instead, one of Largo's sympathetic employees spares her life. She also manages to kill Largo herself and expresses satisfaction in doing so. Interestingly, because Bond does not save her, there is no indication that he and Domino resume their physical relationship at the conclusion of his mission. Bond is not the hero: he neither saves Domino nor kills Largo. Thus, *Thunderball* ends in a manner quite different from the three prior films, wherein Bond disposes of the villains (with the exception of Rosa Klebb) and is seen embracing the primary Bond Girl in the final scene. Here, Domino and Bond climb aboard a raft, with Domino's wet attire revealing her curvaceous figure one last time to the audience. Domino sits apart from Bond, only to eventually crawl into his arms. But any indication that an embrace might occur is short-lived as they are whisked into the air and carried away. It appears that, with the mission complete and Largo dead, both can go their separate ways without the other because, at least for Bond, any usefulness Domino exhibits has run its course.

* * *

Goldfinger and *Thunderball* together represent the height of the Bond series in the 1960s and, some argue, the pinnacle of the entire franchise. *Goldfinger* "remains one of the most memorable and popular films of all time,"[289] while *Thunderball* "transformed James Bond into more than a popular fictional hero: he became and remains a phenomenon."[290] With two rare exceptions (namely the pre-heterosexual and misaligned Pussy Galore and the inherently sinister Fiona), virtually every female character presented in both films serves as a visual stimulant. As *Look* sarcastically noted, "[M]urder can't keep [Bond] from the arms of superwomen . . . [they] don't care that his body is a . . . canvas of reds, blacks, and blues . . . they love him."[291] Indeed, the women in these films are so enthralled by the mere idea of Bond that none of them can resist his charm. They ultimately are willing to accept Bond on his terms or, as Patricia memorably states, anytime and anyplace. Only Paula is left to wonder about the joys accompanying a sexual encounter with Bond.

Fiona's unwillingness to submit to Bond reaffirms her aberrational stature: "Fiona is the only girl Bond beds who still wants to kill him after[wards] . . . slipping Double-0-Seven?"[292] But *Esquire* erroneously placed the blame with Bond, whereas the true failure rests with her flawed character. Notwithstanding Pussy Galore's lesbian tendencies, Fiona possesses considerably masculine traits. Moreover, she shoots to kill, uses sexuality to exploit others, and takes delight in seeing others meet their demise. These qualities contribute to her extreme, over-exaggerated villainy—particularly in contrast to the much calmer Largo. Consequently, the audience is left to question Fiona's overall plausibility, even in an over-the-top Bondian world. Simply stated, Fiona is a hyperbolic representation of an unnatural woman.

* * *

The franchise concluded its first decade in the same way in which it began. The next two films perpetuated and reinforced the original, successful formula of portraying submissive and obedient women—like Jill, Pussy Galore, and Domino—who willingly allow Bond's masculinity to subdue them. In stark contrast to these characters, a strong social movement was rapidly gaining public exposure and political ground, and its participants began demanding that America revisit and ultimately cast aside longstanding, stereotypical representations of and preconceived notions about women in popular culture and beyond.

008

Shaken & Stirred: The Feminist and Women's Liberation Movements in America

Women are an oppressed class. Our oppression is total, affecting every facet of our lives. We are exploited as sex objects, breeders, domestic servants, and cheap labor. We are considered inferior beings, whose only purpose is to enhance men's lives. Our humanity is denied.

—"The Redstockings Manifesto"[1]

There is a lot of evidence that American men always have been afraid of women, and indeed chronically mismanaged them.

—Eleanor Perenyi[2]

This notion [that most men treat women as sexual objects] is now embraced by 57% of American women under 25, according to a recent poll by McCall's *of 20,000 females.*

—Ruth Brine[3]

Anyone who felt that American women had "rights and opportunities today the likes of which the Western world has never seen" and that "women today are in many respects much better off than men" received a rude awakening when *The Feminine Mystique* reached bookshelves.[4] Excerpts of Betty Friedan's work were reprinted in numerous magazines. *The Feminine Mystique*, hailed by some as "a staple item in many a suburban household," soon became a bestseller.[5]

At the same time, Betty Freidan's Nazi concentration camp metaphor, along with other "strong words,"[6] was toned down, and most allusions to oppression instead referenced an invisible cage that enslaved women. The cage image was discussed at length in a 1963 article that appeared in the *Saturday Evening Post*:

> The ingenious point about [a] new-model zoo is that it deceives . . . . [N]ot only cannot the animal see how it is imprisoned, the visitor's conscience is relieved of the unkindness of keeping animals shut up. He can say, "Look, no bars round the animals," just as society can say, "Look, no laws restricting women," even while it keeps women rigidly in place by zones of fierce social pressure. There is, however, one great difference. A woman . . . unable to perceive what is holding her back . . . may accuse herself and her whole sex of craven timidity because women have not jumped at what has the appearance of an offer of freedom.[7]

Indeed, one academic who addressed a seminar for women later that year informed her audience that "women may be accused of being part of the problem. They do not resist change—unless it is one which fashion decrees, or one which simplifies housework."[8]

Were women themselves to blame? One writer recounted that she came upon the heading "Women" while searching for material in a book of quotations and observed that almost half of the entries "suggested that [a woman] is a good deal more attractive when she keeps her mouth shut."[9] Another writer, who noted that women failed to take an active role in elevating their positions in society, argued that "the professions are wide open to American women," though "most jobs that women hold . . . are in the lower-paid, unskilled, semi-skilled, or what might be called 'blue smock' categories."[10]

Women were called upon to "arise as individuals committed to perfect themselves as human beings wherever they are, whatever they do," though it was recognized that such a task was, of course, "not easy."[11] Marjorie Carpenter of Stephens College, an institution established in 1833 in order to "meet[] the changing needs of women,"[12] criticized women for allowing themselves to "be tied to trivia and guided by glamour . . . paralyzed by a fear of not being 'feminine.'"[13] She offered a parody of "The Slave," a poem by James Oppenheim, as a rallying call for women to break free from the so-called invisible cage:

> They set woman free, giving her a vote and job.
> She is still chained to triviality
> She is still manacled to mental indolence

> She is still bound by fear of not being feminine
> By ignorance of what is potentially hers
> Her slavery was not to the home
> But in herself.
> [We] can only set . . . women free . . . .
> Free women set themselves and all men free.[14]

The time to bring down the so-called invisible bars that confined women had arrived.

Tired of being "shamed back into the kitchen . . . and told that she had to find her contentment right [there],"[15] women began exerting pressure upon President Lyndon B. Johnson to elevate and protect the status of American women. Unlike his predecessor, who was criticized for symbolic gestures intended solely to pacify female constituents, President Johnson seemed proactive. He initiated a program of female "affirmative action" designed to appoint more women in higher-level government positions. He directed aides to look "in the baskets on your desks . . . you'll find there are a lot of [applications from] women who've been asking for elevation . . . . [G]et some of them moving [and] report back to me next week [as to] how many you have placed."[16] Almost immediately, the number of female governmental appointments increased. At one point, those numbers reached 1,600.

President Johnson's actions resonated beyond government appointments. Efforts soon mounted to question the determination by President Kennedy's Commission on the Status of Women that "sex discrimination was sufficiently different from race discrimination."[17] A small number of women breathed new life into the fifty year-old National Woman's Party (NWP), which had been founded to promote the elimination of sex discrimination, in an effort to merge women's rights within the larger, ever-increasing civil rights movement. The NWP successfully persuaded legislators to reconsider the commission's findings, which resulted in the inclusion of sexual discrimination provisions in future civil rights legislation. While amendments specifically mentioning "sex" to titles II, III, IV, and V of the new civil rights bill were soundly defeated in the Democrat-controlled House of Representatives, language that included "sex" alongside proscriptions of discrimination based upon race, color, religion, and national origin were ultimately incorporated into title VII.

Signed into law in July 1964, the Civil Rights Act guaranteed constitutional rights in public facilities and public education, extended the Commission on Civil Rights, and established the Equal Employment Opportunity Commission (EEOC). Section 703 of the Civil Rights Act,

"Discrimination Because of Race, Color, Religion, Sex, or National Origins," provides:

> It shall be an unlawful employment practice for an employer—
>
> (1) to fail or refuse to hire or to discharge any individual, or otherwise to discriminate against any individual with respect to his compensation, terms, conditions, or privileges of employment, because of such individual's race, color, religion, sex, or national origin; or
>
> (2) to limit, segregate, or . . . deprive any individual of employment opportunities or otherwise adversely affect his status as an employee, because of such individual's race, color, religion, sex, or national origin . . . .[18]

Although title VII of the Civil Rights Act was not a total victory for advocates, it represented progress toward eliminating inequality in the workplace. Ultimately, it became clear that title VII did nothing to "rescue women trapped in suburban homes[,] . . . but it did hold out the promise of an escape route out of the pink-collar ghetto."[19]

The import of title VII was trivialized by its opponents long before it became law. Representative Howard W. Smith, chairman of the House Rules Committee, publicly proclaimed that he added the word "sex" to title VII as a joke in order to mock the achievements of the NWP and other women's organizations. More importantly, Smith, a Southern Democrat and ardent supporter of segregation, believed that adding the term "sex" to the legislation would undermine the bill and facilitate its defeat. In fact, the "prohibition against discrimination based on sex was added to title VII at the last minute on the floor of the House of Representatives."[20] Smith's plan, of course, backfired, and while he "admitted to being anything but 'serious' about the amendment" and introduced it with "tongue in cheek,"[21] he was quite surprised to see it enacted.

Title VII was virtually ignored once it became law. The EEOC failed to investigate over four thousand cases of sex discrimination filed by women between 1964 and 1966, justifying its inaction by frequently citing an overabundance of "frivolous complaints."[22] The EEOC's apparent "[v]irulent hostility" toward acknowledging sex discrimination and enforcing federal law frustrated feminists, most of whom believed that their hard work was being easily undermined.[23] The EEOC's ability to virtually ignore title VII, these feminists believed, offered opponents justification for the dismissal of gender equality concerns. Indeed, feminists theorized that men would become empowered since women would ultimately resign themselves to returning home to the domestic sphere: "The feminists . . . have interpreted the [opposition] movement as an assault [to maintain] the last stronghold of Victorian culture, the patriarchal family."[24]

Was title VII being deliberately dismissed, or did some legitimate reason exist for the legislation's inability to effect any change? A loophole in the law, referred to as the "bona fide occupational qualification" clause, exempted employers from hiring women for positions that required a male employee. The exemption, some argued, swallowed the rule and undercut the seriousness of the law. Rather than facilitate gender equality in employment, title VII prompted critics to mock the potential effects of the law via tongue-in-cheek counter-examples involving the hiring of male employees. One notable example involved Playboy Bunnies.

During a 1965 White House conference, government officials jokingly remarked that title VII would require Playboy clubs to hire men as "male bunnies." Following the conference, title VII garnered the dubious distinction of being dubbed the "bunny law." Ultimately, the so-called "bunny law" spawned a larger "bunny problem." With slender, attractive, young women receiving employment as "bunnies" at Playboy establishments around the country, Richard K. Berg, the EEOC deputy general counsel, indicated that title VII raised serious issues about these hiring practices: "The bunny question is interesting because everybody considers the answer to be obvious . . . . But in terms of what bunnies do, it is something else—they serve drinks."[25]

The "bunny problem" simply represented a larger criticism of title VII. A 1965 *New York Times* editorial suggested that "it would have been better if Congress had just abolished sex itself"[26] and forecasted the dangerous effects of title VII:

> Everything has to become neuterized. Housemaid becomes a dirty word; it is, of course, discriminatory. Handyman must disappear from the language . . . . Girl Friday is an intolerable offense . . . . Bunny problem, indeed! This is revolution, chaos. You can't even safely advertise for a wife anymore.[27]

Thus, what began as a "bunny joke" transformed into a real and serious issue. Representative Smith's casual inclusion of the term "sex" ultimately carried significant legal consequences that no one had previously contemplated.

In response to the "bunny law" moniker being ascribed to title VII, Democratic Congresswoman Martha Griffiths publicly expressed her resentment over the manner in which the EEOC was dismissing women's claims and targeted the government for "its arbitrary arrogance, disregard of the law and hostility to the human rights of women."[28] In an act of defiance against what they perceived as government inaction, twenty-eight women formed their own organization during the third annual meeting of the National Conference of State Commissions on the Status of Women in June 1966. Advancing a platform that recommended "to take the actions needed to bring women into the mainstream of American society, *now*, full equality for women, in fully equal partnership with men,"[29] the group established the National Organization for Women (NOW).

The most immediate—and perhaps significant—effect stemming from the creation of NOW was a shift of control of the feminist agenda away from the federal government. In fact, one tremendous benefit the private, independent organization possessed was the latitude to formulate its own agenda and define its objectives free from bureaucratic entanglements. NOW rejected the Freudian and widely accepted contention at the time that "biology is destiny,"[30] adopting instead an agenda that heightened similarities between the genders, as opposed to embracing positions that accentuated gender differences. As Betty Friedan recalled, "[i]t wasn't going to be women against men; men had to be included, though women must take the lead."[31]

NOW has been described as the first "militant" feminist group in the twentieth century that addressed and sought to combat sex discrimination.[32] It became the primary organization to formulate a liberal feminist agenda based upon principles of liberal democracy. Betty Friedan, who referred to the women's movement as a "movement for equality" or the "sex role revolution," deliberately refrained from using the term "liberation," which other, more radical groups that formed in the late 1960s and early 1970s ultimately embraced.[33] The initial three hundred charter members of NOW felt a "sense of history [they] all shared as [they] began to make it happen. Here women, for all these years, had done . . . work and helped organize and support causes . . . but now, finally, [they] were doing it for ourselves—for women . . . ."[34] In short, NOW members believed that they "spoke for millions."[35]

Betty Friedan was elected the first president of NOW. She presented a program—initially outlined in her seminal work—that reinforced the principle that "it is no longer either necessary or possible for women to devote the greater part of their lives to child-rearing."[36] Yet NOW bore the difficult task of carefully molding its agenda in such a way to ensure that its message did not reject marriage, family, and motherhood. The organization envisioned that "a true partnership between the sexes demands a different concept of marriage, an equitable sharing of the responsibilities of home and children and of the economic burdens of their support."[37] In fact, the concept of marriage as a contract soon emerged since contractual principles were considered "at its very heart and essence."[38] Handbooks were printed to instruct women on how to draft their own marital contracts, and the concept of "the utopian marriage contract" promoted the idea that a husband and wife equally divided their responsibilities as well as their expenses.[39]

NOW did not merely seek modernization of the institution of marriage. Rather, it adopted a strong political platform through which to promote its wide-ranging agenda. In 1967, the organization formulated a women's bill of rights that was presented to both Democratic and Republican presidential candidates. The bill of rights contained, among other things, a strong endorsement for the ratification of the ERA as a constitutional amendment:

> We demand that the United States Congress immediately pass the Equal Rights Amendment to the Constitution to provide that "Equality of rights under the law shall not be denied or abridged by the United States or by any State on account of sex," and that such then be immediately ratified by the several States.[40]

Immediately following the ERA provision, the NOW bill of rights demanded that the federal government "Enforce Law Banning Sex Discrimination in Employment,"[41] a direct response to years of EEOC inaction concerning women's rights in the workplace. Other bill of rights provisions called for "equal and unsegregated education," "equal job training opportunities and allowances for women in poverty," "maternity leave rights in employment and in Social Security benefits," "child care centers," and "tax deduction[s] for home and child care expenses for working parents."[42] The most contentious and controversial item, "the right of women to control their reproductive lives," expressed a woman's right to "control [her] own reproductive li[fe] by removing from penal codes laws limiting access to contraceptive information and devices and laws governing abortion."[43]

Betty Friedan declared that NOW would "use every political tactic available . . . to end sex discrimination," even if doing so required women to march upon Washington.[44] NOW members composed letters to the president, the Justice Department, and leaders in the Civil Service Commission requesting meetings to discuss ways in which the government could address women's concerns. NOW also established a legal department and began filing lawsuits against employers allegedly engaging in title VII violations. Many women began picketing "all-male" establishments, protesting newspapers that printed highly controversial sex-segregated want ads, and targeting airlines for "running . . . bordello[s] in the sky."[45] During a 1969 demonstration

Women's rights activists protest inside a male-only establishment in New York City, 1971.

(Associated Press)

cosponsored by NOW against a prominent New York hotel that refused to integrate a men's only restaurant, journalist Gloria Steinem decided to join the feminist cause.

The hotel boycott was one of many NOW campaigns against traditionalism. It encouraged protests against Madison Avenue and the images of an apparent cult of femininity perpetuated therein. As one commentator wrote in 1966, women were encouraged to "[l]eave [their magazines] on the stands, cancel [their] subscription[s], and the chances are excellent that women won't be mentioned on Madison Avenue for a long while, perhaps long enough for a whole generation of girls to grow up unscathed."[46] Women were praised for finally beginning to realize that the Madison Avenue establishment had duped them into believing that a woman "must look alluring to hold her husband's love."[47] Indeed, it was argued that cosmetic industries survived only by perpetuating the myth that "the loss of . . . physical beauty has come to mean . . . the loss of . . . womanhood [and] . . . value as a person."[48] Needless to say, the way in which women were utilized as marketing tools to sell products to men—and to suggest that women who did not use certain products would never attract male attention—came under increasing scrutiny.

One goal of a nationwide Women's Strike for Equality, which was held on August 28, 1970, was the boycott of products perpetuating gender stereotypes. Among the companies targeted were Ivory Soap, which was accused of placing too great an emphasis upon women identifying solely with motherhood, and the publisher of *Cosmopolitan*, which was characterized as a mere compilation of articles replete with didactic instructions on how to maximize female sexuality for the purpose of satisfying men. As the feminist movement increased awareness of these marketing ploys and preconceived notions on which the advertising industry was based, one commentator writing in *America* urged Madison Avenue to "run for [its] life."[49]

NOW also advocated for fair media treatment of women. As one author noted, "Those in control of media and politics, far from acknowledging what women encountered, in fact worked to make their situation more difficult."[50] In fact, "nothing drove home the gap between TV land and reality [more] than the civil rights movement."[51] The feminist movement was no different. Mass media "reflected and reinforced an image of the role of women in American society that [was] both unfair and distorted."[52]

In 1970, journalist Helen Dudar suggested that the "TV screen and the ads [portrayed] this person who's either sexy or shrill, and that's what's called a woman."[53] Television situation comedies contained an underlying message that granting women increased independence was ultimately dangerous to society. Situation comedies such as *Green Acres*, *Bewitched*, and *I Dream of Genie* are three poignant examples.

Eva Gabor's character in *Green Acres* always seemed to cause trouble, something she shared with the character of Samantha on *Bewitched.* Portrayed by Elizabeth Montgomery, Samantha was the daughter of a witch who, like her mother, had a penchant for placing her husband Darrin in precarious positions. The theme of *Bewitched* was very similar to the premise of *I Dream of Genie*.

In *I Dream of Genie*, order was maintained—and restored—whenever Barbara Eden's Genie was placed in her bottle by Major Tony Nelson, an astronaut with the National Aeronautics and Space Administration (NASA) and, more notably, her *master*. Each time that Genie emerged from captivity, she caused trouble and wrecked havoc, turning Major Nelson's male-dominated world upside down. The message was clear: men needed to contain and control how much freedom women were permitted to possess. Susan J. Douglas argued that such depictions reflected that "female emancipation turns out to be very bad advice because it undermines the woman's femininity, makes her appear ridiculous," and ultimately constitutes a "parody of feminism."[54]

But scrutiny was not limited to female characters in situation comedies. Walt Disney was criticized for "regularly reaffirm[ing] the importance of the doormat as a role model for little girls."[55] Even *Sesame Street*, the popular children's educational program, was subject to critique for perpetuating the ideal that "motherhood and homemaking [were] the most desirable and only appropriate roles for females."[56]

* * *

Although NOW advanced a mainstream feminist agenda, it soon became viewed by some as "slightly middle-aged, middle-class and tame."[57] As sentiment against the Vietnam War mounted, gender tensions among members of the Student Non-Violence Coordinating Committee (SNCC) and Students for a Democratic Society (SDS) became pronounced. Many women who were involved in the antiwar campaign mobilized around the belief that NOW was ineffective at improving their status. In fact, within the SNCC and SDS, male representatives refused to acknowledge the merits of the feminist movement, used condescending language toward female counterparts, delegated menial tasks to women, and refused to entertain any discussion of women's rights as part of their organizations' platforms.

The civil rights movement actually exacerbated the need for a feminist movement:

> The civil rights movement, in an ironic way, created additional converts to the feminist cause. During the Southern turmoil of the

> middle '60s, many women volunteers found that sexist discrimination extended even to the revolution. "Civil rights," says one organizer, "has always been a very male-dominated movement." Most radical organizations saw to it that the "chicks" operated the mimeograph machines and scampered out for coffee while the men ran the show."[58]

For example, during a meeting of the National Conference for New Politics, delegate William Pepper dismissed his female colleague, Shulamith Firestone, by patting her head and remarking that "we have more important issues to talk about here than women's liberation."[59] During an address to an SDS audience, Marilyn Salzman Webb was shouted offstage by members chanting that they wanted to "take her off the stage and fuck her."[60]

The assassinations of Malcolm X, Martin Luther King Jr., and Robert F. Kennedy facilitated a gravitation toward more left-wing and radical civil, social, and war protest movements. Groups such as the Weathermen and the Black Panther Party garnered notoriety for their overtly militant objectives and violent demonstrations. The Weathermen was formed from within the leadership circles of the SDS. One of its founders, William Ayers, had hoped to unite the group with the Black Panther Party, particularly since both groups "came to consider the police as the focus of their attacks."[61] Ayers, whose close personal association with Barack Hussein Obama was exposed during the 2008 presidential election,[62] was indicted for inciting riots, including a "Days of Rage" rampage in Chicago in 1969, and for bombing the United States Capitol in Washington and other federal buildings.[63]

Groups that focused exclusively upon women's rights were no different. Among those that became prominent were BITCH, the Women's International Terrorist Conspiracy from Hell (WITCH), Bread and Roses, the Redstockings, the Radical Mothers, and Media Women. In 1968, two hundred women from thirty-seven states and Canada gathered in Chicago for the first women's liberation conference. Advocating a radical and aggressive feminist agenda, these conference attendees marked the beginning of an internal fraction from within the feminist movement that would generate friction and discord for years to come. Indeed, as the number of these splinter groups increased, the presence of a strong, single organization such as NOW began to wane, a phenomenon that some feminists reflected was an "unfortunate" consequence.[64] Author and activist Ti-Grace Atkinson remarked that the "whole thing [was] in a mess. We need[ed] a revolution *in* the revolution. We really have to get to the truth, which a lot of women are afraid of doing."[65]

What ultimately resulted was the rise of Women's Liberation, which varied considerably from the "mainstream" feminist agenda that NOW promoted. Author and activist Susan Brownmiller offered her own interpretation of the distinction between the two movements: "NOW's commitment to equal opportunity in employment was its strong suit . . . . NOW preferred to rely on traditional forms of protest: committees[,] . . . lawsuits[,] and lobbying, while Women's Liberation broke new ground through theoretical papers, imaginative confrontation, and inventive direct action."[66]

Women's Liberation groups ultimately staged the single most defining event that effectively ended a media-imposed blackout of the feminist movement: demonstrations against the 1968 Miss America Pageant. An example of "agit-prop," a term used by communists to describe how to make "revolutionary capital out of a current event,"[67] female protestors from New York, Florida, Washington, and New Jersey converged upon the pageant site in Atlantic City. They distributed leaflets to women urging them to "bring old bras, girdles, high-heeled shoes, women's magazines, curlers . . . other instruments of torture to women," as well as *Playboy* magazines, so that they could be deposited into a "Freedom Trash Can."[68]

The protestors, who refused to speak to male reporters or to identify a leader or group affiliation out of fear of collective arrest and prosecution, ultimately crowned a live sheep as the new Miss America. They also marched with signs containing phrases such as "Welcome to the Miss America Cattle Auction" and "The more I see of men, the more I like dogs."[69] The organizers of the Miss America protest later justified their actions: "All women were hurt by beauty competition—Miss America as well as ourselves. We opposed the pageant in . . . the self-interest of all women."[70]

The media responded in kind, depicting feminists as "unfeminine, unappealing women who were denouncing the importance of the lame gaze . . . . [T]he media paid inordinate attention to the way feminists violated physical and social boundaries."[71] More significantly, the media erroneously characterized these protestors as "bra-burners," a description that remains a stereotype for both feminists and liberationists. The symbolic burning of a bra had, in fact, been planned. Indeed, Robin Morgan, one of the pageant demonstrators, conceived of the idea as a symbolic equivalent to "lighting a match to a draft card[, which] has become a standard gambit of protest."[72] But Morgan was unable to secure a permit, and the idea, fittingly, went up in smoke. While no bra was ever set ablaze during the protest, a *New York Post* reporter nevertheless coined the term bra-burning, creating an indelible image of the women's rights struggle. At the same time, others contended that bra-burning was not as substantitive as some believed: "[B]raburning, seen frequently as the symbol of Women's Lib, has more to do with fashion than liberation."[73]

The media's inaccurate portrayals did, to some degree, unite activists from both the feminist and Women's Liberation movements in protest against their depictions. But radical feminists developed their own guidelines that they believed would ensure accurate and objective reporting. Under these rules, male reporters were precluded from attending any function, a move designed, in part, to force the media to take Women's Liberation seriously. On a practical level, the exclusion was intended to provide female journalists with an opportunity to report, write, and publish their own stories:

> We are not adverse to the (cautious) use of mass media, though we are not blind to its corruptions . . . . We will work only with women reporters but will inform and penalize in an appropriate manner any reporter and medium that, for whatever reason, in tone or substance, presents distorted or partial information about our group. We will also seek to form a strong coalition with other women's rights groups in order to deal more effectively with the problems and potential of the media.[74]

These preclusive policies worked.

As one reporter noted in 1970, the media's attention to the feminist and Women's Liberation movements substantially increased:

> In an age of social protest, the old cause of U.S. feminism has flared into new and angry life in the women's liberation movement . . . . [I]t is a phenomenon difficult to cover; most of the feminists won't even talk to male journalists, who are hard put in turn to tell the story with the kind of insight a woman can bring to it.[75]

Fully aware of the media's ability and perceived willingness to sabotage the movement at all costs, Ti-Grace Atkinson promulgated another strategy: a refusal to divulge too much information on the basis that anything "could be used against the movement."[76] Critics, of course, accentuated the absurdities of such tactics, referring to feminists as "hyenas in petticoats."[77] Nonetheless, the importance of factual reporting prompted *Ms.* to identify reporters at *Newsweek*, who, the editors of *Ms.* believed, "succeed[ed] . . . most of the time" at reporting news with "100% objectivity."[78]

Women's Liberation, to a much greater degree than the liberal feminism espoused by NOW and other mainstream organizations, dominated media attention, brought several key figures to prominence, and etched stereotypical portrayals of feminists into the American psyche. Ti-Grace Atkinson abandoned her position as president of the

National Women's Liberation Party members protest the Miss America Pageant in Atlantic City, New Jersey, 1968.
(Associated Press)

New York NOW chapter in order to establish the Feminists, one of the most vocal and anti-male groups in existence at the time. Unlike NOW members, Atkinson's followers rejected the concept of marriage, likening the institution to a form of slavery or legalized rape:

> If you look at the laws, [marriage] is legalized rape, causes unpaid labor, curtails a woman's freedom of movement and requires no assurances of love from a man. [Love is] tied up with a sense of dependency, and we cling to it. Those individuals who are today defined as women must eradicate their own definition. In a sense, women must commit suicide.[79]

Similarly, Shulamith Firestone and Ellen Willis broke away from the New York Radical Women and established a branch of Marxist feminists called the Redstockings. Whereas NOW promoted equal partnership in marriage, the Redstockings urged women to assume greater responsibility and define their relationships on their own terms: "Only when women have the choice . . . to be celibate, the choice to choose their sex partners (male or female) when they want them, will women be sexually free."[80]

After her participation in the Miss America protest, Robin Morgan formed her own group: WITCH. It embraced an anti-marriage platform:

> Marriage is a dehumanizing institution—legal whoredom for women. *Confront* the perpetrators of our exploitation as women. *Confront* the institutions which make us pawns in a male dominated culture . . . . The wedding ceremony is the symbolic ritual of our legal transference from father's property to husband's property. The name is changed from one man's to another's and our role as chattel in a male's house remains the same. SISTERS! Let us confront the whoremakers at the Bridal Fair but more important, confront and overthrow the institutions of marriage and capitalism which make such bridal fairs possible![81]

According to Morgan, the sexual revolution of the early 1960s was "hell on women. It never helped us—it just made us more available."[82] Other smaller groups that advocated women's sexual freedom included BITCH, Bread and Roses, the Radical Mothers, Media Women, and SCUM. SCUM promoted the belief that men were a biological accident because the Y-chromosome was actually an incomplete X-chromosome. As such, SCUM members accused men of making the world a "shitpile."[83]

* * *

NOW distanced itself from the notoriety of these Women's Liberation groups and instead garnered attention through its use of the legal and political systems. NOW's frequent litigation ultimately succeeded in changing EEOC policy by successfully instituting bans against separate male and female want-ads in newspapers and other publications across the country. NOW, together with the Women's Equity Action League, filed sex discrimination lawsuits against numerous institutions, including colleges and universities. In fact, between 1968 and 1970, NOW filed claims against Harvard and Columbia universities, the University of Michigan, and the entire Florida and New York state university systems.

NOW also became a vocal critic before Congress. Betty Friedan testified against G. Harrold Carswell, President Richard M. Nixon's nominee for the United States Supreme Court, alleging that Carswell was "insensitive" to women's issues.[84] Her testimony marked the first time in which the issue of women's rights was raised during confirmation proceedings for a Supreme Court nominee. NOW lobbyists also prompted the Senate Judiciary Subcommittee on the Constitution to hold hearings on the ERA in May 1970. The House of Representatives passed the proposed amendment that August. On March 22, 1972, the ERA was sent to the states for ratification.

Of course, NOW did not limit itself to seeking judicial remedies. As noted above, it staged the Women's Strike for Equality to commemorate the fiftieth anniversary of the passage of the Nineteenth Amendment, which guaranteed women's suffrage. Considered the "largest protest for women's equality in U.S. history," the strike sought, in addition to an end to stereotypical representations of women in the media, the creation of twenty-four-hour child-care facilities, the implementation of equal opportunities in employment and education, and the availability of free abortions.[85] Betty Friedan, who addressed an audience during the strike, recalled that the great debate of the 1960s focused upon the question "Is God Dead?"[86] The 1970s, she opined, would be characterized by the question "Is God He?"[87]

* * *

Radical feminists, as noted previously, pursued their agendas differently. Whereas *Playboy* garnered attention through the derogatory reference to title VII as the "bunny law" earlier in the decade, women began picketing the magazine's buildings as the 1960s neared an end. Students at Grinnell College, enraged by pictorial degradations of women, protested a *Playboy* representative's on-campus visit by staging a "nude-in." The appearance of a Playboy Bunny during a "Men's Day" at the University of Washington sparked numerous protests on that campus. During the summer of 1970, sixty women "seized" the Statue of Liberty, draping the monument with a banner that read "Women of the World Unite!" The protestors explained their choice of Lady Liberty: "[I]t is ironic that a woman symbolizes the abstract idea of liberty, but in reality we are not free."[88] That same year, a group of women interrupted an annual CBS stockholder's meeting and charged that the network distorted the way in which women were portrayed on television.

Another phenomenon unique to Women's Liberation was an increased emphasis upon and enrollment in karate classes. Helen Dudar explained the lure of karate:

> The lib view is that most girls, discouraged from developing their muscles, grow up soft, weak, and without any defense reflexes to speak of . . . . In the new feminist doctrine, karate is not merely a physical or psychological weapon, it is also political [since] knowing a small bit of karate is really remarkable [in that] you don't feel impotent.[89]

Karate also signaled to men that women would not tolerate being "leered at, smirked at, whistled at by men enjoying their private fantasies of rape . . . ."[90]

Liberationists addressed a wider range of women's issues than NOW. These women "gave the movement its intellectual structure" by reinterpreting the female experience and placing women at the foreground of current issues.[91] Susan Brownmiller attributed "the explosive creation of the anti-violence issues—rape, battery, incest and child molestation, sexual harassment[,] . . . anti-pornography theory[,] . . . lesbian feminism and the rise of a vital, alternative feminist press"—to Women's Liberation.[92] Underground papers such as *off our backs* and *Ain't I a Woman?* proliferated within radical feminist groups, but similar messages slowly percolated to well-established journals, albeit in more marketable manifestations.

For example, *Newsweek* featured a story describing the release of a new *Liberated Woman's Appointment Calendar and Survival Handbook*. The handbook offered karate lessons to women, quoted from "the enemy," and provided a list of survivor goals that included "[t]he first female editor of *Playboy* whose job lasts only one day because she suspends publication."[93] These themes, which originated from within radical liberationist groups, ultimately became mainstream and demonstrated that "women's lib will become part of our everyday lives."[94]

Women's rights activists place a "Women of the World Unite!" banner on the Statue of Liberty, 1970.

(CSU Archives / Everett Collection/Rex USA)

* * *

When the 1970s began, the motto "Sisterhood is powerful" was frequently shouted by many strong voices expressing discontent.[95] Yet as the decade moved forward, Women's Liberation gradually lost its momentum. In its place reemerged the mainstream feminism promoted by NOW and, with it, a change in leadership. Whereas Betty Friedan represented the voice of 1960s feminism, Gloria Steinem ultimately eclipsed her during the next decade. The waning of Women's Liberation corresponded with the rise of a conservative feminist backlash movement composed of both men and women that soon became powerful and influential. While mainstream feminism and Women's Liberation clashed against traditional gender politics and each other, the Bond franchise endured, serving as a medium through which opposition to the new gender politics could be passively promoted by perpetuating the Bond Girl archetype.

009

Perpetuating an Archetype: *You Only Live Twice* and *On Her Majesty's Secret Service*

Japanese women are just not sexy.

—Sean Connery[1]

I'm looking forward to being Bond for the broads and bread . . . . I wouldn't even care if they didn't put my name up on the marquee . . . . I've done things Bond never did—things you couldn't print.

—George Lazenby[2]

The fantasy of this superman who at the same time makes love to this series of women who fall in love with him . . . is the reality. On the other hand, there's the pure fantasy of the fact that he always gets away scot-free at the end with a lovely girl in his arms.

—Diana Rigg[3]

The publicity campaign associated with the James Bond films advanced the notion that the Bond Girl was an extremely independent, modern, and liberated woman. Claudine Auger maintained the Domino Derval, whom she portrayed in *Thunderball*, was "the ultimate in [a] modern, emancipated woman."[4] Director Terence Young characterized the Bond Girls as "women of the nuclear age, freer and able to make love when they want to without worrying about it,"[5] a sentiment that another *Thunderball* actress, Luciana Paluzzi, echoed: "All of [the Bond Girls] seem to be smart. They are not just an adornment. They always have a brain."[6] But the presentations of these characters on screen belied the platitudes that were presented to the press. Indeed, each of these descriptions reinforces a male-oriented view of female sexuality.

The Bond Girl's apparent "sexual liberation" may have simply been "enhanced liberation for men, a grand occasion for the even more ruthless sexual exploitation of women."[7] The Bond Girl, according to Luciana Paluzzi, was *not just* an adornment, though her observation implicitly conceded that the Bond Girl was an adornment of some kind. Whether these characters are depicted as free, modern, intelligent, and emancipated women, of course, is subject to considerable debate. Certainly, the casting of fashion models, pageant winners, and *Playboy* centerfolds suggests that serving as an adornment is a key—and perhaps the sole—Bond Girl attribute. In this regard, producers' focus upon aesthetics and, for example, the presentation in *Goldfinger* of the homosexual Pussy Galore within the mold of a heterosexual male fantasy, suggests that these characters are solely intended to enhance male sexual fantasy. Of course, the opinions advanced by Claudine Auger and Paluzzi must be discounted due to the actresses' vested interest in justifying the vitality of the characters they portrayed and immortalized on screen.

As the decade of the 1960s drew toward a close, the fifth and sixth installments in the franchise, *You Only Live Twice* and *On Her Majesty's Secret Service*, respectively, continued to employ the successful cinematographic formula of their predecessors. In so doing, these two films consciously and unabashedly focused upon enhancing male sexual freedom at the expense of female independence. Indeed, the Bond Girl archetype became more fully entrenched, paving the foundation for what would become a second successful decade of Bond on the big screen.

You Only Live Twice

Released in 1967, *You Only Live Twice* is the first Bond film that bears little resemblance to the Ian Fleming novel of the same name.[8] One account cited the novel's plot as too violent and sadistic for a cinematic version, so a new plot had to be devised in order to "protect the box office."[9] When screenwriter Richard Maibaum was unavailable, Cubby Broccoli and Harry Saltzman turned to noted short story writer Roald Dahl to develop a screenplay that would fit within the milieu of the series, although Dahl had no experience writing screenplays.[10] Dahl described Fleming's original novel as a travelogue rather than a workable plot,[11] recalling that *You Only Live Twice* "had virtually no semblance of a plot that could be made into a movie[, though] I could retain only four or five of the original novel's story ideas."[12] Thus, a new, original plot "us[ing] very little from Fleming's novel" was needed.[13]

When he began writing the screenplay, Roald Dahl adhered to what is referred to as the "Bond Formula," a term that describes the overall structure of and sequence in each film. Maryam d'Abo and John Cork noted that the first four Bond films incorporated three types of Bond Girls:

> There were the naïve beauties like Sylvia Trench and Patricia Fearing[,] who had no direct connection to the world of espionage, the *femme fatales* like Miss Taro and Fiona Volpe, and the 'angels with a wing down' like Tatiana Romanova, Jill Masterson, and Domino[,] who were held under the thumb of a villain.[14]

You Only Live Twice reveals a fourth type: the comrade-in-arms, a Bond Girl who is allied with Bond and finds herself on the same or similar mission.[15] In an article published in *Playboy*, Dahl revealed that he was given free reign over the plot, but "'[t]here [we]re two things you mustn't mess about with. The first is the character of Bond. That's fixed. The second is the girl formula. That is also fixed.'"[16]

The so-called "girl formula," as communicated to Roald Dahl by Broccoli and Saltzman themselves, apparently had "nothing to it."[17] Dahl recounted his conversation:

> "You use three different girls and Bond has them all . . . . So you put in three girls. No more and no less. Girl number one is violently pro-Bond. She stays around roughly through the first reel of the picture. Then she is bumped off by the enemy, preferably in Bond's arms."
>
> "In bed or not in bed?" [Dahl] asked.
>
> "Wherever you like, so long as it's in good taste. Girl number two is anti-Bond. She works for the enemy and stays around throughout the middle third of the picture. She must capture Bond, and Bond must save himself by bowling her over with sheer sexual magnetism. This girl should also be bumped off, preferably in an original fashion."
>
> "There aren't many of those left," [Dahl] said.
>
> "We'll find one," they answered. "Girl number three is violently pro-Bond. She occupies the final third of the picture, and she must on no account be killed. Nor must she permit Bond to take any lecherous liberties with her until the very end of the story. We keep that for the fade-out."[18]

Although Dahl retained Fleming's original heroine, Kissy Suzuki, another "cock-fodder" name that followed in Fleming's tradition,[19] he created the characters of Aki and Helga Brandt, the latter derived from Fiona Volpe in *Thunderball*. Thus, *You Only Live Twice* would feature an "economy of women" that was no different than its predecessors.[20]

Of course, this fact did not go unnoticed. *Time* noted that Bond was "surrounded by a scare'em harem, this time peach-skinned almond-eyed Japanese dishes."[21] One critic observed in *The New Yorker* that sexuality existed in *You Only Live Twice* "not so much in the girls themselves as in Bond's achievement of getting through as many of them as possible."[22]

The Bond Girl was everywhere in the film's advertising campaign, and for good reason. In 1967, *You Only Live Twice* was competing with the Charles K. Feldman production of *Casino Royale*,[23] which featured a "mammoth cast" of actors, including Bond alumna Ursula Andress, Peter Sellers, David Niven, Orson Wells, and John Huston.[24] Advertisements for *Casino Royale* featured the now-iconic image of a naked, tattooed woman, and *Playboy* printed a feature of the *Casino Royale* actresses. With numerous beautiful women appearing in *Casino Royale*, promoters of *You Only Live Twice* had to highlight their Bond Girls over those in Feldman's film.

Three months after the *Casino Royale* pictorial appeared in *Playboy*, the magazine presented the Bond Girls of *You Only Live Twice*. Other advertisements reflected a vigorous campaign by Broccoli and Saltzman to promote their Bond Girls over Feldman's so-called imitations. One such *You Only Live Twice* print advertisement teased audiences that "'TWICE' is much *Bondgirls!*" and contained the following quote from the *Daily News*: "For openers, 007 gets himself killed in a bedroom with a Chinese girl. But that is not the end of James Bond . . . ."[25] The saturation of Bond Girls did not go unnoticed by any means: "[L]eave it to these guys to give you what you expect, in spades: naked (well, almost) diving girls, [and] massage girls . . . ."[26] Despite the competition between *You Only Live Twice* and "the false James Bonds of *Casino Royale*,"[27] there really was no rivalry. *Casino Royale* simply could not hold its own against the Broccoli and Saltzman production.[28]

Despite the vigorous media campaign to promote the Bond Girls, producers encountered substantial difficulty casting actresses to portray the three roles.[29] For example, "Japanese officials insisted that they would only co-operate with the production if the two female leads were played by Japanese actresses."[30] Accordingly, numerous Japanese women performed screen tests. Producers quickly discovered that very few of these actresses could speak English or act, and not a single woman who auditioned for the part possessed both skills.[31] Indeed, assistant director

Poster art for the Charles K. Feldman production of *Casino Royale*, 1967.
(G. Garratt/Rex USA)

William P. Cartlidge recalled that "there was not a single Japanese actress [who] spoke English."[32]

Despite the painstaking process, the candidates were narrowed to two women, Akiko Wakabayashi and Mie Hama, both of whom were contract artists at Toho Studios.[33] Hama, "[t]he most photographed girl in her country, . . . was often described as the Japanese Brigitte Bardot."[34] *Esquire* opined that Hama was "precisely the kind of Japanese girl that will make American audiences forget Pearl Harbor."[35] *Playboy* noted that Wakabayashi, with 35-23-35½ measurements, sported a fuller mouth and darker skin than her counterpart.[36]

Both Hama and Wakabayashi were sent to England for three months in order to learn English.[37] Hama could not master the language, a problem that nearly cost her the part.[38] Ultimately, she and Wakabayashi were retained and appeared in the "007's Oriental Eyefuls" pictorial in *Playboy*'s June 1967 issue.

The next casting challenge producers encountered involved finding a "blonde, blue-eyed, tall, German girl" to portray the villain Helga.[39] Hundreds of European women interviewed and auditioned for the part. Ultimately, West German actress Karin Dor, described by Roald Dahl as "well-built,"[40] was cast, though she was nothing like what producers envisioned for Helga. Instead, producers dyed Dor's hair red and required that she wear high-heeled shoes to compensate for her short height.[41] Prior to her casting, Dor had never seen a Bond film and was entirely unfamiliar with Sean Connery.[42]

* * *

You Only Live Twice introduces an interesting twist to the Bond formula: Bond exchanges nuptials for the first—but not the last—time. During this mission, the marriage is arranged solely as a cover that will enable Bond to complete his assignment. When Bond first learns that he must "take a wife" in order to adequately pose as a Japanese man, he registers a look of shock.[43] Once this reality sets in, Bond's primary concern shifts to whether his future (and faux) wife is attractive. His inquiry prompts Tiger Tanaka, head of the Japanese Secret Service, to respond sarcastically that the putative bride has "a face like a pig."[44] Bond promptly objects: "To hell with that idea."[45] Although one critic thought Bond's concern was superfluous and wrote, in a particularly racist manner, that Asian women "could surely be told apart only by their mothers,"[46] the Far East element in *You Only Live Twice* effectuated two purposes. First, it added a visual and cultural aesthetic that was previously absent in the Caribbean, European, and American locales of the previous films. Second, it provided a built-in subtext in which the

West German actress Karin Dor, British actor Donald Pleasance, and Japanese actress Mie Hama pose on the set of *You Only Live Twice*, 1966.
(Larry Ellis/Stringer/Hulton Archive/Getty Images)

film could reinforce the beliefs and practices of a patriarchal society in which females served at the pleasure of their men.

* * *

The film's title sequence reveals at least two themes. First, the audience observes numerous images of boiling lava, which foreshadow the film's plot and, specifically, Ernst Stavro Blofeld's elaborate lair that is hidden deep within a volcano. Second, the trademark images of female silhouettes are projected against this backdrop, though the figures do not gyrate as in previous title sequences. Instead, in keeping with an Asian theme, the silhouettes feature Japanese women attired in traditional garments. Most of these silhouettes are stationary, and the women are depicted either fanning themselves or assuming traditional prayer positions. It is not until the end of the sequence that several of these women begin moving to bathe. A clear outline of their breasts, including an exposed breast, is noticeable, though the image is tastefully presented. Despite the exposed breast, the title sequence is relatively innocuous.[47] Rather than frontload the sexism, *You Only Live Twice* reserves it for later, although audiences are treated to a teaser before the credits appear.

In the pre-title sequence, Bond appears in bed with a "delectable" Chinese agent named Ling, who was portrayed by actress Tsai Chin.[48] After he embraces Ling, Bond bluntly asks, "Why do Chinese girls taste different from all other girls?"[49] Ling, smiling and displaying a slight sense of pride, asks if Bond thinks Chinese women are better, but he refuses to humor her with a definitive response. Instead, Bond responds, "No, just different. Like Peking duck is different from Russian caviar, but I love them both."[50]

Ling is an "amalgam of almost every Chinese female stereotype: a submissive sex nymph speaking in breathy, broken English, and a calculating dragon lady."[51] Having arisen from the bed, Ling stands at the doorway and replies, "Darling, I give you very best duck."[52] She then engages a button that causes Bond's bed to fold up into the wall. Ling then permits two men with machine guns to enter the room and fire at the closed bed, facilitating what ultimately becomes Bond's faux death. As soon as these assassins enter, Ling runs away and never appears again.

Ling, therefore, serves two functions. First, she is a visual stimulus. At best, she represents Bond's first sexual conquest (though it appears, as noted below, Bond and Ling do not have the time to consummate their newfound friendship) and, at worst, offers sexual innuendo to whet the audience's appetite for more. Second, she executes an order, which has been assigned to her by a nameless, faceless, and presumably male superior who requires her participation in precipitating Bond's fake demise. Later, Miss Moneypenny playfully teases Bond about Ling:

> *Moneypenny* (*typing at her desk*): Oh, by the way, how was the girl?
> *Bond* (*tilting her desk lamp so that the light is directly in her face*): Which girl?
> *Moneypenny*: The Chinese one we fixed you up with.
> *Bond*: Oh, another five minutes, and I'd have found out.
> *Moneypenny*: Hmm, she'll never know what she missed.[53]

Neither will Bond, who had to "duck" out early. It is interesting to note that Miss Moneypenny herself refers to Ling as a "girl," not as a "woman."

* * *

A "wondrously vivid" Japanese locale,[54] as noted above, enabled producers to highlight—both explicitly and implicitly—the traditional, subservient roles prescribed for women in Eastern culture. The underlying message to a Western male audience is that unwavering devotion should be universally expected from a woman, and this theme permeates the film's dialogue and its characters' actions. A careful examination reveals that the women of *You Only Live Twice* are presented primarily in service capacities, accomplishing tasks that require little, if any, mental faculties or exertion.

First, Ling arguably does not particularly aid in staging the illusion of Bond's demise, unless pressing a button on a wall constitutes aid. She neither fires a weapon nor engages in any additional conduct. Instead, the automatic mechanism of the bed essentially does all the work for her, and the two men who unload their rounds of ammunition at the folded bed finish the task. Once she opens the door to permit their entry, Ling simply escapes. None of Ling's acts is particularly compelling.

Second, most of the women of *You Only Live Twice* merely take "their place as incidentals"[55] throughout the film and are blatantly characterized as property to be used as the owner deems fit. When Tanaka invites Bond to his home, he states, "Consider my house yours, including all of my possessions, naturally."[56] As he makes this remark, the scene shifts to the interior of Tanaka's home, where four scantily clad women present themselves. The suggestion, of course, is that these women, along with inanimate objects contained in Tanaka's residence, are rightfully his "possessions."

John Brosnan characterized these women as Tanaka's "servant girls," and they serve both Bond and Tanaka with great devotion and pleasure.[57]

Bond, apparently unaccustomed to such treatment, stares at these women with admiration as he intently listens to Tanaka explain Japanese custom:

> *Tanaka*: My friend, now you take your first civilized bath.
> *Bond* (*staring as the women gather around him*): Really? Well, I like the plumbing.
> *Tanaka*: Place yourself entirely in their hands, my dear Bond-san. Rule number one is never do anything for yourself when someone else can do it for you.
> *Bond*: And rule number two?
> *Tanaka*: Rule number two: in Japan, men always come first, women come second.
> *Bond*: I might just retire to here.
> *Tanaka*: Your English girls would never perform this simple service.
> *Bond* (*suggesting his sexual prowess and usual effect upon women, particularly Miss Moneypenny*): I think I know one or two who might get around to it.[58]

As Bond and Tanaka converse, the women continue to attend to Bond. In effect, as one review sarcastically noted, "[t]heir job in the movie is to bathe Bond. A good time is had by all. The most fun is hunting for the soap."[59] When Tanaka requires their attention, he simply claps his hands and issues them further directives.

In the next bathing scene, Bond and Tanaka are soaking in separate small pools with the so-called servant girls perched next to them obsequiously watching and waiting, presumably with anticipation, for Tanaka's next command. None of these women appears particularly comfortable in their half-sitting, half-squatting positions, yet each maintains a constant gaze upon both men. Tanaka asks Bond to select a "girl," and he seems to have a difficult time making a choice. Finally, Bond makes a selection and receives approval from Tanaka, who describes the chosen woman as "very sexy-ful."[60] The chosen servant rises, gathers a towel for Bond, and, with legs outstretched, holds it out for him. The camera angle is quite effective: Bond's face is directly between her outstretched legs with his eyes looking upward, thereby creating a powerful sexual mystique. She is next seen providing Bond with a body massage, at which point Aki, unbeknownst to Bond, relieves her of her duty.

* * *

The audience is, in fact, first introduced to Aki earlier in the film when Bond attends a sumo wrestling match. There, he meets Aki, to whom he reluctantly reveals the coded message to which both the British

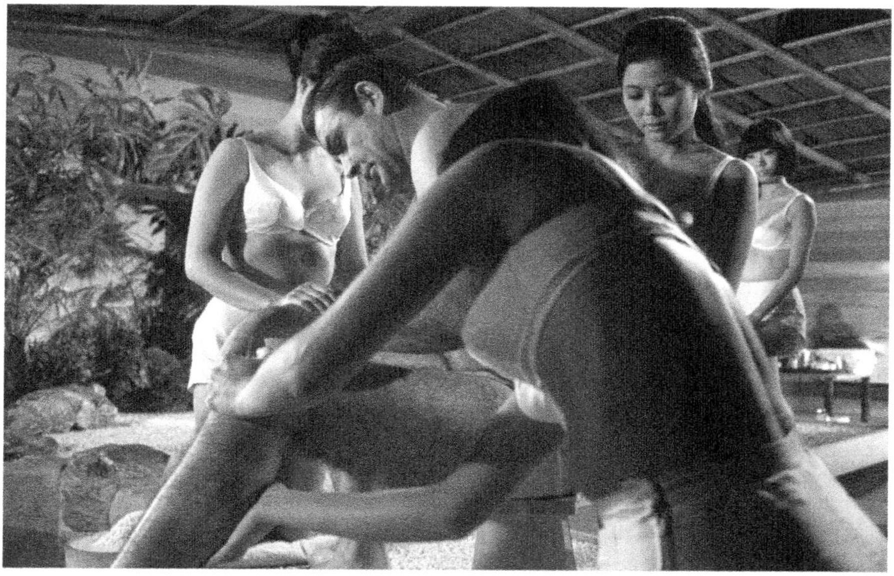

Tiger Tanaka's "servant girls" attend to James Bond (Sean Connery) in *You Only Live Twice*.
(Rex USA)

and Japanese intelligence bureaus agree for this mission: "I love you."[61] Of course, the mere thought that Bond would voluntarily express such sentiment toward a woman is fanciful, but it is for that precise reason that the message is humorous. Once contact has been successfully made, Aki indicates that she has a car waiting to transport Bond to meet a man named Henderson, who is ultimately stabbed in the back while speaking with Bond.

Aki, whom *Esquire* dubbed "Girl Friday of Tiger Tanaka" and "Tiger's Pussycat,"[62] can be best characterized as "sexual set-dressing,"[63] though she is actually a member of the Japanese Secret Service. By contrast, *Playboy* described Aki as Tanaka's "sexy secretary."[64] Most of her on-screen time involves fulfilling the role of Bond's chauffeur or participating in some type of chase, whether by car or on foot. For example, when Bond escapes from the Osato chemical plant, Aki is waiting to pick him up in a sports car. But Bond is not thoroughly convinced that Aki is an ally he can trust. Instead, his tone is firm with her as he demands answers during their getaway ride:

> *Bond*: Now what the hell's the score?
> *Aki*: What do you mean? My job is to help you.
> *Bond*: Like you helped Henderson?
> *Aki*: I'm taking you to a place of safety.
> *Bond*: No, this time, I'm taking you. I want some information and I want it now.
> *Aki*: I have no information to give you.
> *Bond*: We'll see about that. Slow down.[65]

Instead of slowing down, Aki pulls the car up to a building and runs away. Bond pursues her and eventually finds himself before Tanaka. Tanaka is amused by the "ease with which I could pull you in," suggesting that Aki is also a form of bait that Tanaka uses to facilitate their first in-person meeting.[66] He admonishes Bond: "The one thing my honorable mother taught me long ago was never to get into a car with a strange girl. But you, I'm afraid, will get into anything with any girl."[67]

Bond's relationship with Aki thaws, and when she replaces the servant girl who had been massaging Bond, she kisses him on the ear. The two embrace, and Bond picks Aki up in his arms. She responds by indicating that she "will enjoy very much serving under" Bond.[68] Her comment has two meanings. First, Aki indicates that she serves *under*, rather than *with*, Bond on this mission, thereby reaffirming Bond's authority and her subservient role. Yet it must be remembered that Aki is a member of the Japanese Secret Service, and her government is supposedly working together with MI6 on the mission. Serving *under* Bond suggests that MI6

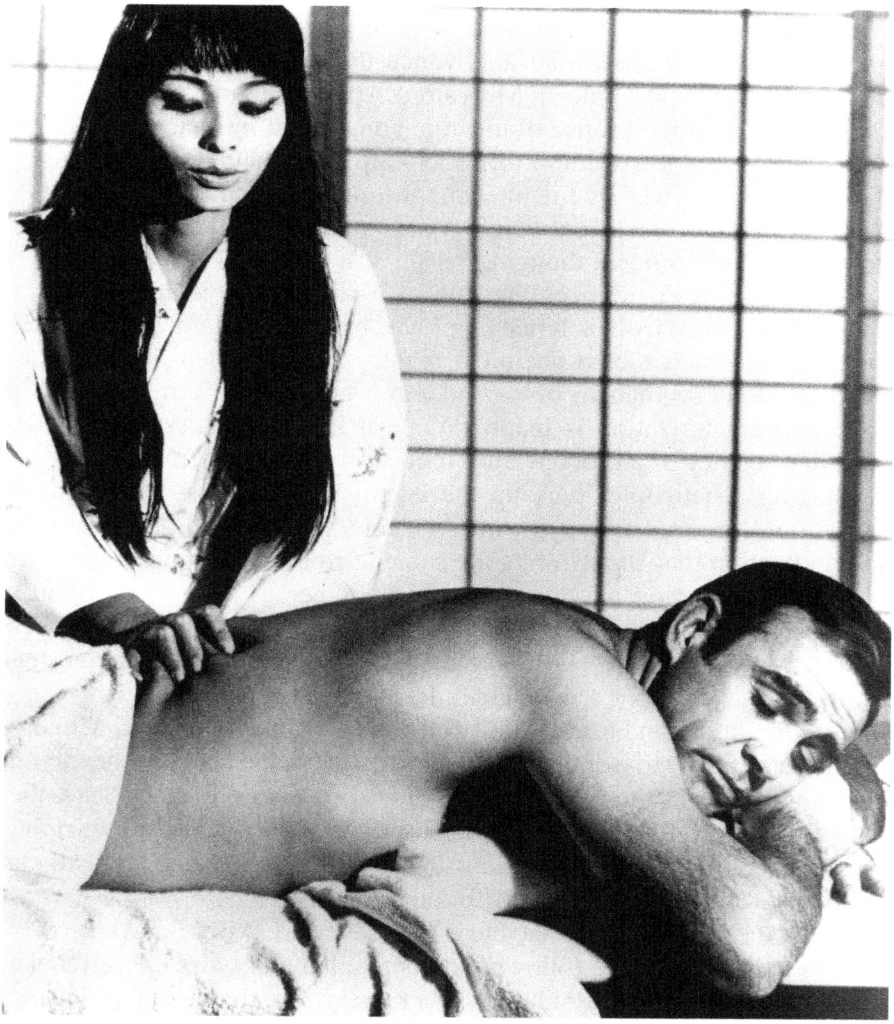

Aki (Akiko Wakabayashi) teaches James Bond (Sean Connery) the Japanese custom that "men come first" in *You Only Live Twice*.
(Everett Collection/Rex USA)

is really in charge of the operation. Second, Aki's statement is sexual innuendo, representing the fait accompli that Bond will consummate their working relationship on his terms and be both literally and figuratively in a dominant role.

It is with regard to this second interpretation that the absurdity of Aki's comment is revealed. Given that she and Bond have had very limited interaction, it is not plausible that she is already completely enamored with Bond. Their most substantive conversation, which is quoted above, produces more annoyance than anything else, let alone feelings of adoration. Indeed, Maryam d'Abo and John Cork noted that Aki exhibits a "forced sense of unearned emotional intimacy,"[69] and her immediate ability to succumb to Bond—after all, they "are not brought together through a trial by fire or even job-imposed sexual fireworks"[70]—demonstrates the extent to which Aki is pliable, impressionable, and incapable of independent thought.

Later, Aki again reprises the role of a chauffeur, picking up Bond while he is pursued by henchmen employed by Mister Osato, a SPECTRE operative and owner of a chemical plant. She has been described as the "first Bond woman to be considered a comrade in arms to 007,"[71] but this characterization is inapt. While it is true that Aki is familiar with her agency's protocols and requests the "usual reception"[72]—*i.e.*, having a helicopter pick up the enemy's automobile with a large magnet and proceed to drop it into the middle of the harbor—there is little indication that she exhibits the same attributes Bond possesses. In fact, notwithstanding another description of her as "every bit Bond's equal—in driving, fighting, running, shooting and seducing"[73]—Aki only demonstrates her driving skills, and there is little to no indication that she can fight, run, shoot, or seduce at all, let alone as well as Bond.

Indeed, during an ensuing fight scene at the Kobe docks, Aki actually offers no assistance to Bond. Instead, he grabs her hand and pulls her along with him in an effort to elude their attackers. As she follows his lead, the audience quickly forgets that Aki is supposedly a spy in her own right. She, apparently, forgets herself, refusing to leave Bond when he instructs her to contact Tanaka. Ultimately, Bond sends her away.

Later, the depth of Aki's naïvete is fully revealed. After Bond narrowly escapes a crashing plane following an entanglement with Helga, Tanaka once again admonishes Bond for his recklessness with women: "Chasing girls will be the end of you, Bond-san, I have told you that before."[74] Aki immediately comes to Bond's defense:

> *Aki*: He didn't chase her. He did it so I could get away. He wouldn't touch that horrible girl. You wouldn't, would you?
> *Bond*: Oh, heaven forbid . . . .[75]

At the beginning of her comment, Aki honestly believes that Bond would never involve himself with Helga. Yet by the end of his remark, Aki herself is no longer convinced, and her assured demeanor quickly transforms into tentativeness and speculation. Of course, Aki has no idea what Bond's motivations might be for becoming entangled with Helga. Furthermore, as Aki herself admits, Bond and Helga cross paths in order for Bond to facilitate Aki's escape. Therefore, Aki essentially can only blame herself for whatever danger befalls Bond.

Aki ultimately accompanies Bond and Tanaka on the mission, despite the fact that she is a mere accessory whose actions consist of standing and smiling. She exhibits a beaming smile across her face at the prospect of serving as Bond's wife[76] and is present at his side during Bond's plastic surgery procedure that is intended to give him a Japanese appearance. Yet Tanaka's servant girls perform the modifications. Aki does not participate, other than to watch and joke with the women throughout the procedure. Curiously, she is the only woman fully attired in the scene, which is supposed to replicate an operating room. Of the scene, John Cork and Bruce Scivally noted that "[o]nly in a 007 film will you find women in bikinis in an operating theatre."[77]

In their last scene together, Aki reminds Bond that he henceforth must do "everything Japanese style."[78] He kisses her, and there is a suggestion that the two proceed to engage in sexual relations. Later, as the two are asleep, a SPECTRE agent sent by Mister Osato attempts to kill Bond by dripping poison onto a black thread, which is slowly lowered over his mouth. Interestingly, this technique was rated by *Playboy* as the best weapon not envisioned by the Second Amendment.[79] As the poison "slides evilly down" the thread, Aki inadvertently turns her head, causing the poison to drip onto her lips.[80]

Bond is awoken by Aki's gasps and kills the intruder. He does not, however, initially respond to her. Instead, he examines the dead intruder before turning his attention to Aki. Once Tanaka arrives, Bond simply informs his counterpart that Aki is dead, he must proceed forward with the mission, and he can no longer waste time training to become Japanese. Aki ultimately dies "demurely,"[81] and Bond simply walks away.

Aki is credited with "savi[ing Bond's] life on several occasions,"[82] but this observation is misleading. By her own admission, Aki places Bond in danger by facilitating his encounter with Helga. Moreover, while she "dies in bed with 007, poisoned in an assassination attempt on his life,"[83] Aki does not intentionally save Bond from the poison drip. Rather, her involuntary movement precipitates her accidental demise. It is not possible to interpret this action, which occurs while she is asleep, in any other manner. Ultimately, Aki's importance is underscored by the fact that she is quickly forgotten, replaced entirely by another fungible woman: Kissy Suzuki.

* * *

Helga Brandt is Roald Dahl's version of an "anti-Bond bitch,"[84] a "ravishing redhead" reminiscent of Fiona Volpe.[85] Also known as Number Eleven in SPECTRE, Helga is an accomplished pilot, seductress, and assassin.[86] Yet as part of her assignment, she is relegated to assuming the stereotypical female role of a secretary to Mister Osato. Like Fiona, Helga similarly "fails to get rid of Bond with her lipstick,"[87] despite the fact that she tries multiple times to eliminate Double-O-Seven.

Helga first appears descending from Mister Osato's helicopter to attend a meeting with Bond. She wears a bright orange blouse that practically matches her hair color, carries Mister Osato's briefcase, and walks behind him at all times. Although Bond gazes at her while she prepares a cocktail for him, it is apparent that he is more interested in the liquor cabinet where he previously disposed of a body. Although he initially declines a drink, Bond ultimately accepts one from Helga, who bends down to serve him. The camera focuses upward on her figure, which produces the effect of making her bosom the centerpiece of the image. As she rises, Helga thrusts her chest forward, remarking that "Mister Osato believes in a healthy chest."[88] Once Bond leaves, Mister Osato instructs Helga to kill Bond, and she immediately endeavors to carry out this order.

Though Mister Osato instructs her to kill Bond, Helga does not actually execute what amounts to her first attempt. Instead, she sends male henchmen to do the job for her. Pulling up in a black sedan slowly behind Bond, Helga's associates proceed to shoot at him from the passenger window. Their efforts, of course, fail, and they ultimately succumb to the "usual reception" to which Aki refers: a helicopter equipped with a magnet pulls their vehicle over the harbor and strategically deposits them into the water.

Helga has another opportunity to redeem herself once Bond is captured by SPECTRE at the docks. In the following scene in Helga's cabin aboard the boat *Ning-Po*, Bond is restrained to a chair. John Brosnan described the scene: "For once[,] he's in a situation where the girl has the advantage . . . ."[89] Helga is sitting on a couch and wearing what appears to be a black cocktail dress. She instructs her henchmen to wake Bond up and to "[l]eave him to me now. Wait in there, and shut the door."[90] Standing over Bond with her hands crossed, she seductively states, "I've got you now."[91] Bond's reply, "Well, enjoy yourself," prompts her to slap him across the face.[92]

Helga immediately begins interrogating Bond, but Bond's calm and adept answers lead her to believe that he is lying. Her initial reaction, of course, is correct, and she proceeds to open a drawer containing various medical instruments. Hoisting a scalpel, she waves the instrument in Bond's face:

> *Helga*: Do you know what this is?
> *Bond*: I'd rather not.
> *Helga*: Plastic surgeons call it a dermatome. They use it to slice off skin. I hope you won't force me to use it.[93]

Notwithstanding her apparent threat and the instrument with which to carry it out close at hand, Helga simply lacks conviction. She expresses *hope* that Bond will not force her to use it. In essence, she presents Bond with a hollow threat. Although she seems to exert authority over Bond by wielding the weapon, Helga inexplicably places the dermatome into Bond's jacket pocket. As she leans in close to him, Bond seizes the opportunity to begin a seduction that is designed to facilitate his physical release on multiple levels.

Interestingly, Bond need not say much to disarm Helga. In fact, it is through Helga that "Bond demonstrates his incredible sexual magnetism."[94] As soon as he asks her what "a nice girl like you [is] doing in a place like this," Helga begins kissing him.[95] Given the expression on her face, it is apparent that Helga is captivated by Bond and physically aroused by their kiss. Bond, of course, sees the opportunity to capitalize upon Helga's weaknesses.

In this regard, Helga is quite more malleable than Fiona, who is simply incapable of being diverted from her mission to kill Bond. Bond devises a ploy to convince Helga to release him from bondage, feigning a confession that he is an industrial spy. Helga, however, claims that she already knows this and continues to kiss him. Either she has not fully understood what Bond has just revealed due to her preoccupation, or she is easily duped. Regardless, Bond elaborates, explaining that he has stolen Mister Osato's process for making monosodium glutamate and that industrial secrets are big business. Helga is unimpressed by this revelation and remains preoccupied with her own arousal. Thus, Bond persists, suggesting that he will split with her the proceeds from this stolen process, which he estimates is worth $300,000, if Helga "get[s] me out of here and back to Tokyo."[96]

Helga removes the dermatome from Bond's jacket pocket, remarks that Mister Osato would kill her, and declines Bond's offer. She immediately changes her mind when Bond suggests that they could fly to Europe together the next day. Bond then completely disarms her, removing the dermatome from her hand and "return[ing] the favor by cutting her free of her dress."[97] As she embraces him, Bond offers a brief soliloquy, "Oh, the things I do for England,"[98] and the scene fades out. Helga has now failed twice in her attempt to kill Bond.

Bond has successfully diverted Helga's focus away from her assignment. Of course, she has Bond bound and in a compromising position that easily affords her an opportunity to eliminate him. Yet she succumbs to Bond's charm and becomes easily distracted, characteristics that are certainly unbecoming of a supposed professional assassin. Once their sexual encounter has concluded, Helga proceeds, once again, to plot Bond's demise.

In the next scene, Helga appears to be piloting a small plane with Bond as the passenger behind her, but the audience only sees her applying makeup. She intentionally drops her lipstick, which explodes and fills the cabin with smoke. Thereafter, she disengages a bar that constrains Bond's hands and jumps out of the plane with a parachute. Her intention is to leave Bond in the rapidly descending plane, but Bond narrowly escapes before it crashes. Helga has now failed to kill Bond for the third time.

Helga is not extended another opportunity to complete her assignment, her third strike constituting her last. When she next appears, Helga is summoned, along with Mister Osato, by Blofeld. Blofeld deliberately refuses to acknowledge her presence. Instead, all of his questions are directed toward Mister Osato. Again standing behind Mister Osato, Helga is unnerved. As Blofeld reveals that Bond is alive, Helga's eyes move rapidly to each side, further evidence of her culpability and failure to carry out her orders. Of course, both she and Mister Osato are shocked by Blofeld's revelation, but Mister Osato attributes the failure to kill Bond to Helga:

> *Blofeld*: Bond is alive. Unless you killed him, Mister Osato? Don't tell me you let him go.
> *Mister Osato*: I gave Number Eleven the strictest orders to eliminate him.
> *Blofeld*: And did she?
> *Mister Osato*: She failed.
> *Helga*: You should have killed him yourself! You had plenty of opportunity!
> *Blofeld*: This organization does not tolerate failure.[99]

Of note is the fact that neither Blofeld nor Mister Osato refers to Helga as if she is present, but she lingers before Blofeld as if paralyzed. Finally, she is ordered to leave. While Helga follows Mister Osato toward the

Helga Brandt (Karin Dor) pilots an ill-fated flight in her latest attempt to kill James Bond in *You Only Live Twice*.
(Everett Collection/Rex USA)

exit, Blofeld causes a section of a bridge, over which is a small pool filled with piranhas, to give way. Consequently, Helga experiences a highly sadistic and painful death as she is "eaten alive, dropped into a private pool of man-eaters through a trick floor."[100] One article described Helga as suffering "a death worse than fate: dumped into a pool of hot lava."[101]

It is possible to view Helga as a step backward in Bond villainy, particularly when compared to Fiona. At the same time, Helga represents a much more traditional female character than Fiona. While Fiona is stubborn, obstinate, and hypersexual, Helga displays some degree of plausible vulnerability. Fiona continually pursues Bond with reckless abandon, yet Helga is not as intent. Helga is presented with at least three opportunities to kill Bond, but she cannot follow through at all, compromising SPECTRE's mission in the process. While Helga may have ample opportunity to dispose of Bond, she is more detached from the plot, exhibiting a willingness to defer to others, which permits her to deflect responsibility for shortcomings or to fall back upon the malfunctions of modern technology. Fiona, by contrast, seems more willing to actively participate in her assassinations. Essentially, Helga "is given little to do in comparison with Fiona,"[102] and what little she is given is performed with ineptitude, save for her ability to succumb to Bond, which is achieved with great aplomb. Imbued with more traditional traits than Fiona, Helga is practically a villainous mirror image of Aki.

* * *

Aki is succeeded by Kissy, who "suffers the indignity of receiving no on-screen introduction . . . ."[103] A "pearl-diving *ama* girl,"[104] Kissy is, for the most part, seen wearing bikinis, much like Domino before her. Her attire essentially defines the substance of her character. As *Esquire* noted in its pictorial of Hama, Kissy simply "wears the hell out of this white bikini . . . ."[105]

Kissy has the distinction of becoming Bond's first wife, though, as noted above, Bond is distraught over the fact that she will have the "face of a pig."[106] His nervousness, however, turns to pleasant delight when he sees Kissy for the first time at their arranged faux wedding. Although their marriage is purely an affront, Bond nonetheless attempts to convince Kissy that they should consummate their union, expressing disappointment that he will endure an "unsatisfactory wedding night"[107] with her:

> *Kissy*: This is my house. My friend has made us some food.
>
> *Bond*: Do you live here alone?
>
> *Kissy*: Yes. My parents are dead. Sit down, please.

> *Bond*: Oysters. Is this the only room there is?
> *Kissy*: Yes. (*pointing behind him*) That is your bed. I shall sleep over there. (*pointing in a different direction*)
> *Bond*: We're supposed to be married.
> *Kissy*: Think again, please. You gave false name to priest.
> *Bond*: Yes, but we must keep up our appearances. We're on our honeymoon.
> *Kissy*: No honeymoon. This is business.[108]

Bond pushes away the oysters, concluding that their aphrodisiac qualities are wasted since he will not be engaging in any bedroom activities thereafter. While this dialogue suggests that Bond feels confined or restricted by this so-called "marriage" and that Kissy seems to have the upper hand, her pushback is only temporary and merely delays the inevitable. In fact, Kissy's initial refusal of Bond's advances only encourages him to seduce her with renewed effort.

Although she does not permit Bond to consummate their "marriage," Kissy willingly submits to Bond in every other respect. She wears a bikini while they scale a volcano together, despite the fact that Bond is fully clothed. Bond expresses uncertainty that she can handle the physical exertion, but Kissy follows him because "it's business."[109] Yet at the same time, Kissy has to request permission to rest along the way. Sprawling out and supporting her weight with her arms to thrust her bosom forward, Kissy informs Bond that it is hard work to scale the volcano. Her comment actually empowers Bond, who utilizes her apparent exhaustion as an opportunity to kiss her. But Bond is not focused upon Kissy. Instead, even as his lips are locked with hers, Bond's attention is on the mission as his eyes follow a helicopter that seems to descend into the volcano. A completely subservient Kissy is then instructed to "get back to Tanaka, tell him to come here with every man he's got."[110] She obligingly replies, "Yes," and leaves.[111]

Gary Giblin and Lisa Neyhouse suggested that Kissy "indirectly saves Bond's life by sending for the Cavalry,"[112] but it is clear that she does so only upon his instruction. They characterized Kissy as a strong feminist, noting that she "swims, dives, runs, climbs, [and] shoots and dodges bullets as well as Bond,"[113] but the ability to swim, dive, run, and climb hardly qualifies Kissy as an admirable character. She does dodge rifle fire from a helicopter as she swims, but Giblin and Neyhouse's assessment of Kissy is hardly complimentary. Moreover, Kissy is forced to participate in a sham marriage in order to advance Bond's mission and Tanaka's objectives. In this respect, she actually serves two masters.

During the climactic fight scene in Blofeld's volcanic headquarters, Kissy is seen firing a gun once, but she hides behind Tanaka the remainder of the time. In fact, she shadows Tanaka and offers no additional assistance. Instead, Tanaka discharges his weapon while Kissy merely grimaces from behind his shoulder. In essence, she is potentially a liability as both Bond and Tanaka are obligated to watch after her and ensure that she emerges unharmed. Once the conflict concludes and she and Bond are safely aboard a raft, Bond commands her to "stay,"[114] much like he would instruct a dog. When he suggests that they actually commence a honeymoon, Kissy now offers no objection, instead expressing concern that her rendezvous with Bond would be short-lived since he would not remain in Japan.

Kissy, therefore, is hardly the "thorough, no-nonsense professional" that Gary Giblin and Lisa Neyhouse perceived.[115] Maryam D'Abo and John Cork conceded that Kissy, along with the other female characters in the film, "have little impact on the plot. Bond does not save them and they do not make an important choice to save Bond."[116] In many respects, Kissy resembles Honey Ryder, who finds herself entangled in Bond's mission on Crab Key. Kissy intends to keep her relationship with Bond strictly professional, but she fails to maintain the appropriate distance and easily succumbs to Bond's charm. She accompanies Bond but offers no aid. Instead, she adeptly follows orders: first from Tanaka, who requires that she portray Bond's wife, and then from Bond, who requires her to accompany him to Blofeld's volcano and later report to Tanaka. As a conduit between Bond and Tanaka, Aki serves no more meaningful a role. Rather, it is apparent that the film highlights expedient dynamics that are framed by Bond's need to successfully complete the mission.

* * *

You Only Live Twice presents the archetype of an extremely willing, submissive female. Its incorporation of traditional Japanese gender roles reinforces the notion that men not only should, but actually do, take precedence over women. In this regard, the Bond Girls seem like an afterthought. None is particularly memorable. Aki, of course, is completely forgotten within the film itself, and Helga leaves no comparable impression to Fiona Volpe. Moreover, Aki and Kissy are virtually indistinguishable from each other, and neither character has any development or story to which the audience can relate. Indeed, one critic relegated both Aki and Kissy to the realm of mere "scenery."[117] And yet, even the scenery was deemed unsexy by some. According to critic Penelope Gilliatt, *You Only Live Twice* presented Bond with "numb leading ladies" who, as "affable sexpots[,] . . . are killed off at a rate of knots and . . . are subsumed into one long, cool act of painless ditching."[118]

After defeating Ernst Stavro Blofeld, James Bond (Sean Connery) embraces Kissy Suzuki (Mie Hama) aboard a raft in *You Only Live Twice*.

(Keystone Features/Stringer/Hulton Archive/Getty Images)

Bond, too, succumbed to criticism, even though the film was described as "'a good buy,' the best package of entertainment that skill and ingenuity and money can provide" and "probably the best of the Bonds to date."[119] *Time* characterized Sean Connery as "uncomfortable and fatigued,"[120] while one critic noted that the "sex is minimal. But, then, Bond is getting old."[121] *Newsweek*'s Paul D. Zimmerman observed that "Connery himself looks worn, playing out his mission with little more than impeccable good manners and a firm sense of smile."[122] Another critic characterized *You Only Live Twice* as lame,[123] while Simon Winder described the film to *New York Times* readers as "too bloated and depressing," which required "a corrective process . . . of weaning Bond off his gadgets . . . in favor of the small scale and mildly realistic."[124]

When Bond returned two years later in *On Her Majesty's Secret Service*, producer Peter Hunt did exactly that, modeling the screenplay after Fleming's novel, disposing of lavish sets, and concentrating upon the personalities of the characters[125] in what would be a "fine adventure story with plenty of human interest . . . ."[126] Of course, particular interest was placed upon Bond and perpetuating the franchise, especially given Sean Connery's eventual departure. As in *You Only Live Twice*, Bond marries, though the wedding in which he participates in *On Her Majesty's Secret Service* is separate and distinct from any mission objective. As explained below, Bond's initial intentions to wed are far from sincere or genuine, and the primary Bond Girl, who would continue along her preordained path, ultimately suffers dire consequences.

On Her Majesty's Secret Service

The 1969 film was actually planned to succeed *Goldfinger*, but plans to bring it to the screen were delayed for several years. Following the filming of *Thunderball*, producers again slated *On Her Majesty's Secret Service* as the next installment and initiated an "expensive talent hunt for twelve international beauties to appear in the film with Sean Connery."[127] Nevertheless, filming did not materialize, and the casting call was abandoned.

Once Sean Connery informed Broccoli and Saltzman that *You Only Live Twice* was his last Bond film, the two producers were left, on one hand, with the unenviable and "formidable" task of finding a replacement for *On Her Majesty's Secret Service*.[128] On the other hand, the head-to-head competition between *Casino Royale* and *You Only Live Twice* signaled to Broccoli and Saltzman that "James Bond the character was the key ingredient" to the future success of the franchise, rather than the actor portraying Bond.[129] The casting change enabled producers to reassess the substance of the next Bond as the late 1960s brought about substantial social change.

Producers and directors interviewed and screen-tested hundreds of actors for the role of Bond during the course of four months,[130] eventually realizing that they were seeking, in essence, a second Connery.[131] Peter Hunt recalled: "[I]t was agreed by practically everybody in the end that . . . what we wanted was another Sean Connery."[132] Australian George Lazenby, who had minimal acting experience in small television commercial roles and had modeled in England,[133] was ultimately selected.

Despite their choice, producers continued searching for another actor.[134] George Lazenby was ultimately retained because, as Peter Hunt explained, he exuded "an air of sexual confidence" much like Sean Connery had before him.[135] It was also generally agreed that Lazenby could be "groom[ed] for the role."[136] Whereas *You Only Live Twice* "can be easily differentiated from the other James Bond movies because it's the Japanese one,"[137] *On Her Majesty's Secret Service* is easily distinguishable as Lazenby's sole performance as Bond.

Without Sean Connery, the film's advertising campaign downplayed the casting of George Lazenby and the introduction of a new Bond. Although producers initially intended for Lazenby to continue as Bond in future films, that scenario would not occur, but it was not merely the result of what was described as the "strait-laced gaffe" of Lazenby's casting.[138] After several behind-the-scenes conflicts and a public relations nightmare, Saltzman decided to pull the plug on Lazenby:

> I think it's true that they like Lazenby's Bond in America. I also think it's true that the man who plays Bond is not the most important thing in the films. We've discovered that since Sean left us. We have not even started looking for a man to play Bond yet. But you can take it as sure that it will not be George Lazenby.[139]

Despite the notion that *On Her Majesty's Secret Service* was "fatally flawed" on account of Lazenby,[140] whom *The Times* noted brought "to his part all the expressiveness of an Easter Island statue"[141] and one American critic described as filling the role of Bond "the way concrete fills a hole,"[142] the film still ranked as the most successful in Great Britain throughout 1970.[143] Indeed, one columnist noted that an assessment of the film should not succumb to the confusion of "George Lazenby's patent unsuitability for the role of 007—his one and only assumption of it—with the overall quality of the film itself."[144]

Maryam d'Abo and John Cork wrote that the only real agreement about *On Her Majesty's Secret Service* has been its atypical departure from the remainder of the Bond franchise.[145] Of course, the popularity of

On Her Majesty's Secret Service stemmed from the fact that it displayed "the usual acreage of female flesh."[146] Furthermore, the film's success can be attributed to the fact that George Lazenby "play[ed] a decidedly second fiddle to an overabundance of continuous action" taking place around Bond.[147]

Alongside George Lazenby, producers featured a strong supporting cast of well-known actors, most notably with their casting of the primary Bond Girl in the film, Countess Teresa "Tracy" di Vicenzo. After attempts to secure French actress and "sex kitten" Brigitte Bardot failed, the part went to seasoned Shakespearean actress Diana Rigg, who was one of the most popular British actresses at the time and who had replaced Honor Blackman on *The Avengers*.[148] In a deliberate attempt to eschew the "Bond woman iconography" that had been developed since *Dr. No*, producers selected Rigg because she "look[ed] the part," had the experience needed to "hedge against box office disaster,"[149] and could "increase the power of the film's romantic scenes."[150] According to Graham Rye, Rigg "brought a freshness and vitality to the part,"[151] though *The Times* noted that Rigg portrayed "the future Mrs. Bond with more wit and intelligence than the lines deserve."[152] Critiquing the film in the *New York Times*, Vincent Canby echoed a similar sentiment, suggesting that Rigg's "presence makes everything around her look even more dull and foolish than is absolutely necessary."[153]

* * *

On Her Majesty's Secret Service features many firsts. In addition to the significant casting change and effort to imbue the series with a more humanistic approach, the film prominently displays an issue of *Playboy*. Bond breaks into an office and discovers the magazine hidden within a newspaper. Apparently delighted by his discovery, Bond is then seen smirking as he turns the magazine sideways to view the entire centerfold pictorial. Of course, he leaves the office with the *Playboy*, continuing to view it unabashedly with delight while he walks down the hallway.[154]

The film also introduces a harem theme. Twelve beautiful women, who are admitted to Ernst Stavro Blofeld's Swiss clinic under the guise of patients seeking treatment for numerous allergies, are introduced to Bond and the audience over a sultry soundtrack, a similar device employed in *Goldfinger* when Pussy Galore's Flying Circus pilots appear. Dubbed by Blofeld as his Angels of Death, these women hail from various locations around the world, having been handpicked so that they can be brainwashed and "return[ed] to their homes across the globe with a bacteriological agent that can devastate crops and livestock, throwing the global economy into turmoil."[155] As Blofeld informs Bond, these women will unwittingly aid in his dissemination of Virus Omega, a disease that will induce "total infertility in plants and animals."[156]

The Angels of Death appear in various forms of attire, some more revealing than others. They also engage in a variety of activities, from crocheting to playing dice, while the main henchwoman of the film, Irma Bunt, supervises them. The Angels of Death are captivated by Bond's presence and are extremely inquisitive as they gather around him. For example, a feisty woman with short curly hair and an impish smile named Ruby Bartlett states that "it's a treat having a man here for once."[157] Similarly, a blonde woman named Nancy sits perched on the floor and desperately implores Bond, who has assumed the alias of genealogist Sir Hilary Bray, to explain his line of work. In fact, each seems extremely interested in Bond's genealogy book. Young, attractive, impressionable, submissive, and passive, these Angels of Death are merely "playthings"[158] in all respects, and Bond does not pass up an opportunity to enjoy them, regardless of whether it compromises his cover and the mission.

* * *

Bond's first conquest of an Angel of Death occurs with Ruby, whose blatant flirtations with Bond culminate with her writing her room number on the inside of Bond's thigh with lipstick during a communal dinner. Ruby was portrayed by British actress Angela Scoular, who died tragically in 2011.[159] Afterwards, Bond sneaks into her room, where he discovers her naked in bed. His seduction of her is virtually effortless:

> *Bond*: I've brought you the book.
> *Ruby*: The illustrated book? (*reaching to turn on the light*)
> *Bond*: No, don't turn it on.
> *Ruby*: I want to see the pictures.
> *Bond*: But you're a picture yourself, and twice as lovely in the firelight.
> *Ruby*: You are funny at pretending not to like girls.
> *Bond*: Well, I don't usually, but you're not usual. That lipstick was an inspiration. So are you.[160]

Bond and Ruby consummate their newfound friendship, and afterwards she smiles and seems fully satisfied when she turns over to kiss Bond. Any further embrace, however, is interrupted by the timed commencement of Blofeld's alleged cure of Ruby's supposed allergy, which places Ruby into a hypnotic state. Bond leaves her room when it becomes clear to him that Ruby is nonresponsive.

James Bond (George Lazenby) enjoys the company of Ernst Stavo Blofeld's "Angels of Death" in *On Her Majesty's Secret Service*.
(Apic/Hulton Archive/Getty Images)

But all is not lost for Bond, who returns to his room and discovers that Nancy is waiting for him. She, like Ruby, is interested in seeing the genealogy book, but Bond has other ideas. His seduction of her, too, is virtually effortless. At the same time, it is comical, given the striking similarities he employs with Ruby earlier that same evening:

> *Nancy*: I come to see the book, the pictures, yes?
> *Bond*: Oh, jolly good idea. Now, where did I put it? Hmm, I had it a few moments ago.
> *Nancy*: Perhaps if we turn on the light. (*reaching for the lamp*)
> *Bond*: No. (*grabbing her hand*) You're a picture yourself. And twice as lovely in the firelight.
> *Nancy*: But, Sir Hilary.
> *Bond*: Hilly.
> *Nancy*: But I think you do not like girls, Hilly.
> *Bond*: Usually I don't, but you're not usual. Coming here like this was an inspiration, and so are you.
> *Nancy*: Mmm.
> *Bond* (*mumbling to himself*): You'll need to be.
> *Nancy*: What you say?
> *Bond* (*correcting himself*) I said a miracle our meeting like this. I don't even know your name.
> *Nancy*: I tell you all about myself later . . . (*wrapping her arms around Bond, falling backward onto the bed, and bringing him atop her*) . . . in the morning.[161]

Bond has now enjoyed the pleasure of two women, back-to-back, in one night. As Maryam d'Abo and John Cork suggested, the introduction of these two sexual interests and the Angels of Death represented "a nod from the filmmakers and Fleming to the audience's desire to see Bond surrounded by more than one beautiful woman, even in a film where he marries the heroine."[162] Of note is Bond's remark that Nancy must be an inspiration for him, a reality check that even the sexually potent Bond can only take so much stimulation in a short period of time.

Interestingly, the Angels of Death are, in essence, a precursor to the characters in the popular television drama *Charlie's Angels*. They represent instruments through which an enigmatic commander, here represented as Blofeld, carries out his plans in order to achieve a particular outcome. Blofeld does not, of course, intend to release the Virus Omega himself. Instead, he controls the women's actions, much to the same degree that the mysterious Charlie tasks his "angels" with a mission and relies upon them to complete it. The following dialogue between Bond and M highlights the extent to which Blofeld's Angels of Death are pawns:

> *M*: Those girls. God knows how many, let alone where.
> *Bond*: Sir, if we destroy the center of communication that controls those girls, without Blofeld's voice those girls can do nothing.[163]

The key word employed is "control," which makes clear that the Angels of Death simply have no will of their own. Both their anonymity and superfluity are confirmed by the film's own credits wherein only Ruby and Nancy are listed as character names under the heading "The Girls."[164] The credits then display the remaining Angels of Death based upon their ethnicity or geographical origin: American, Australian, Chinese, English, German, Indian, Irish, Israeli, Jamaican, and Scandinavian.[165]

As noted previously, Bond's desire to have affairs with these women ultimately compromises both his cover and his mission. Sneaking into Ruby's room once again, he unexpectedly encounters Irma Bunt in bed: "Fancy meeting you here, Fraulein."[166] He is then hit in the head by a henchmen and brought to Blofeld, who informs Bond that "[r]espectable baronets from the college of heralds do not seduce female patients in clinics."[167]

* * *

Irma Bunt is essentially an homage to Rosa Klebb. Middle-aged, toady, and displaying a constant scowl across her brow, Bunt, who was portrayed by German actress Ilse Steppat, carefully monitors the Angels of Death to ensure that their interactions with Bond are minimal. She also drugs these women as part of the final stage of Blofeld's brainwashing scheme.

While it is not suggested that Bunt shares the same sexual proclivities as Klebb, she does share Klebb's strict disciplinarian constitution and executes Blofeld's orders with neither hesitation nor reservation. Just as Bond fails to kill Klebb, he also is unable to dispose of Bunt, and Bunt therefore is able to carry out her most significant action at the conclusion of the film. In his fictional biography of Bond, John Pearson described Double-O-Seven embarking on a trip to Australia to pursue Bunt and exact revenge.

* * *

Perhaps the most memorable element of *On Her Majesty's Secret Service* is that Bond marries Tracy, the film's most tragic figure. Diana

Rigg described Tracy as “a bit of a mixed up lady,”[168] and she is unlike any other Bond Girl who precedes her. The “emotionally distraught daughter” of Marc-Ange Draco, himself the leader of an influential crime syndicate,[169] Tracy’s introduction to the audience is aberrational. Whereas each previous Bond Girl is initially presented in a sexually charged atmosphere, Tracy is first seen attempting suicide by drowning herself into the ocean “in a shimmering emerald dress.”[170]

The film opens with her attempting her own death. Bond is driving along the Portuguese coastline when a red sports car driven by a young woman speeds past him. In a scene reminiscent of *Goldfinger* in which Bond and Tilly Masterson engage in a high-speed chase, Bond seems intrigued and “overtaken,”[171] coolly contemplating whether he should follow the sports car as he lights a cigarette. Turning a curve in the road, Bond finds the sports car abandoned with its door open. Using a telescope, he observes the woman walking into the surf fully clothed. John Brosnan described the scene as “beautifully photographed . . . with the girl, dressed in a flimsy gown that makes her look like a large butterfly, walking into a huge moonlit sea.”[172] Indeed, the scene evokes the image of author Kate Chopin’s protagonist Edna Pontellier in her groundbreaking 1899 novel *The Awakening*,[173] though Tracy’s attempt to commit suicide is interrupted. Bond, “always ready to help a lady in distress,”[174] immediately drives his car down the hill toward the shore and runs into the water after her.

Bond grabs Tracy from behind, prompting her to scream “No,” but while his efforts are initially met with protest, she ultimately collapses into Bond’s arms.[175] Bond then smacks her face to induce consciousness, but their encounter is interrupted by two henchmen, one of whom drags Tracy away. Tracy eventually escapes and speeds away in her automobile, leaving Bond on the beach. No Bond Girl previously exhibited such behavior, but producers created the perfect moment in which to introduce audiences to George Lazenby’s version of Bond. Reflecting upon the entire ordeal he has just experienced, Bond sarcastically quips, “This never happened to the other fellow!”[176]

* * *

The title credits that follow the self-destructive imagery of the pre-title sequence bring the audience back to traditional elements of the franchise. Although naked silhouettes of “writhing nymphets” with flowing hair are presented throughout,[177] they are secondary to the overall theme, which is designed to provide continuity following Sean Connery’s departure. Scenes from previous films are superimposed within the image of an hourglass, creating a sense of nostalgia as the hands of a clock move in a counterclockwise direction. Maurice Binder chose this theme in order to reassure audiences that "while the actor may have changed, the character is the same."[178] Not surprisingly, the images chosen to represent Bond's prior missions are his sexual conquests: Honey Ryder, Tatiana Romanova, Pussy Galore, Domino Derval, Aki, and Kissy. The sequence concludes with six naked silhouettes kneeling. The audience is left to wonder whether Tracy will survive long enough to include herself in exclusive company.

* * *

Bond is both puzzled and intrigued by the mysterious woman he encounters at the beach. He notices her car at a hotel and inquires to whom it belongs. That evening, Bond finds Tracy at the *chemin de fer* table. Wearing all white, she bends down to reveal her bosom and places a substantial bet she cannot cover, itself another "self-destructive act."[179] When she loses, Tracy expresses her inability to pay. Bond, who is distracted by her appearance, comes to her rescue yet again: "Forgive me, my mind was elsewhere. Madame has forgotten we agreed to be partners this evening."[180] Tracy, visibly agitated, walks away, but Bond, once again, follows.

Tracy reveals a cold demeanor accompanied by general disinterest, leaning her head against her palm and exhibiting body language that indicates she has no desire to converse with Bond. And yet, Tracy turns the tables on him:

> *Tracy*: Why do you persist on rescuing me, Mister Bond?
> *Bond*: It's becoming a habit, isn't it, Contessa Teresa?
> *Tracy*: Teresa was a saint. I'm known as Tracy.
> *Bond*: Well, Tracy, next time play it safe and stand on five.
> *Tracy*: People who want to stay alive play it safe.
> *Bond*: Please stay alive, at least for tonight.
> *Tracy* (*getting up and throwing her room key on the table*): Come later. I hope you'll be worth it, partner.[181]

Bond is perplexed by what has just unfolded, but it is apparent that Tracy believes that submitting herself to Bond is the most convenient way to repay him for covering her debt. For Bond, Tracy's sexual offer simply cannot be passed up.

Tracy, however, is not in her hotel when Bond arrives. Instead, he encounters a henchman and, having disposed of him, returns to his own suite. There, he discovers Tracy, who has stealthily removed Bond's gun from his holster. Wearing a brassier that is exposed underneath an open

James Bond (George Lazenby) rescues a suicidal Countess Teresa "Tracy" di Vicenzo (Diana Rigg) and encounters an adversary, Raphael (Terry Mountain), in *On Her Majesty's Secret Service*.

(Larry Ellis Collection/Hulton Archive/Getty Images)

bathrobe, Tracy points the gun at Bond. Exhibiting a cool and calculating demeanor, Tracy approaches Bond. Although the gun is pointed in his direction, Bond remains in complete control of the situation:

> *Bond*: You're full of surprises, Contessa.
> *Tracy*: So are you, Mister Bond. Do you always arm yourself for a rendezvous?
> *Bond* (*approaching her*): Occasionally, I seem to be accident prone. I'll take that, if you don't mind? (*holding out his hand to take back his gun*)
> *Tracy*: You're very sure of yourself, aren't you? Suppose I were to kill you for a thrill?
> *Bond*: I can think of something more sociable to do.[182]

While it has been suggested that Tracy is simply "playing hard to get" in these scenes,[183] her behavior is both erratic and puzzling. In order to effectively put Tracy in her place, Bond resorts to physical aggression, firmly grabbing her wrist and causing her to drop the gun. As he literally twists her arm, Bond directs Tracy to "stop playing games."[184] Her only response is that Bond is hurting her. Bond simply does not care, responding callously, "I thought that was the idea."[185]

Bond's interrogation to ascertain who assailed him in Tracy's suite yields no answer, and as such, Bond slaps her across the face. His resort to physical violence with Tracy is swift, even suggesting that he can subject her to even greater pain: "I can be a lot more persuasive," he remarks.[186] Tracy, clearly shaken by his conduct, simply replies, "I'm sure you can," as she attempts to maintain her composure.[187] Thereafter, Bond forcefully pushes her away and commands her to dress. The scene essentially channels the violence Bond exhibits toward Tatiana Romanova during their train ride in *From Russia With Love*.

Their dynamic thus far is characterized solely in terms of tension and conflict. Tracy makes matters worse by disobeying Bond. Rather than dress, Tracy gets into Bond's bed and stares blankly in front of her, detaching herself from the reality in which she finds herself. Bond's forcefulness is soon replaced with concern as Tracy provides a slight glimpse of her fractured psyche:

> *Bond*: You know, you're the most extraordinary girl.
> *Tracy*: I'm not interested in your opinion of me, Mister Bond. I'm here for a business transaction.
> *Bond*: Really? (*holding up her wrist to his nose and smelling her perfurme*) Isn't Le Bleu a bit heady for that?
> *Tracy*: So, you know your perfumes, what else do you know?

Countess Teresa "Tracy" di Vicenzo (Diana Rigg) surprises James Bond in his hotel suite in *On Her Majesty's Secret Service*.
(Everett Collection/Rex USA)

> *Bond*: A little about women.
> *Tracy* (*turning her head to face him*): Think about me as a woman you've just bought.
> *Bond*: Who needs to buy? (*moving to kiss her, though she turns her head away*) Look, you don't owe me a thing. (*taking her hand in his*) I think you're in some sort of trouble. Would you like to talk about it?
> *Tracy*: No, Mister Bond. The only thing you need know about me is that I pay my debts.
> *Bond*: Twenty thousand francs is a lot of money.
> *Tracy* (*nodding*): Mmm.[188]

Rather than reveal too much, Tracy reaches up and embraces Bond.

Tracy pays her debt to Bond by submitting to him sexually, despite the fact that Bond no longer seems interested in a sexual encounter. He does not object, of course, to her initiation. At the same time, this encounter ultimately begins Bond's process of repositioning Tracy, slowly reining in her reckless, wild, destructive personality and beginning her transition toward becoming a more "respectable" woman.

The next morning, Bond awakens to an empty bed, with Tracy having adopted the Ian Fleming habit of not remaining with a lover overnight. Although Bond's gun is missing, he finds twenty thousand francs in his night table drawer. He reflects aloud, with a bit of a smirk, "Paid in full as well."[189] Tracy has, in fact, paid her debt, but at what price to her? The free-spirited, independent behavior she displays is ultimately self-destructive and must be stripped from her if she is to survive. Indeed, the film's focus upon Tracy turns toward subduing her and reforming her conduct so that she can exhibit socially acceptable behavior that is becoming of a woman. Bond is tasked with the unenviable task of serving as her personal savior.

* * *

Bond meets Draco in his office, where he is seen playing chess with his mistress, a fulsome brunette named Olympe. Draco instructs Olympe to bring Bond his signature drink, to which she responds, "A pleasure."[190] As she rises, Olympe twirls her purple skirt, highlighting her subservience. Draco recounts the extent of Olympe's skills, which include serving drinks and playing chess. He informs her that they will continue their chess game later, to which she obsequiously responds, "As you wish."[191]

Olympe, of course, is not the primary focus of this meeting. Instead, Draco has summoned Bond to discuss his daughter. The audience learns that Tracy is his only daughter, the product of his marriage to an "English girl" who discovered him hiding from police in the mountains.[192] Draco's wife died when Tracy was twenty years old, and Draco sent her to Switzerland to complete her studies. He speculates as to why she is not a respectable woman, *i.e.*, submissive and subservient to men:

> Unfortunately, I didn't give her a proper home. She was without supervision. So, she joined the fast international set. One scandal after another. When I disapproved, I cut off her allowance, she committed some greater folly—to spite me. Yet, behind her bravado, something was eating away at her soul. This can happen to men and women. They burn the heart out of themselves by living too greedily. And suddenly, all is finished . . . . Without telling me, she married—an Italian count who killed himself in a Maserati with one of his mistresses. I gave her too much, and it brought her nothing.[193]

Bond does not understand why Draco has chosen to reveal this information to him.

Ultimately, Draco offers a lucrative—and curious—proposal that he hopes Bond will accept. He explains:

> *Draco*: What you did, the way you behaved, might be the beginning of some kind of therapy. She needs help—your help.
> *Bond*: I find her fascinating, but she needs a psychiatrist, not me.
> *Draco*: What she needs is a man to dominate her. To make love to her enough to make her love him. A man like you.
> *Bond*: You overestimate me, Draco. She's very attractive, but what you ask is not for me.[194]

This dialogue is direct and brutally revealing. Draco, who is distraught over the fact that his daughter "is fast heading for disaster" with her self-destructive tendencies,[195] believes that Bond can *dominate* Tracy, prevent her from spiraling out of control, and mold her into a respectable woman who can learn to love a man through prolonged sexual intercourse. Bond's response—that Tracy is attractive—indicates what he believes is most important.

It is apparent that one sexual encounter with Bond has, at least temporarily, evaporated Tracy's thoughts about suicide.[196] Such a remarkable turnaround is reminiscent of Pussy Galore's metamorphosis, having been sexually and ideologically misaligned before she succumbs to Bond. Bond is disinterested in mentoring Tracy in this manner, recognizing that her problems far exceed his expertise or capability. Indeed, Draco himself accepts blame for his poor parenting, but his responsibility for her current condition is downplayed. Instead, the focus is solely upon Tracy's recklessness. Bond, naturally, is more concerned about his own self-preservation.

Draco sweetens his offer to Bond, explaining that Bond will reap both financial and professional rewards by accepting this curious arrangement:

> *Draco*: Listen to me. On the day you marry her, I'll give you a personal dowry of one million pounds in gold.
> *Bond*: That's quite an inducement. But I don't need a million pounds.
> *Draco*: Stupido!
> *Bond*: And I've a bachelor's taste for freedom.
> *Draco*: Please, just see her some more. Who knows what will come of it?[197]

Once again, Bond declines. Draco's persistence seems futile.

But Bond suddenly realizes that Draco could aid him in completing his mission. Now Bond finds himself in a precarious and compromised position:

> *Bond*: You have connections not open to me. Where is Ernst Stavro Blofeld?
> *Draco*: Blofeld? Some of my men have recently defected to him. I don't know where he is.
> *Bond*: Can you find out?
> *Draco*: If I could, I wouldn't tell Her Majesty's Secret Service. But I might tell my future son-in-law.[198]

Draco's desire to no longer worry about Tracy's mental and physical well-being is as great as Bond's desire to defeat his nemesis, and Bond is willing to become entangled with Tracy if doing so facilitates defeating Blofeld. For Bond, his "courtship of Tracy [is] a way of furthering his mission," and he will accept Draco's proposition if doing so enables him to obtain valuable information.[199]

Under these circumstances, Tracy is merely a pawn in a scheme devised by two men who are only interested in furthering their own agendas. Bond may genuinely care about Tracy's well-being. He seems concerned enough to broach the topic with Tracy in his hotel suite. Yet the only plausible explanation for Bond's willingness to pursue Tracy and forego his bachelor lifestyle is successful completion of a mission. Absent that objective, Bond has clearly and unequivocally indicated his unwillingness to accept Draco's offer.

* * *

The audience next discovers Tracy en route to see her father in Portugal. It is the first time in the film that she exhibits a smile across her face. Her apparent jovial spirits, however, abruptly end when Draco introduces her to Bond. The encounter is so distasteful that she leaves immediately. Draco interprets her behavior as a sign of her interest in Bond, but Bond suggests that Draco "give [him] the name of your oculist."[200]

Tracy correctly believes—and confides to Olympe—that Draco "is up to something, I'm sure of it," and Olympe does not state otherwise.[201] Instead, Olympe implies that Draco has, in fact, already set a scheme in motion, stating "[w]hatever he may arrange, I know it's for your happiness."[202] A curious and annoyed Tracy, returning to Bond and Draco, demands to know the reason for Bond's presence. The answer offered—that Bond and Draco are conducting business (indeed, Bond's courtship of Tracy has already become a business transaction)—is not to Tracy's satisfaction:

> *Tracy*: I suggest you revise the terms of your contract, Mister Bond. You'll find your liability too expensive.
>
> *Bond*: Ah, now there you're mistaken.
>
> *Tracy*: Papa.
>
> *Draco*: Yes?
>
> *Tracy*: Mister Bond wants information.[203]

Tracy's petulance elevates to the threat that Draco will never see her again. Having manipulated the conversation, Tracy compels her father to divulge Blofeld's whereabouts. Thereafter, she declares that Bond "need have no further interest" in her and leaves.[204]

Tracy's display of bravado belies her fragility. Bond discovers her weeping, but he does not attempt to seduce her. Rather, a courtship sequence ensues, depicting "a montage containing lyrical, slow-motion scenes of a horseback ride, lyrical slow-motion running along a beach and so on—all of it given a vocal blessing by the late Louis Armstrong."[205] These scenes reveal little in terms of substance of their relationship, "but by the end, Bond and Tracy are seen eyeing wedding rings."[206] Glistening sunshine suggests that this all is a mirage, but the sequence ends with a love-struck couple incapable of taking their eyes off each other. Interestingly, one critique of *On Her Majesty's Secret Service* noted how Bond "seems principally interested in seducing everything in sight—especially girls with emotional problems."[207]

Bond later discovers Tracy ice skating in Switzerland after he escapes Blofeld's compound. It has been written that Tracy "rescues" Bond.[208] This is a complete overstatement, despite the fact that Bond informs M that he was rescued by her. Although Tracy provides an escape vehicle that she drives, Bond retains control. It is *she* who asks where they are heading, and it is *he* who tells her their destination. Bond approves of her compliance, leaning over to kiss her and stating, "Good girl."[209]

Is Bond in love with Tracy? According to Tracy, she remains hopeful that he will be at some point:

> *Tracy* (*laughing and smiling*): But what can be better than being in love?
> *Draco*: Mister Bond, he's in love with you?
> *Tracy* (*hoping*): That may come, too, someday.
> *Draco*: Life's too short for someday, Teresa.[210]

Finding themselves trapped for a night in a deserted barn during a storm, Bond and Tracy discuss the future, with Bond acknowledging that he "has to find something else to do."[211] He then professes his love and proposes marriage. Just as shocking is Bond's declaration of a moratorium on lovemaking until after the wedding, which he describes as his New Year's resolution. Tracy simply responds, "Whatever you say, darling,"[212] a signal that Bond has succeeded in asserting himself over her and effectuated her submission. Although his sexual moratorium lasts fewer than five minutes, Bond has transformed Tracy from an "aimless, self-destructive, even suicidal" woman into a subservient, attentive bride, just as Draco desires.[213]

Ultimately, Blofeld captures Tracy, and Bond must rescue her. He must do so, however, without the aid of MI6, as M indicates that the mission is too risky and Bond must separate his personal affairs from his professional responsibilities. To her credit, Tracy is proactive, resourcefully distracting Blofeld during Bond's impending aerial assault. She even disposes of one of Blofeld's henchmen, an act that was "unprecedented in a Bond film."[214] Yet considering that Tatiana Romanova disposes of Rosa Klebb in *From Russia With Love* and Domino Derval kills Emilio Largo in *Thunderball*, Tracy's act, standing alone, does not justify characterizing her as a strong, independent, and capable woman. In fact, Tracy's sudden ability to engage in physical combat is out of character and is more reflective of Rigg's former role as Miss Emma Peel on *The Avengers*.

The film's penultimate scene depicts the wedding ceremony. Draco offers the new bride instruction, but Tracy dismisses it entirely:

> *Draco*: Remember, obey your husband in all things. You promise me?
>
> *Tracy*: But of course I will. As I always obeyed you.[215]

Tracy submits to Bond, but she nevertheless remains somewhat defiant of male authority. Such a glimmer of independence foreshadows her demise as she refuses to place herself entirely in the hands of a man. Nevertheless, Tracy's reformation is substantial, and Draco delivers to Bond an envelope containing the payment he promised. Bond declines: "An old proverb, 'Her price is far above rubies,' or even your million pounds."[216] Despite his questionable intentions when he initially accepts Draco's scheme, Bond has clearly been affected by Tracy.

Although Tracy believes that Bond offers her a future, he simply cannot save her. Moments after the wedding ceremony concludes, Bond and Tracy depart and stop briefly along the side of the road. While the vehicle is parked, an automobile driven by Blofeld approaches, and Bunt, sitting in the backseat, unloads a round of machine gun fire. Bond's *first* reaction is instinctive: he leaps into the car with the intent of chasing after Blofeld. He exhibits no concern for Tracy and, in fact, neglects her entirely. When she is nonresponsive, Bond realizes that Tracy is dead. Her lifeless body collapses into his arms.

Thereafter, the film abruptly concludes, though it ultimately comes full circle. Having opened with a depiction of Bond saving Tracy from her own demise, it concludes with his inability to continue serving in such capacity. The scene has been criticized as "totally incongruous" with the remainder of the film, which contains "light-hearted action."[217] Yet it is also one of "the most moving scene[s] in any Bond picture" and required several takes for George Lazenby to convey the appropriate restraint that the directors sought.[218]

* * *

Tracy, at first glance, appears to constitute a complete departure from the prototypical Bond Girl archetype. Unlike her predecessors, she is not an "object of to-be-looked-at-ness."[219] Nevertheless, Tracy is ultimately best characterized as an amalgam of various Bond Girls.

Like Pussy Galore, she exhibits a strong will and seems defiant at times. Both women require that Bond reposition them to conform to societal conceptions of normalcy. For Pussy Galore, the realignment is *sexual* and *ideological*, removing her lesbian tendencies and extricating herself from Auric Goldfinger. By contrast, Tracy's realignment is *psychological*, chiseling away at her independence and subduing her destructive free spirit. Like Domino Derval, Tracy "has no job, no position, no real responsibility."[220] Like Honey Ryder, Tracy initially is skeptical of Bond, but she eventually opens up to him and exhibits a strong sense of attachment.

Moreover, Tracy is the pawn in a scheme devised by Draco, a similar circumstance in which Tatiana Romanova finds herself. Tatiana, under the threat of death, is expected to deliver a Lektor device to Bond and to obey his orders. Tracy, having threatened and attempted suicide, is expected to deliver herself to Bond and to obey his orders. Diana Rigg described her character as follows: "[A]t a moment in her life when she wishes to destroy everything, and everything doesn't seem worthwhile at all, she meets and falls in love with James Bond."[221]

Tracy's self-destructiveness undermines her entire psyche. Her so-called independence is more akin to arrogance, and her demeanor toward her father is accusatory and defiant. The free-spiritedness Tracy exhibits is not channeled in a positive manner. Instead, it provides her with opportunities to destroy herself, rather than to facilitate any liberation. Her emotional and psychological disturbances further marginalize her, and her suicidal tendencies suggest an inherent imbalance that a romantic relationship simply cannot remedy. Indeed, it is wholly implausible that Bond is able to transform Tracy, though it is equally implausible that his sexual prowess can dissolve Pussy Galore's homosexual proclivities. But the plausibility of Bond's effect is immaterial. The remedy he provides is defined in terms of male assertiveness, rather than the female's willingness to adapt.

Indeed, Bond's potency is so concentrated with Tracy that she appears to accept the role of a subservient dutiful wife. As soon as they are married, Tracy immediately requests that Bond give her six children. The film's conclusion demonstrates that Tracy's abrupt and untimely death prevents her from fulfilling this destiny.

Notwithstanding her desire to rear several children and fulfill her destiny as Bond's subservient wife, it is apparent that Bond may encounter difficulty harnessing Tracy, who may also be interpreted as the embodiment of "second wave" feminism. She may wed Bond, but her comment to Draco suggests that she will maintain her independence, balancing a woman's traditional maternal role with her own separate interests. Such beliefs, of course, are consistent with the mainstream feminist ideology advanced by NOW. But Tracy's death serves as a stark reminder that such radical reinterpretations of traditional gender roles are ultimately unsustainable.

Tracy is a memorable addition to the Bond Girl sorority, serving as an apt metaphor for the dangerous and destructive consequences that result from bestowing upon women too much freedom and independence. Too unpredictable and unwilling to obey authority, Tracy falls outside the ideal perpetuated throughout the 1950s and early 1960s that marriage was the appropriate role for women. At the same time, Tracy also cannot survive under a feminist conception of a woman's role in society because her independence is defined in terms of self-destructiveness. Neither liberated nor entirely subservient, Tracy is an enigma for which there is simply no place in the Bond mythology or beyond.

* * *

On Her Majesty's Secret Service was described as "deservedly forgotten" on account of the casting of George Lazenby,[222] which was ranked among the one hundred worst ideas of the twentieth century.[223] Following its release, the film received the dubious distinction of being named one of the ten worst films of 1969,[224] though it is held in much higher regard today.[225] Although *On Her Majesty's Secret Service* is best remembered for Lazenby's sole performance as Bond, the presentation of Tracy is a significant contribution to the development of the Bond Girl archetype.

As the franchise entered the 1970s, the Bond Girl would continue her journey. The juxtaposition of a traditional patriarchal order and the new feminist ideal that is explored through and manifested in Tracy's character is strikingly absent. Instead, the Bond Girl is refined, accentuating a more suitable role that modern women should fulfill in both the Bondian and real worlds. Whether intentional or otherwise, the Bond Girl of the early 1970s became a powerful reactionary character during a time of social upheaval that witnessed the rise of a significant and vocal antifeminism movement.

0010

Shaken, Stirred, and Undeterred: The Antifeminism Movement and Backlash Across America

[T]he women's liberation movement . . . is not a reflection of and response to the actual life experience of women in our society but an ideological movement whose aim is the subversion of human experience and the avoidance of that necessary anguish which lets us know we are responsible adults.

—Robert Boyers[1]

Women's Liberation has really made it in our neighborhood. Last night I was held up by a gunperson.

—Robert Orben[2]

The only alliance I would make with the Women's Liberation Movement is in bed.

—Abbie Hoffman[3]

Newsweek reported that 1970 "was the year in which American women became intellectually aware of the modern feminist movement" and forecasted that Women's Liberation would become commonplace in America within one year.[4] By 1972, NOW had established more than 250 chapters across 48 states and boasted a membership exceeding 18,000 men and women.[5] As one writer summarized,

> the feminists urged women to aspire to something better than domestic drudgery. Some feminists pressed their campaign against

> the bourgeois cult of the family to the logical conclusion of attacking marriage itself. Most . . . were satisfied with advocating careers outside the home. All . . . opposed the proposition that women's place was in the home, and for that reason . . . the feminists . . . have interpreted the movement as an assault against the last stronghold of Victorian culture, the patriarchal family . . . .[6]

Meanwhile, members of Women's Liberation continued to advance their own agendas, urging women to "learn some sort of martial arts" and protect themselves from "male chauvinist pigs."[7] Within the network of women's underground press, posters that illustrated vital male areas in which to inflict pain circulated alongside images of Wonder Woman. Slowly, these messages filtered into the mainstream. As previously noted, karate workshops burgeoned with participants who rejected a woman's submissive and passive role in society: "She is not yet out of diapers when she learns that girls [only] play with baby dolls . . . she becomes a secretary, a teacher, a nurse."[8]

Gloria Steinem remarked that "police [now] understand that women are just as likely to be pushers or bombers."[9] Yet she and other members of the mainstream feminist movement preferred words as the weapon to challenge the male establishment. For example, Steinem wrote that if men were biologically capable of menstruation, they would likely "brag about how long and how much" and partake in ceremonies marking their initiation into manhood.[10] She even theorized that "men would claim greater sexual powers [and] heightened intellectual skills [during] their 'time of the month.'"[11]

The only monthly changes that were noticeable were reflected in women's magazines, which quickly began scrambling to adjust their own portrayals of women. This phenomenon demonstrated the beginning of the industry's "liberation." *Good Housekeeping*, for example, began publishing articles and book reviews advocating "practical action" and recommending that "protesting in the street and burning bras" was an ineffective and counterproductive method for making a lasting impact.[12] Magazine fiction that previously accentuated the benefits of motherhood and the importance of preserving the domestic sphere now began highlighting, albeit slightly, the importance of a woman pursuing her own professional career. These vignettes also provided women with insights into how they could begin their career search. New magazines, including *You* and *New Woman*, offered alternatives to *Cosmopolitan* for those readers who "want[ed] . . . a slice of the 'man's world.'"[13] One women's magazine editor remarked that the term "women's lib" "turn[ed] a lot of women off" and recommended use of "womankind" as an appropriate and less offensive alternative.[14]

Author and women's rights activist Robin Morgan (right) attends a karate workshop for women, 1970.

(Sahm Doherty/TIME & LIFE Images/ Time & Life Pictures/Getty Images)

While periodicals tailored specifically to a female audience actively sought to maintain their readership by "hurriedly changing in taste and tone as they strive[d] furiously to keep pace with changing times," most of these magazines preserved the traditional notion that a woman's first and foremost duty was to her family.[15] The unwillingness to abandon these engrained notions of femininity suggested that an undercurrent of opposition to the feminist and Women's Liberation movements was percolating. Indeed, it began brewing among women, many of whom felt "[s]ecure and happy in their traditional roles . . . [and] reject[ed] any drastic change in their status. They also resent[ed] what they regard[ed] as a kind of propaganda designed to either force them into more active lives or make them feel guilty about staying home."[16]

Liberationists dismissed mainstream women's periodicals, believing that any modifications that were reflected therein were simply "cop-outs" and contending that the truly substantive and meaningful feminist publications remained underground.[17] The works advanced by radical feminists often were of a "shrill tenor."[18] But the substance of these works was not the only objectionable material. In fact, members of Women's Liberation soon focused upon both the message and the English language that they used to convey their messages.

Women's Liberation utilized numerous new words and phrases that immediately became commonplace in the English language. "Male chauvinist pig," "sex role," "sexist," "sisterhood," "machismo," and "son of a bitch" are typical examples.[19] These lexicographical additions soon spawned an interest in analyzing the syntax and structure of the English language itself, and an entire movement developed that was devoted to reforming rules and guidelines for both grammar and usage. Calling themselves the "Manglish" reformers, proponents of English language modification decried "the use of the masculine singular pronoun in which the subject is not necessarily male," contending that such devices were "blatantly sexist."[20] They noted that subjects taking female pronouns were typically derogatory, including names of tropical storms and hurricanes.

An article appearing in the inaugural issue of *Ms.*, which was first published as part of a double-issue in *New York Magazine*, argued that English language rules adversely affected young girls:

> The grammar of English dictates that when a referent is either of indeterminate sex or both sexes, it shall be considered masculine. The penetration of this habit of language into the minds of little girls as they grow up to be women is more profound than most people . . . have recognized: for it implies that personality is really a male attribute, and that women are human subspecies.[21]

Reformers decried the usage of "ettes" and "esses" plurals that were applied to female members of a particular profession—*i.e.*, waitress, stewardess, ambassadress—and sought their complete elimination on the basis that such suffixes reinforced the idea that women "do not qualify for membership in . . . a central type of humanity."[22] Others noted that the English language contained approximately sixty-seven synonyms for "whore," bolstering their belief that the language itself "function[ed] as a heavy whip-wielding master to keep women in their place."[23]

These criticisms culminated in the issuance of a new Feminist English Dictionary, which was designed to demonstrate that the "English language is a tool of repression."[24] Over 441 so-called sexist terms were listed in the work, which also highlighted words derived from *man*, *master*, and *father*.[25] The concept of a common-gender pronoun in the singular form was proposed: "Once [such] a word is adopted, *he* can become exclusively masculine, just as *she* is now exclusively feminine. The new program will thus accentuate the significant and valuable differences between females and males . . . while affirming the essential unity and equality of the two sexes within the same species."[26] Other neutered or feminine replacements for words such as "chairperson" were advocated. Additional modifications were imposed upon words such as "sportsmanship," "spokesman," and "history," which, under the new language system, would become "sportsoneship," "spokesone," and "herstory," respectively. The editors of *Time* rejected these proposals, contending that "if the feminists have their way," then those and other "absurd" suggestions would infiltrate the vernacular language.[27]

Time also devoted particular attention to another contentious language and gender issue: usage of "Mr." and "Mrs." in formal address. Feminists began utilizing and advocating "Ms." as an alternative to "Mrs." and "Miss." Yet critics quickly emphasized that "Ms." was a common abbreviation for other things, namely "mail streamer," "master sergeant," and "manuscript." Feminists ignored these critics, and the abbreviation became widely accepted after *Ms.* was published in the spring of 1972. Nevertheless, the editors of *Time* defiantly eschewed utilizing "Ms." in the magazine, instead determining that "Miss and Mrs. convey valid information."[28] A war of words had been declared.

* * *

In 1971, authors Judith Hole and Ellen Levine wrote that "[f]eminism by definition challenges the status quo. It questions political, social and cultural institutions, ways of thinking and the very articulation of those thoughts . . . resistance from men is perhaps most understandable."[29] Even though the success of feminism "[was]n't a media trick" and was instead "a consequence of the fact that those ideas have always been there,"[30] backlash and opposition were a constant:

> Backlash didn't need time to build up; backlash didn't wait for feminism to settle in. Backlash was there from the moment women took to the streets, barking and nipping at their heels. The war between feminism and antifeminism in the early 1970s raged throughout the media in an explicit, no-holds-barred action.[31]

The first line of defense against feminism and Women's Liberation involved sarcasm and humor: "No cocktail party can be considered top drawer without at least one reference to the 'myth of the vaginal orgasm' or to some 'phallustine,'" which referred to a male chauvinistic pig philistine.[32] *Time* sarcastically suggested that "both men and women should be addressed as Mm., as in Mm. and Mm. Smith. Or when in doubt, mumble."[33] Satirists claimed that women's concerns about language were merely part of a great "Msapprehension," that their objectives were "msguided" attempts to rewrite and speak "herstory," and were generally "msanthropic."[34] One columnist recounted an instance in which she overheard a young boy approach her daughter and ask whether the girl had an interest in his personality or his body.[35]

In July 1973, *Esquire* published "302 Women Who Are Cute When They're Mad" and awarded Simone de Beauvior the title of "Mother of Us All."[36] Suggesting a hierarchy within a royal family of fledging feminists, the slightly lower-ranked "Other Mothers of Us All" included Robin Morgan, Shulamith Firestone, Betty Friedan, and Ti-Grace Atkinson. *Ms.* was dubbed the "Official House Organ," while Virginia Woolf, Zelda Fitzgerald, Janis Joplin, and Norman Mailer's four ex-wives were named "Martyrs."[37]

Television also became an effective medium for backlash against feminism and Women's Liberation. During an interview with Dick Cavett in 1971, Gloria Steinem was asked whether her new article about a recent lecture tour would be entitled "Bra-less in Boise."[38] Meanwhile, journalist Harry Reasoner offered commentary on a December 21, 1971 broadcast of *ABC News* about *Ms.*, which he described as a "pretty sad" attempt at a "shock magazine" that would likely "last about three issues."[39]

Groundbreaking situation comedies like *All in the Family* and *Maude*, which frequently tackled issues such as Women's Liberation and abortion, became extremely popular with American audiences. At the same time, both shows portrayed feminists in a harsh light. In *All in the Family*, Edith, the matriarch of the Bunker family portrayed by Jean Stapleton, represented a traditional, subservient wife and mother who never asserted or stood up for herself. By contrast, her daughter Gloria Bunker Stivic, played by Sally Struthers, was a vocal, progressive, post-civil rights era activist. Although Gloria was opinionated, she was usually overpowered by both her father Archie and husband Michael Stivic. Stapleton publicly acknowledged that "as Edith Bunker I don't have equal rights,"[40] but for all her efforts, Gloria never seemed to achieve equality either, a much more subtle reality that the program presented. Indeed, Edith did not actively *seek* equality, and Gloria's efforts fell short. By contrast, the character of Maude, portrayed by Beatrice Arthur, was an unmistakable stereotype of the feminist movement. Described as a "strident, loud, unfeminine bruiser," Maude's voice sounded like a "diesel truck in second gear."[41] Despite the popularity of *All in the Family* and *Maude*, both programs were off the air by 1978,[42] evidence that the gender movement had run its course.

The sudden explosion of police dramas depicting female victims of rape or abuse, one scholar argued, suggested that Women's Liberation "became an excuse to terrorize" women.[43] By contrast, the rise of "bionic bimbo" programs such as *The Bionic Woman* and *Wonder Woman* presented audiences with images suggesting that strong, independent women were more science fiction fantasy than reality. Wonder Woman's truth lasso, however, was symbolic of a more disturbing theme. Able to maintain justice only by using her lasso to tie and constrain her typically male criminals, Wonder Woman implied to audiences that a strong, powerful woman was, in fact, a visible constraint upon a male-centric society.

Charlie's Angels, another popular 1970s television drama, placed three beautiful women in very realistic settings, but it ultimately presented "a version of the pimp and his girls. Charlie dispatches his streetwise girls to use their sexual wiles on the world while he reaps the profits."[44] In fact, *Charlie's Angels* single-handedly exploited the tensions between the feminist and Women's Liberation movements and the mounting backlash response. The mysterious Charlie appears as a great liberator, but it is merely a façade:

> We hear the voice of the great white patriarch, Charlie, announcing, "Once upon a time, there were three little girls who went to the police academy." But . . . we see three buxom women grimly shooting guns, using judo to flip men over their heads and onto the ground, and writing traffic tickets. Then Charlie says sarcastically, "And they were each assigned very hazardous duties," as we see them stuck in . . . dead-end jobs . . . doing clerical work and serving as crossing guards for schoolchildren . . . . Charlie announces proudly, "But I took them away from all that, and now they work for me."[45]

Gloria Steinem appears on *The Helen Reddy Show*, 1973.
(CSU Archives / Everett Collection/Rex USA)

While Charlie's Angels carry weapons, drive fast sports cars, apprehend villains, and "do what men do," all of their actions stem from and are directed by the omnipresent, albeit invisible, Charlie, who is "commanding, unseen, permeating everything, issuing orders and instructions the girls must obey."[46]

The attractive, feminine women of *Charlie's Angels* stood in sharp contrast to the perceptions of feminists and Women's Liberationists, who were generally described as "bitches," "man-haters," "sexually and emotionally frustrated," and "lesbians." One NOW member claimed that "the most serious opposition to the women's movement" was from men, who "are like the plantation owners who argued that life wouldn't be the same without slaves. They are right. Life won't be the same, and if you own even a small plantation, you may not like it."[47] The so-called "man-hating, lesbian" core of Women's Liberation was described as a "buncha dykes" that were perpetuating political and social unrest.[48] *Time* suggested that activist Kate Millett's revelation of her bisexuality undermined her work and actually validated critics' claims that lesbians had assumed control of the movement:

> Kate Millett herself contributed to the growing skepticism . . . by acknowledging at a recent meeting that she is bisexual. The disclosure is bound to discredit her as a spokeswoman for her cause, cast further doubt on her theories, and reinforce the views of those skeptics who routinely dismiss all liberationists as lesbians.[49]

Indeed, one way to "deal" with the movement was to "stress adamantly that it is by and about . . . Commies, freaks, lesbians, [and] neurotics."[50]

While lesbians and Women's Liberation activists were typically branded as the source of anti-male rhetoric, mainstream feminists and NOW quickly were characterized as the "man-hating part of the movement" due to NOW's status as the first and most prominent organization advancing feminist ideals. Firing back at "feminists who espouse masturbatory clitoral orgasm as a political weapon against men," many antifeminists maintained that liberationists unknowingly "ha[d] made themselves sexual objects."[51] Senator Barry Goldwater of Arizona expressed his own opinion about feminism when he remarked that he had "nothing against a woman just [as long as] she can cook and get home on time."[52]

Of course, "[p]redictably, much female backlash is a result of male backlash."[53] Yet while many perceived the backlash movement as one dominated by men, large numbers of women, in fact, expressed opposition to feminism and Women's Liberation. For example, Golda Meir, who served as Israel's first female prime minster and was, at the time, the third female to lead a nation, described feminists as "nuts that burn their bras

Members of Women's Liberation demonstrate on Fifth Avenue in New York City, 1971.

(New York Daily News Archive/New York Daily News/NY Daily News via Getty Images)

and walk around disheveled and hate men."[54] One female interviewee offered the following reaction to depictions of feminists on television: "I saw one of those Lib women on TV. She ranted and raved so, I thought maybe she just had a bad day."[55]

Numerous groups and organizations emerged as part of a larger conservative New Right movement that challenged the way in which feminists promoted a "deliberate departure from traditional expectations of female images and roles."[56] Many participants believed that "Gloria Steinem needs a good husband and three children" and that the "style" of the feminist and Women's Liberation movements was highly offensive.[57] Many women reacted negatively to Women's Liberation because they felt "alienated" by the way in which the issues were addressed, though they were ultimately "glad that the issues [we]re being raised . . . ."[58] At the same time, backlash from women was "based on style or on misunderstanding . . . what Women's Liberation [wa]s."[59] In this regard, many women could not identify with a movement that was perceived as being dominated by homosexuals or individuals who, at the very least, "find . . . men sexually distasteful."[60]

Many organizations, notably the Women Against the Ratification of the ERA, Females Opposed to Equality, Happiness of Motherhood Eternal, Women Who Want to Be Women, the Eagle Forum, the Pussycats, and Happiness of Womanhood! garnered national support. Happiness of Womanhood! members objected to the way in which Women's Liberation undermined the traditional role of the family: "God commanded Eve, 'Thy desire shall be to thy husband and he shall rule over thee' . . . a man is the head of the family."[61] Members of these groups dismissed liberationists' "radical changes in sexual socialization and identity, radical changes in the nature of the family, or its dissolution altogether" as simply "extravagant."[62] A small group of women in California protested what they believed was a denunciation of femininity by Women's Liberation, instead claiming a "love [for] the idea of looking delectable and having men whistle."[63]

In addition to advocating a National Celebration of Womanhood Day, many groups suggested that "each wife should wear her most frilly, feminine dress and should 'sing before breakfast,' serve her husband breakfast in bed and 'tell him how great he is.'"[64] One theory emerged that liberationists simply "eschewed housework, not because it is dullard's work, but because it is perpetually decision demanding and women simply aren't up to it."[65] Liberationists, it was argued, were not overburdened by marriage but instead preferred to dismiss the institution on account of selfishness: they simply "cannot stand to give."[66] Members of the Pussycats, described as a "cutie-poo anti-Lib group,"[67] protested feminism because it "mean[t] giving up black-lace underwear."[68] Armed with buttons and slogans such as "The lamb chop is mightier than the karate chop" and "Purr, Baby, Purr," the Pussycats likened Women's Liberation to communism, describing liberationists as "malcontents" who failed to comprehend or acknowledge that women had already achieved total equality.[69]

"Pangs of souring sisterhood" began to develop across the country as men and women increasingly responded negatively to feminism and Women's Liberation.[70] *Ms.* reported the extent to which "trashing," a form of character assassination that amounted to "psychological rape," was becoming rampant within liberationist circles themselves.[71] An aura of elitism among feminists developed that further alienated other women from the movement: "I'm-more-liberated-that-you-are" quickly dissolved into accusations that "I-take-my-work-more-seriously-than-you-do" and, ultimately, claims that "My-work-is-more-important-than-yours."[72] Many older women became "just plain jealous of younger women who not only have options—to get married, have children, have careers, or not—but use them."[73] Indeed, when NOW called upon women to stage a national "Alice Doesn't"—*i.e.*, doesn't work, cook, clean, or parent—strike in 1975, its request fell upon deaf ears. Betty Friedan later reflected that "there was no real reason to strike" since President Gerald R. Ford had previously proclaimed a Women's Equality Day.[74]

Indeed, President Ford, by designating Women's Equality Day, suggested that the time had "now come to institutionalize the gains of the past five years," suggesting that a "truce" was imminent.[75] Consequently, the press began referring to feminism as a "nonissue," indicating that women's rights had been recognized and that the discussion was over.[76] Shortly thereafter, one journalist noted that "the shriller and more aggressive feminists have become less audible and visible. All signs point to the end of a revolution."[77] The decline of the feminist and Women's Liberation movements ultimately was hastened by one final campaign that seemed to bring the new gender revolution to an apparent end. Ironically, it was spearheaded by a woman.

* * *

Phyllis Schlafly, who, according to one scholar, "made the Wicked Witch of the West look like Mary Poppins,"[78] has been credited with mounting a successful campaign that defeated ratification of the ERA and effectively undermined the feminist and Women's Liberation movements. Although the ERA was passed in the United States Senate on March 22, 1972, many senators "remained at heart opposed to dealing with the issue of an amendment even as they voted for it."[79] In fact, Democratic Senator Sam Ervin of North Carolina lamented, "Father, forgive them, they know not what they do . . . . American womanhood [will be] crucified on a cross of dubious equality and specious uniformity."[80] The ERA, of course, had been one of NOW's primary objectives during Betty Friedan's tenure as president, and feminists successfully lobbied thirty state legislatures to ratify the amendment in 1972 alone. The deadline imposed for ratification of the ERA was March 22, 1979.

The United States Supreme Court's decision in *Roe v. Wade*, which was issued in 1973, contributed to a united attack against the ERA's ratification from conservatives. Schlafly founded the National Committee to Stop ERA, and opponents focused upon lobbying state legislatures to prevent ratification. By contrast, NOW had succeeded in helping elect pro-ERA candidates to these legislative bodies.[81] Yet momentum soon stalled. Whereas thirty states ratified the ERA in 1972, only eight joined the following year. That number dropped to three in 1974 and was reduced to only one state in 1975. Not a single state ratified the ERA in 1976.[82] By 1977, proponents of the ERA sought an extension of time for ratification. Eventually, the deadline was extended to June 30, 1982.

Unlike the Nineteenth Amendment, which was clearly defined in scope and purpose, the exact effects of the ERA were unclear: "The ERA is less tangible . . . . [What] it will do, over the long run and on a most basic level, is to prevent the government from determining the rights of women and men on the basis of sex."[83] Phyllis Schlafly capitalized upon this uncertainty, arguing that the ERA would no longer distinguish between the genders and have unintended consequences. It would, Schlafly maintained, establish unisex public facilities, permit unlimited abortions, recognize homosexual marriages, send women into war, and absolve men from any obligation to support their spouses. A monthly newsletter, the *Phyllis Schlafly Report*, was circulated to advance these positions and the belief that "men and women are different, and that those very differences provide the key to her success as a person and fulfillment as a woman."[84]

Implementing a grassroots campaign, Phyllis Schlafly appealed to women to reject feminists as a "bunch of anti-family radicals and lesbians and elitists."[85] Feminists were, according to Schlafly, "petty . . . and vindictive" individuals who thought "it is unequal that mothers have to take care of their babies."[86] Furthermore, feminists "just don't want to be nice. They want to be ugly."[87] Arguing that the ERA would encourage a greater number of dissolutions of marriage and would compel women to work in order to provide for themselves, Schlafly found a sympathetic audience: "If ERA is ratified, the aged and faithful mother, who has made her family her lifetime career, would have no legal right[s] . . . . [S]he would have to take any menial job she could get or go on welfare if her husband and children did not voluntarily choose to support her."[88]

Phyllis Schlafly leads a protest inside the Illinois state capitol as the legislature considers ratifying the ERA, 1975.

(Michael Mauney/TIME & LIFE Images/Time & Life Pictures/Getty Images)

Making the anti-ERA campaign "more newsworthy" than the campaign for its ratification, Schlafly asserted that "[t]he American people do not want the ERA."[89]

Ultimately, she was right. Along with her own followers and support from other antifeminist groups, Phyllis Schlafly forecasted that the ERA would become a moot issue. Despite NOW's efforts—both political and legal—to advocate vigorously, the ERA fell three states short of ratification and never took effect.[90] Gathering at an "Over the Rainbow" victory celebration immediately following the June 30, 1982 expiration of the ratification deadline, Schlafly proclaimed that the "defeat of the Equal Rights Amendment [wa]s the greatest victory for women's rights since the women's suffrage amendment of 1920" and urged women to preserve the family and moral values that she believed feminists and liberationists sought to destroy.[91]

* * *

The ERA has been introduced in each session of Congress since 1982. The unsuccessful ratification campaign, together with the efforts of the backlash movement, extracted momentum from the feminist and Women's Liberation movements. As early as 1974, one journalist wrote that "[a]ll signs point to the end of a revolution,"[92] but the failure to ratify the ERA was the most memorable act of finality for an era.

Although the formal "revolution" may have fallen into decline, those who participated in the movement achieved significant legal, social, and political gains:

> Higher-status jobs, plentiful role models, fairer household sharing, and quality day care—all imply that women deserve both more opportunity and more freedom than they have enjoyed in the past . . . . [T]he women's movement is part of a much larger change, a change away from stereotypical thinking in our national life.[93]

As early as 1972, "everyone believe[d] in equal pay for equal work . . . everyone believe[d] that women should not be sharply limited in the economic roles available to them."[94] But the "second-wave" of feminism[95] that came to life in the 1960s and 1970s did much more, having successfully initiated a process that changed men's views about gender[96] and left a significant mark on the American social and political landscapes.

* * *

Feminism "speak[s] from women's experience."[97] As one author acknowledged, "[t]here's a lot of feminism out there—and you should check it all out,"[98] and American women "owe an incalculable debt" to those who fought for women's rights during the latter half of the twentieth century.[99] Indeed, as one scholar reflected, there is "no turning back from a feminist future."[100] Robin Morgan recently wrote, "No matter how they try to marginalize it, trivialize it, stereotype it, mourn it, or demonize it: the U.S. Women's Movement, *Still here*—and further reinventing itself."[101]

And the feminist and Women's Liberation movements ultimately influenced the world of James Bond, which entered the 1970s with a refined Bond Girl archetype that would serve as its own unique response to new conceptions of gender rights and equality.

0011

Refining an Archetype: *Diamonds Are Forever, Live and Let Die,* and *The Man With the Golden Gun*

[Sean] Connery had brought with him a hint of macho relish. The retiring Bond had learnt to wear his wardrobe as if he had grown into it.

—Alexander Walker[1]

[Roger Moore] makes Bond a more sophisticated character; he doesn't project the innate toughness that Sean [Connery] had . . . . Therefore, we had to be more extreme with Roger and find places for him to knock girls around and that sort of thing.

—Richard Maibaum[2]

Bond women are larger than life. They're not meant to represent the real woman. They're meant to represent almost a dreamlike quality, it's a fantasy quality.

—Jill St. John[3]

I knew this was a very decorative part.

—Maud Adams[4]

The James Bond franchise found itself in a state of transition in the early 1970s. On one hand, it needed to successfully translate a 1960s mentality into the new decade: "James Bond movies belong to the 1960s, especially the early '60s, when the adventures of 007 reflected a public fascination with modern technology, *Playboy* sexuality and the kind of elegant style embodied in the short reign of John F. Kennedy."[5] On the other hand, producers faced the reality that over the course of three films and four years—*On Her Majesty's Secret Service* in 1969, *Diamonds Are Forever* in 1971, and *Live and Let Die* in 1973—three actors portrayed Double-O-Seven.

Following what was described as Lazenby's "still and lifeless"[6] performance in *On Her Majesty's Secret Service* and the film's relatively lackluster box office performance in comparison to its predecessors,[7] producers decided that *Diamonds Are Forever* would "be light and breezy, full of humour, in contrast to the darker, more serious tone of the previous 007 adventure."[8] They turned to Bond franchise veterans Richard Maibaum to write the screenplay and Guy Hamilton to direct the film. When United Artists sought a screenplay that was imbued with more humor, Tom Mankiewicz was brought aboard.[9] With a writing and production crew established, producers focused upon casting a new Bond.

While United Artists wanted Sean Connery to return, Cubby Broccoli and Harry Saltzman deemed it inappropriate to beg the actor to reprise a role he did not desire.[10] Consequently, an international search was conducted that also included American actors. Burt Reynolds, along with Adam West, who portrayed Batman on the popular television series, were both considered for the part.[11] Clint Eastwood and Steve McQueen were also named as possible candidates.[12] Eventually, John Gavin, who was known for his role in Alfred Hitchcock's *Psycho*, was signed.[13] Nevertheless, United Artists wanted Connery and enlisted the assistance of Ursula Andress to convince him to return.[14] Once Connery agreed, Gavin was excused from his contract. *Diamonds Are Forever* would be Connery's "one last fling as 007" in an EON Productions film.[15]

In 1972, producers again faced a casting change. After Sean Connery's second departure, Broccoli turned to Roger Moore, who had an established acting career and "carried himself with an air of assured sophistication."[16] Moore was the producer's first choice for the role and was a leading candidate for the part back in 1962. Ultimately, the decade wait afforded him the opportunity to become "very familiar to American audiences via the various TV series" in which he starred.[17]

Roger Moore's long-awaited debut as Bond, however, received mixed reviews. While *Time* described him as "more like the original 007 in the late Ian Fleming's novels than was Connery,"[18] critic John Russell Taylor indicated that the actor "trie[d] too hard, and seem[ed] even more titillated by the outrageousness (mild enough anyway by today's standards) of the things he is supposed to do than anyone in the audience."[19] *Time* critiqued Moore as an actor who "lack[ed] all Connery's strengths" and possessed "several deep deficiencies."[20] In 1974, *Newsweek*'s film critic opined: "Sean Connery was a cool Bond. Moore is a cold one. Connery invested his counterspy Casanova with a playful sensuality that signaled he was having fun. Moore has no sense of fun, only a mannequin's good looks and a priggishness that turns second-rate sexual innuendos into fifth-rate stag-part boffolas."[21]

Nevertheless, Roger Moore was given the latitude to "play James Bond as Moore," rather than attempt to replicate Sean Connery's version of the protagonist.[22] The formula worked. For the next twelve years, Moore brought continuity to the franchise, ending his tenure after seven missions with *A View To A Kill* in 1985.

Despite the myriad changes between 1969 and 1974, Guy Hamilton was a constant throughout the trilogy consisting of *Diamonds Are Forever*, *Live and Let Die*, and *The Man With the Golden Gun*. Hamilton brought a slightly different approach to the Bond Girl: "His women played up to Bond by having a go at him and finding, after a lot of knockabout humour, that he was well worth the trouble."[23] James Chapman suggested that these three films were "transitional in that they offered various strategies by which the Bond series attempted to reinvent itself and keep apace of changing popular tastes at a time when many critics were saying loudly that in style and outlook it belonged to the 1960s."[24] John Brosnan, however, emphasized that beginning with *Diamonds Are Forever*, the franchise simply "revert[ed] . . . completely back to the old-pre-*OHMSS* formula."[25]

Both assessments are valid. Yet Maryam d'Abo and John Cork suggested that *Diamonds Are Forever* signaled an "adjustment in the way women were portrayed in the Bond films."[26] Unlike the Bond Girls of the 1960s, the Bond Girls of the 1970s, they maintained, "became stronger in some ways," including exhibiting greater confidence, stability, and independence while simultaneously presenting character attributes that are less serious and complex.[27] As will be seen, this assessment is inaccurate, particularly with respect to the Guy Hamilton trilogy considered in this chapter. Although it is certainly true that the franchise reinvented itself, it did so, in part, by demonstrating with greater urgency and emphasis that liberated, independent women did *not* have a place in Bond's world.

Consequently, the franchise depicted female characters that became more detached from reality. As critic Roger Greenspun observed in 1973, "[y]ou don't identify with James Bond—*nobody* is that tacky any more—but you might admire the apparent ease with which such ancient attitudes manipulate the anxieties of the modern world."[28] Not surprisingly, the Bond Girls presented in the Guy Hamilton trilogy leave much to be desired in terms of strong leading women. At the same time,

Diamonds Are Forever introduced a new Bondian twist: a critique of and commentary about male chauvinism.

Diamonds Are Forever

Although it was the most popular film of 1972, *Diamonds Are Forever* was nevertheless perceived as "faded and formularized,"[29] "not exactly tops in the Bond film canon,"[30] and "pallid" in comparison to previous Bond productions.[31] Gary Giblin and Lisa Neyhouse characterized the film as "the absolute nadir of the Bond series."[32] Yet one critic suggested that "an old adventure . . . is better than no Bond at all," even if that adventure is "downright imbecilic."[33] Simultaneously juggling an emasculatory and antifeminist agenda, *Diamonds Are Forever*, at least with regard to the former, suggests that the rugged masculinity inherent in Sean Connery's earlier films no longer seemed relevant in the new decade.[34]

The Bond presented in *Diamonds Are Forever* is much slower, and Sean Connery appears fatigued throughout the film: "Connery himself looks a bit long in the tooth to be running around the world . . . ."[35] Indeed, *The Times* noted that Connery "is now 40 and not 30 and his hair [is] thinning and graying a little."[36] One critic observed that Connery "was now packing flab as well as a Walther PPK" and that his style "resemble[d] an elder statesman of espionage with an implanted pacemaker."[37] Apparently gone was the youthfulness that Connery brought to the role just five years earlier in *You Only Live Twice*.[38]

Also gone was the seriousness with which he imbued Bond: "From the start, . . . the idea was to give the character humour. This is his answer to the charge of harmful violence: humour is the release."[39] Even Sean Connery noted that he infused humor into the role, stating that the film was "just another strip cartoon for adults, which is why I've never really understood the idea of Bond as a vicious, sadistic killer. There are too many laughs for that."[40]

But the Bond that the audience discovers in *Diamonds Are Forever* also brings a callous aggressiveness heretofore unseen, as evidenced by his conduct during the pre-title sequence. Presumably, Bond is in pursuit of Ernst Stavro Blofeld in an effort to avenge Tracy di Vicenzo's murder, though this theme is not expressly revealed in the film and is therefore pure speculation. John Brosnan described the pre-title sequence as "a lot of fun. We see Bond beating up various people . . . ."[41]

One of Bond's victims is a woman named Marie, whom he discovers at Blofeld's coastal compound.[42] She is wearing a brown bikini as she sunbathes and reads a magazine. When she discovers Bond, Marie turns her body to reveal her chest and slender figure. She asks, "Is there something I can do for you?"[43] Bond, as he kneels down in front of her, responds that there is, and he reaches his hands behind her back. He meets no objection from Marie as his hands begin to wander, and she even registers a look of interest in him.

Bond's intent, however, is not to seduce her. He coldly states, "There's something I'd like for you to get off your chest," pulls her bikini top off her body, and uses it to choke her.[44] Deliberately tightening his grip around Marie's neck, Bond demands to know the whereabouts of Blofeld, even mockingly imploring her to "speak up, darling, I can't hear you" as he continues to strangle her and she desperately gasps for air.[45] Breath deprivation is a theme that reemerges later in the film.

This act of hypermasculinity is sharply contrasted by the campy, effeminate portrayal of the male characters, including Bond himself, throughout the film.[46] In fact, *Diamonds Are Forever* has been described as "a mixed bag of viciousness and camp humour."[47] As defined by critic Jack Babuscio, camp "is a way of poking fun at the whole . . . of restrictive sex roles and sexual identifications which our society uses to oppress its women and repress its men."[48] At one point, Bond adorns a short pink necktie, attire that not only seems out of place, but also out of character:

> The pink tie has had Bond fans and fashion gurus hanging their heads in embarrassment for 30 years now . . . . The fact that the tie is pink is pretty bad, but that's not the worst of it[: it's] so short, barely going halfway down his shirt, it looks ridiculous.[49]

Perhaps it is Bond who invented the wardrobe malfunction.

Blofeld, too, gets into the wardrobe act. In an effort to elude surveillance, he appears in full drag, complete with a wig, bright red lipstick, and blue eyeliner. As he expresses delight to see Tiffany Case, Blofeld caresses his cat in a manner that is extremely effeminate, prompting critiques that actor Charles Gray's performance was "a trifle too camp for comfort,"[50] "extremely unconvincing," and "miserably incompetent."[51] One scholar opined that Blofeld's drag routine is a subtle suggestion "that Blofeld might be gay,"[52] but any homosexual overtones inherent in Gray's presentation of Blofeld are ultimately negated by his slight interest, whether feigned or otherwise, in Tiffany.

In this regard, the calculating, asexual villainy that Blofeld exhibits in *You Only Live Twice* and *On Her Majesty's Secret Service* is wholly absent from *Diamonds Are Forever*.[53] In fact, Charles Gray's Blofeld is entirely devoid of menace,[54] the result of a miscasting that Raymond Benson described as the "third infuriating time the character has been misrepresented."[55] Blofeld is simply "too charming and poised,"[56] lacking any characteristics befitting a leader of an international terrorist organization such as SPECTRE.[57]

Indeed, *Diamonds Are Forever* suggests that "what appears virile may not be, and one of the anxieties underlying *Diamonds* is the realization that . . . not everyone who looks like a man is really a man. Some of them, it turns out, may actually be 'pussies.'"[58] Blofeld, who at one point remarks that the global powers "flex[] their military muscle like so many impotent beach boys,"[59] is one example, as is Bond's pink necktie, which clearly undercuts his masculinity. One might claim that these are isolated incidents, but numerous other male characters appear nothing short of incompetent, fallible, or emasculated. In fact, Bond even finds himself locked inside a coffin about to succumb to his own cremation. Interestingly enough, two male villains are portrayed as openly homosexual.

Incompetence is first exemplified by British customs officials, who fail to keep diamond smuggler Peter Franks in custody. Consequently, Franks escapes in an effort to rendezvous with Tiffany.[60] Later, Bond, who poses as Franks in order to meet Tiffany himself, encounters the real Franks, and an elevator fight ensues. Bond ultimately prevails, but, in order to maintain his cover, mocks himself. To that end, he places his wallet (containing, among other things, a Playboy Club membership card) into the jacket of the dead Franks so that Tiffany will discover it and believe that Franks is, in fact, Bond. The ploy works as she acts stunned: "My god, you've just killed James Bond!"[61] Bond-as-Franks responds, "That just proves no one's indestructible."[62] Bond then uses the real Franks's body as a vessel in which to transport diamonds from Europe to the United States, suggesting that Franks's true resourcefulness is fully realized only upon death, a metaphor for men's usefulness in general. Although James Chapman suggested that the scene is imbued with comic irony,[63] it serves a greater, overarching purpose by accentuating male vulnerability.

The ineptitude exhibited by the British customs officials is reflected across the Atlantic, as the CIA is similarly presented as incompetent and ineffective. Bond arranges with Felix Leiter to deliver the diamonds to Tiffany in a stuffed animal at a Las Vegas circus. The objective of this arrangement is to place Tiffany under CIA surveillance in order to ascertain the final destination of the diamonds. Bond warns Felix that Tiffany better not "give[] your men the slip," but Felix reassures him: "Relax, I've got upwards of thirty agents down there. A mouse with sneakers couldn't get through."[64] What appears to be a well-planned operation rapidly dissolves, and Bond's worst fear is realized. Not even thirty agents can track Tiffany. Her escape baffles Felix and his associates, who inform a frustrated Bond that "we lost her."[65] In essence, one woman carrying a very noticeable stuffed animal filled with diamonds has managed to evade the CIA, requiring Bond to start anew in his efforts to locate her.

Later, Tiffany sarcastically quips that the CIA's surveillance of Bond outside his hotel suite is "a switch . . . the wolf being guarded by the *three little pigs*."[66] Adding insult to injury is an agreed-upon signal for the release of weather balloons to alert Felix and the CIA to commence their aerial assault against Blofeld. John Brosnan aptly described the signal as "embarrassingly inept."[67]

The Las Vegas police department, replete with male officers, is depicted as bumbling and useless. During a night chase on the Las Vegas strip and a nearby parking lot, Bond evades capture while police vehicles crash into each other and are otherwise destroyed. At one point, a sheriff believes that Bond has been caught, only to have his deputy inform him that Bond is fleeing the scene right before his eyes.

Diamonds Are Forever also features the symbolically castrated Willard Whyte, a billionaire recluse loosely modeled after Howard Hughes who is held captive by SPECTRE within his own estate.[68] Whyte's assets have been stolen from under him and are being utilized by SPECTRE, and only with Bond's assistance can he reclaim his empire from Blofeld's grasp. His first question to Bond when Double-O-Seven liberates him, "What the hell has happened to me, and what can I do about it,"[69] clearly demonstrates the extent to which Whyte has been stripped of any control over himself or his empire. Moreover, Whyte has been described as a weird,[70] an essentially impotent character who tries to catch up to what happens around him in a reactive, rather than proactive, manner.

Finally, the film's focus upon "anality" is exemplified through the presentation of Mister Wint and Mister Kidd, two homosexual assassins[71] portrayed by Bruce Glover and Putter Smith, respectively. Glover, who brought a "studied creepiness" to the role of Mister Wint that appealed to filmmakers,[72] recalled that producers sought "weird physical types," so he approached the role with a possessiveness that suggested that Mister Kidd was his "toy."[73] Smith noted that, because the audience already knew the character's sexual preference, "you don't need to act like you're gay."[74] Ultimately, their portrayal reflects the extent to which the film's homophobia was both "trite and distasteful,"[75] though the Wint-Kidd relationship was "treated in tongue-in-cheek fashion" on account of the fact that homosexuality was "a tad spicy in 1971."[76] Nevertheless, Mister Wint and Mister Kidd have been described as "two camp serial-killer baddies"[77] who are "[a]s cringe-making now as they were in 1971."[78]

Mister Wint and Mister Kidd are "the first gay villains to appear in a Bond movie and two of the first openly gay characters to appear in any Hollywood film."[79] Indeed, they are presented "through a series of familiar cultural and filmic codes—in short, gay stereotypes, including various tropes of effeminancy—in order to clearly demarcate them as gay."[80] Both hold hands immediately after sadistically using a scorpion to commit murder, though they "are never . . . able to produce a threatening effect."[81] Mister Wint is prone to wearing too much cologne, which serves as an identifying characteristic.

For example, Mister Wint and Mister Kidd attempt to dispose of Bond after he is knocked unconscious. As they place Bond into the trunk of their vehicle, Mister Wint accidentally (or carelessly) drops his cologne bottle, which cracks when Bond is placed atop it. Later, Bond awakens in a pipeline to a pungent odor. Encountering a sewer rat, he is "initially unable to tell which of the two of them smells . . . 'like a tart's handkerchief.'"[82] Thereafter, Mister Wint and Mister Kidd become associated with the rat itself, with Bond informing them that he's "smelled that aftershave before, and both times I've smelled a rat."[83]

The rat metaphor further demonstrates the extent to which the characters of Mister Wint and Mister Kidd are "wrong not only morally but as men."[84] Professor Dennis Allen suggested that the rat "becomes a central symbol of anal intercourse,"[85] though it is more likely that the rat possesses a more general meaning. Mister Wint and Mister Kidd are unnatural, not merely because they are homosexual, but rather because they are extremely callous and ruthless in their apparent passion for murder. Throughout the film, they assassinate with "cold aplomb."[86] More importantly, like Donald "Red" Grant in *From Russia With Love*, Mister Wint and Mister Kidd are imposters whose real identities are revealed only through Bond's particular attention to detail. Bond exposes Grant when he mistakenly orders red wine with fish. In *Diamonds Are Forever*, Bond exposes Mister Wint and Mister Kidd "after finding out they don't know claret from crumpets."[87]

Mister Wint and Mister Kidd are ultimately not as menacing or threatening as Grant. While they "look an evil-enough pair, . . . they act more like a comedy team than a murder squad,"[88] and their demise is imbued with homophobic humor. Mister Kidd is lit ablaze, literally transforming him into a "flaming queen."[89] Mister Wint, by contrast, meets his end when Bond "pull[s] Wint's arms between his legs in what is very clearly an emasculating maneuver and then, attaching [a] bomb to Wint's coattails, flings him over the side of the ship, where he explodes."[90] Mister Wint even registers slight pleasure from this act, but Bond's quip that Mister Wint "certainly left with his tails between his legs"[91] reaffirms that Bond's elimination of these two villains represents a restoration of order and the preservation of heterosexual masculinity that the film itself challenges.

The over-arching theme of emasculation and, to some degree, male superfluity is also explored through the lyrics of the title song. Performed by Shirley Bassey, who previously made "Goldfinger" a hit on the recording charts, "Diamonds Are Forever" serves as another tutorial for women. Its comparison of men to diamonds is striking. Forget men, the anthem suggests, because diamonds not only last forever but are also all that a woman ultimately needs for satisfaction. Diamonds, unlike men, "stimulate and tease" and "won't leave in the night."[92] Furthermore, diamonds are transparent: "nothing hides in the heart" to cause pain.[93] More importantly, diamonds "never lie," while men "are mere mortals who are not worth going to your grave for."[94] For Raymond Benson, however, the song lacked impact and came off "corny."[95] Considering that composer John Barry reportedly suggested that Bassey imagine she was singing about a penis,[96] Benson's characterization may be quite apt. In fact, Saltzman reportedly requested that Bassey's performance be removed "because of its sexual innuendo."[97]

* * *

In addition to the emasculatory theme, *Diamonds Are Forever* presents four female characters that range the entire spectrum. Tiffany, the primary Bond Girl in the film, was portrayed by American actress Jill St. John.[98] St. John received the screenplay from Broccoli himself,[99] who believed that she should be cast as Plenty O'Toole, an ancillary character.[100] Ultimately, Guy Hamilton thought she was better suited to portray Tiffany.[101] St. John was "thrilled" when she was offered the role, recalling that she "wanted to look glamorous."[102] But not everyone shared her definition of glamour. Critic Thomas Berger described St. John as follows: "[Her] breezy California voice has always previously set . . . teeth on edge."[103] *Newsweek* even conferred upon St. John the title of "the world's worst actress"[104] and questioned "[w]hat movie would be idiotic enough to [cast St. John] and not strip every last bit of lace from her body?"[105]

The role of Plenty was awarded to Lana Wood, the younger sister of actress Natalie Wood. Wood was cast at the suggestion of Tom Mankiewicz, who thought she was "perfect" for the part,[106] although *Playboy* credited Wood's casting to her appearance in one of its pictorials.[107] One description of both Tiffany and Plenty noted that these "ladies of sinister sexuality look[ed] like randy and overweight cheerleaders beside the likes of Domino and Pussy Galore. They furnish 007 with a few pleasant pit stops, but the real adventure lies elsewhere."[108] Bambi and Thumper, portrayed by Lola Larson and Trina Parks, respectively, round out the cast of female characters in *Diamonds Are Forever*.[109]

On one hand, it has been stated that Bond "moves to bed the more natural kind of Bond girl."[110] Yet on the other hand, *Diamonds Are Forever* did not compare well with its predecessors: "The early Bond bashes, with their luscious women and racy puns, seemed sexy in the '60s."[111] By contrast, *Diamonds Are Forever*, wrote one critic, featured women who, "for all their exotic names, are [merely] *Playboy* mannequins."[112]

* * *

The first noteworthy female character in *Diamonds Are Forever* is Plenty. As her name suggests, Plenty is buxom. Best described as a "Las Vegas B girl,"[113] Plenty has also been characterized as a "floozy"[114] and a "casino gold digger"[115] who is more than willing to employ her sex appeal in exchange for a financial incentive.[116] Perhaps the most hyperbolic caricature of the traditional Bond Girl, Plenty is "a plot device with a serious cleavage"[117] and a character completely devoid of substance.

The audience is first introduced to Plenty in Whyte's casino. She is standing next to a heavyset man wearing a salmon-colored shirt (note, once again, the attribution of pink to male characters) who informs Plenty, whom he has dubbed his "pussycat," that he just "shot the whole wad" on a losing bet at the craps table (similarly note the recurrence of failure and ineptitude attributed to men).[118] This risqué but veiled sexual reference is countenanced by Plenty's immediate disinterest, and she rejects his offer to return to his hotel room.

As she walks away, Plenty registers a curious and interested expression when she hears Bond-as-Franks requesting $10,000 in chips. The camera eventually returns to Bond, who now has the pleasure of Plenty's presence beside him. She wears a purple dress that practically exposes her entire chest, and a long necklace calls further attention to her ample cleavage.

Plenty immediately introduces herself, prompting Bond to turn around and immediately focus upon her chest:

> *Plenty*: Hi, I'm Plenty.
>
> *Bond* (*gazing at her bosom*): But of course you are.
>
> *Plenty*: Plenty O'Toole.
>
> *Bond* (*rising*): Named after your father perhaps?
>
> *Plenty*: Would you like some help? On the craps, I mean.[119]

Bond's snide quip is lost on Plenty, whose tone and manner are extremely superficial. Certainly, her offer of assistance could, under the circumstances, only reference the game of craps. The fact that she must qualify her offer suggests that she is not particularly sharp.

Bond nonetheless permits Plenty to feel useful, and she initially rolls the dice on his behalf. For the audience and the rest of the men around the table—indeed, only one woman is at this particular craps table—this is another opportunity for Plenty's chest to figure prominently. When she loses, Bond takes over, displaying an adeptness that is extremely puzzling to Plenty. She places one hand on her hip and states with cool incredulity, "Say, you've played this game before."[120] Bond's response, "Just once," does not immediately register as sarcasm to Plenty, who then has a noticeably delayed reaction of bewilderment.[121] Once Bond leaves the table with $50,000 in winnings, Plenty is pleasantly surprised: "You handled those cubes like a monkey handles coconuts!"[122] Plenty is further captivated by Bond's generous gift of $5,000, which she receives for essentially doing absolutely nothing.

Although Bond walks away from the table, Plenty obsequiously follows, grabbing hold of his arm. She declares that Bond is terrific, albeit weird, but his purported weirdness does not deter her. Rather, Plenty immediately invites Bond to have a drink with her. The suggestion is merely a polite way of offering herself to Bond. In fact, she slightly stumbles over the word "drink," perhaps a not-so-subtle indication that Plenty has other things in mind. In a scene that did not make the final cut, Bond and Plenty do share a drink, but Plenty's dialogue verges on the absurd. Bond not only dislikes the wine he orders, he also seems thoroughly disinterested in Plenty herself. The scene, like the wine, is stale.

Here is what the audience does not see in the original film. After tasting stale wine, Bond returns the bottle, an act that shocks Plenty: "Hey, I didn't think you could really do that. I bet they charge you for it."[123] She loses Bond's interest because she simply cannot engage in coherent conversation, and she stumbles over Bond's suggestion that she should be paying for dinner given the windfall he has given her at the casino. Plenty inquires if Bond is a knight, but she reassures him that his commoner status is fine with her because she is a member of the Democratic Party. Plenty, rather than Bond, suggests that she has "had enough of this," but Bond is in no apparent rush to leave, inquiring whether Plenty is enjoying herself.[124] While Plenty seems anxious to wind up in bed with him, Bond appears to exhibit a look of complete apathy.[125] Noticing that her opportunity to sleep with Bond is waning, Plenty suggests that she properly thank Bond for his generosity by walking him to his hotel suite. Bond's apathy is inherent in his noncommittal response: "If you insist."[126]

In the film's next scene, Plenty barrels through the door of Bond's hotel suite, which prompts him to sarcastically suggest that she come in. Lacking any *savior-faire*, Plenty essentially throws herself at Bond. Whether she feels some sense of obligation to Bond for his monetary gift

Plenty O'Toole (Lana Wood) offers assistance to James Bond (Sean Connery) at the craps table in *Diamonds Are Forever.*

(Everett Collection/Rex USA)

or not, it is apparent that Plenty believes the only way she can reciprocate Bond's generosity is to offer her body in return, much in the same manner as Tracy di Vicenzo in *On Her Majesty's Secret Service*. But while she endeavors to act in a sexy manner, Plenty's entire essence is comical. Indeed, her declaration that Bond's hotel suite is a "super place" is delivered in a thick American accent that is comical.[127]

Presented with a woman who is more than willing to serve as an empty sexual vessel, Bond accepts the invitation. But it is Plenty, not Bond, who initiates their embrace, again a suggestion that Bond is not particularly interested. That said, he hastens the encounter by removing her dress. Wearing only undergarments, Plenty excuses herself, which enables Bond to discover Tiffany's henchmen pointing guns at him. Bond confesses that he's been caught "with more than my hands up," and Plenty is carried out of the bedroom toward the window by Tiffany's men.[128] Even the protestations she lodges against them verge on the ridiculous: "What the hell is this, a pervert's convention or something? Hey, listen, you can't do this to me. Stop that, I've got friends in this town!"[129]

Plenty's superfluity has already been established through her dialogue and demeanor. Yet her expendability is fully realized when she is thrown out the window. Coincidentally, and unbeknownst to Tiffany's henchmen, Plenty lands in the hotel's swimming pool. Bond is impressed by the marksmanship, noting that it is an "exceptionally fine shot."[130] The response he receives is that the henchmen "didn't know there was a pool down there,"[131] a quip that one critic characterized as a "harmlessly sadistic joke."[132]

In a second deleted scene, a drenched—and determined—Plenty returns to Bond's suite in the hope of capitalizing upon the sexual encounter that previously eludes her. Her efforts are thwarted when she discovers Tiffany with him. Plenty registers both a shocked and stumped expression on her face, but she decides to rummage through Tiffany's purse in order to find her address. She eventually presents herself at Tiffany's, and, as the film moves forward, Bond and Tiffany discover her body in the swimming pool with her legs bound to a concrete block. What the audience does not know but can infer is that Mister Wint and Mister Kidd mistake Plenty for Tiffany (another indication of male incompetence) and kill her in error.[133]

As Raymond Benson noted, Plenty's "presence is gratuitous, especially since most of her scenes were cut from the final print."[134] Although Plenty is the "Obligatory Sacrificial Lamb,"[135] there is really no reason for Plenty to die, a fate that John Brosnan stated he "cannot grasp."[136] Indeed, Plenty's character *appears* to serve no real purpose. Moreover, she essentially personifies *coitus interruptus* through her failed efforts to sleep with Bond, and her irrelevance is only overshadowed by the annoyance she generates. The audience, which presumably lets out a "schoolboy giggle" just from her name alone, cannot help but chuckle at her entire on-film persona.[137]

Plenty clearly serves an aesthetic purpose. At the same time, she also represents one extreme of the 1970s female archetype that is presented in *Diamonds Are Forever*. Unlike her predecessors, Plenty lacks the most basic attributes, and her character suffers from anemic dialogue and puzzling or absurd reactions to that which occurs around her. Gary Giblin and Lisa Neyhouse described Plenty as "a true bimbo, 100% at odds with the female characters of every film before and since."[138] Anything that Plenty finds foreign or incomprehensible is defined in terms of being "a little weird."[139] And yet, Plenty herself can be characterized in a similar manner, leeching on to seemingly wealthy male gamblers in the hope of reaping a financial gain and expressing some willingness to engage in sexual activity if the men present her with a windfall. In this regard, Plenty can be viewed as predatory, her behavior subdued to some degree by grossly and overly exaggerated ineptitude.

* * *

The hyperbole inherent in Plenty is also present at the opposite end of the spectrum through the characters of Bambi and Thumper, whom James Chapman completely dismissed as simply "two athletic women."[140] Bambi and Thumper arguably represent the franchise's first direct response to the feminist and Women's Liberation movements, though it has been suggested that characters named Bambi and Thumper "would never be mistaken for feminists."[141] Regardless of the descriptions—from "bikinied bodyguards,"[142] "lesbian karate experts,"[143] "SPECTRE martial arts experts,"[144] and "black and white Amazons,"[145] to representatives of the "man-hating branch of women's lib"[146]—attributed to them, Bambi and Thumper are presented in a highly unflattering light. Given the countless number of Bond Girl alumnae who appeared in *Playboy*, it is not at all surprising that neither Lola Larson nor Trina Parks graced the magazine's pages.[147]

In light of the stereotypical critique of feminists and liberationists as lesbians, Bambi and Thumper may also succumb to such a characterization, having also been branded "a couple of butch beauties."[148] Slender, athletic, devoid of makeup, and lacking any accentuating or flattering curves on their bodies, Bambi and Thumper are nothing like Pussy Galore, who represents the ideal heterosexual lesbian fantasy. Whereas Pussy Galore participates in Auric Goldfinger's scheme for profit, maintaining a charming, mysterious, and seductive persona throughout, Bambi and

Thumper waste no time trapping Bond and physically assaulting him. Their disdain for Bond and a desire to eliminate him is more akin to the toad-like Rosa Klebb in *From Russia With Love*. Moreover, their unflattering and sexless attire further deemphasizes any feminine qualities they may possess. Bambi's tank top and shorts are both brown, while Thumper sports a bright yellow bikini that clashes with her dark skin tone. If these two characters were intended to represent so-called gorgeous amazons, then the on-screen translation misses the mark.

Bambi and Thumper "strike a gymnastic blow for Women's Lib by effortlessly bouncing Bond, the sexist pig."[149] Regardless of their sexual preferences, the characters ultimately lend support to those who assumed that liberationists were lesbians[150] and that "'feminism is lesbianism.'"[151] That Bambi and Thumper are portrayed in a manner to suggest that they are imbued with such characteristics[152] reflects the extent to which they are anomalous and out of place in Bond's world.

Their sexless characteristics aside (indeed, the most arousing image in the scene is the shape of the chair—resembling a bosom or buttocks—from which Bambi rises to introduce herself),[153] Bambi and Thumper arguably pose a very real threat to Bond's masculinity. They are unafraid to attack Bond, proving that the karate chop is, in fact, mightier than the lamb chop. For this reason alone, Bond must assert himself over them if he (and a patriarchal order) can survive. At the same time, it must be remembered that, notwithstanding their supposed independent, liberationist characteristics, Bambi and Thumper are ultimately aligned with a villain, Blofeld's associate Bert Saxby, and, by extension, ideologically represent Blofeld and SPECTRE.[154] They also serve male superiors and are therefore not independent.

Their introduction can be characterized as both "mocking insouciance and seductive warmth."[155] Bambi greets Bond by rising from the shapely furniture and performing cartwheels for him. Thumper, who is sprawled on a large rock much like a lizard tanning in the sunlight, asks Bond if there is something they can do for him. Bond, briefly assessing the situation, replies with innuendo: "I can think of several things off hand."[156] After Bond states the reason for his presence, Thumper points him in the proper direction. But she requests Bond's aid in order to descend from the rock. Bond, believing he has obtained the information he needs, states that is "all there is to it," but Thumper disagrees: "Not quite. We're going to have a ball."[157] Detaining Bond by placing her arms around him, Thumper delivers a blow to his groin.

What ensues quickly turns into a performance for Bambi and Thumper, replete with their own cues for each other's entry and reentry into the fight. With Bond on the ground wincing in pain, Thumper defers: "All yours, Bambi!"[158] Bambi then proceeds to perform flips toward Bond, kicking him in the chest. Bond flies backwards and again falls to the ground, while Bambi laughs and smiles. Thumper proceeds to perform cartwheels and, once again, cues Bambi: "You're on again, Bambi."[159] Bambi obliges, jumping up onto a fixture hanging from the ceiling and deferring again to Thumper for the next strike. Although Bond subdues Thumper, the elevated Bambi kicks him in the face and then succeeds in gripping Bond's head between her thighs. Meanwhile, Thumper, who remains on the ground after Bond strikes her, writhes with diabolical, spiderlike movements that are accompanied by fierce facial expressions. As a finale, both Bambi and Thumper push Bond into a swimming pool and dive in after him to continue their assault.

John Brosnan opined that Bond "met his match" with Bambi and Thumper,[160] and others have similarly noted that these two women simply trounce Bond,[161] who gets "dusted up."[162] This is only partially true. As soon as Bambi and Thumper throw Bond into the swimming pool, the tide, so to speak, turns against them. Once again, the swimming pool theme figures prominently,[163] and nothing good seems to result for the women submerged therein. Plenty, of course, lands in a swimming pool after being thrown out a hotel window and ultimately dies in a second swimming pool.

With their effort to drown Bond unsuccessful, Bambi and Thumper are forced beneath the water by Bond's overpowering hands and arms. In the same manner in which Bond constrains Marie's breathing at the beginning of the film, Bambi and Thumper suffer a similar fate. Bond pulls them up by their hair briefly enough to compel an answer to his demand, but neither capitulates. Bond then pushes their heads down beneath the surface again in an effort to make them talk. Finally, Thumper acquiesces. She breaks free from Bond, swims to the edge of the pool and, coughing as she struggles to gasp for air, motions in the direction where Whyte is held captive. Bond has effectively defeated Bambi and Thumper.

The symbolic drowning of Bambi and Thumper is somewhat prophetic: that both the feminist and Women's Liberation movements, while seeming to gain momentum when *Diamonds Are Forever* was released, will ultimately succumb to the weight of reality. Bambi and Thumper threaten the establishment, and Bond must literally deprive them of air in order to preserve the system and order from which he derives strength. The audience emerges from this scene with a sense that, after sufficient effort, Bambi and Thumper can be subdued and relegated to positions in which they can no longer challenge traditional societal mores.

Moreover, the supposed liberationist tendencies that Bambi and Thumper exhibit, no matter how stereotypical they may be, are revealed as nothing more than a façade. Absent their physical bruteness, Bambi and Thumper have no substance. Instead, they merely represent physical

James Bond (Sean Connery) encounters Thumper (Trina Parks) in *Diamonds Are Forever*.

(Rex USA)

obstacles around which Bond must navigate, a fact that is corroborated by Raymond Benson's assessment that neither Bambi nor Thumper ultimately poses a real threat to Bond at all.[164]

* * *

Having explored those female characters that stand at opposite ends of the spectrum, only Tiffany, the primary Bond Girl, remains. Tiffany initially presents herself as confident, if not arrogant, with a detached condescension that suggests she is a primary player in the diamond smuggling operation of which she is a part. But this, too, is merely a façade as Tiffany ultimately demonstrates that she is both "ineffective" and "all mouth and no mind."[165] Although Jill St. John believed that her character "had no problem with who she was and what she represented,"[166] Tiffany is hardly a laudable feminist figure. In fact, one critic characterized St. John's performance as merely "funny,"[167] a sentiment later shared by Gary Giblin and Lisa Neyhouse, who described St. John as a "Borscht-belt comedienne in search of an audience."[168]

So who is Tiffany, and what does she represent? According to Jill St. John, Tiffany is a true woman of the 1970s, a character who is "starting to take charge" of her own life.[169] Tiffany's first cinematic appearance in the film, however, suggests otherwise. Bond-as-Franks arrives at Tiffany's apartment in Amsterdam and observes a scantily clad blonde wearing skin-colored lingerie walking into her bedroom. Tiffany informs Bond-as-Franks that she will be out momentarily, a signal presuming that she will dress and present herself to her guest. Bond-as-Franks, in the interim, engages in conversation with her from the other room, and Tiffany reveals that she is unmarried.

"Tiffany Case? Definitely distinctive," Bond-as-Franks quips as he discovers her complete name.[170] Tiffany reveals that she was born on the first floor of the jewelry store after which she is named while her mother searched for a wedding ring. Bond-as-Franks, endeavoring to display charm and, hopefully, his art of seduction, responds, "I'm glad for your sake it wasn't Van Cleef and Arpels."[171]

The function of this exchange is to confirm Tiffany's availability for Bond-as-Franks's sexual conquest. Curiously, when Tiffany does reemerge, she is wearing the same lingerie. The only difference in her appearance is that she now adorns a brunette wig. Standing confidently at the threshold of her bedroom door in minimal clothing, Tiffany presents herself as a pure object of sexual desire. The ensuing dialogue is wrought with innuendo:

Bond-as-Franks: Weren't you a blonde when I came in?
Tiffany: Could be.
Bond-as-Franks: I tend to notice little things like that, whether a girl's a blonde or a brunette.
Tiffany: And which do you prefer?
Bond-as-Franks (*fixating his glance upon Tiffany's bosom*): Well, providing the collars and cuffs match.
Tiffany: We'll talk about that later . . . .[172]

Bond-as-Franks continues to stare at Tiffany as she walks away. He is absolutely captivated, and his interest is clearly piqued.

Tiffany is a peculiar character, and it is unclear to both Bond-as-Franks and the audience how she should be initially perceived. Tiffany countenances her aesthetic objectification with a persona that, at least initially, indicates resourcefulness and authority. As Lee Pfeiffer and Dave Worrall observed, "[w]hen Bond first meets [Tiffany], she is hard-edged and intriguing, as befitting a professional smuggler."[173] With respect to her supposed hard-edged, smuggling persona, Tiffany takes the drinking glass under the pretext of providing Bond-as-Franks with ice. Instead, she returns to her bedroom, adds a few ice cubes, dusts the glass for a thumbprint, and photographs the print in an effort to verify that the man in her apartment is, in fact, Franks. Inside her dresser, Tiffany accesses a large projector, which she uses to compare a file image of Franks's thumbprint with the thumbprint she obtains from the glass. Although Tiffany is no forensic scientist, she concludes, following a cursory review of the two images, that the thumbprints are identical. As such, Tiffany easily succumbs to the deception occurring right in front of her.

Tiffany returns to the living room now wearing a transparent black negligee over her lingerie. Bond-as-Franks remarks, "That's quite a nice little nothing you're almost wearing. I approve," but Tiffany is wholly unimpressed.[174] She condescendingly responds, "I don't dress for the hired help. Let's see your passport, Franks."[175] With Bond-as-Franks reduced to the status of "hired help," Tiffany's remark suggests that her role within the diamond smuggling hierarchy is of far greater importance and that she holds a high position in the chain of command. She also rejects each sexual insinuation presented to her without hesitation or reservation:

Tiffany: I never mix business with pleasure.
Bond-as-Franks: Well neither do I.
Tiffany: Good! Then we can start by saving the cute remarks until after you get the diamonds into Los Angeles.

> *Bond-as-Franks*: Well where are they are now?
> *Tiffany*: That's not your problem. Your problem is getting them in.[176]

Tiffany directs the conversation, ensuring that the focus remains upon the task at hand: Bond-as-Franks's responsibility to smuggle 50,000 carats across the Atlantic Ocean. In short, Tiffany's introduction suggests that, at least initially, she exhibits the traits befitting a professional jewel smuggler.

Later, Tiffany, still under the false impression that Bond is Franks, infiltrates Bond's hotel suite in Las Vegas in an effort to obtain the diamonds. Bond discovers her in his bed after his rendezvous with Plenty is prematurely interrupted. But the falsity flows both ways, as Tiffany continues to present an erroneous aura of authority over Bond. Indeed, the audience continues to believe that she is one of the masterminds of the smuggling scheme. Condescending in tone, Tiffany is sprawled out in the bed as if perched on a throne:

> *Bond-as-Franks*: Good evening, Miss Case.
> *Tiffany*: Sorry about your fulsome friend. I bet you really missed something.
> *Bond-as-Franks* (*approaching the bed*): Well, the evening may not be a total loss after all.
> *Tiffany*: Why don't we talk a bit first?
> *Bond-as-Franks*: First? (*sitting down on the bed*) Well, what would you like to talk about?
> *Tiffany* (*rubbing her foot casually, but seductively, along Bond's side*): You pick a subject.
> *Bond-as-Franks*: Diamonds?
> *Tiffany* (*condescending*): Good boy.
> *Bond-as-Franks*: And you want to know where they are, and whether I'm working alone or not.
> *Tiffany*: So far, so good. Keeping going.
> *Bond-as-Franks*: And if not, then with whom, so you can inform your superiors and acquire the diamonds.
> *Tiffany* (*condescending*): Peter, I'm very impressed. There's a lot more to you than I had expected.[177]

Tiffany has both orchestrated this encounter and directed the conversation. Yet Bond has begun to significantly cut holes into Tiffany's purported authority, exposing her true role in the scheme.

These holes, nevertheless, are very much discernible earlier. Tiffany's chameleon-like wig and hair color changes reflect the pervasive theme in *Diamonds Are Forever* that things are not as they appear. First appearing as a blonde, Tiffany inexplicably becomes a brunette. It is entirely unclear why she replaces the wig as it serves no practical function. Once she emerges as a natural redhead, Bond-as-Franks comments, "Eh, I don't care much for redheads, terrible tempers. But somehow it seems to suit you."[178]

It is also curious that someone as indecisive as Tiffany is tasked with responsibility in an elaborate diamond smuggling operation. Nevertheless, it later becomes apparent that Tiffany's role in the scheme is simply to direct others, actions that are, in turn, directives assigned to her. Moreover, Tiffany seems to lack focus. Although she informs Bond-as-Franks at her apartment that she needs to "finish dressing," it is unclear when she ever *begins* dressing.[179]

These peculiarities foreshadow what is revealed in Bond's Las Vegas hotel suite, where Tiffany tacitly acknowledges that her authority within the diamond smuggling hierarchy is limited. Indeed, Tiffany is wholly exposed as her true self, a "naïve and easily manipulated" character.[180] Once he has undressed, Bond-as-Franks notes that, as a "condemned man," Tiffany represents his "hearty breakfast."[181] While Tiffany previously emphasizes her refusal to coalesce business with pleasure, this principle apparently has no application at this juncture in the film. In fact, Tiffany offers no protest to Bond-as-Franks's declaration that he is, in essence, *entitled* to possess her sexually.

In the scene immediately following their sexual counter, Tiffany's façade of independence and authority is virtually stripped. She no longer directs the conversation:

> *Tiffany*: You're not going to tell me where the diamonds are, are you?
> *Bond-as-Franks*: What diamonds?
> *Tiffany*: Sooner or later, you'll have to talk. *They'll make* you . . . .[182]

Tiffany's frustration outweighs the import of her comment. The "they" to whom she refers are the diamond smugglers. She is simply a conduit. Although Tiffany attempts to regain some authority, suggesting that she and Bond-as-Franks work together (she proposes "a fifty-fifty split. You get the diamonds, I get us out!"[183]), and that she will retrieve the diamonds while Bond-as-Franks secures a rental car to facilitate their escape, she ultimately becomes an unwitting participant in another elaborate scheme. This time, the orchestrator is the CIA. Even in her effort to free herself from one burden, Tiffany becomes entangled in another mess.

In order to gain possession of the diamonds, Tiffany must navigate around and leap through various hoops during a circus. She ultimately criticizes Bond-as-Franks for "letting me freeze my behind off at a blackjack table for two hours waiting for some nonexistent diamonds,"[184] but it is apparent that Tiffany is simply unaccustomed to taking action on her own. Apparently tasked with smuggling the diamonds into the United States, Tiffany nevertheless places all responsibility upon Bond-as-Franks while presenting the illusion that she is acting to further that result. For example, she previously informs Bond-as-Franks that "*we've* got to get those diamonds out of here and fast," but the audience can point to no specific act on Tiffany's part that moves the diamonds into Los Angeles.[185]

Bond's conquest of Tiffany exposes her character weakness and confirms that she is entirely expendable. He informs Tiffany that she has stumbled upon circumstances that are far beyond what she previously imagined, admonishing her for getting in over her head. It is at this point, finally, that Tiffany discovers Bond is not Peter Franks. In response to her skepticism, Bond smacks Tiffany across the face with his necktie and demands that she reveal her connections. Her response is indicative of her low-level participation in the operation: "All I know is voices on a phone. They got me this place and told me to wait for further instructions."[186] Later, Tiffany finally acknowledges that she has stepped into quicksand: "Listen, you can drop me off at the next corner. This whole thing is getting a little out of hand."[187]

Whereas Tiffany once exudes arrogant confidence and self-assuredness, she begins to express perpetual concern over her eventual fate. In one scene in which she and Bond are in bed together in the bridal suite of the Whyte House (Bond explains that they are there in order "to form a more perfect union"), Tiffany inquires, "[W]hat's going to happen to me?"[188] She persists:

> *Tiffany*: You did talk to your friend Felix about me?
>
> *Bond*: Mmhmm.
>
> *Tiffany*: Well, what did he say?
>
> *Bond*: Something about twenty years to life, nothing important.
>
> *Tiffany*: Twenty years to life!
>
> *Bond* (*rolling on top of her*): Relax, darling. I'm on top of the situation.[189]

Felix later reveals that Tiffany has a "lifetime reservation" in a federal penitentiary,[190] but she, determined to avoid prison, seeks aid from whomever is available, including Q: "Listen, Mister Q, I was wondering, have you heard any talk about me from Felix or James?"[191] Tiffany explains: "I guess I'm working for the good guys now, but I'm still only two steps away from the slammer if they want me there. I thought you might be able to put in a good word."[192] As expected, Q offers no assistance, and her self-serving efforts to avoid the ramifications of her actions prove fruitless.

While she acts out of self-interest to avoid prison, Tiffany also functions as an accessory. She either receives directives from Bond or displays considerable ineptitude and, as such, is imbued with dependence and vulnerability, two traditional Bond Girl traits. Although Bond directs Tiffany to cause a commotion at a gas station in order to facilitate his entry into a van that transports the diamonds, she accomplishes the objective in the most visible manner possible, replete with brash, disruptive, and unpredictable behavior. Later, Tiffany stumbles upon Blofeld and becomes his hostage, requiring Bond to rescue her.

Yet Bond discovers that Tiffany is not held in traditional captivity and is in absolutely no physical harm. Instead, she is with Blofeld on an offshore oil rig, sporting a purple bikini, and relaxing on a chaise lounge while casually reading a magazine. Indeed, as Blofeld informs Bond, Tiffany "has taken a terribly reasonable attitude about all this. Like any sensible animal, she's only threatening when she's threatened."[193] The "animal" is also relatively quiet, as if she has been muzzled, a clear and stark contrast to her previous obnoxious loquaciousness. Nevertheless, Blofeld admonishes Tiffany because her scantily clad figure is distracting his all-male crew and, by extension, interfering with his operation.

Although Tiffany attempts to assist Bond and serve a useful purpose while they are on the oil rig, the "dragon lady," as Bond dubs her, ultimately causes greater harm than good.[194] She confiscates a cassette tape that she believes controls Blofeld's satellite and gives it to Bond. Bond switches the tape and, calling her a "bitch," slips the second tape down the bottom of her bikini.[195] Tiffany then inserts the tape that Bond places in her bikini into the satellite controls. She informs Bond of her action, feeling triumphant about her accomplishment. Bond, however, is less than pleased: "You stupid twit, you put the real one back in."[196] In response, Tiffany can only register a puzzled and bewildered look upon her face, and her attempt to correct her own error fails. Blofeld discovers the concealed tape in her bikini bottom, remarks that she is displaying a bit too much cheek, and demands that she forfeit the tape. After she complies, Blofeld offers a sexist critique of Tiffany's aptitude: "What a pity, such nice cheeks, too. If only they were brains."[197]

After Bond defeats Blofeld and rescues Tiffany, she stubbornly remains obsessed with reacquiring the diamonds, which are now part of a satellite in orbit around the earth. This unrealistic desire underscores Tiffany as a character who lacks potential. Throughout the entire film, she desires the diamonds, but she lacks the acumen or gumption to devise her own plan to obtain them. Instead, Tiffany relies upon others to implement the plan for her, and she repeatedly finds herself caught as a mere player in others'

Tiffany Case (Jill St. John) displays "too much cheek" aboard Ernst Stavro Blofeld's oil rig in *Diamonds Are Forever.*

(United Artists/Archive Photos/Getty Images)

schemes. In this regard, Jill St. John's characterization of Tiffany as a woman taking charge of her own life is both inaccurate and unsupported.

Yet even if Jill St. John's assessment is true, then *Diamonds Are Forever* advances a message that the ideal 1970s woman is reactive rather than proactive. Tiffany possesses no initiative and instead permits others to direct her actions. When a moment arises during which she must exert effort on her own, she complains. But she also brings upon herself the predicaments in which she finds herself, willingly becoming engulfed by matters that she cannot fully comprehend. To compensate, she enlists the efforts of others to accomplish her tasks and bears the burden of their shortcomings. Thus, the image Tiffany advances of the ideal 1970s woman is one who is best relegated to an object to be viewed, *i.e.*, lounging on Blofeld's oil rig reading magazines—like Marie at the beginning of the film—and silent. Even producer Barbara Broccoli conceded that the Bond Girls "'went through a period . . . when they became more window dressing. They were draped around swimming pools and that sort of thing.'"[198] Tiffany fits nicely within the period to which Broccoli referred.

* * *

Taken together, Plenty and Tiffany paint a bleak portrait of a feminine ideal for a new decade. Of course, it must be remembered that the 1970s Bond was "still very much a figure of the more conservative 1960's."[199] Far from women of substance, independence, and capability, these characters serve as a springboard for refining the 1970s Bond Girl archetype. Whereas Bambi and Thumper are abhorrent because they blatantly display the elements associated with Women's Liberation, the reactionary nature of Plenty and Tiffany is much more subtle. Both Plenty and Tiffany demonstrate that physical attributes, submissive demeanor, and naïve personas are preferable over women who exhibit intellectual acumen or independence. Moreover, to the extent that both Plenty and Tiffany insert themselves into the patriarchal order, they are disruptive and burdensome.

Diamonds Are Forever "reestablishes Double-O-Seven as the classic British secret agent."[200] But the film ultimately offers audiences "requisite come-ons from Tiffany Case . . . and three or four certified Bondettes,"[201] and "the most ineffective and contemptible female leads and supporting characters in the series."[202] The nascent incapacity inherent in Plenty and Tiffany provides fertile ground for development over the course of the next two films, which introduce audiences to the likes of Rosie Carver, Solitaire, Andrea Anders, and Mary Goodnight.

Live and Let Die

By 1972, *Diamonds Are Forever* and the 1960s were both relegated to distant memory. Indeed, many believed that "James Bond [was] dead"[203] in the new decade. Released in 1973, *Live and Let Die* was criticized for what was perceived as its "[u]nashamedly out-of-date" presentation.[204] *Live and Let Die*, it was written, "aims to be the biggest and most expensive B feature ever made,"[205] and *The Times* questioned, "[W]ill James Bond live on in the 1970s? Not much farther, if this episode is anything to go by."[206] *Time* suggested that *Live and Let Die* was part of a series "that has long since outlived its brief historical moment—if not, alas, its profitability."[207]

A so-called anachronistic formula was not the only complaint. *Live and Let Die* was also described as "the most vulgar addition" to the Bond series.[208] The novel, which was Fleming's second Bond adventure, is "the most violent and sadistic of all . . . when Bond himself was at his toughest, running up his highest body count . . . ."[209] The film greatly subdued the violence, but it was difficult to garner acclaim nonetheless. Raymond Benson suggested that the film's plot did not measure up to the novel, though he described the screenplay as both "witty and entertaining."[210] For one critic, Roger Moore's debut as Bond was the "worst" he had seen,[211] while another noted that *Live and Let Die* was "both perfunctory and predictable—leaving the mind free to wander into the question of its overall taste. Or lack of it."[212]

One legacy of *Live and Let Die* is the extent to which it incorporates blaxploitation, which was a "particular cultural and industrial phenomenon of Hollywood at the time."[213] The "common denominator" in a successful blaxploitation film is that the black criminal element contains "a black fantasy figure who ripped off 'Whitey.'"[214] The franchise's foray into this genre and the race politics associated therewith also proved ripe for critique. The *New York Times* noted that "[m]erely to make a new adventure movie in which all the bad guys are black and almost all the good guys are white, and which includes in its climax the (near) sacrifice of a (recent) virgin—takes nerve."[215] Critic Vincent Canby observed:

> Just how civilized the film is, I think, is reflected in the fact that it is able to exploit, in a single coherent narrative, sinister Caribbean voodoo rites, a crooked black island dictator, a sense of real black brotherhood, the supremacy of James Bond at almost everything, and a red-neck Louisiana sheriff who . . . becomes one of the funniest characters you'll probably see on screen all year.[216]

With an outrageous plot featuring African Americans entangled in fantastic and unrealistic voodoo magic that originates from a Caribbean epicenter, the film was described as "superfluous."[217] Despite its focus on the occult, *Live and Let Die* apparently offered "nothing frightening . . . and nothing greedy or snobbish."[218]

Perhaps the most important legacy of *Live and Let Die* is its treatment of the Bond Girl. The three female characters that appear in the film suffer from suppression, subordination, and outright ineptitude. Critics certainly took note. *Time*, for example, observed that Solitaire, Rosie, and Miss Caruso—portrayed by Jane Seymour, Gloria Hendry, and Madeline Smith, respectively—"suffer a sport of weightlessness, a lack of humanness."[219] According to *The New Yorker*, in

> the new "007" movie[,] . . . the girls are made to seem unreal, with minds the size of moths' as they flicker round the irresistible flame of the caddish 007. There is one beautiful broad in *Live and Let Die* who is directed so as to seem such a hilariously hopeless actress that when she is supposed to be simulating terror of death . . . she squints with about as much alarm as a fashion model trying to see her nose because she is afraid there is a smudge on it . . . you can't exactly admire [their] character.[220]

Such a resounding endorsement was echoed by Taylor, who, writing in *The Times*, suggested that the antiquated values presented in *Live and Let Die* ensured that "[a]s long as they keep on making James Bond films, the 1960s will never die."[221]

Interestingly, the representations of the Bond Girl are contrasted by the film's title song. In "Live and Let Die," recording artist Paul McCartney reminds audiences that they are living amidst an "ever changing world" in 1973.[222] It is therefore not unreasonable to believe that, with a successful Bondian formula producing highly grossing films, a "live and let live," laissez-faire approach was extended to the Bond Girl archetype.

* * *

The *Live and Let Die* title sequence features Maurice Binder's "familiar surreal nudes."[223] It opens by depicting a statuesque, nude Nubian woman attired in a native necklace. Then, with flames emanating from her head, which now displays her eyes opened widely, the woman's face transforms into a burning skull. The face-skull dichotomy continues briefly as each image flashes across the screen, incorporating the voodoo and occult themes of the film and blurring the distinction between the living and the dead. Finally, nude silhouettes appear through the nasal

American actress Gloria Hendry, British actor Roger Moore, and British actress Jane Seymour pose on the set of *Live and Let Die*, 1973.
(Terry O'Neill/Terry O'Neill/Getty Images)

passage of the skull, and a woman is depicted kneeling and writhing in slow motion.

As the sequence progresses, tribal religious themes also emerge. For example, a woman with tribal symbols across her arms kneels and presumably prays as brightly colored sparks and flames emanate nearby. A second nude female silhouette dances and waves her hands and arms toward the sky. A sea of colorful hands and arms then emerges from the bottom of the screen, rising and reaching toward the heavens for salvation. Finally, a Caucasian woman appears stretching or reaching out, perhaps for salvation, amid a wash of color simulating fire and burning rocks. The sequence retains the sexual energy of its previous manifestations, though the only element connecting these images to the film's plot is the human skull. The nearly ubiquitous dancing silhouettes merely add to the visual spectacle and increase the sexually suggestive nature of the scene.

* * *

After the title sequence concludes, the audience is presented with its "first introduction to Roger Moore as James Bond. This takes place in Bond's apartment where he is, of course, in bed with a girl."[224] She is a voluptuous brunette named Miss Caruso, a character that is virtually indistinguishable from Plenty O'Toole, save for the fact that Miss Caruso actually succeeds in reaching the bedroom with Bond. The part of Miss Caruso is so insignificant that it was credited simply as the "Beautiful Girl" at the film's conclusion.[225]

Both Bond and Miss Caruso are asleep when Bond is awoken by a visitor ringing his doorbell. Though John Brosnan suggested that the encounter succumbed to *coitus interruptus*,[226] it is apparent that the scene occurs after Bond and Miss Caruso have engaged in sexual relations, an observation confirmed by Miss Caruso's plea, "One more time again?"[227] Bond, walking toward the door, mumbles the first of many sarcastic remarks: "Not married by any chance, are you?"[228] Bond leaves Miss Caruso in bed, but she disappears by the time M, rather than a jealous boyfriend or husband, enters Bond's apartment. The reason for Miss Caruso's disappearance is initially unclear, and Bond is visibly perplexed by it. At the same time, he is relieved that M does not discover her.

Accompanying M is Miss Moneypenny, who discovers Miss Caruso tiptoeing partially naked across Bond's apartment in an effort to find her clothing. Stumbling upon Miss Moneypenny, she implores her not to reveal her presence. Miss Caruso then scampers into Bond's closet, a theme that reemerges in *The Man With the Golden Gun*. While Miss Caruso hides, M informs Bond that his previous mission in Rome was successful despite the Italians' complaint that they are missing one of their agents—a woman named Miss Caruso.

It is not revealed whether Miss Caruso follows Bond to London on account of his "sheer magnetism."[229] Nevertheless, once M and Miss Moneypenny depart, Bond utilizes a magnetic wristwatch to slide open his closet door and expose Miss Caruso. Her back is facing the closet door with her face buried toward the back of the closet in an over-the-top and anemic effort to avoid discovery. When she turns around, her face registers sheer alarm and fear until Bond reassures her. If Miss Caruso is, in fact, an Italian agent, then this behavior is certainly implausible. She then proceeds to embrace Bond lustfully, sighing as she lays her head on his chest and shoulder. Bond again turns to his magnetic wristwatch, this time using it to unzip her dress.[230]

Raymond Benson suggested that the scene was designed to provide comedic relief,[231] but it serves a greater purpose. Miss Caruso's brief appearance and quick disappearance make it clear that she serves a functional role. Virtually indistinguishable from Sylvia Trench in *Dr. No* and *From Russia With Love,* Miss Caruso simply permits Bond to increase his on-screen sexual exploits without sacrificing plot. A pure sexual conquest requires no character development and little dialogue. It also reassures audiences that Bond's sexual potency is wholly unaffected by a casting change.

* * *

When Bond arrives in Jamaica in pursuit of the film's villain, Dr. Kananga (and his alter-ego, Mister Big), he encounters Rosie, who reveals herself as an incompetent and inept CIA agent. Gloria Hendry, a former Playboy Bunny, became the first African American actress to portray a substantial Bond Girl role in the franchise (Trina Parks portrayed the less significant role of Thumper in *Diamonds Are Forever*),[232] and she arguably treats the audience to "a much more spirited performance than the leading lady."[233] Rosie is presented through a lens of timidity, insecurity, and inexperience. She is devoid of the requisite traits exhibited by an effective agent. In fact, as it later becomes clear, Rosie is actually double-crossing the CIA as one of Dr. Kananga's associates. Unfortunately for her, Rosie manages to demonstrate her incompetence in both roles.

Rosie's ineptitude is established from the moment she appears. Partially opening the door to Bond's hotel suite, she points a gun toward the bed in what appears to constitute an assassination attempt. Bond thwarts her effort by burning her hand with his cigar, pulling her into the suite, and throwing her onto the bed. She readily admits to Bond, rather timidly, that she has "a little explaining to do,"[234] but her explanation is wrought with shrugging and careless gestures. The justification she provides to Bond is that she is "just trying to be careful."[235] With Rosie's shortcomings readily apparent, Bond offers a recommendation: "Perhaps you better start by getting your head together."[236]

Rosie also informs Bond, rather enthusiastically and with an air of importance, that Bond is only her second assignment, the first of which ended when Baines, the British agent to whom she was assigned, was murdered. In response, Bond sarcastically remarks that "it's a relief to know I'm next in line for the same kind of aid."[237] Rosie simply smiles in response. Her credibility has been entirely stripped away within moments of her introduction.

Rosie also has a penchant for screaming in sheer terror, another trait that contradicts her supposed status as a CIA agent trained in clandestine surveillance and to act inconspicuously. The first scream occurs in Bond's hotel suite bathroom after Rosie finds a dead snake. Completely exasperated by this discovery, Rosie runs out of the bathroom, exclaiming, "Oh, I should have never gotten into any of this!"[238] The fright induces tears, and Rosie forecasts that she "is going to be completely useless" to Bond.[239] A reassuring Bond responds that he can "lick [her] into shape."[240] Again, as a supposed CIA agent, it is conceivable that Rosie has encountered much more frightening situations, whether simulated during training or in the field. And yet, Rosie's behavior can only be described as puzzling.

Rosie's weakness affords Bond an opportunity to seduce her, and any interracial romance suggests to the audience "that 007 appreciated beauty, whatever the colour."[241] As he explains what assistance he needs from her the following day, Bond's tone is both condescending and irreverent. By contrast, his physical conduct is disarming as he caresses Rosie's shoulders and turns her around to face him. His physical actions are initiated under the pretext that she is posing as his wife. At first, Rosie resists:

> *Bond* (*caressing her shoulders*): That, I'm afraid, only leaves us tonight to, well, catch up on old times.
> *Rosie*: Felix told me there'd be moments like this.
> *Bond* (*moving his hands towards her face*): What did good old Felix suggest?
> *Rosie*: If all else failed, cyanide pills. I settled for two bedrooms. (*stepping back toward the bedroom door threshold and extending her arm to shake Bond's hand*) Good night, Mister Bond.
> *Bond*: Mrs. Bond.[242]

As she leaves to enter the bedroom, the smile across Rosie's face appears fake and manufactured. Her resistance to Bond, however, is short-lived.

Immediately thereafter, Rosie shrieks a second time when she discovers a small hat with a bloodied feather—an apparent voodoo symbol—on the bed. Bond carelessly characterizes the item as "just a hat . . . belonging to a small-headed man of limited means who lost a fight with a chicken."[243] But for Rosie, the symbol is "a warning"[244] so dire that she is completely paralyzed by its presence. Scared and fearful, she runs into Bond's arms and pleads with him to stay with her the remainder of the night.

Rosie's implausibility and incapability worsen as the film progresses. First, she inadvertently discovers communications equipment and weapons aboard a boat on which she, Bond, and Bond's assistant, Quarrel Jr., are traveling. Believing that Quarrel Jr. (the son of Quarrel, who aids Bond in his mission on Crab Key in *Dr. No*) is about to strangle Bond with rope, Rosie emerges from beneath the deck—wearing a bikini that reveals a highly toned, athletic figure—and points her gun at Quarrel Jr. What happens next is humiliating for her:

> *Rosie*: Keep your hands up!
> *Bond*: As I was saying, Quarrel, a lousy agent. But the compensations speak for themselves. Rosie Carver, meet the man who shares my hairbrush, Quarrel Jr.
> *Rosie*: I'm really sorry. I could've shot you.
> *Quarrel Jr.* (*taking the gun from her hands*): You might have even killed me if you'd taken off the safety catch.[245]

A sulking Rosie then approaches Bond in an attempt to receive some form of reassurance. Shortly thereafter, Rosie indicates that she can locate an automobile, prompting Bond to offer mild encouragement: "Ah, beautiful, brave, and now resourceful. Rosie, you seem to be staging a remarkable comeback."[246]

Second, Bond informs Rosie that her primary responsibility is to identify the location where Baines was murdered. From their boat, Rosie points to the location, stating that it is "up in the hills, just after we clear the next cove."[247] Later, her assuredness is rapidly replaced by equivocation:

> *Rosie* (*pointing*): It's down there.
> *Bond*: But, I thought you said Baines was killed up in the hills, darling.
> *Rosie* (*indicating bewilderment*): Up in the hills, down there.[248]

Rosie Carver (Gloria Hendry) and James Bond (Roger Moore) consummate their relationship in *Live and Let Die*.
(Everett Collection/Rex USA)

So much for her comeback. Bond convinces Rosie that they should discuss the disparity over lunch, and they ultimately supplement their meal with a sexual rendezvous. The subsequent discussion permits Bond to expose Rosie as a fraud. When confronted, however, Rosie's first reaction is to scream.

By the time Rosie screams for the third time in the film, Bond already is fully aware that her antics are a ploy. In fact, he previously received a tip—a tarot card of the Queen of Cups positioned upside down—indicating that Rosie cannot be trusted. Conveniently, Bond does not reveal his knowledge of her true identity until *after* he possesses her sexually. He displays the Queen of Cups tarot card: "You do know what the Queen of Cups means in an upside-down position—a deceitful, perverse woman, a liar, a cheat—and I'd like some answers now."[249] Of note is Bond's use of the word *woman* rather than *girl*, the implication being that naïve and innocent *girls* are incapable of such reprehensible, deceitful behavior.

Interestingly, Rosie does not contest Bond's accusation. Rather, her response is imbued with toady insouciance: "Please, uh, you don't understand, sir. They'll kill me if I do."[250] Her use of the word "sir" reaffirms that Bond, a male authority figure, controls the situation.[251] Rosie, of course, finds herself in the most untenable position since she cannot advance the interests of both Bond and Dr. Kananga. On one hand, Dr. Kananga will kill her if she divulges the information Bond demands. On the other hand, Bond will kill Rosie if she refuses to talk. Either way, her fate is sealed.

With few options, Rosie attempts to obfuscate by using her sexual encounter with Bond as leverage.[252] But this tactic, much like her other actions, fails. Although Rosie may have been forewarned by Felix about the possibility of sexual relations, she forgets that Bond's allegiance rests first with Queen and country. Bond responds that he "certainly wouldn't have killed [her] before" they engaged in sexual relations, and Rosie screams again:

> *Bond*: It used to be a convincing act, Rosie. It's wearing a little thin now.
> *Rosie*: It's not an act.
> *Bond* (*pointing his gun at her right temple*): Make your choice.[253]

Rather than make a choice, Rosie scampers off into the jungle.

Ultimately, Rosie does not live long enough to disclose the truth. Contrary to John Brosnan's assertion that Rosie is "accidentally shot"[254] while she attempts to escape into the jungle, she is, in fact, murdered by Dr. Kananga.[255] Tee Hee, one of Dr. Kananga's henchmen, later remarks that "[t]he girl was about to confess, we had to kill her."[256] Given that

Rosie "is just another variation on the female villain ploy,"[257] she must die. Indeed, Bond's failure to convert Rosie ideologically through sexual intercourse requires that Rosie meet a fate previously reserved for Fiona Volpe in *Thunderball* and Helga Brandt in *You Only Live Twice*.

The preceding assessment of Rosie is derived from Bond's perspective. Perhaps it is Rosie's unconvincing and transparent performance as a CIA agent that seals her fate, particularly since Bond seems to view her with extreme skepticism from the moment he encounters her. But Rosie fares no better when analyzed from Dr. Kananga's perspective. Fundamentally, Rosie is an expendable pawn whose sole utility is setting a trap that will facilitate Bond's death. Once Bond is delivered to Dr. Kananga, Rosie serves no additional purpose, much like Tatiana Romanova serves no purpose after Bond retrieves the Lektor decoding device in *From Russia With Love*. Although Dr. Kananga initially demonstrates satisfaction with the fact that Rosie "has been more efficient than I anticipated" by luring Bond to him, he is exasperated when the outcome deviates from that which he expects.[258] He interrogates Solitaire after she fails to forecast the events that unfolded: "The trap was set. Tee Hee was waiting. And you saw death."[259]

As noted above, Rosie is destined to perish. Nevertheless, she lacks any ability to prolong her life and instead, by committing blatant and glaring errors, hastens her demise. She simply cannot recover from her lost credibility with Bond or her failure to help seal Bond's fate with Dr. Kananga. Although her cinematic appearance is brief, prompting Raymond Benson to describe the character as "simply provid[ing] another Obligatory Sacrificial Lamb" for the Bond mythology,[260] her symbolism endures.

* * *

Rosie's weaknesses are eclipsed by Solitaire, the tarot card-reading, virginal, "timid little waif."[261] Arguably representing the nadir of Bond Girl individuality, assertiveness, and independence, Solitaire is, perhaps, the most reactionary female character in the entire franchise, though Mary Goodnight follows closely behind in *The Man With the Golden Gun*. Whereas the hyperbolic implausibility and stereotypical presentation of Plenty O'Toole is secondary to Tiffany Case in *Diamonds Are Forever*, *Live and Let Die* transitions those attributes to the primary Bond Girl. Solitaire's introduction as the female lead in the film incorporates two new elements: (1) timid inexperience and naïvete (both sexually and worldly); and (2) literal objectification.

Broccoli and Saltzman initially envisioned actress and singer Diana Ross for the role of Solitaire, but they ultimately remained true to

Fleming's conception of the character as a Caucasian woman.[262] While searching for an actress who could "capture the sensuality of a Bond woman and the virginal innocence of the character," producers discovered Jane Seymour, who captivated Saltzman with her long-flowing brunette hair after he directed her to remove her hat; she reportedly earned the part at that moment.[263] At twenty years of age, Seymour was one of the youngest actresses to costar in a Bond film.[264]

In retrospect, Jane Seymour was miscast for the role.[265] Tom Mankiewicz recalled that "a much flashier girl should have been used . . . . Jane was so sweet and adorable looking that when Roger got into bed with her . . . it almost looked as if she was being taken advantage of. She's the type of girl you . . . bring home to your mother, as opposed to a Bond girl."[266] One critic observed: "As Solitaire, to whom the cards speak truth only so long as she remains a virgin, Jane Seymour is beautiful enough, but too submissive even for this scale of fantasy."[267] John Brosnan described Seymour as "attractive but a little *too* virginal in appearance" and suggested that Solitaire "comes across as being rather insipid."[268] Seymour mitigated some of these concerns when she posed in the July 1973 issue of *Playboy* that featured Bond's "Sainted" beauties. Notwithstanding the shortcomings Seymour may have possessed, the part itself may have been deficient: "Most disappointing is the development of Solitaire, who could have been used to much greater force."[269]

Solitaire is a sorceress who possesses the supernatural power of the "obeah," also referred to as the "second sight." Like her mother and grandmother before her, she predicts the future for Dr. Kananga through a deck of tarot cards. Whereas previous Bond Girls are *employed* by or *aligned* with the villain, Solitaire is, in essence, the *property* of Dr. Kananga. Indeed, at best, Solitaire is indentured to him.[270] Her main purpose is to service him when and how he wishes.

Solitaire's "psychic powers are linked in the film to her virginity[,] and therefore Mr. Big has a vested interest in keeping her 'pure' and untouched."[271] It is Dr. Kananga who will determine when her sexual awakening will occur, and he will serve as the man who bestows this awakening upon her, a fact that is communicated to Solitaire in no uncertain terms: "Your power exists to serve me, and it is mine to control. If and when the time comes I decide you are to lose it, I myself will take it away."[272] Although the theme of realignment via sexual conquest has been pervasive throughout the series, most notably demonstrated in *Goldfinger* with Pussy Galore, *Live and Let Die*, through Solitaire, takes the notion that "there is a woman waiting to be converted by the power of sex" to the extreme.[273]

Utilizing a deck of tarot cards, Solitaire (Jane Seymour) forecasts the future for Dr. Kananga in *Live and Let Die*.
(Brian Moody/Rex USA)

Solitaire possesses no voice of her own. Rather, she relies exclusively upon the tarot cards to guide her, as evidenced by her initial dialogue with Bond:

> *Bond*: Black queen on the red king, Miss—
> *Solitaire*: Solitaire.
> *Bond*: My name's Bond. James Bond.
> *Solitaire*: I know who you are, what you are, and why you've come. You have made a mistake. You will not succeed.
> *Bond*: Rather a sweeping statement considering we've never met.
> *Solitaire*: The cards have followed you for me.[274]

Bond, curious if his likeness appears in Solitaire's tarot deck, selects a card at Solitaire's encouragement. After he selects the Fool, Solitaire detachedly remarks that Bond has found himself and seems satisfied that the tarot cards have proven their accuracy once again. Believing in the cards, Solitaire seemingly derives any strength she may possess exclusively from them.

Her firm resolve, however, is shaken when Bond selects a second card, the Lovers, and inquires whether it represents him and Solitaire. Her face registers an expression of incredulity and shock. As Maryam d'Abo and John Cork noted, the impact of Bond's selection upon Solitaire is "profound":[275] the "tarot cards have revealed that she and Bond are destined to be lovers,"[276] so it must be her destiny to experience sexuality for the first time with him. Later, Solitaire herself uncovers the Lovers card while providing a reading for Dr. Kananga, reinforcing for her the reality that she believes has been predetermined. As one critic observed, "James Bond's card keeps coming up 'Lovers,' though she thinks she is hoping for 'Death.'"[277]

Solitaire's blind allegiance to the tarot cards affords Bond the ideal opportunity to exploit her for his gain. Bond breaks into Solitaire's quarters and begins shuffling and playing with her tarot deck. Solitaire emerges in a white gown, symbolic of her virginity and purity, enraged that Bond sits atop her throne partially adorned in her ceremonial garb: "Put down those cards! It is a blasphemy. They tell nothing to those who cannot see."[278] Bond disagrees, reminding Solitaire that the cards indicate that they will be lovers. Once again, Solitaire is visibly shocked and overwhelmed. Unsure of a response, she ultimately replies that Bond is mistaken, adding that the possibility of a sexual relationship is "impossible, forbidden."[279] Bond persists:

> *Bond*: But you do believe, I mean, really believe in the cards.
> *Solitaire*: Well they have never lied to me.

> *Bond*: Then they won't now. (*unfolding a deck of cards in his hand*) Pick one.[280]

Reluctantly, Solitaire complies and selects a card bearing the Lovers.

Completely dumbfounded and perplexed, Solitaire's lips quiver, and she turns away, unable to accept what has transpired. Bond explains: "You knew the answer before it was given. Strangely enough, so did I."[281] As Bond embraces her, he tosses an entire deck comprised solely of the Lovers tarot cards onto the table, revealing to the audience the extent of his manipulation. Maryam d'Abo and John Cork described the scene—and Bond's tactics—as "one of the most amusingly mercenary seductions in the film series."[282]

The irony, of course, is that nothing compels Solitaire to do anything on the basis of what the tarot cards purport to represent. The meaning of the Lovers card is derived from *Bond*'s interpretation of to whom the card refers. At no time does Solitaire, who apparently possesses the power to read and interpret the cards, offer a contradictory explanation—let alone *any* explanation—for Bond's initial selection of the Lovers and presumption that it refers to them. Even when she uncovers the Lovers herself while reading the cards for Dr. Kananga, Solitaire resigns herself to believing the cards speak of her and Bond, even though Bond advances this interpretation. Thus, not only does Solitaire succumb to her own unwavering allegiance to the cards, she defers to another to illuminate their meaning.

These character flaws enable Bond to maneuver himself into the positions of awakening Solitaire sexually and becoming her physical liberator. In the next scene, which depicts Solitaire and Bond in bed following their first sexual encounter, Solitaire stares blankly toward the ceiling with an expression of despair and resigned shock across her face. The scene demonstrates the extent to which "Solitaire comes off as an unintelligent little girl":[283]

> *Solitaire*: So it's finally happened. Just as it did to my mother and her mother before her.
> *Bond*: Of course it did, you're visual proof of that, aren't you? (*rolling toward her*) Come on, cheer up, darling. (*caressing her chin*) There has to be a first time for everyone.[284]

There is a first time, and then there is a first time with Bond. For better or worse, Solitaire experiences both simultaneously, though the gravity of the moment is lost upon Bond. Instead, he immediately and audaciously resumes his mission by questioning Solitaire about Dr. Kananga's whereabouts.

An exasperated Solitaire, who has just lost her virginity, now fears for her life as she reveals that her psychic powers are lost. Bond, at first, fails to comprehend her predicament and offers to retrieve the tarot deck. In her metaphorical lament, Solitaire explains:

> *Solitaire*: The power . . . I've lost it. The high priestess is wife to the prince no longer of this world. The spiritual bridge to the secret church. It was my fate. By compelling me to earthly love, the cards themselves have taken away my powers.
> *Bond*: Darling, I've a small confession to make, now try not to be too upset. The deck was slightly stacked in my favor.
> *Solitaire*: It makes no difference. Physical violation cannot be undone. When he finds out I've lost my power, he'll kill me.[285]

Of note is Solitaire's characterization of the sexual encounter as a "physical violation," which suggests that her consent was wholly absent. For Bond (and the audience), his encounter with Solitaire represents the fruits of a successful seduction. Not so for Solitaire. The implications of her statement are substantial but are left entirely unaddressed.

In an effort to induce Solitaire to provide information about Dr. Kananga, Bond reveals that he has arranged for a boat and that she "can be on it" to escape Dr. Kananga if she reveals what is being hidden "in voodoo land."[286] Although initially hesitant, Solitaire becomes more receptive, oddly enough, once the prospect of a second sexual encounter presents itself. Suddenly the "physical violation" she previously endured is forgotten. Much to her delight, Bond determines that "there's no sense in going off half-cocked,"[287] and a fully sexually awakened Solitaire later reveals that "for the first time in my life, I feel like a complete woman. The slightest touch of your hand, oh I was always so afraid that a part of me would stay with the past. But now I know there's no chance of that any longer."[288]

Solitaire's belief that her sexual awakening has transformed her into a complete woman is a flawed one. From the moment she appears on screen, Solitaire is treated like a possession, and that role does not change once she and Bond consummate their relationship. Prior to meeting Bond, Solitaire lacks independence and accompanies Dr. Kananga everywhere. She is even referred to as "the Kananga woman" by Quarrel Jr.,[289] further evidence that she is perceived as a possession whose value is determined by her owner.

When Dr. Kananga demands that she "[t]ell me about the future,"[290] Solitaire complies without hesitation, dutifully serving her master. In the event that circumstances do not correspond to Solitaire's predictions, Dr. Kananga unleashes his wrath upon her:

> *Dr. Kananga*: You will explain what went wrong . . . . The trap was set. Tee Hee was waiting. (*pointing at Solitaire*) And you saw death.
> *Solitaire*: It must have been the girl's death. If you do not ask specific questions, I cannot be responsible for your misinterpretation of the answers.
> *Dr. Kananga* (*approaching her, pointing again*): These growing signs of impertinence begin to disturb me, Solitaire, even as they did with your mother before you. She had the power and lost it, became useless to me. You will not make the same mistake. Solitaire, where is Bond now? (*repeating the question in a demanding and angry tone*) Where is Bond now?!
> *Solitaire* (*getting up*): I cannot see when you are this way with me. Things become unclear.
> *Dr. Kananga*: Let us hope these momentary lapses do not become a habit.[291]

Solitaire ultimately complies with her master's orders, regardless of the tone in his delivery.

Bond himself perpetuates Solitaire's status as a possession. Whereas previous Bond Girls aligned with the villain survive or die predicated upon Bond's ability to reposition them, Solitaire requires no such realignment because she is perceived and treated as an object. Dr. Kananga exploits her for her soothsaying, but Bond exploits her *value to Dr. Kananga* as part of his effort to successfully complete his mission.

Although Bond frames his desire that Solitaire accompany him in terms of offering her protection, even reassuring her that everything is "all over" with Dr. Kananga,[292] his objectives are more selfish. Bond realizes that Dr. Kananga will pursue him in order to secure Solitaire's return, and it is therefore apparent that Solitaire is used as bait to trap Dr. Kananga. In fact, Bond says as much himself, reminding Quarrel Jr. that Solitaire is "a valuable piece of merchandise we're carrying, which, with any luck, they'll want back."[293] In essence, Bond has confiscated a piece of personal property that he knows its original owner will seek to recover.

But Solitaire is used merchandise, and she endures significant repercussions for losing her supernatural powers. Bond is informed by Dr. Kananga's henchmen that he apparently "took something that didn't belong" to him.[294] Telling is the use of the word *something* rather than *someone*, further dehumanizing Solitaire and relegating her to the status of an object. Dr. Kananga ultimately recaptures Solitaire, and the notion of Solitaire as an object culminates during a confrontation between

Bond and Mister Big, who ultimately reveals himself as Dr. Kananga, in Solitaire's presence:

> *Mister Big*: Well then, you go and steal this valuable young lady from my good friend Dr. Kananga.
> *Bond*: Well, possession being nine points of the law, I would say Kananga is your problem.
> *Mister Big*: [T]here's one little question that [Kananga] wants answers for.
> *Bond*: In that case, you better ship me back to the islands and let him ask in person. I'm not in the habit of giving answers to lackeys.
> *Mister Big*: You damn lucky you got an ear left to hear the question with, which is (*pointing at Solitaire*) did you mess with that?[295]

Mister Big does not ask Bond if he has messed with *her*, yet another indication that reinforces the fact that Solitaire's status has not changed once she becomes entangled with Bond.

Dr. Kananga utilizes this confrontation as an opportunity to test Solitaire's powers in order to determine whether Bond has, in fact, engaged in relations with her. He declares: "Tee Hee, on the first wrong answer from Miss Solitaire, you will snip the little finger of Mister Bond's right hand. Starting with the second wrong answer, you will proceed to the more vital areas."[296] Dr. Kananga challenges Solitaire to confirm whether he accurately recites the registration number of Bond's wristwatch. A distressed Solitaire stares at the cards before her but seems uncertain. She ultimately confirms the truth of Dr. Kananga's statement. Tee Hee does not snip any finger. Bond is taken away. The audience is led to presume that Solitaire is correct.

Solitaire is wrong. Dr. Kananga admonishes her: "Solitaire, why? I treated you well, you lacked for nothing. Mister Bond's watch, my dear, I gave you every break possible. You had a fifty-fifty chance. You weren't even close."[297] Her response—that she simply believes in what the cards indicate to her—falls upon deaf ears, and Dr. Kananga violently strikes her face with such force that Solitaire is thrown to the ground. Standing over her, Dr. Kananga reminds Solitaire that "[w]hen the time came, I myself would have given you love. You knew that. You knew that!"[298]

For her betrayal, Solitaire is marked for death, and she is next seen on a Caribbean island bound to two poles awaiting the bite of a poisonous snake during a voodoo ritual.

Bond, once again, rescues Solitaire and, in a moment reminiscent of his dismissal of Dink in *Goldfinger*, tells her to "say good-bye to Felix, darling" when the two board a train.[299] For saving her, Bond is rewarded with the opportunity to resume Solitaire's sexual education. The train ride also affords him an opportunity to acclimate Solitaire to modern society, including teaching her how to play gin rummy. When Bond loses the card game to his novice counterpart, he pulls down the bed in their train cabin in order to "test[] an old adage, 'Unlucky at cards.'"[300] Solitaire registers a pleased look on her face, which comports with her earlier expression of satisfaction about sharing a bed with Bond. The shock and anguish she initially felt after her first experience with Bond is nothing more than a distant memory.

Maryam d'Abo and John Cork suggested that Solitaire's character "has an interesting journey" and noted that she transforms from believing in superstition into someone who "embraces the more temporal pleasures of James Bond's world."[301] It is wholly unclear what Solitaire embraces. Rather, it seems that Solitaire passively accepts whatever is placed before her. When she is with Dr. Kananga, she resigns herself to reading tarot cards. When she is with Bond, she accepts playing gin rummy with a deck of playing cards.

Born into servitude, Solitaire is weak, impressionable, and malleable. Susceptible to capture, violation, and dehumanization, she does not, as Maryam d'Abo and John Cork maintained, "live for the moment."[302] Rather, accustomed to male domination and manipulation, Solitaire submits to the male authority figure who claims ownership of her. Although she passes from Dr. Kananga's hands to Bond's bed, Solitaire's status never changes.

"[T]he first and only virgin deflower[ed in] the Bond film series,"[303] Solitaire is entirely out of place in a world devoid of voodoo magic or tarot cards. And yet, she actually represents the ideal woman in the Bond mythology: obedient, subservient, impressionable, and an overall object of visual and physical pleasure. In sum, Solitaire merely "tak[es] up space."[304]

* * *

Taken together, "Jane Seymour, Gloria Hendry and Madeline Smith are comely enough but curiously sexless sex objects."[305] More significantly, the Bond Girls in *Live and Let Die* are not characters who possess laudable strengths. Miss Caruso serves solely as a sexual conquest. To the extent that she is an Italian agent, Miss Caruso's behavior renders her implausible. Rosie suffers from gross incompetence, and her errors and omissions are so glaring that Bond himself admonishes her for her shortcomings. In some respects, Rosie's premature death spares her from further embarrassment and humiliation.

Having betrayed Dr. Kananga, Solitaire is marked for death at the hands of a voodoo worshiper wielding a venomous snake in *Live and Let Die*.
(Popperfoto/Popperfoto/Getty Images)

As for Solitaire, she is an objectified girl who finds herself thrust into womanhood against her will, assuming that womanhood is even defined solely in terms of a sexual awakening. Once Bond conquers her and she loses her soothsaying capabilities, Solitaire serves no purpose for Dr. Kananga, and she ultimately lacks any information that is beneficial to Bond. Instead, Solitaire becomes an empty vessel that Bond strategically carries with him in an effort to defeat Dr. Kananga and complete his mission.

The message *Live and Let Die* conveys about the Bond Girl archetype generally, and Solitaire specifically, is that women, in particular "dumb women,"[306] are best kept away from the real world. Injecting these characters into Bond's world only causes harm to befall them. Moreover, their interference jeopardizes those around them, particularly with respect to Rosie and Solitaire. The first British agent assigned to Rosie is murdered, and Bond almost meets a similar fate. Instead, Rosie serves as the requisite sacrifice. Bond's entanglements with Solitaire generate the wrath of Dr. Kananga, and his ability to complete the mission is substantially diverted by his focus and attention upon the "possession" he carries with him. In essence, relegating these female characters to positions that limit their interactions with the outside world would, it seems, benefit everyone, including themselves.

Although it underperformed *Diamonds Are Forever*,[307] *Live and Let Die* sold the most box office tickets than any other film released in 1973,[308] a strong indication that audiences either did not object to or were entertained by the Bond Girl archetype the film advanced. *The Man With the Golden Gun* ultimately reinforces the themes underlying the portrayal of the female characters in *Live and Let Die*, depicting in no uncertain terms the consequences of involving inexperienced women in men's affairs and the dangers they pose to those around them. Presenting another iteration of a mistress-turned-concubine, the film again reprises the theme of repositioning female alliances through sexual conquest.

The Man With the Golden Gun

When it reached theaters in 1974, *The Man With the Golden Gun* was characterized as "weak."[309] One critic recommended that audiences "better skip this one,"[310] noting that the film was "doggishly faithful" to its literary counterpart, which was Fleming's last and perhaps least accomplished novel.[311] Another described the film as "a considerable letdown."[312]

Roger Moore's performance as Bond, in addition to supposedly lacking a sense of fun,[313] was also apparently plagued by "deep deficiencies."[314] A *New York Times* review of the film elaborated:

> Mr. Moore functions like a vast garden ornament. Pedantic, sluggish on the uptake, incapable of even swaggering, he's also clumsy at innuendo. (While Sean Connery wasn't the wit of the century, he did manage to be impudent, and there were those pleasing moments of self-parody.) But . . . [Moore] merely makes you miss his predecessor.[315]

Moore "ma[de] fewer attempts to toughen the character than he did in *Live and Let Die*,"[316] and laments continued throughout the 1970s that the franchise had "lost its edge" when Moore was cast for the role of Double-O-Seven. According to a *New York* reviewer, "[t]he figure of James Bond . . . ha[d] long since ceased to mean anything."[317] In the United States, box office receipts confirmed that Moore's Bond was not as financially successful as Sean Connery's Bond.[318]

Notwithstanding Roger Moore's supposed lackluster performance as Bond generally, *The Man With the Golden Gun* is significant in that it widened the interstice between the Bond Girl archetype and the reality of gender politics during the volatile 1970s. Unlike *Diamonds Are Forever*, which addresses Women's Liberation directly with its introduction of Bambi and Thumper, *The Man With the Golden Gun* implicitly rejects the gender movement by reaffirming its commitment to an ideal that had essentially become antiquated and anachronistic in light of contemporary social and political developments. Indeed, *Time* observed that "nothing much happens" to the Bond Girls portrayed by Maud Adams and Britt Ekland, though both characters "make a couple of mildly decorative . . . heroines."[319] Consequently, *The Man With the Golden Gun* earned the distinction of being named the "egg" of 1974.[320]

* * *

The title sequence structure in *The Man With the Golden Gun* may be described as representing the entire act of coitus, complete with foreplay, intercourse, climax, and a post-coital tease. As foreplay, an Asian woman seductively moves her hands, replete with brightly polished nails, across her face. While it appears that she may form a gun with her thumb and index finger, it is also plausible that her fingers are gesturing for her lover to approach, an act that is reinforced by a facial expression suggesting piqued curiosity and desire. A rippling water theme, which virtually permeates the entire title sequence, partially obscures her features, adding another element of mystery.

Once this seduction is complete, the sequence transitions to intercourse, which begins with the background image of a woman, again obscured by rippling water, outstretching her hands in an expression of physical pleasure. As this occurs, the title song, which was performed by recording artist Lulu, describes her lover, a mysterious man with a golden gun whose most striking feature is his "powerful weapon."[321] Thereafter, another woman is shown sprawled partially on her stomach with her posterior facing the camera, a suggestion that a change in sexual position has occurred. Several other women appear plunging into water, visually depicting their journey into the depths of pleasure. Another woman lying on her back repeatedly strokes the barrel of a golden gun in a suggestive manner. The lyrics of the title song transition to the following: "[W]ho will he bang? We shall see!"[322]

The phallic allusion is heightened—and the question answered—when the rippling water theme is interrupted by the climax, a bright explosion of red sparklers behind the dancing and gyrating silhouette of an athletic, naked woman. Although the initial focus on this silhouette is the woman's entire figure, the climax scene carefully focuses upon her pelvic region as Lulu declares that the man with the golden gun "comes just before the kill."[323] Once the climax is complete, the rippling water theme reemerges in a post-coital tease sequence, which features one naked woman on her side, a second on her back caressing herself, and a third stroking the long barrel of the golden gun with her middle finger.

Interestingly, neither the title sequence nor the title song has anything to do with Bond. Rather, the primary focus is the man with the golden gun, though he shares a commonality with Double-O-Seven. As the scene suggests, the man with the golden gun ensures that the sexual encounter is about himself and possesses a cavalier attitude that enables him to prey upon women for his own gain.[324] The sexual overtones are not subtle. In fact, filmmakers deliberately sought to "pok[e] fun at the sexual misadventures of 007"[325] and did so in *The Man With the Golden Gun* by accentuating his nemesis's conquest capabilities. Overall, the entire title sequence was considered "too, too much" for some,[326] and it arguably precedes the one of the most reactionary depictions of women in the series.[327]

* * *

Two primary Bond Girls are featured in *The Man With the Golden Gun*. The first is Andrea, portrayed by Maud Adams. A former Swedish model who later made a second appearance as the title character in the 1983 film *Octopussy*, Adams was described as an "alluring, fashionable figure."[328] Her portrayal of Andrea, who has been described as villain Francisco Scaramanga's "girlfriend,"[329] a "scared seductress,"[330] and a "lethal human weapon,"[331] accentuates the fact that her character is a "kept woman."[332] Adams later recalled that portraying a damsel in distress was "not really the most wonderful part to play," but she recognized that her role in *The Man With the Golden Gun* was "a very decorative part."[333]

Andrea appears in the film's pre-title sequence relaxing along the coast of a Southeast Asian island. She is interrupted when Scaramanga's diminutive servant, Nick Nack, approaches with drinks, a sign that essentially summons Andrea to attend to Scaramanga. She quickly rises and gathers two towels for Scaramanga, who emerges from the water. She acts like a servant, handing Scaramanga one towel and using the second to dry him. Indeed, she crouches submissively to reach his legs, all the while in silence, with a clear expectation that the conduct in which she engages is demanded of her. Only after Scaramanga walks away does she return to her feet. Once Scaramanga is dry and her immediate duties are performed, Andrea is next observed sprawled out and tanning in a chair, presumably until she is summoned to perform her next task for Scaramanga.

Drying Scaramanga is perhaps Andrea's most innocuous task. The extent to which she serves him is eventually fully revealed. First, Andrea is Scaramanga's sexual concubine. Part of his preparation for a hired assassination involves his physical violation of Andrea, and he ensures that the gratification derived therefrom is one-sided and in his favor. Indeed, the only so-called affection Scaramanga exhibits during his pre-kill exercise is to caress Andrea's body with the barrel of a golden gun, actions that he believes are seductive but actually cause her tremendous discomfort. According to Andrea, Scaramanga is a lover "only before he kills."[334]

Second, Andrea serves a more practical function by advancing the film's plot. Scaramanga, a "million-dollar-a-shot hitman,"[335] is the only man who utilizes golden bullets,[336] and one of his "prized golden bullets" mysteriously finds its way "to Her Majesty's Secret Service inscribed with Bond's number."[337] Bond investigates and soon discovers Andrea in Hong Kong retrieving golden bullets for Scaramanga. Indeed, the audience learns that it is Andrea who performs Scaramanga's drop-offs and pickups.

Bond infiltrates Andrea's hotel suite in an attempt to extract information from her about Scaramanga. The method he utilizes is particularly brutal. Indeed, the "script allows [him] to beat [her] up,"[338] and Bond's reckless display of violence, coupled with an apparent sadistic disassociation from his actions, is reminiscent of Sean Connery's bikini choking of Marie in *Diamonds Are Forever*. Maryam d'Abo and John Cork described the scene as "uncomfortable" and "disturbingly violent."[339] Raymond Benson, however, found Bond's behavior implausible, arguing that his "harshness is contradictory. It's difficult to accept Roger Moore slapping

Swedish actresses Maud Adams (left) and Britt Ekland, and British actor Roger Moore pose on the set of *The Man With the Golden Gun*, 1974.

(Everett Collection/Rex USA)

anyone, much less a pretty girl."[340] Written depictions of the scene cannot ultimately capture the degree of hostility Bond exhibits toward Andrea,[341] but the fact remains that, regardless of its plausibility, it is a part of the film that cannot be ignored or discounted.

Slapping her, throwing her onto the bed, pulling on her hair, and constraining her arms behind her back, Bond demands answers from Andrea. Though she pleads with Bond that he is hurting her arm, Bond responds with a threat that he will break it if she refuses to talk.[342] Andrea's failure to respond to this demeaning treatment suggests that she is accustomed to a certain amount of physical abuse, but her silence prompts Bond to increase his forcefulness. He slaps Andrea across the face, grabs her robe, and raises his hand in anticipation of another strike. Fearful, Andrea finally submits herself to Bond, who reminds her that she is in a particularly compromising position and must follow his explicit instructions. Otherwise, Bond warns, Scaramanga "may even use one of those little golden bullets on you, and that will be a pity because they're very expensive."[343] The implication is that Andrea is trivial and insignificant, and her life is worth even less than the bullet that would forever silence her.

It becomes apparent that Scaramanga has no intention of killing Bond. Rather, Andrea herself sends a golden bullet marked for Bond to MI6 in the hope that Bond will assassinate Scaramanga and facilitate her liberation.[344] For some reason, Andrea refuses to initially reveal this information to Bond.[345] Later, Andrea enters Bond's hotel suite. Bond already knows that Scaramanga is not interested in killing him, though the entire situation has not yet come into focus. With her plan unraveling, Andrea pleads for Bond to serve as her veritable "knight in shining armor,"[346] declaring that Scaramanga is a "monster" whom she despises.[347] She asserts that she cannot simply walk away from Scaramanga because "[t]here's no place he wouldn't find me."[348] Bond initially wants no part of her assassination fantasy, but he seems more receptive once Andrea suggests that he will reap sexual rewards:

> *Andrea*: I need Double-O-Seven. Who do you think sent that bullet to London with your number on it? (*pausing*) I did. And it wasn't easy getting his fingerprint on the note.
> *Bond*: You'll forgive me if I've been a little slow on the uptake.
> *Andrea*: Don't you see you're the only man in the world who can kill him?
> *Bond*: And what gives you that idea?
> *Andrea*: The way Scaramanga speaks about you. He even has a likeness of you . . . . I want him dead. Name your price, anything,

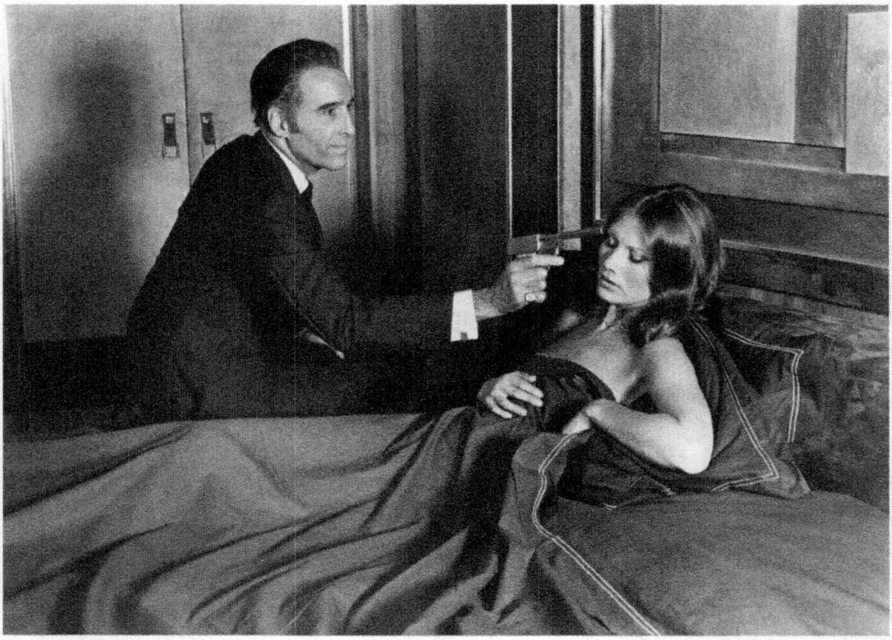

Francisco Scaramanga (Christopher Lee) caresses Andrea Anders (Maud Adams) with the barrel of his golden gun in *The Man With the Golden Gun*.
(Everett Collection/Rex USA)

> I'll pay it. (*pausing*) You can have me, too, if you like. I'm not unattractive?
> *Bond*: At last you're starting to tell the truth.
> *Andrea* (*approaching Bond to embrace him*): I've dreamed about you setting me free.[349]

For Bond, Andrea's confession is more about sexual conquest than the substance of her statement.

Unable to effectuate her own liberation from Scaramanga, Andrea requires Bond's facilitation. The *quid pro quo* she offers is purely sexual in nature since she apparently can offer nothing more. Yet, at the same time, Bond capitalizes upon Andrea's vulnerability by requiring sex *and* action that advances his mission, namely demanding that she deliver to him a coveted Solex Agitator, "a vital piece of equipment intended for use in the first completely efficient solar energy generator"[350] that Scaramanga has stolen in order to sell to the highest-bidding superpower. Just as Scaramanga requires that Andrea perform his tasks, so, too, does Bond require that Andrea place herself in harm's way to acquire that which he seeks.

Andrea's character advances the ideal that a woman's independence cannot be achieved by her own efforts. Rather, her release must be effectuated by a man, notably Bond. In this regard, Andrea is entirely "out of control"[351] of her life, as Maud Adams later described the character. Although she boldly sets into motion a sequence of events that brings Bond to her, Andrea requires Bond's actions and reactions to bring about the change that she seeks. In the process, Bond manipulates her to serve him, both sexually and otherwise. Andrea's lack of assertiveness, dependence upon Bond, and ease with which she can be realigned to serve Bond's interests all foreshadow her final unraveling. Ultimately, Bond discovers Andrea with a single bullet lodged in her chest. As Scaramanga aptly explains, "A mistress cannot serve two *masters*."[352]

* * *

Andrea's passive, "Sacrificial Lamb"[353] character is complemented by Goodnight. Britt Ekland, also from Sweden, "lobbied" to portray Goodnight, but her initial efforts were unsuccessful.[354] In fact, Ekland expressed a desire to appear in a Bond film for many years,[355] recalling that she resented not being cast prior to *The Man With the Golden Gun*.[356] Although Broccoli initially informed Ekland that the role of Goodnight would not be included in the film,[357] producers ultimately incorporated Goodnight into the script and awarded Ekland the part. As one critic wrote, "Britt Ekland embarrasses herself as Bond's blundering Girl Friday,"[358] though her acting was constrained by the role.

Goodnight is, for lack of a better description, a "beautiful, idiot side-kick" who represents "the least appealing of Bond heroines."[359] Lee Pfeiffer and Dave Worrall characterized Goodnight as "so inept she makes Inspector Clouseau seem like Sherlock Holmes."[360] Indeed, Goodnight "makes one wonder how she ever managed to pass her Secret Service entrance exam."[361] The audience easily forgets that Goodnight is a British intelligence agent who supposedly possesses field experience.[362]

A "scatter-brained bimbo in a bikini,"[363] Goodnight is, according to some, comedic relief, a character that is "played for laughs"[364] and an "amusing ally"[365] to Bond. This description, however, misses the mark. Although Maryam d'Abo and John Cork described Goodnight as "an appendage—a loyal, lovesick, and . . . incompetent assistant who does not really fit into the James Bond universe,"[366] Goodnight, in fact, serves a vital role in the Bond mythology: she reinforces the archetype that women belong in a separate and distinct sphere from men. More importantly, Goodnight exemplifies the dangers inherent in permitting women entry into a man's world based upon the assumption that women are equal in status, acumen, and capability. Raymond Benson's description of Goodnight—that "the character, *though attractive, is basically an idiot*"[367]—was apt, though idiocy is not, under any circumstance, mitigated by or excused based upon aesthetics. Goodnight's ineptitude ultimately rivals—and even surpasses—the naïvete of Solitaire. Indeed, she serves as the final representation of a no-longer-extant ideal.

Goodnight's first tragic character flaw is her omnipresent, unrequited love for Bond. At her first opportunity, and throughout the entire film, Goodnight indicates her interest in Bond, usually with an overtone of yearning: "James, it's wonderful to see you."[368] As quickly as Goodnight expresses her interest, Bond responds with absolute apathy:

> *Bond*: The subject under surveillance [Andrea] is occupying room 602. I'll buy you dinner, tonight, Goodnight, but first I have a little official business to attend to.
>
> *Goodnight*: Yes, I saw the official business.
>
> *Bond*: Goodnight, would I do that to you after two years?
>
> *Goodnight*: Yes, you bloody well would![369]

Bond is acutely aware of Goodnight's feelings. But rather than address them directly, Bond deliberately obfuscates. His behavior enrages her:

> *Bond*: Goodnight, you know I'd much rather have dinner with you.
>
> *Goodnight*: Oh, I understand, James. Please hurry back.
>
> *Bond*: I'll ring as soon as I do. A midnight snack might be just the thing.

> *Goodnight*: I'll keep the wine properly chilled.
>
> *Bond*: And everything else warm, I trust.
>
> *Goodnight (fuming upon Bond's departure)*: And everything else warm?![370]

Despite Bond's "hopelessly obvious"[371] comments and behavior, Goodnight's desire remains. In fact, it increases as she continues to pine for him.

While Bond seemingly plays hard to get, Goodnight attempts to adopt a similar approach. During dinner, Bond compliments Goodnight on her attire, which is "tight in all the right places, not too many buttons."[372] Although he seduces her by essentially indicating that he has nothing better to do for the night, Goodnight declines, expressing her desire for something more than a fleeting sexual encounter: "I'm tempted, but killing a few hours as one of your passing fancies isn't quite my scene."[373] She rises from the table and walks away, seemingly "relish[ing] her enjoyment of rebuking Bond."[374]

Yet when Bond returns to his hotel suite, he finds that Goodnight is already there. "My hard-to-get act didn't last very long, did it,"[375] she asks before leaping into his arms. Once she is in Bond's bed, Goodnight indicates that she never believed her moment with Bond would happen. She also acknowledges that her sudden change of heart stems from the following revelation: "I'm weak."[376]

Goodnight's apparent triumph is short-lived when Andrea appears in Bond's hotel suite and interrupts her rendezvous. Bond, scrambling to conceal Goodnight, realizes that she is a liability who would effectively preclude him from seducing Andrea. The actions he takes deliberately reduce Goodnight to complete irrelevance.

First, Bond covers Goodnight with sheets, suggesting that he utilizes a "pillow trick" as a decoy for his own protection. He even goes so far as to hit the pillows, effectively smacking Goodnight underneath. Second, once Andrea excuses herself to undress, Bond removes Goodnight from the bed and throws her into a tight closet, where she remains for over two hours while Bond and Andrea utilize the bed several feet away. Bond "even leaves Goodnight inside long enough for Andrea to return to Scaramanga[]."[377]

Goodnight is understandably furious when Bond finally releases her from the closet, but he wholly dismisses her concerns:

> *Goodnight*: You mean I've been in here for two hours?
>
> *Bond (smoking a cigar)*: All in the line of duty.
>
> *Goodnight*: Duty? I'm resigning in the morning.

> *Bond*: Oh, Goodnight, come on, don't let us down. The Service needs women like you.
> *Goodnight*: Well, obviously you don't.[378]

Bond chooses Andrea over Goodnight, having no qualms about discarding Goodnight for another and tossing her into a closet while he conquers Andrea. Yet the source of Goodnight's frustration, interestingly enough, is her inability to be with Bond, not her reprehensible experience in the closet. Her only consolation is Bond's manipulative reassurance that her "turn will come."[379] Remarkably, Bond's comment seems to allay her anger and frustration.

Ultimately, Goodnight's opportunity to experience lovemaking with Bond is realized. It comes with a heavy price for Bond, whose mission becomes more difficult and deadly due to Goodnight's ineptitude. In effect, Bond's conquest of Goodnight serves more as a reward for his need to address and navigate around her errors and omissions than her fulfillment of a dream.

Goodnight's second and most significant character flaw is her complete incompetence. Every opportunity in which Goodnight offers or believes she is providing assistance transforms into a calamity that highlights the degree to which she is a "clumsy fool."[380] During an attempt to place a tracking device on Scaramanga's automobile without being noticed, Goodnight, "through sheer idiocy," finds herself thrown and locked into the trunk of the vehicle.[381] She inadvertently becomes Scaramanga's kidnapping victim in the process.

Bond, who is now unable to locate her and is frustrated as a result, makes a disparaging remark about women and their unreliability. An annoyed Bond attempts to communicate with Goodnight via walkie-talkie, but this becomes an exasperating ordeal. Once Bond locates Scaramanga's automobile, he tries to follow it in his own vehicle, but Goodnight has the keys with her inside Scaramanga's trunk. Although she informs Bond triumphantly that she possesses the keys, Goodnight is oblivious that her predicament has become Bond's dilemma since she has no ability to give Bond the keys and he cannot follow close behind to secure her release.

Ultimately, Bond commands Goodnight to remain in Scaramanga's trunk, as though she has a choice. But this instruction is no different than the closet incident in Bond's hotel suite. In fact, it reveals a theme: Goodnight is best kept in an isolated place without an escape so that those around her are not subjected to the calamities she creates.

This is but one example of how Goodnight "blithely caus[es] problems" for Bond.[382] While Goodnight takes pride in her ability to dispose of one of Scaramanga's henchmen by throwing him into freezing liquid helium, she is entirely unaware of the fact that her action "sets the solar complex on the inevitable path of self-destruction."[383] It is Bond who informs Goodnight that her actions destabilize the temperature, catalyze a chemical reaction, and initiate a complete meltdown. Yet she does not grasp the magnitude of her behavior. Bond even calls to her attention a large sign warning that absolute zero temperature must be maintained. In an annoyed tone, Bond scolds Goodnight: "Don't you believe in signs? We've got about five minutes before his body temperature raises that helium well above zero. Then this whole damn place will go sky-high!"[384] While Bond scurries to fix her blunder, Goodnight simply responds, "I'm sorry, I didn't know."[385]

But Goodnight has not completed creating havoc. As Bond attempts to remove the Solex Agitator from a laser capable of massive destruction, Goodnight commits "another boob":[386] rather than help Bond, she leans her body against the control panel and accidentally activates the device. An unsuspecting Bond suddenly finds himself in the path of the laser. The look of bewilderment on Goodnight's face as she sets into motion this chain of events reveals how quickly her carelessness escalates to a deadly level. Her behavior reflects the extent to which she is over her head and is an unfit intelligence agent:

> *Bond*: Kill the beam! Hit the master override switch!
> *Goodnight*: The what??
> *Bond* (*speaking in a commanding and condescending tone*): Goodnight?
> *Goodnight* (*answering in a submissive and ashamed manner*): Yes, James?
> *Bond*: Now listen carefully. There's a console up there. Now there must be a "scanner interlock button" on it. Push it! Goodnight, are you still there? It'll be on the auxiliary feedback circuit![387]

Goodnight is thoroughly overwhelmed by these simple instructions.

She identifies a series of buttons labeled "Computers Controlled Lock In," which she interprets as the scanner interlock button. With time of the essence, Goodnight pauses to inquire. A thoroughly disgusted Bond, who is trying to avoid contact with the deadly laser beam, commands Goodnight to simply "push every damn button."[388] This is one order that Goodnight seems to understand.

Unbeknownst to them both, Goodnight's desperate engagement of each button on the panel coincides with the movement of a cloud that obstructs the sun, thereby temporarily disengaging the laser beam that relies upon direct solar energy for activation. Bond believes that Goodnight succeeds in deactivating the device, condescendingly praising her: "Good girl, Goodnight, you've done it!"[389] Goodnight, however, has no idea what, if anything, she has done, but she nevertheless accepts Bond's compliment: "Oh, I have?"[390] In fact, Goodnight has done nothing to deactivate the machine.

Fortunately, Bond removes the solar component immediately before the sun reemerges from behind the cloud and reactivates the laser. His success, therefore, is wholly independent of Goodnight's assistance. In fact, she fails entirely to remedy the predicament that she herself creates, instead setting off a chain reaction that destroys the entire facility. Despite Goodnight's "exasperating" conduct, Bond nevertheless embraces her at the conclusion of the mission.[391]

Finally, Goodnight's character succumbs to complete implausibility throughout the film. In addition to the examples cited above, another encounter with Bond is worth mention. Upon his arrival in Hong Kong from Macau, Bond meets Goodnight, who arrives late to retrieve him from the airport. He instructs her to contact the license bureau and to trace a green Rolls-Royce. In response, Goodnight attempts to display her resourcefulness:

> *Goodnight*: A green Rolls?
> *Bond* (*repeating in an annoyed tone*): A green Rolls-Royce. There can't be that many in Hong Kong.
> *Goodnight* (*laughing*): Courtesy cars. All green Rolls-Royces belong to the Peninsual Hotel. You see what a two-year posting to Staff Intelligence does for a girl?[392]

Goodnight's observation, of course, does not require two years of duty. Indeed, she should be able to discern the common ownership of these vehicles in a relatively short period of time if she, in fact, engages in intelligence gathering in Hong Kong. The fact that Goodnight appears entirely satisfied with herself for reciting easily ascertainable information—and laughing about it, no less—illustrates the depth of her ineptitude as a member of the espionage community. Goodnight is essentially unhelpful, a fact that does not go unnoticed. Indeed, Bond can only state with dry sarcasm: "[Y]ou're a great help, Goodnight."[393]

Goodnight is a clear example of how so-called stereotypical "dumb blonde" aesthetics supersede productivity and intelligence.[394] Indeed, she appears wearing a bikini that accentuates her slender, athletic figure toward the conclusion of the film (Scaramanga offers his own commentary about Goodnight's attire: "I like a girl in a bikini—no concealed weapons."[395]), but her body should not become her focal point. In essence, Goodnight's ineptitude is forgiven because of her physical attractiveness. She reminds the audience that skill, qualification, and aptitude are traits that are not as important as appearance. So long as a woman is visually appealing and can serve as an object of desire, she will be tolerated.

Yet Goodnight also reinforces the extent to which women are inherently out of their element in a man's world. Women are, her character suggests, wholly unreliable, highly destructive, and virtually incapable of responding to pressure or adapting to rapidly changing circumstances. Goodnight functions in a perpetual state of oblivion. She lacks the capacity to understand that her actions affect those around her, and she fails to understand how her efforts to assist actually cause greater harm. Goodnight is therefore a dangerous symbol, representing the archetype of a misplaced woman who, even in 1974, should eschew ambition and a career that will disrupt her life and the lives of those around her. Goodnight ultimately instructs the audience that women should avoid the complexities of a patriarchal society and embrace a more appropriate and traditional role.

A comparison between Goodnight and a modern-day, 1970s woman reveals the extent to which Goodnight is unrealistic, anachronistic, and reactionary. Indeed, the comedy of Goodnight is how far she deviates from a character to which the audience can relate. As such, Goodnight represents the last manifestation of a Bond Girl archetype imbued with a nostalgic longing for the preservation of traditional, pre-feminist gender politics. The Bond Girl archetype that created Goodnight is taken to its farthest extreme in *The Man With the Golden Gun*, and the hyperbole Goodnight represents signaled that the Bond Girl in her then-current form could no longer remain viable.

* * *

After the release of *The Man With the Golden Gun*, Broccoli and Saltzman began production of the next Bond film. By the spring of 1975, Saltzman's own financial difficulties prompted him to sell his interest in EON Productions, effectively ending his affiliation with the franchise and longtime collaboration with Broccoli.[396] The departure of Saltzman also coincided with a substantial overhaul of the Bond Girl archetype for the final two films of the decade. The Bond Girl of the early 1970s no longer represented a viable vehicle through which to promote and preserve the social mores of the 1960s. Consequently, in order to preserve the franchise's vitality, the Bond Girl of the late 1970s warranted an overdue reconsideration that reconciled the successful Bond formula with modern female attributes.[397] The Bond Girl's survival depended upon her plausibility and sustainability, particularly since the feminist and Women's Liberation movements could no longer be ignored or discounted.

Mary Goodnight (Britt Ekland) sits idly while Francisco Scaramanga (Christopher Lee) challenges James Bond (Roger Moore) to a duel in *The Man With the Golden Gun*.

(Everett Collection/Rex USA)

The first attempt at achieving a balance occurred in 1977 with the release of *The Spy Who Loved Me*. Its successor, *Moonraker*, continued the trend two years later. In both films, producers introduced "engaging female" spies who reluctantly work alongside Bond but generally represent his equals.[398] These Bond Girls are nothing like Goodnight, Rosie, or any of their predecessors and are imbued with characteristics heretofore unexplored by the franchise. Together, *The Spy Who Loved Me* and *Moonraker* ushered in a new era in which the thematic premise of Double-O-Seven could survive—and, indeed thrive—within a paradigm that presents the Bond Girl as an assertive woman who eschews traditional gender roles and functions as an equal and productive member of society. The Bond Girl archetype presented in *The Spy Who Loved Me* and *Moonraker* preserved the character's cultural relevance and became an essential foundation for the franchise's success during the next three decades.

0012

Reconsidering an Archetype: *The Spy Who Loved Me* and *Moonraker*

Anya [Amasova] was really not one of Bond's girls so to speak. She's in the film doing her own bit . . . . [M]ost of the girls in the Bond films have just been merely beautiful girls that you know have small parts and come in and go out. Anya stays from the beginning to the end.

—Barbara Bach[1]

In 1979, it was a funny time to be a Bond Girl . . . because, at that time, women were protesting their image in the movies, how they had been portrayed. It was a conflicted time to be a Bond Girl.

—Lois Chiles[2]

Bond's attitudes to women caused outrage, titillation and amusement in roughly equal parts: they made a generation of men and boys very overexcited, and a generation of feminists extremely angry.

—Ben Macintyre[3]

It has been written that *The Man With the Golden Gun* represented "a low point in the series."[4] Due, in part, to the dissolution of the Cubby Broccoli-Harry Saltzman collaboration,[5] three years passed before the release of *The Spy Who Loved Me*. Broccoli assumed all production responsibilities, endeavoring to explore and develop James Bond's relationship with the Bond Girl.[6] To the extent that previous films presented what were perceived as strong female characters, these characters were aligned against Bond, and their hyperbolic representations ultimately offset the "little more than eye-catching adornments" that comprised the heroic Bond Girls.[7] As explained in the preceding chapter, the Bond Girl eventually succumbed to her own fantasy archetype, deviating far from any plausible female character model as the 1970s progressed.[8]

The Spy Who Loved Me ultimately refocused the lens on the Bond Girl, replacing her prior manifestation as an aesthetic accessory with an independent, more developed character. Indeed, the film became the first in the franchise that challenged Bond as "the archetypal male chauvinistic pig [who] uses . . . women."[9] The Bond Girl of yesteryear, the so-called "bosomy female of the 1960s,"[10] had reached her twilight. In her place emerged "a more believable female protagonist."[11]

The transformation, naturally, was not without criticism and a nostalgic longing for the less assertive Bond Girl character that was exalted in the previous nine films.[12] Ultimately, audiences accepted the new Bond Girl archetype, as evidenced by then-record-setting box office receipts.[13] In fact, *The Spy Who Loved Me* was the highest-grossing Bond film since *Thunderball.*[14] Two years later, *Moonraker* expanded upon and refined the presentation of the new Bond Girl archetype, again making a strong showing at the box office.

The Spy Who Loved Me

John Brosnan observed that *The Spy Who Loved Me* is "basically an anthology of all the Bond films that have gone before."[15] The description is apt, particularly since the film can be viewed as a series of reconfigured sequences featuring the following elements: ski chases reminiscent of *On Her Majesty's Secret Service,* fighting aboard trains in the style of *From Russia With Love* and *Live and Let Die*, and *Thunderball*-style underwater combat.[16] In fact, a theatrical trailer for *The Spy Who Loved Me* employed a device that harkened back to the days of *Dr. No*: narration by the actor portraying Bond.[17] Aside from marketing and aesthetic similarities, James Chapman argued that *The Spy Who Loved Me* was most akin to *You Only Live Twice* in both narrative and plot.[18] Considering the "lukewarm reception" received by *The Man With the Golden Gun,*[19] it is plausible that producers deliberately sought to rekindle the sparks enjoyed by predecessor installments of the Bond mythology.

These elements are ultimately subtle compared to the progressive, groundbreaking presentation of the Bond Girl that is displayed in *The Spy Who Loved Me*. According to Maryam d'Abo and John Cork, the Equal Pay Act, previously enacted in 1970 by the British Parliament, finally took effect in 1975, thereby enabling the "concept of 'equal pay for equal work'" to serve as an inspiration behind the female protagonist in the film.[20] Yet Congress had enacted similar legislation as far back as 1963,[21] and that law seemingly had little effect upon the presentation of the Bond Girl in the previous nine films. Moreover, while the ERA enjoyed rapid ratification by state legislatures in the early 1970s, that rate immediately halted in 1974 and 1975, ultimately yielding not a single state ratification in 1976. It is therefore apparent that legislative developments in both the United States and Great Britain had little effect upon facilitating a new era for the Bond Girl.

A more plausible reason for the significant narrative and substantive shift in the Bond Girl was an anachronistic model that required a modern update. Simply put, the time was ripe to address the following question: "What if Bond were confronted with his equal in every respect, and she was a woman?"[22] In fact, speculated Janet Woollacott, the franchise likely would have benefitted from a Bond Girl "whose challenge to Bond was more contemporary and more direct, and seen to be more relevant."[23] Ultimately, what producers sought to present in *The Spy Who Loved Me* was a Bond Girl of whom "women's lib would be rather proud."[24] At the same time, the Bond Girl had to fit within the established parameters of the Bondian formula. Therefore, it is quite possible that underneath the façade of equality "beats the heart of a pure sex object."[25]

The film's official poster design foreshadowed the introduction of a new Bond Girl archetype. The female lead is displayed with her back against Bond. The juxtaposition serves two important purposes. First, it visualizes opposing ideological representations—East versus West—and therefore advances the plot narrative. Second, it visualizes the perception of gender equality that the film explores. Like Bond, the Bond Girl is fully clothed, and she also clenches a weapon. Her eyes, however, depict skepticism as she gazes suspiciously toward Bond. It is readily apparent that she mistrusts him while he does not seem slightly fazed by the fact that she presents a challenge greater than his most dangerous enemy. Audiences were on notice that they would be in for a treat.

* * *

The Spy Who Loved Me is not about Bond. The audience, however, is initially led to believe otherwise. In the pre-title sequence, M learns that a British nuclear submarine has disappeared under mysterious circumstances. He immediately promises the prime minister that MI6 will send its "best man" to investigate.[26] Accordingly, M summons Bond, who is currently on a separate mission in Austria.

In the next scene, the audience discovers Bond in a rustic mountain log cabin in Austria romancing a blonde woman. His art of seduction is confirmed by the extent to which the woman experiences pleasure:

"Oh, James, I cannot find the words."[27] Her comment is perceived as a confession,[28] which is followed by Bond's testimonial, "Well, let me try to enlarge your vocabulary."[29] His encounter is interrupted by an electronic summons from M, and he quickly departs. The woman with whom Bond "has his hands full in the Austrian log cabin"[30] reveals herself as a Soviet spy and informs a group of assassins that Bond's arrival is imminent. A ski chase ensues, during which a KGB agent named Sergei Barzov is killed. Bond ultimately skis off the edge of a cliff, a moment John Brosnan described as "a sheer precipice to his apparent doom."[31] Yet Bond proves his superiority and virility by defeating his assailants and safely landing with the aid of a Union Jack parachute.

Both the ensuing title sequence and title song, "Nobody Does It Better," further suggest that Bond is the centerpiece of the film. The song, which was composed by Marvin Hamlisch and performed by Carly Simon, stands in sharp contrast to Lulu's "The Man With the Golden Gun," which focuses upon the prowess of the villain in the 1974 film. Bond is the clear subject of "Nobody Does It Better." According to the lyrics, no one does it "half as good" as Bond, and Bond is ultimately declared "the best."[32] As the song unfolds, the audience learns that Bond sparks "some kind of magic" in women.[33] In fact, the song hypothetically inquires as to how Bond "learned the things [he] do[es]."[34] The ballad eventually peaked on the recording charts[35] and earned an Oscar nomination for Best Song.[36]

While this apparent ode to Bond is performed, the audience is treated to another trademark title sequence created by Maurice Binder that features images of both Roger Moore and his Double-O-Seven silhouette firing weapons. The sequence is the first to incorporate images of the actor portraying Bond, another subtle suggestion of the extent to which the audience believes that Bond is the primary focus.[37] Other female silhouettes appear, and the most sexually suggestive activity in which one silhouette engages is the performance of acrobatics off the barrel of a gun. Bond also encounters a silhouette phalanx of military-attired women that immediately falls like dominos upon his approach, a visual representation of the extent to which his charm is "disarming." Considered one of Binder's greatest efforts,[38] the title sequence in *The Spy Who Loved Me* was designed to channel the story of the film.[39] Given the presentation of the Bond Girl that follows, it is understandable that the title sequence is not imbued with the sexually charged imagery of several of the previous films.

* * *

Before focusing upon Anya Amasova, the centerpiece of the film, a brief discussion of a secondary Bond Girl is warranted. As John Cork and

Bruce Scivally noted, the film's plot was "populated by uncomplicated characters."[40] One such character is Naomi, a helicopter pilot employed by villain Karl Stromberg. Although she is described as both Stromberg's "luscious assistant"[41] and "mistress,"[42] it is unclear whether any romantic elements supplement their professional relationship. Unlike Jill Masterson, who explicitly denies a physical relationship with Auric Goldfinger, Naomi reveals nothing.

Broccoli cast Caroline Munro for the role after he saw her wearing a wetsuit and wielding a knife in an advertising campaign.[43] Despite the suggestive pictorial, Munro refused to pose naked in *Playboy*.[44] The former model's "sultry presence and perfect figure (barely covered in a bikini)"[45] are immediately apparent in her first scene, where she displays her athletic figure. Naomi is sent by Stromberg in a speedboat to retrieve Bond and Anya, who are traveling under aliases as married marine biologists, for a meeting at Stromberg's Atlantis lair. As she returns to the speedboat, Bond remarks, "What a handsome craft. Such lovely lines."[46]

A brief, nonverbal flirtation ensues between her and Bond during their speedboat journey, much to the frustration of Anya. An element of sexual tension develops with an intriguing female villain persona that is somewhat reminiscent of Fiona Volpe in *Thunderball* or Helga Brandt in *You Only Live Twice*,[47] particularly since Naomi's "obvious interest in 007"[48] is cause for concern to Anya. The tension between the two women inexplicably thaws in a subsequent scene. Nevertheless, battle lines have been drawn between the two women.

Following Bond's encounter with Stromberg, Naomi is ordered to kill Bond and Anya. Piloting a helicopter equipped with machine guns, Naomi playfully winks at Bond while initiating a high-stakes game of cat-and-mouse. Ultimately, Bond launches a missile from his aquatic Lotus Esprit, bringing Naomi's role in the film to a "sudden, regretful end."[49]

Although Maryam d'Abo and John Cork characterized Naomi as a strong character,[50] she is more akin to the villainesses who precede her in implausibility and unsustainability. Raymond Benson observed that "the script gives her nothing to do,"[51] and, aside from her aesthetic appearance, Naomi serves little substantive purpose. In fact, her presence is purely facilitative. Upon Stromberg's order, she delivers Bond to him and later initiates a helicopter attack that provides an "excitingly filmed" chase sequence.[52] Moreover, she is an object of sexual desire who exhibits complete subservience to her male superior. In this regard, she is not unlike the "throwaway harem from which Bond is invited to choose a partner for the night" during a scene in Egypt,[53] another passing moment in a film that suggests that the archetype of a woman as a mere

British actress Caroline Munro poses on the set of *The Spy Who Loved Me*, 1977.
(Everett Collection/Rex USA)

aesthetically pleasing object of desire no longer deserves a prominent depiction.

* * *

The role of Anya, who is also known as Agent Triple X in the KGB, was awarded to Barbara Bach, who became only the second American actress to portray a primary Bond Girl—after Jill St. John in *Diamonds Are Forever*—and fourth overall, after Lana Wood, also in *Diamonds Are Forever*,[54] and Gloria Hendry in *Live and Let Die*. Finding a new leading actress for *The Spy Who Loved Me*, director Lewis Gilbert recalled, proved difficult because "they've got to be able to act a bit."[55] Ultimately, Bach "jogged the memory" of Broccoli when producers searched for a "spectacular Kremlin spychick,"[56] and she exhibited the traits that producers were seeking:

> Barbara was a very serene kind of girl, very quiet, and thus very effective as the Russian agent. We didn't want anyone flashy or loud. And we couldn't have someone too young either—a girl in her early twenties—because she wouldn't match up with Roger. She had to be a mature woman, especially since she was playing a top KGB assassin.[57]

Moreover, Broccoli believed that Bach, who was relatively unknown, would "bring[] a certain freshness" to the film.[58] Of course, Bach also possessed the physical attributes necessary to successfully portray a Bond Girl. Although she was a professional model for over a decade before landing the female lead in *The Spy Who Loved Me*,[59] Bach recalled that her casting was her "first really big lucky break."[60]

Barbara Bach introduced a new attitude about the role of a Bond Girl, recalling that Anya was "a very nice character, and . . . probably the best female character that's ever been in a Bond film."[61] Her approach also suggested that "she was to play a different sort of Bond girl."[62] For example, Bach generally resisted posing in a bikini for publicity photos, preferring instead to appear in character by adorning a Russian military uniform.[63] In so doing, Bach "wanted to avoid the 'cheesecake' image of much accepted 'Bond girl' publicity."[64] The official film poster similarly depicted a fully clothed Anya, whereas previous film art depicted the Bond Girl in less attire. Indeed, Bach's character "remains fully dressed" throughout the entire film, a true rarity.[65]

Interestingly, Barbara Bach, like Ursula Andress before her, preferred to appear on the set without wearing a brassier. Whereas Andress's

American actress Barbara Bach poses on the set of *The Spy Who Loved Me*, 1977.
(Everett Collection/Rex USA)

decision to do so was celebrated during the filming of *Dr. No*, the reaction to Bach was markedly different:

> Barbara Bach, latest of a beautiful line of Bond Birds, feels she is a liberated enough creature of the 1970s not to wear a bra. But when she turned up on the set of the new James Bond epic, *The Spy Who Loved Me*, there was a shock for this russet-haired American beauty. "Go and buy a bra," she was politely but firmly told.[66]

Bach ultimately did not deviate from her predecessors when she agreed to pose for *Playboy*,[67] a decision that, according to one writer, "undid the good work" of the film.[68]

* * *

Anya is introduced during the film's pre-title sequence after the Soviets discover that one of their nuclear submarines has mysteriously vanished. General Anatol Alexis Gogol, upon learning this sensitive information, commits himself to assigning "our best agent immediately."[69] He summons for Agent Triple X, who is currently on leave at a convalescence center.

The audience is then taken to the convalescence center, where Barzov and a woman are making love. When they conclude, the woman asks when they can meet again, to which Barzov responds, "As soon as my mission is accomplished."[70] Barzov rises, stating that he must depart for Austria. All indications are that Barzov, who is tasked with assassinating Bond while in Austria, is the Agent Triple X to whom General Gogol refers.

Indeed, when a music box on the night table begins playing, Barzov reaches to open it and listen to General Gogol's message: "Agent Triple X, calling Agent Triple X. You will report to headquarters immediately. Agent Triple X, acknowledge and verify."[71] Thereafter, Barzov gets out of the bed. The woman, however, remains in bed and moves toward the music box. At this moment, the camera quickly draws closer to her face, highlighting the surprise the audience experiences as *she* identifies herself as Agent Triple X. The KGB's best agent is a woman who, as it becomes clear throughout the film, represents a veritable "equal of Bond in every way."[72]

Janet Woollacott described this revelation as a "joke" perpetrated on the audience.[73] But it is far from a joke. If Anya is essentially "a female James Bond,"[74] then the parallel structure inherent in the "simultaneous calling of the top British and top Russian agents by their respective governments"[75] is both apt and creative. And yet, the revelation that the

KGB's top agent is a woman ultimately should not have been surprising to audiences in 1977, even within Bond's fictional world.

The parallelism inherent in the manner in which Anya and Bond are assigned their missions is but one example of the similarities between the two characters. Most obvious are the titles bestowed upon each spy by their respective governments. Whereas Bond possesses a Double-O moniker at MI6, Anya is the KGB's Agent Triple X . Although the Triple X title is sexually suggestive, it does not detract from the strength of Anya's character. In fact, in terms of sexual prowess, Anya's drive is as strong and verile as Bond's, as evidenced by her bedroom scene with Barzov. Like Bond, whose utmost devotion is to country and the mission, Anya approaches her mission with an unemotional, detached sense of duty. When she learns that Bond was responsible for killing Barzov, Anya's first reaction is to conclude her joint mission with Bond and, only upon its completion, avenge his murder.

Anya and Bond first encounter each other at the Mojaba Club in Cairo, where both hope to obtain a microfilm copy of a nuclear submarine tracking system that "is being peddled on the open market."[76] Their introduction is more akin to a battle of wits than a conversation, with each agent attempting to display more knowledge of the other's dossier. Wearing a black formal gown as she enters the club, Anya is approached from across the room by Bond. Offering to buy her a drink, Bond asks whether she would prefer he call her Triple X, a question that exposes her true identify. Anya is unaffected by Bond's remark and instead dismisses him. Once they approach the bar, Bond takes the liberty of ordering Anya her signature drink. She, in turn, orders him a vodka martini, shaken not stirred. This first round is a virtual stalemate, as Bond's "touché" response indicates.[77]

Anya then turns the table on Bond, evidencing a wide-eyed glance as she proudly, but nonchalantly, displays her knowledge of the British agent, all while casually resting her head on her left arm. Her recitation is both unexpected for and unnerving to Bond, whose facial expression gradually changes from a slight arrogant smirk when Anya begins recounting Bond's attributes to annoyance. Finally, he must interrupt her:

> *Anya*: Commander James Bond. Recruited to the British Secret Service from the Royal Navy. Licensed to kill and has done so on numerous occasions. Many lady friends, but married only once. Wife killed . . . .
>
> *Bond* (*interrupting*): All right, you've made your point.
>
> *Anya*: You're sensitive, Mister Bond.
>
> *Bond*: About certain things, yes.[78]

Bond immediately rises from the bar, excusing himself: "[T]ragically, I have a previous engagement."[79] "Happily enough," Anya responds, "so do I."[80] Their second round of sparring belongs to Anya, who has shaken Bond's resolve by referencing Tracy di Vicenzo's death. Interestingly, her statement is the first direct reference to Bond's marriage in *On Her Majesty's Secret Service*, and it is not mentioned again until Bond is seen visiting her gravesite in *For Your Eyes Only* in 1981.

The apparently separate engagements both Bond and Anya reference are, in fact, with the same individual: Max Kalba, owner of the Mojaba Club and a black market trader who currently possesses the microfilm that both the British and Soviets seek. Bond begins to converse with Kalba, but Anya interrupts, bringing Bond's drink that he leaves behind at the bar. Their encounter with Kalba reflects the extent to which Anya employs her sexuality as a weapon. As it appears that a bidding war will commence between Bond and Anya, Kalba, noticing Anya's low-cut gown, cautions Bond: "From where I sit, I fancy you will find the lady's figure hard to match."[81] The auction between the two spies for the microfilm ultimately does not come to fruition as Kalba is called away. Bond then discovers that Kalba is murdered by Jaws, the "[e]normous, apparently invulnerable steel-toothed assassin."[82] Before killing Kalba, Jaws takes the microfilm from him. Although Bond and Anya cannot bid on the merchandise, it is clear that Anya remains a step ahead of Bond at the Mojaba Club and that Bond finds himself struggling to catch up to her.

Bond decides to pursue Jaws, but Anya refuses to extend any latitude to him or to allow him out of her sight. Instead, she follows Bond, and while they both are sitting in the back of the van that Jaws drives into the desert, Anya makes her intentions clear: "Make no mistake, Mister Bond, I want that microfilm. And I'm going to get it."[83] Anya is clearly not intimidated by Bond. Assertive, confident, and knowledgeable, she presents a formidable challenge that Bond has never encountered from a member of the opposite sex. His only response to her declaration, a bland "[u]nless I get it first,"[84] is his best and only effort to counter her commanding attitude and presence.

Bond and Anya pursue Jaws at an Egyptian archaeological site, but it is Anya who assumes a leading role. It is her adeptness and perceptiveness that enable her to observe a falling boulder heading toward Bond, and she forces Jaws to relinquish the microfilm, which he tosses to the ground. Although it seems that Anya has obtained what she has sought, she makes one critical mistake by momentarily taking her eyes off Jaws as she looks to the ground to pick up the microfilm. Doing so enables Jaws to kick her weapon aside. But her mistake also permits her to flee with the microfilm while Bond is left behind to fight Jaws.

In pursuit of microfilm, James Bond (Roger Moore) and Anya Amasova (Barbara Bach) follow Jaws to an Egyptian archaeological site in *The Spy Who Loved Me*.

(Everett Collection/Rex USA)

Anya's escape is short-lived because Bond ultimately possesses the keys to the getaway van. After temporarily disabling Jaws, Bond returns to the vehicle, dangling the keys before her in a taunting manner. He also seizes the microfilm that Anya casually places on the dashboard: "Sorry," he says as he forcefully removes her hand, "you're just too late."[85]

Bond may have matched wits with Anya and won this battle, but Anya, once again, triumphs. Her sense of emotional detachment and fidelity to the mission are clear to the audience once she and Bond escape from Jaws:

> *Bond (smirking, and with sarcasm)*: Oh, by the way, thanks for deserting me back there.
> *Anya (focusing upon driving, without expression)*: Every woman for herself, remember?
> *Bond (smirking)*: Still, you did save my life.
> *Anya (lacking expression)*: We all make mistakes, Mister Bond.[86]

Ultimately, Bond and Anya, still in their formalwear from the previous night, traverse across the desert until they approach a small riverboat that takes them to Cairo.

While aboard the riverboat, Bond analyzes and copies the microfilm without Anya's knowledge. She remains intent upon obtaining the microfilm and employs her own method of seduction as the means to that end. Anya begins to describe how she learned to keep warm during training missions to Siberia, a discussion that prompts her to embrace Bond. At the same time, she is fully cognizant of Bond's wandering hands and questions whether *he* is trying to take advantage of her. Anya then presents a cigarette containing a stun gas, which she proceeds to blow into Bond's face. Once he is subdued, Anya takes the microfilm and disappears. Bond awakens aboard the riverboat by himself, clearly agitated that he has been compromised. Anya, once again, has outwitted Bond, leaving him to contemplate his embarrassment.

Their rivalry, however, has only just begun. Bond reports to an ancient Egyptian monument where MI6 has established a temporary headquarters. After Bond encounters General Gogol, M advises Bond that the British and Soviet governments have agreed to cooperate in a joint effort to retrieve their stolen submarines, a collaboration that one critic claimed places Bond "hand-in-blouse with the KGB."[87] As a gesture of good faith, General Gogol offers MI6 the opportunity to view the microfilm that, he emphasizes, was "recovered by Agent Triple X."[88] Bond winces at this remark, though Anya adds insult to injury by noting her retrieval was effectuated "[w]ith considerable ease."[89] Humiliated in the presence of his superior, Bond attempts to take control, noting that he previously examined the microfilm, a statement that places Anya on the defensive for the first time during the course of the mission.

Anya and Bond again lock horns when they engage in a joint analysis of the microfilm with M, General Gogol, and Q. Anya continues to remain one step ahead, and it becomes clear to the audience that her rivalry with Bond is an extension of their respective governments' efforts to outperform each other. Regardless, Anya's resourcefulness and intellect far surpass any of her Bond Girl predecessors and keep Bond struggling to catch up.

General Gogol inquires as to the meaning of a partially obscured word, "oratory," on the enlarged microfilm image. Bond quickly responds: "It's another word for chapel."[90] Anya, however, carefully analyzes the image further and concludes that "[i]t is a fish. That is the symbol of the Stromberg shipping line."[91] Bond rolls his eyes rapidly and offers an alternative interpretation, claiming that the term is "laboratory" and that Stromberg has a marine research laboratory in Corsica. His comment receives warm praise from M, but it is short-lived. Anya promptly corrects him: "Actually, sir, it is in Sardinia."[92] A wide-eyed Bond is shocked, and the tit-for-tat sparring prompts laughter from General Gogol, who concludes that "two such perceptive talents will enjoy working together in Sardinia."[93]

Ironically, the atmosphere of cooperation that develops between Bond and Anya thaws not only their rivalry but also Anya's independence. Although Anya heretofore keeps a physical distance from Bond, utilizing her sexuality and skill of seduction to her advantage, her ability to continue repelling Bond's advances begins to wane. Although she declines a nightcap aboard the train en route to Sardinia and retires to her separate room, Anya is certainly tempted to take Bond up on his offer. The smile on her face as she undresses indicates her satisfaction in knowing that she has whetted Bond's sexual appetite. Yet after Bond saves her from Jaws, who appears aboard the train in an attempt to dispose of both agents, Anya quickly elevates Bond to the role of savior and submits to him.

For the remainder of the film, Anya exhibits slightly more traditional Bond Girl attributes that emerge alongside the independence and resourcefulness she exhibits prior to her sexual encounter with Bond. For example, it is Anya who discovers a peculiarity in the shape of Stromberg's model supertanker and calls it to Bond's attention when they are hosted by Stromberg. She also appears more adept at operating Bond's Lotus Esprit underwater while Bond encounters difficulty. Releasing a smokescreen and an explosive device when Bond seems uncertain of the vehicle's capabilities, Anya confesses that she "saw the blueprints of this car two years ago."[94] At the same time, her statement stands in sharp contrast to the expressions of shock and amazement she exhibits when Bond first submerges the Lotus and transforms it into a submarine. Had Anya previously viewed the blueprints as she claims, she certainly would have been aware of its capabilities. Her reaction of bewilderment, therefore, is inexplicable.

There are also glimpses of relegating Anya to a status subordinate to her male counterparts. Bond, who assumes an alias as a marine biologist, introduces Anya as his wife and "assistant."[95] In effect, Bond has no shame placing her in such a traditional role, though it is clear that Anya expresses disgust with Bond's characterization. At MI6 headquarters in Egypt, General Gogol, having declared a new era of Anglo-Soviet relations, quickly snaps his finger at Anya, a nonverbal command inducing her to immediately produce the microfilm.

Moreover, although she initially conducts the mission objectively and without emotional attachment, Anya is imbued with greater plausibility when it is apparent that her pain over the loss of a lover can no longer be concealed. Once it is revealed that Bond kills Barzov in Austria, Anya vows to kill Bond once their mission is complete. It is Bond who must remind Anya about the nature of their profession: "In our business, Anya, people get killed. We both know that, and so did he. It was either him or me . . . . Yes, I did kill him."[96]

While aboard the USS *Wayne* in pursuit of Stromberg's supertanker, Anya surprises Commander Carter, who is not expecting a female crew member. Although Anya declares that "[a]board this vessel, Commander, I am Major Amasova of the Russian army," Commander Carter's response is dismissive, "Yeah, sure."[97] At first, Anya refuses to receive special accommodations, but she ultimately utilizes private quarters to shower in light of the logistical realities of being aboard a submarine populated by an entirely male crew.

Most significant is that Anya must disguise her femininity once the USS *Wayne* is intentionally captured by Stromberg. Bond has the foresight to instruct her to remain inconspicuous as she, along with the remaining male crew, is under constant surveillance. Anya resists, unashamed of her identity, and strikes one of Stromberg's men in the face. Her actions remind the audience that she is, in fact, a "dangerous spy."[98] Thus, Anya inherently eschews concealing her gender in order to remain inconspicuous.

At the same time, her conduct results in her captivity, and she is taken by Stromberg back to his Atlantis compound. Bound and confined, Stromberg apologizes for her current predicament, justifying it on the basis that her violent proclivities—or assertiveness—require "control[]."[99] At this point, Anya is effectively removed from the mission, leaving Bond with the task of averting nuclear annihilation and dismantling an atomic warhead. Whereas Anya previously declares that she "never failed on a mission,"[100] it appears that this mission has, to some degree, gotten the better of her. Her status as "a strong, equal, and interesting character,"[101] particularly once she is imprisoned by Stromberg, is diminished. Indeed, one critic observed that Anya "makes no sense as a master spy who is almost (but not quite) as ingenious as 007 himself."[102]

Bond eventually "locates Amasova just as Atlantis is hit by torpedoes and the whole establishment begins to fill up with water."[103] Whereas she previously expresses gratitude to Bond for saving her from Jaws on the train, Anya is now wholly unimpressed and remains intent upon avenging her lover's death until the last moments of the film: "The mission is over, Commander."[104] Notwithstanding her strong resolve, Anya "quickly melts"[105] after Bond timely pops the cork of a champagne bottle. She falls into his embrace, even asking him what their superiors would think of their union. Authority ultimately rests with Bond, but virtually the entire film plays out before he acquires it. One might argue that it is not until the end of their mission that Anya herself cedes any authority to Bond.

* * *

As Janet Woollacott observed, "Anya is set up as a challenge to Bond, but one to be subordinated by Bond in the characteristic development of the Bond narrative."[106] Ultimately, Bond "beds [every woman] to his will,"[107] and Anya is no exception. After all, Anya is, by definition, a Bond Girl who exists within the parameters of a prescribed formula. Described as a Barbie doll, one critic wrote that Anya "look[s] ridiculous" as her disdain for Bond evaporates as their mission progresses.[108] Although John Brosnan lamented that *The Spy Who Loved Me* is "without an original bone in its body,"[109] the observation ultimately discounts the extent to which Anya's character is groundbreaking within the Bond Girl paradigm.

Anya is "one of the best comrade-in-arms characters in the series because even until the very end, there is a wonderful tension between her and 007."[110] More importantly, Anya is imbued with a plausibility that surpasses her predecessors, effectively ushering in a "new breed of heroine for the series."[111] Regardless of how her significant moments of independence and assertiveness are tempered by the constraints inherent in the successful Bondian formula, the character of Anya effectively provides the first glimpse of the franchise's balance between the realities of the gender movement and the presentation of a strong and attractive female lead character that is both modern and sustainable. Although the Bond Girl archetype exemplified by Anya would likely not "win votes at a NOW convention," Broccoli conceded in 1979 that "'[t]he feminist viewpoint is very strong today and we can't ignore it.'"[112]

Separate and distinct from Mary Goodnight and those characters that precede her, Anya represents the first in a succession of viable and sustainable female characters within the Bond mythology. As the series approached the conclusion of its second successful decade, producers refined this reconsidered Bond Girl archetype with the next iteration, which was "very similar" to, but also light-years ahead of, its predecessor.[113]

Moonraker

The success of *The Spy Who Loved Me*—the film generated "twice as much business" than any other Bond film[114]—enabled Broccoli to exercise "financial free reign" over the next film in the series.[115] Initially, producers intended to release *For Your Eyes Only*, which had been announced as the next installment in the ending credits of *The Spy Who Loved Me*. The success of *Star Wars* and *Close Encounters of the Third Kind*, however, prompted producers to reconsider: "The public wanted outer-space adventure, and Broccoli felt that in *Moonraker* . . . he had a story and a title that were ripe for the times."[116]

Indeed, Broccoli explained that "[p]art of the formula is taking James Bond where he hasn't been before . . . ."[117] Raymond Benson lamented that "the entire concept behind choosing *Moonraker* for the next film emphasize[d] the Bond series' inability to maintain its originality."[118] Nevertheless, *Moonraker* was a conscious effort to replicate the tremendous success of *The Spy Who Loved Me*.[119] Described by one critic as "cheerful, splashy entertainment,"[120] *Moonraker* delivered at the box office.[121]

But, as with each Bond film, *Moonraker* garnered its fair share of criticism. Described as another low point in the series,[122] *Moonraker* was dismissed as having "nothing on its mind except dizzying entertainment."[123] Roger Moore's eyes, according to one review, "no longer twinkle[d] with the old multiple lust for danger, bimbos and gadgets that made James Bond the ultimate Playboy male fantasy."[124] One critic asked, "Is *Moonraker* the best or the most boring of the Bonds?"[125] Yet the most scathing attacks, interestingly enough, focused upon the film's progressive portrayal of the Bond Girl.

* * *

Dr. Holly Goodhead, described as "rather bland and . . . one of the least memorable of Bond's onscreen lovers,"[126] was portrayed by American actress Lois Chiles, whose previous film experience included *The Way We Were* and *The Great Gatsby*.[127] Gilbert, who returned to

American actress Lois Chiles and British actor Roger Moore pose on the set of *Moonraker*, 1978.

(Associated Press)

direct *Moonraker*, met Chiles aboard an airplane and was impressed with her "very cool exterior,"[128] a description suggesting that Chiles could bring depth, realism, and a sense of independence to the Bond Girl role. Chiles's "devil-may-care attitude" ultimately attracted her to the role of Holly,[129] and she later admitted that she took delight in possessing one of the more obscene names in the franchise.[130] Chiles nostalgically joked: "The name 'Dr. Holly Goodhead.' How am I going to explain that to my parents?"[131]

Although John Brosnan applauded the casting of Lois Chiles, whom he described as a "great improvement on Barbara Bach, being not only a better actress but also possessing a much more interesting screen presence,"[132] not all agreed. Chiles's cool exterior did not sit well with many critics, who described her as "lovely," but ultimately "just one of the sexually tireless Bond's conquests."[133] Another reviewer described Chiles as "charmless,"[134] and she was branded as "beautiful but bland."[135] Steven Jay Rubin described her as "an ice machine in the charisma department."[136] The *Los Angeles Times* characterized Chiles as "very attractive, although as an actress she makes one wince for the unkind things that have been said about Ali MacGraw."[137] Playing Holly "a bit too coldly,"[138] Chiles brought to the screen a Bond Girl who apparently was "all too sexless"[139] and "cares more for karate than kisses."[140] Like Caroline Munro, Chiles declined to pose in *Playboy*.[141]

The critiques of Lois Chiles merely reflected a broader criticism of the film's female characters. The "Broccoli factory," as it was dubbed, was accused of failing to "alter the basic formula" despite two decades of "sexual and political developments."[142] Yet after the franchise began reassessing and reconsidering the Bond Girl archetype, *Moonraker* ultimately prompted lamentations. For example, the *National Review* suggested that "[a]fter we have had our fill of . . . Lois Chiles's less than stellar glamor, we have ample time to reflect on how much more fun the lines, gimmicks, and plot twists used to be in the days of Sean Connery. Why, even the girls were prettier then."[143] *Moonraker*'s female actresses were described as "more slimline-decorative instead of protruding too bustily,"[144] an insinuation that the franchise succumbed to elevating political correctness over entertainment. For some, *Moonraker* simply proved too sterile: "Even the sex isn't very sexy."[145]

* * *

But *Moonraker* is replete with traditional Bond Girl elements that balance the presentation of Holly, who has been dubbed the "feminist icon in the Bond saga."[146] First, the title sequence reprises images of diving, somersaulting, and flying naked female silhouettes, sexually suggestive elements that are entirely absent from *The Spy Who Loved Me*. Despite its reincorporation of these features, the title sequence is subdued and stands in sharp contrast to the sexually charged title sequence in *The Man With the Golden Gun*.

Second, *Moonraker* features two ancillary Bond Girl characters that enable Bond to demonstrate his sexual prowess and, to some degree, preserve the Bondian formula. Their presence balances the strong, feminist protagonist that Bond ultimately encounters during his mission. The fact that *Moonraker* features two such characters evidences the extent to which the film advances the Bond Girl archetype beyond the presentation initially introduced in *The Spy Who Loved Me*, which juxtaposes Anya Amasova alongside only Naomi. By further refining the attributes of its female lead, *Moonraker* tempers its groundbreaking portrayal while simultaneously veering away from the traditional Bond Girl archetype by attributing those seemingly antiquated ideals to two throwaway characters that demonstrate for the audience the long and circuitous path the Bond Girl has traversed to reach her 1979 potential.

The first such character is Corinne Dufour. Portrayed by French actress Corinne Clery, Corinne is villain Hugo Drax's personal assistant and pilot. In essence, she is akin to Stromberg's Naomi. Corinne serves both an aesthetic and narrative function. The audience is introduced to her when she meets Bond at the airport and transports him to Drax's California estate. Describing herself as a "humble pilot in the service of the Drax Corporation," Corrine's attire suggests otherwise as she adorns a white-and-orange dress that features a plunging neckline. Indeed, Corinne's fulsome chest and ample cleavage leave little to the imagination, and her physical attributes are not lost upon Bond. After Corinne welcomes him to California, Bond, referring to her, responds, "I like it already."[147] Once she facilitates Bond's introduction to Drax, Corinne is called upon to escort Bond to meet Holly, after which she disappears.

Later, Bond, who remains at the Drax residence overnight, enters Corinne's bedroom. He is uninvited, but this fact is quickly forgotten. Seated at a table wearing a silver nightgown as she combs her hair, Corinne believes that Bond appears to seduce her. She smiles coyly and cautions him: "My mother gave me a list of things not to do on a first date."[148] Bond responds, "Maybe you won't need it,"[149] and instead indicates that he seeks information. Oddly enough, Corinne seems somewhat dejected by this revelation, though Bond's information-gathering expedition quickly dissolves into a successful seduction. Corinne rises, and Bond escorts her toward the bed. After their first embrace, Corinne remains slightly skeptical of Bond, but she quickly succumbs to him once they embrace again.

Having "turn[ed] on the charm," Bond, in usual fashion, causes Corinne to "switch[] her allegiance"[150] and turn against her own employer. Her behavior is virtually indistinguishable from all of those characters that precede her and experience the same effect. Sitting on the bed, Corinne dutifully responds to Bond's question concerning the activities that occur on the Drax estate. Maryam d'Abo and John Cork described the scene as follows: "Bond offers to sleep with her if she will help uncover information. Corinne goes for the idea . . . ."[151] "What about that list of your mother's," Bond asks.[152] "I never learned to read," Corinne responds.[153] In the next post-coital scene, Corinne discovers Bond inside Drax's office seeking "information" and stands idly next to Bond as he accesses Drax's safe.

Unbeknownst to Bond or Corinne, their activities are being observed by Chang, one of Drax's servants and henchmen. Chang ultimately reports Corinne's betrayal to Drax, who orders that she be killed. The "just reward" for assisting Bond, Drax determines, is that Corinne be fed to his Doberman pinschers.[154] He summons Corinne, who appears wearing a white dress that conceals her entire figure, an allusion to the sacrificial role that she now unwittingly assumes.[155] Terminating her employment despite her weak denials that she assisted Bond and revealed the safe to him, Drax unleashes the Dobermans, which chase her into the forest. The scene omits the violence inherent in the punishment, so much so that Raymond Benson described it as "lush and soft focused" and therefore unworkable.[156] The scene was also characterized as one containing "all the lush romanticism of a hair spray commercial, . . . one with Drax offering her as breakfast on the hoof to his two dogs."[157]

Regardless of the cinematography, Corinne is simply a sexual exploit for Bond. Once Bond conquers her physically, Corinne's usefulness runs its course. Although the film seemingly portrays her as an adept pilot, Corinne lacks any independent or assertive attributes. She works for a male employer and must comply with his directives. Appearing somewhat naïve, Corinne permits Bond to seduce her under the pretense that she provides information to him. Although Maryam d'Abo and John Cork declared that Corinne, in fact, "aids 007,"[158] such an assessment is a slight exaggeration. Before their sexual encounter, Corinne reveals that something "very secretive" occurs at the Drax compound, but she indicates that everything has been moved elsewhere.[159] In essence, she knows neither the substance of the work nor the new location. Corinne does, however, direct Bond to Drax's safe, though she does so with a vague nonverbal cue. Bond assumes the remainder of the work on his own.

The second character is Manuela, Bond's contact at Station VH in Rio de Janeiro.[160] Manuela, who was portrayed by the "[b]eautiful, exotic

French actress Corinne Clery poses on the set of *Moonraker*, 1979.

(U.A./Everett/Rex USA)

actress" Emily Bolton,[161] initially appears trailing Bond's car from the airport with a camera, an image reminiscent of the Jamaican photographer Bond encounters in *Dr. No*. Manuela then appears in Bond's hotel suite preparing his signature drink. "She makes it clear that she definitely prefers to mix business and pleasure,"[162] and Bond does not pass up the opportunity. Manuela then positions herself on a couch wearing a transparent white gown with a blue ribbon around her waist with white lingerie underneath. Bond approaches her and asks, "How do you kill five hours in Rio if you don't samba?"[163] Bond then proceeds to remove the ribbon, initiating what is undoubtedly his "fastest seduction."[164] Indeed, "Manuela and Bond have been in each other's presence on screen for exactly one minute before Bond propositions her."[165]

One minute is all that is required, as Manuela's entire function is to elevate the number of Bond's sexual conquests. After apparently killing several hours in bed together, the next scene takes Manuela and Bond to one of Drax's facilities. Although Manuela is presumably an intelligence agent herself, Bond curiously instructs her to wait outside for him while he explores the facility on his own. Also curious is that Manuela offers no protest to this directive. Perhaps he has learned his lesson during his mission with Goodnight.

Although she is relegated to standing idly in an alleyway during Carnival, Manuela, much like Goodnight, becomes a magnet for trouble. She is approached by a large clown that is revealed to be the assassin Jaws. Her reaction to impending death at the hands of the steel-jawed villain is entirely implausible, particularly for an intelligence agent: she pulls out a knife but finds herself easily overcome by the much stronger and larger adversary. In fact, Manuela, "obviously more skilled in the boudoir than in fieldwork—barely makes a token attempt at resistance and has to be rescued by 007."[166]

Although she survives the assault, Manuela does not reappear in the film. Since Bond has already conquered her sexually, there is little purpose to developing her character. Indeed, the longest activity she is capable of sustaining is several hours of intercourse with Bond, and that occurs entirely off-screen. In essence, Manuela's unconvincing performance as a member of the espionage community renders her character easily forgettable and insignificant.

* * *

Ultimately, the primary Bond Girl of the film demonstrates the extent to which Corinne and Manuela are antiquated feminine ideals. The name "Holly Goodhead," which has been described as "cleverly named mattress candy,"[167] was the creation of screenwriter Christopher Wood, who described it as "very, very Fleming."[168] It is, of course, one of many in the franchise that "incite[] schoolboy giggles."[169]

Yet Holly's name does her character disservice and serves only to undermine the traits and principles for which she stands.[170] An undercover CIA agent working as a NASA scientist who is "[o]n loan to Drax Industries,"[171] Holly is both an astrophysicist and a fully trained astronaut.[172] The audience learns that Holly is a college graduate, presumably the first Bond Girl to have earned a degree from an institution of higher learning. An alumna of Vassar College, Holly boasts to Bond that she learned hand-to-hand combat, as well as acquired her scientific training, in school, as opposed to during her tenure at NASA. Lois Chiles described the character as a "'concession to women's lib,'" recalling that "'[i]t was 1979 and women were burning their bras still, so the Bond woman as such in its old form, they sort of had to update it. They called her Dr. Holly Goodhead.'"[173]

The selection of Vassar as Holly's alma mater is fitting and acknowledges a significant moment in higher education. Along with Barnard, Bryn Mawr, Mount Holyoke, Radcliffe, Smith, and Wellesley colleges, Vassar is one of what is termed the Seven Sisters, institutions that were founded as women's colleges. Beginning in the 1960s, pressure mounted to merge these colleges with the men's colleges with which they were generally associated. Vassar, however, refused to merge with Yale University[174] and instead became the first among these women's colleges to open its doors to male students.[175] Today, only five Seven Sisters institutions—Barnard, Bryn Mawr, Mount Holyoke, Smith, and Wellesley—remain women's colleges, with Radcliffe having merged with Harvard University in 1999.[176] Reference to Vassar, which has been recognized for its "curricular innovation,"[177] therefore demonstrates a conscious commitment in the late 1970s to bridging the expansive divide between the portrayal of the fictional Bond Girl and the backdrop of the real gender equality movement.

Holly has been described as "very similar" to Anya Amasova insofar as she "joins forces, reluctantly, with Bond in order to vanquish the villain."[178] Yet *Moonraker* modifies this theme, ultimately creating a Bond Girl character that, unlike any other preceding her, can truly be described as Bond's equal within the parameters of the Bondian formula. Fittingly, Holly is arguably the first Bond Girl who possesses a "narratively important skill" that Bond lacks: commanding a space shuttle.[179]

* * *

Holly's introduction sets a clear and deliberate tone and exhibits, in no uncertain terms, Bond's—and the franchise's—recognition of the achievements inherent in the feminist and Women's Liberation movements. Until his initial encounter with Holly, all references to Dr. Goodhead have been intentionally gender neutral, setting the stage for what is arguably the most uncomfortable surprise Bond encounters. Arriving for a previously scheduled appointment with Dr. Goodhead, Bond observes a woman in a corner office engaging in scientific calculations. Clearing his voice to gain her attention, she approaches, revealing a beige dress that fully conceals her figure. Although her demeanor is not overly friendly, she is nevertheless pleasant. Bond states that he is looking for Dr. Goodhead. The woman responds, with a proud smile, "You just found her."[180] A clear expression of shock registers across Bond's face, and the encounter quickly dissolves into contentious and condescending verbal sparring:

> *Bond* (*indicating shock, but registering an approving smirk*): A woman!
> *Holly* (*glaring and in a snide tone*): Your powers of observation do you credit, Mister Bond.[181]

The cinematography brilliantly depicts the battle of wits that has commenced. At each turn, the camera focuses upon Bond or Holly individually, creating a back-and-forth that draws the audience into the ensuing dispute. This process continues throughout the remainder of the scene.

In an effort to dispense with formality and forge a truce, Bond extends his hand to shake hers. Holly, whose facial expression demonstrates considerable disgust as a result of Bond's audacious presumption that Dr. Goodhead could not possibly be female, reluctantly extends hers in return. Of course, Bond finds it difficult to accept the reality that the intelligent, attractive woman before him is the Dr. Goodhead he is scheduled to meet. In an effort to regain control of the conversation, he condescendingly inquires as to whether Holly is training to become an astronaut. She tersely responds in an equally condescending tone: "I'm fully trained, on loan from NASA, the space administration."[182] The camera again focuses upon Bond, whose practically nonverbal "Oh" response is overshadowed by an apathetic, dismissive, and unimpressed facial expression that is accompanied by a blatant roll of his eyes.[183]

Just as he finds himself caught off-guard by Anya Amasova at the Mojaba Club in *The Spy Who Loved Me*, Bond is similarly taken aback. Whereas he can simply walk away from Anya, Bond is unable to do so here. In fact, his success on the mission, in part, depends upon following Holly as she proceeds to tour him around Drax's facilities.

During the course of this tour, Bond finds himself spun around, literally, but he does enjoy two brief moments of what he perceives as small triumphs. First, he interrupts Holly as she explains the *Moonraker* shuttle's features, completing her sentence for her and prompting her to register an expression of annoyance and disdain. As she walks away to continue the tour, Bond briefly remains behind, smirking. Second, Holly takes Bond to the centrifuge training room, which simulates G-force. There, Bond takes it upon himself to display his knowledge to Holly, who is not amused. Again, her glare is countered by Bond's smirk.

Holly ultimately gets the last laugh when she straps Bond into the centrifuge machine in order to demonstrate the machine's capabilities and simulate a zero-gravity environment. Bond, who appears slightly unwilling, is reassured by Holly, who condescendingly explains that 3G-force simulates takeoff pressure: "C'mon, Mister Bond. A seventy year-old can take 3Gs."[184] But Chang assumes control of the machine while Holly is called away and subjects Bond to forces equivalent to 13G. Bond stumbles out of the machine, declines assistance from Holly when she reappears, and walks away. Like Patricia Fearing in *Thunderball*, Holly is shocked and embarrassed by the incident. Unlike Patricia, Holly is not subjected to Bond's sexual exploitation, and she is unconcerned about any ramifications the occurrence might have upon her employment.

Holly next appears in Venice, where Bond has been investigating Drax's operations. Bond discovers Holly on a public tour of a glass gallery and follows her. His presence shocks her, and another combative dialogue ensues:

> *Bond*: Dr. Goodhead!
> *Holly*: I can only hope your presence here is a coincidence, Mister Bond. I dislike being spied on.
> *Bond*: Well, don't we all?
> *Holly* (*walking away*): Hmmpf.[185]

Although she dismisses him and walks away, Bond attempts to recover from what appears as another failure at thawing tensions. His methods, however, are imbued with sexual innuendo and sexist overtones, and it is therefore not surprising that Holly fails to succumb to what Bond perceives as charm:

> *Bond* (*following Holly*): You're staying at the Danieli [hotel], aren't you?
> *Holly* (*turning to Bond*): Yes, how did you know?
> *Bond*: Well, I like to keep abreast of things.
> *Holly*: Hmmpf.

Bond: May I ask what you're doing in Venice?
Holly: I'm addressing a seminar of the European Space Commission.
Bond: Ahh, heavy stuff. But there again, I keep forgetting that you are more than just a very beautiful woman.
Holly (*stopping*): If you're trying to be ingratiating, Mister Bond, don't bother. I have more important things on my mind.
Bond: Ah, that's what I'd like to talk to you about. Dinner this evening?
Holly: This evening I'm giving my address. (*smiling*)
Bond: Then can you think of a reason why we don't have a drink afterwards?
Holly: Not immediately, but I'm sure I shall.[186]

Holly again walks away, leaving both Bond and the audience to ponder the significance of their encounter. It is clear that a trend develops: Bond attempts to engage Holly by making sexist remarks, and Holly, in response, discredits Bond and extricates herself by walking away.

Maryam d'Abo and John Cork believed that the "conflict between Holly and Bond is played for comic relief,"[187] but their dynamic has greater significance. *Moonraker* "mocks Bond's male chauvinism"[188] without reservation, depicting Bond as a man who is overwhelmed by the accomplishments of Holly. In fact, Bond finds it difficult to comprehend that intelligence and beauty are not mutually exclusive elements. Bond continually remains a step behind Holly, and her dismissals of him further reveal the extent to which her presence overpowers him. This is an element that is completely absent from *The Spy Who Loved Me*, wherein Anya Amasova acknowledges that she and Bond work for rival governments but can maintain what appears to constitute a sustainable, professional relationship. Bond is generally at ease around Anya, though her acumen and skill equal, if not surpass, his versatility.

The same cannot be said with regard to Holly. Unlike Anya, who ultimately follows Bond in pursuit of the microfilm, Holly remains entirely independent through this point in the film. Whereas Anya's intentions are clear from the beginning, Holly deliberately obfuscates and reveals nothing. Neither Bond nor the audience understands the role Holly plays in the Drax Corporation and with which side she is aligned. Holly's cold, virtually emotionless demeanor is difficult to thaw, and her adversarial disposition toward Bond is firmly entrenched.

At the same time, Holly's skepticism toward Bond is defined in terms of her personal reaction to Bond. By contrast, the lines that are drawn between Bond and Anya in *The Spy Who Loved Me* are ideological and professional. Needless to say, Bond continues to grate against Holly in order to ascertain her true intentions.

Bond, wearing all black, eventually surprises Holly, who is wearing a backless white gown, in her hotel suite. The juxtaposition of his black against her white attire visually affirms the extent to which the two characters are diametrically opposed, and they, in effect, represent a real-life chess match in which neither party wishes to relinquish any piece. As he inspects her personal effects, Bond inquires what Drax is doing, but Holly is not forthcoming: "Why don't you ask him yourself?"[189] Bond then uncovers a poison pen, a daily diary that conceals a poison dart, flame perfume, and a transmitting device, materials he declares are standard CIA-issued equipment. His discoveries prompt Bond to surmise that Holly has been placed with Drax by the CIA. She responds that Bond is astute, though he dismisses the compliment, noting that he has "friends in low places."[190] His comment is revealing. If Bond, in fact, already knows Holly's role in the Drax Corporation, then his item-by-item discovery is merely for her—or the audience's—benefit. Indeed, it affords Bond the opportunity to exhibit his skill.

Yet, for all his effort, Holly is wholly unimpressed and retains control throughout the scene. In fact, it is apparent that she *intends* for Bond to reveal her true identity. Noticing a bottle of Bollinger champagne, Bond states, "You were expecting me."[191] As it turns out, Holly orchestrates the entire encounter, and the surprise she exhibits upon discovering Bond is decidedly feigned.

Their embrace, immediately preceded by Holly's inquiry if this "could . . . possibly be the moment for us to pool our resources,"[192] does not, however, result in an immediate thawing. Unlike previous films in which Bond's seduction and sexual conquest effectively strip the female character of whatever independent traits she may possess, Holly does not become subservient to Bond. Although Bond discovers an airplane ticket to Rio de Janeiro, Holly claims (falsely) that she has no intention of traveling anywhere. The camera then focuses upon a pile of luggage and a smiling Holly, who remains satisfied with her deception. Mistrust and skepticism plague their dynamic:

> *Bond*: We would be better off working together. Détente?
> *Holly*: (*feigning enthusiasm*) Agreed.
> *Bond*: Understanding?
> *Holly*: Possibly.
> *Bond*: Cooperation?
> *Holly* (*smirking*): Maybe.
> *Bond*: Trust?
> *Holly*: (*shaking her head, smiling*) Out of the question.[193]

Bond poses the questions, but Holly sets the parameters.

Ultimately, Bond and Holly wind up in bed together. In the next scene, Bond plays a card from the Ian Fleming deck, departing the hotel suite while he believes Holly is still asleep. Yet as soon as he departs, Holly opens her eyes, revealing the extent to which she is "just as conniving . . . when it comes to the mercenary use of sex."[194] She immediately calls for a night porter to retrieve her luggage and departs for Rio de Janeiro.

Bond may have achieved the sexual conquest he seeks, but Holly also capitalizes upon a sexual exploit of her own. Indeed, notwithstanding her name, Holly "is supposed to represent the New Woman and be an equal as opposed to simply being Bond's sexual plaything."[195] At this juncture, nothing in her character suggests or indicates that Holly is Bond's plaything. In fact, the audience still has no indication that they have truly agreed to work together. All that remains clear is Holly's immunity to Bond's charm, and her immunity has not been compromised following their bedroom rendezvous.

The tenuous, strained dynamic they enjoy in California and Italy resumes in Rio de Janeiro. Bond, using an observatory telescope, notices Drax's aircraft taking off from an airfield. He then notices the figure of a woman, which is revealed as Holly. As he views her, she simultaneously views him from her own telescope. Her facial expression becomes one of substantial displeasure. Bond, not Holly, makes an initial approach, again evidencing her desire to remain unencumbered. He asks, with a smirk, "Haven't we met before somewhere,"[196] and places his hand over Holly's hand that rests on the telescope. She disapproves of this action and quickly removes her hand, responding, "The face is familiar, as is the manner."[197] Despite her rebuke, Bond inexplicably appears more confident in her presence, ultimately obtaining the cooperation he seeks despite Holly's reluctance:

> *Bond*: It's become distinctly chilly since Venice.
>
> *Holly*: Well that was before you walked out on me.
>
> *Bond*: Yes, nearly tripping over your suitcase on the way through the door.
>
> *Holly*: So?
>
> *Bond*: So why waste time working against each other?[198]

Holly's only response is to shrug her shoulders. This time, Bond begins walking and Holly, continuing to express skepticism about his trustworthiness, follows. But Bond ultimately shares a similar skepticism, and the two agents proceed on the mission together under the pretext of obtaining the cooperation they need but do not necessarily desire. Pragmatism and professionalism seem to supplant ego.

Dr. Holly Goodhead (Lois Chiles) and James Bond (Roger Moore) work together to destroy Hugo Drax's space station and prevent global destruction in *Moonraker*.

(United/Everett/Rex USA)

Shortly thereafter, the chill thaws. Although Holly assists Bond in defeating Jaws atop a cable car, she credits him fully with saving her life, rewarding him with a kiss that prompts a longer embrace. Henceforth, Bond is imbued with greater authority, directing Holly to distract a man holding them captive in an ambulance, outmaneuvering Jaws again, discovering the truth behind the missing *Moonraker* shuttle, and rescuing her. A description of Bond and Holly as "a true team, mutually dependent upon each other, neither of whom could have done the job alone"[199] is therefore not entirely accurate. Their forged alliance is brief prior to Holly's capture, and the extent of their true collaboration is somewhat limited.

By contrast, Holly's most meaningful contributions occur above the earth's atmosphere, a place that is completely foreign to Bond. Holly's training as an astronaut is a vital asset when she and Bond pursue Drax into space. As Lois Chiles recalled, Holly represented the "first time that a woman could do what Bond could do, she could fly the plane, she was a scientist."[200] Holly is in her element at the flight controls of the space shuttle, although the initial launch is dictated by preset computers and, in effect, requires little, if any, navigation. Bond, on the other hand, is entirely overwhelmed by his surroundings.

Holly explains to Bond the significance of the parallel flight patterns for five space shuttles, an indication that each will approach an orbiting satellite. Once Drax's space station comes into view, it is Holly, not Bond, who hypothesizes that the space station is a city in space concealed from radar by use of a jamming system. Aboard the station, it is Holly, not Bond, who determines the location of that system, and she leads Bond to it. During the course of their deactivation of the system, Holly exhibits considerable adeptness at handling a laser gun and disposing of two male technicians without Bond's assistance or intervention. The athleticism and fighting skills that she possesses from her Vassar education are on full display for both Bond and the audience, and it is clear that Holly can hold her own. In fact, Bond's participation at this point is ancillary.

Ultimately, Holly and Bond destroy Drax's space station in a joint effort. Bond, of course, disposes of Drax himself, and later Holly navigates one of the space shuttles back toward Earth. During their reentry into the Earth's atmosphere, Bond destroys three orbs containing a toxic nerve gas that Drax launches to destroy mankind. In return for essentially saving the world, Bond and Holly enjoy a zero-gravity sexual encounter during which Holly makes the following request: "Take me around the world one more time, James?"[201] While Bond may have spared the planet from devastation, he cannot succeed absent Holly's involvement. Indeed, they both enjoy physical pleasure as a just reward for their joint, successful completion of the mission.

Holly's complexity and strength distinguish *Moonraker* from its predecessors insofar as it became "the ultimate James Bond film in that it doesn't need a Bond at all."[202] Holly, recalled Lois Chiles, "was capable of doing everything that Bond could do. It was a real step forward in the James Bond genre in terms of modernization."[203] Indeed, unlike prior Bond Girl manifestations, Holly "removes a minimum of clothing during the film."[204] In fact, she is seen in a yellow space suit for a large portion of the film, attire that is hardly flattering and does not accentuate her physical features.

Thus, it is clear that *Moonraker* effectively elevates the Bond Girl's substantive attributes, downplays the importance of her aesthetics, and conveys a message that the former is not in any way dependent upon the latter. In fact, the substance of the character ultimately enhances her appeal and attractiveness. The Bond Girl archetype would never be the same again.

* * *

The franchise revitalized the Bond Girl when it introduced Anya Amasova in *The Spy Who Loved Me* and Holly Goodhead in *Moonraker*, combining well-celebrated Bond Girl aesthetics with a greater sense of independence and plausibility that enabled the character to transition from accessory to substantive contributor. The reconsidered Bond Girl archetype translated into a complete character, a female protagonist whose strength, capability, and resourcefulness never encroached upon her femininity and ultimately did not compromise the successful Bondian formula.

Nevertheless, questions remain, particularly given the critiques directed at *Moonraker* generally and Holly specifically. Did the transformation of the Bond Girl exhibited through Anya and Holly deviate too far from the Bond Girl archetype? Would the newly reconsidered Bond Girl require even further reconsideration? Did the franchise incorporate the necessary elements into the Bond Girl character that made her wholly plausible in light of the feminist and Women's Liberation movements? Could the franchise reinvent a post-feminist, liberated Bond Girl character? If so, how would it present her? After *Moonraker*, one critic opined that "007 had nowhere to go but down to earth."[205]

0013

Reconciling an Archetype: A *Quantum of Solace* for the Next Generation

To many modern men, the Bond Girl myth is still a powerful fantasy; for many modern women, to be called a Bond Girl would be an unforgivable insult.

—Ben Macintyre[1]

In the old days, the Bond girl was the blonde girl in the swimming pool. We're going into the 21st century and women are not just gorgeous to look at but smart. They're intelligent and just as smart as Bond.

—Michelle Yeoh[2]

Beautiful women are always part of the story. In the past maybe they were more objectified. They were just eye candy. Now they're integral and powerful in their own right.

—Daniel Craig[3]

Moonraker may have been an example of significant overreaching. According to Raymond Benson, "*Moonraker* went as far as [Cubby] Broccoli could go with outlandishness. The only direction possible for the Bond films of the eighties was backwards."[4]

While *Moonraker*'s plot mirrored science fiction more than reality, the observation may aptly describe the fate of the Bond Girl. The character witnessed a rapid and compressed reinvention in which her iteration in *The Spy Who Loved Me* was immediately imbued with characteristics heretofore unseen. During an interview in 1981, Broccoli recognized that, beginning with Anya Amasova and Dr. Holly Goodhead, "'[w]e've tried to portray a more modern woman in the last few years . . . . We haven't done anything because of the E.R.A., but because it suits the story and the place that women have in today's world.'"[5]

Moonraker's presentation of Holly, characterized as the "most qualified of all the Bond Girls,"[6] effectively carried the torch lit by Anya, and both characters belong to a unique sorority within a sorority insofar as they represent the franchise's first conceptions of a viable and sustainable feminist counterpart to its male protagonist. But both characters, while equally as capable and adept as James Bond, are nevertheless incomplete. Anya's desire to avenge the death of Sergei Barzov evaporates too quickly, trivializing her emotional turmoil, and Holly's cold demeanor keeps Bond and the audience at a guarded distance throughout the mission. Whereas Anya's physical attributes are accentuated in *The Spy Who Loved Me*, Holly's sex appeal is virtually absent in *Moonraker*. Indeed, Lois Chiles recalled that it "wasn't a good thing to be sexy" during the late 1970s, noting that there was nothing sexy about being in a spacesuit.[7]

In short, while both films made substantial and important progress with their Bond Girl presentations, they ultimately struggled to harmonize aesthetics with substance. Together, *The Spy Who Loved Me* and *Moonraker* represent a significant milestone in the franchise. And yet, they are also the final chapters of an era in the Bond mythology.

* * *

The continuity of the Bond franchise places it in the unique position of portraying female characters before, during, and following the feminist and Women's Liberation movements in the United States. While the franchise's twenty-two films are frequently classified based upon numerous criteria, including the actors portraying Bond or geopolitical themes, they may also be classified based upon their presentations of their female characters. The first eleven films discussed in this book represent the first phase of the Bond Girl archetype, and they constitute what is referred to here as the Golden Era of the Bond Girl. The next eight films, beginning with *For Your Eyes Only* in 1981 and ending with *The World Is Not Enough* in 1999, build upon the Bond Girl archetype that was introduced during the Golden Era of the Bond Girl. In effect, these films transition audiences to the Post-Feminist Bond Woman Era. Finally, beginning with *Die Another Day* in 2002, the franchise charts another path of reinvention, and its presentation of female characters ushers in the Revisionist Bond Girl Era.

To better understand the trends of these three distinct periods within the Bond mythology, several factors are considered.

The Golden Era of the Bond Girl, 1962-1979

In the Golden Era of the Bond Girl, thirty-three female characters are identifiable as primary, secondary, or tertiary Bond Girls.* Of these thirty-three, twenty-four (73%) are (a) allies of Bond, (b) brought into some type of alliance with Bond, or (c) of a neutral allegiance. They include familiar names: Sylvia Trench, Honey Ryder, Tatiana Romanova, Dink, Jill and Tilly Masterson, Pussy Galore, Patricia Fearing, Paula Caplan, Domino Derval, Ling, Aki, Kissy Suzuki, Tracy di Vicenzo, Tiffany Case, Plenty O'Toole, Miss Caruso, Solitaire, Andrea Anders, Mary Goodnight, Anya Amasova, Corinne Dufour, Manuela, and Holly Goodhead. The remaining nine (27%) characters—Miss Taro, Bonita, Mei Lei, Fiona Volpe, Helga Brandt, Bambi, Thumper, Rosie Carver, and Naomi—retain their status as villains. Two additional female characters, Rosa Klebb and Irma Bunt, are not deemed traditional Bond Girl roles and are therefore excluded from this calculus.

Occupations attributed to these thirty-three characters vary, but they can be classified into general categories. Spies and government agents account for fifteen (45.5%) characters: Miss Taro, Tatiana Romanova, Bonita, Paula Caplan, Fiona Volpe, Ling, Aki, Kissy Suzuki, Helga Brandt, Miss Caruso, Rosie Carver, Mary Goodnight, Anya Amasova, Manuela, and Holly Goodhead.** Four (12.1%) characters—Sylvia Trench, Tracy di Vicenzo, Tilly Masterson, and Plenty O'Toole—are socialites, heiresses, or individuals without a specified profession. Another five (15.1%) are employed by a villain in various capacities, typically as pilots or personal assistants: Jill Masterson, Pussy Galore, Mei Lei, Naomi, and Corinne Dufour. Three (9.1%) characters are villains' mistresses or so-called kept women: Domino Derval, Andrea Anders, and Solitaire. Two (6.1%) characters work in the health care field: Patricia Fearing as a nurse and Dink as a masseuse. The remaining four (12.1%) characters belong to an "other professional" category, namely entrepreneurs (Honey Ryder), smugglers (Tiffany Case), or security personnel (Bambi and Thumper).

The Post-Feminist Bond Woman Era, 1981-1999

Beginning with *For Your Eyes Only*, the franchise entered an eighteen-year period called the Post-Feminist Bond Woman Era. During this span,

* Miss Moneypenny, a unique character in her own right, is not part of the calculus in any era.

** Bonita appears as a flamenco dancer, but she is actually a double agent. Although Holly is an astrophysicist and would therefore also be classified as a scientist, her primary occupation is that of a CIA agent. She has been classified accordingly.

twenty-two female characters are identified as primary, secondary, or tertiary Bond Women appearing in eight films. Of these twenty-two, seventeen (77%) characters are (a) allies of Bond, (b) brought into some type of alliance with Bond, or (c) of a neutral allegiance. They include: Melina Havelock, Bibi Dahl, Countess Lisl Von Schlaf, Octopussy, Magda, Kimberley Jones, Stacey Sutton, May Day, Kara Milovy, Pam Bouvier, Lupe Lamora, Natalya Simonova, Caroline, Wai Lin, Paris Carver, Christmas Jones, and Molly Warmflash. The remaining five (23%) characters—Pola Ivanova, Jenny Flex, Xenia Onatopp, Guilietta da Vinci, and Elektra King—retain their status as villains.

The occupations of female characters presented in the films of the Post-Feminist Bond Woman Era can be categorized in a manner similar to their Golden Era of the Bond Girl predecessors. Spies or double agents account for seven (32%) characters: Kimberley Jones, Pola Ivanova, Pam Bouvier, Xenia Onatopp, Caroline, Wai Lin, and Guilietta da Vinci. Two (9%) characters are socialites, heiresses, or individuals without professions: Paris Carver and Elektra King. Three (14%) are employed by either a Bond ally (Magda for Octopussy) or villain (May Day and Jenny Flex for Max Zorin). Two (9%) are mistresses: Countess Lisl Von Schlaf and Lupe Lamora. Four (18%) are scientists or physicians: Melina Havelock (marine biology), Stacey Sutton (geology), Christmas Jones (nuclear physics), and Molly Warmflash (physician).* The remaining four (18%) characters belong to an "other professional" category, which includes athletes (Bibi Dahl), entrepreneurs (Octopussy), musicians (Kara Milovy), and computer programmers (Natalya Simonova).

The Revisionist Bond Girl Era, 2002—

Four films—*Die Another Day*, *Casino Royale*, *Quantum of Solace*, and *Skyfall*—comprise the Revisionist Bond Girl Era, though *Skyfall* will not be released in the United States until November 2012. *Die Another Day*, *Casino Royale*, and *Quantum of Solace* feature seven Revisionist Bond Girls who are identified as primary, secondary, or tertiary characters. Of these seven, five (71.4%) characters are (a) allies of Bond, (b) brought into some type of alliance with Bond, or (c) of a neutral allegiance. They include: Jinx, Vesper Lynd, Solange Dimitrios, Camille Montes Rivero, and Strawberry Fields. The remaining two (28.6%) characters, Miranda Frost and Valenka, retain their status as villains. Additionally, in terms of occupations, five (71.4%) are spies or government agents—Jinx,

* Although Molly Warmflash is employed by MI6, her primary function is that of a physician. She is classified accordingly.

Miranda Frost,* Vesper Lynd, Camille Montes Rivero, and Strawberry Fields. One (14.3%) falls into the category of socialites, heiresses, or individuals without professions: Solange Dimitrios, an associate villain's spouse. One (14.3%) serves as a villain's mistress (Valenka).

Several conclusions can be drawn from these statistics. First, as Chart A demonstrates, the percentage of female characters who are allies of Bond, are brought into some type of alliance with Bond, or are neutral increases between the Golden Era of the Bond Girl and the Post-Feminist Bond Woman Era. Although the percentage decreases during the Revisionist Bond Girl Era, this period currently includes only three films, and it is likely that the percentage will continue to increase over the course of time. Accordingly, the franchise seems committed to portraying its female characters in an increasingly positive light by allying them or their interests with the protagonist. Chart B reflects these trends by number.

The positive portrayal of female characters is also evident in the declining depiction of mistresses. During the seventeen years spanning the Golden Era of the Bond Girl, three characters are mistresses, the same number presented during the long span of twenty-seven years encompassed by the Post-Feminist Bond Woman and Revisionist Bond Girl eras. The same trend is discernible with respect to socialites, heiresses, or individuals without professions. Four such characters are presented in the Golden Era of the Bond Girl, but only three and one are presented in the Post-Feminist Bond Woman and Revisionist Bond Girl eras, respectively. This trend suggests that female characters are portrayed as more self-sufficient and independent both socially and financially over the course of time.

Second, the number of female characters employed as spies or government agents decreases in the Post-Feminist Bond Woman Era, during which period audiences are exposed to a significantly wider array of professional choices for women. Two characters in the Golden Era of the Bond Girl hold traditional, stereotypical gender roles: nurse and masseuse. These occupations are eliminated in subsequent eras. In their place, the Post-Feminist Bond Woman Era introduces a female physician and other occupations heretofore unrepresented in the Bond mythology: scientists, athletes, musicians, and computer engineers.

Interestingly, none of the characters currently presented in the Revisionist Bond Girl Era is employed in any of these diverse fields. Similarly, the number of female villains also decreases significantly

---

* Although she is a world-class athlete, having won an Olympic gold medal in fencing, Miranda Frost's primary role is that of a spy: she poses as an MI6 agent while employed as villain Gustav Graves's publicist and fencing partner. She is classified accordingly.

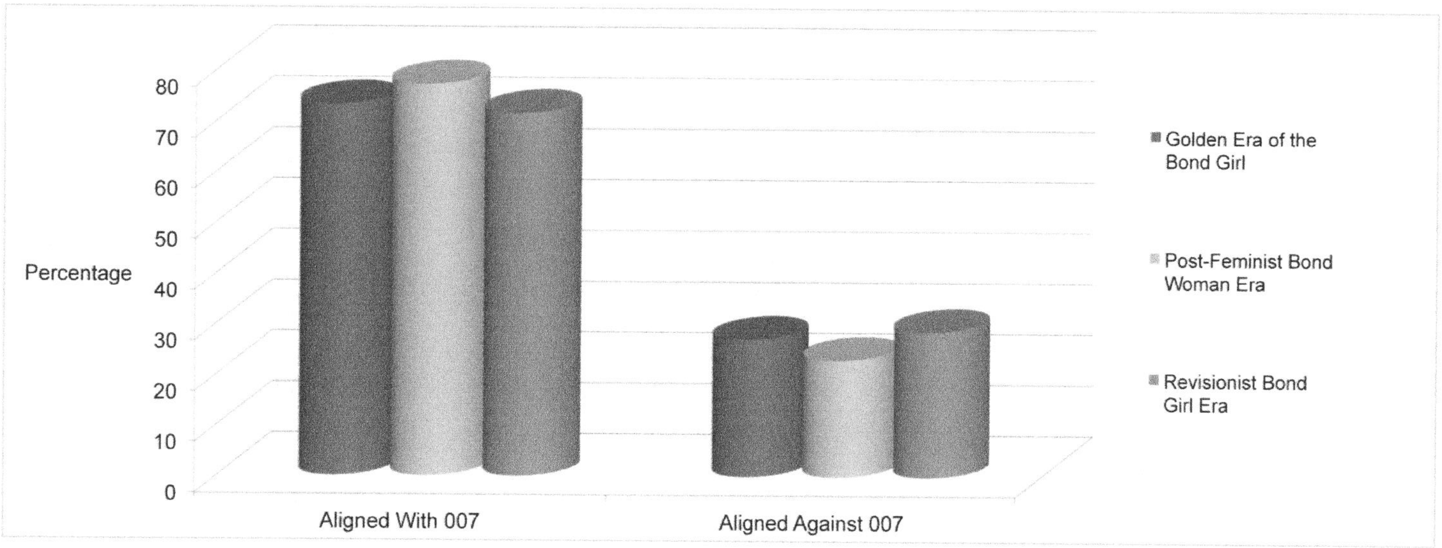

Chart A: Ideology of Female Characters By Percentage, 1962-2008

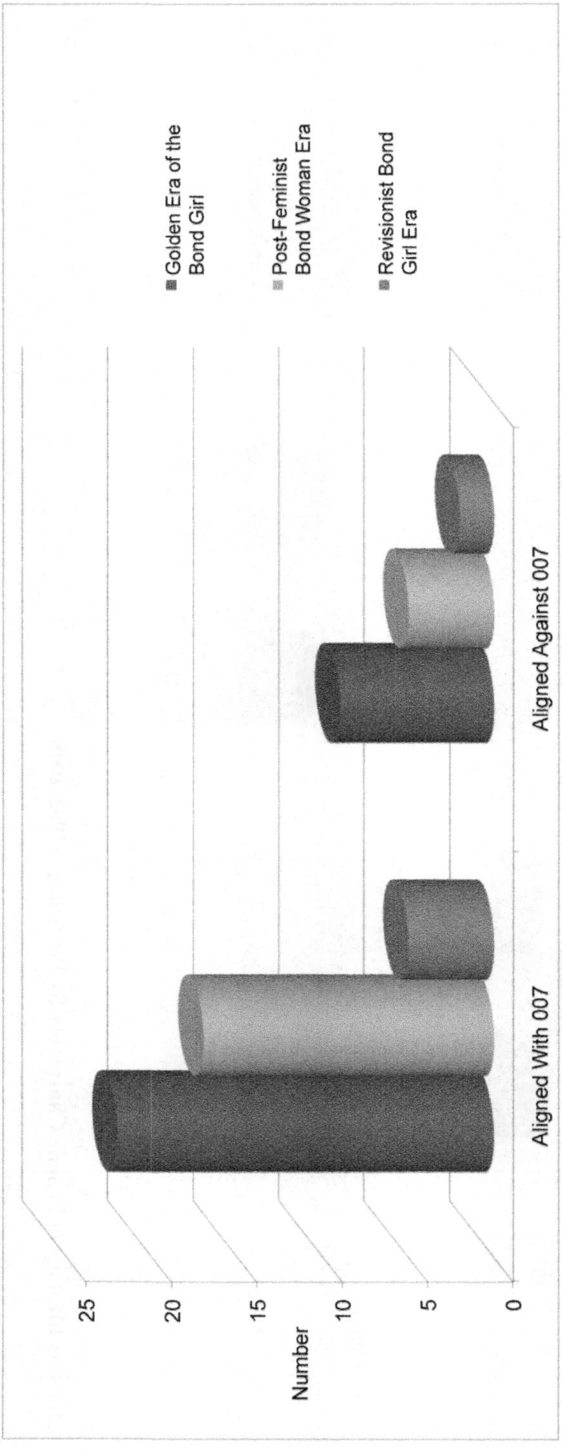

Chart B: Ideology of Female Characters By Number, 1962-2008

during the Post-Feminist Bond Woman Era. The franchise, therefore, consciously shifts away from characters such as Fiona Volpe, instead accentuating portrayals of women who have achieved new, positive societal statuses and imbuing female villains with more plausible attributes. Since it appears that the Revisionist Bond Girl Era will witness an increase in the number of female villains, as compared to the number appearing during the Post-Feminist Bond Woman Era, the franchise likely seeks a return to juxtaposing varying female allegiances and adding new, complex relationships and dynamics. Charts C and D summarize these occupational observations by percentage and number, respectively.

Third, the frequency of character names imbued with trademark sexual overtones in the style of Ian Fleming decreases over the course of time. During the Golden Era of the Bond Girl, eight characters—Sylvia Trench, Honey Rider, Pussy Galore, Kissy Suzuki, Plenty O'Toole, Holly Goodhead, Bambi, and Thumper—possess such names. That number decreases by almost half during the Post-Feminist Bond Woman Era, with only five such characters: Bibi Dahl, Octopussy, Jenny Flex, Molly Warmflash, and Xenia Onatopp.* To date, the Revisionist Bond Girl Era features only one such character: Strawberry Fields. Although Strawberry Fields appears to represent a deliberate attempt by producers to connect the franchise to the Golden Era of the Bond Girl (and an homage to The Beatles' song "Strawberry Fields Forever"), particularly with a new actor portraying Double-O-Seven, the overall lack of sexual innuendo in this area evidences a conscious effort to portray women whose character attributes are neither undermined nor compromised by their name. Indeed, Strawberry Fields is only referred to as Agent Fields in the film; the audience does not learn her given name until it appears in the credits. Initial indications suggest that *Skyfall* will continue the trend of avoiding sexually suggestive names for female characters.

* * *

The evolution described above is also apparent in the title sequences featured in the twenty-two films currently released. Generally speaking, the title sequences during the Golden Era of the Bond Girl are moderately sexual in nature. These films introduce audiences to images of dressed and naked female silhouettes that engage in various acts, namely dancing, swimming, jumping, and leaping. Most of their movements

---

* In *Octopussy*, Penelope Smallbone is introduced as Miss Moneypenny's secretary. Because the character is on screen very briefly, she is not considered in this calculation.

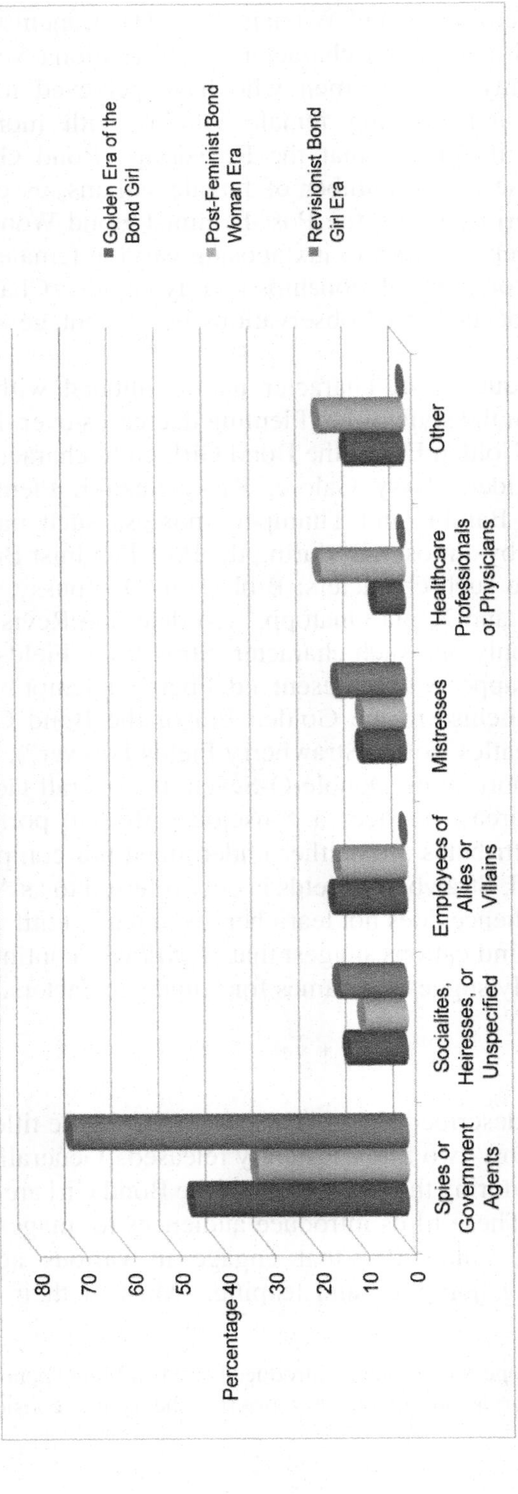

Chart C: Professions of Female Characters By Percentage, 1962-2008

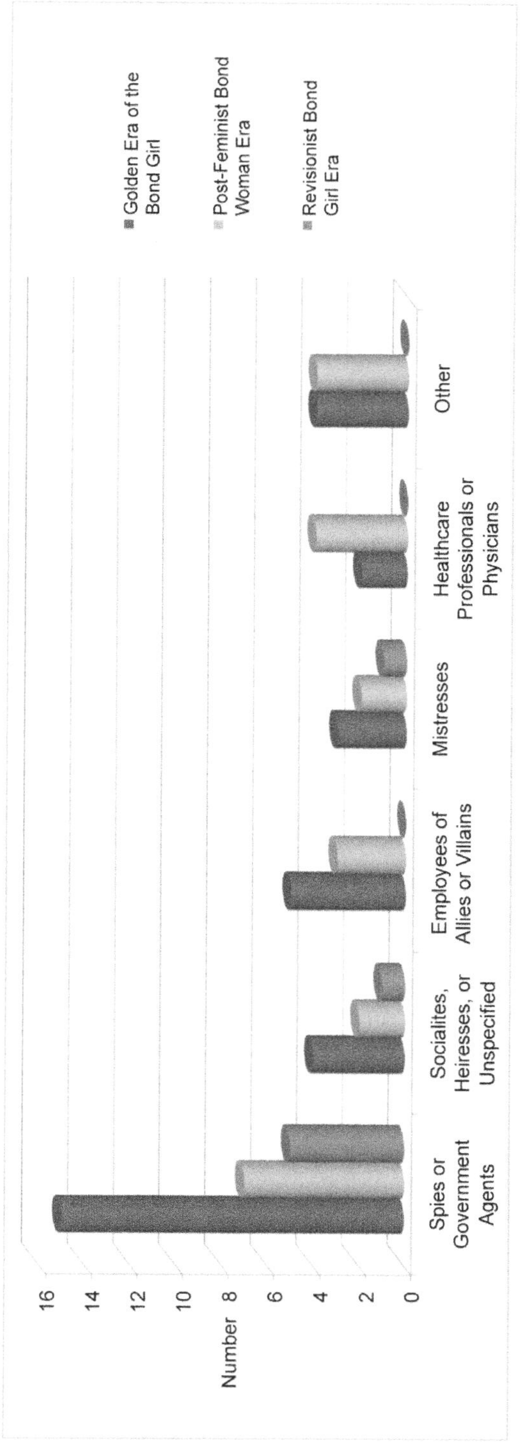

Chart D: Professions of Female Characters By Number, 1962-2008

are not overtly sexual, though each title sequence is certainly both sexy and alluring. There are, of course two notable exceptions with *From Russia With Love* and *The Man With the Golden Gun*. As previously noted, the title sequence in *From Russia With Love* features images and text superimposed across the gyrating, partially clothed figure of a belly dancer, creating an arousing display of color as well as sexual anticipation. And the title sequence featured in *The Man With the Golden Gun*, with its overarching coital metaphor, exudes sex. Although *Goldfinger*'s title sequence is similar in style to its predecessor, the image of the golden girl remains stationary throughout. The image of a woman painted in gold is provocative and alluring, and perhaps even scandalous, but it is ultimately benign.

The same can be said for virtually all the remaining title sequences from the Golden Era of the Bond Girl films. The female silhouettes primarily add visual stimulus and do not engage in any conduct that is overly arousing. In the title sequence in *The Spy Who Loved Me*, a female silhouette wields a gun. Her arm, however, is rapidly set down by the male silhouette representing Bond, suggesting that she is either unprepared to handle the weapon or does not belong doing so. Accordingly, this image disappears in the title sequence for *Moonraker*. *The Spy Who Loved Me* therefore represents the only title sequence during the Golden Era of the Bond Girl in which a female silhouette holds a weapon.[8]

Interestingly, the image of women holding weapons becomes a dominant trademark of the title sequences in the Post-Feminist Bond Woman Era films, an apparent acknowledgment that women are certainly capable of handling guns. In *For Your Eyes Only*, the armed female silhouette image is prominently displayed, despite the fact that the title sequence's primary focus is upon recording artist Sheena Easton, who performed "For Your Eyes Only" and became "the only musical performer ever to sing on camera in the series."[9] *Octopussy* features female silhouettes and other photographed women handling weapons: "[A]s smoke billows, psychedelic reds and greens wash across the screen and the silhouettes of nubile ladies interact meaningfully with large pistols and other big guns, including the silhouette of James Bond."[10] *A View To A Kill* replicates its predecessor, adding glowing fluorescent guns. Although the elaborate color scheme depicted in *A View To A Kill* is eliminated in *The Living Daylights* and *Licence to Kill*, the overall weapon theme remains unchanged.

In the *GoldenEye* title sequence, the female silhouettes exchange their firearms for hammers, which they use to dismantle and destroy former Soviet statues in a post-Cold War, post-Soviet era. Nevertheless, the gun image remains intertwined with these women, some of whom dance atop the barrels of guns as they rise vertically across the screen. In the next film, *Tomorrow Never Dies*, the hammers displayed in *GoldenEye* are replaced with guns, and the traditional silhouettes are given a modern, digital update with painted circuitry across their bodies. Women dance inside bullet casings and atop a sea of firearms. In a visually impressive sequence employing a film negative technique, a woman loads bullets into the chamber of a gun that she ultimately discharges, setting off a chain reaction. The stark lines of the computer circuitry that are superimposed across the silhouettes' bodies in *Tomorrow Never Dies* give way to visually impressive amorphous, viscous black silhouettes dripping in oil, watercolored silhouettes rising from a dark sea, and other spectrally enhanced silhouettes in *The World Is Not Enough*, though not a single silhouette handles a weapon in the title sequence, making it a true aberration for its era in this regard.

The absence of women handling weapons in *The World Is Not Enough* continues in the title sequences in the Revisionist Bond Girl Era films, which reprise the phenomenon observed during the Golden Era of the Bond Girl. In *Die Another Day*, black silhouettes appear in the shadows of scorpions, engulfed in flames, and comprised entirely of ice, visually depicting the contrasts of heat and cold as part of a torture theme that is relevant to the plot. The title sequence in *Casino Royale* contains not a single female silhouette, and while silhouettes appear rising from the desert sand and dancing around a source of intense light in *Quantum of Solace*, Bond alone is depicted handling a weapon.

It is also apparent that the title sequences become more sexually charged over the course of time, particularly during the Post-Feminist Bond Woman Era. This trend suggests that the franchise utilizes the title sequence to balance the portrayal of increasingly assertive and independent female characters that appear throughout the film while preserving the Bondian formula without having to resort to undermining the characters. The increased use of photography rather than silhouettes and particular attention to the women's curvaceous bodies highlight traditional conceptions of beauty and femininity and permit the audience to see more skin, thereby heightening titillation and tease. This theme is discernible in *Octopussy*, *A View To A Kill*, *The Living Daylights*, and *Licence to Kill*, but some elements also appear in *Tomorrow Never Dies*.

For example, the title sequence in *Octopussy* features naked women whose seductively sprawled bodies, like the belly dancer in *From Russia With Love*, project images of the Double-O-Seven logo and a neon octopus. *Octopussy*'s title sequence was described as plagued by "leering sexism," featuring "obviously naked women [who] cavort with obviously clothed men."[11] The title sequence in *A View To A Kill* unfolds with the unzipping of a woman's ski jacket, which expands as two fulsome breasts are released from captivity while a Double-O-Seven logo appears across her cleavage. Later, women adorned in glowing neon lipstick, nail polish, and body art dance and slither across the screen, with one eventually emerging from fire, a moment that is vaguely reminiscent of *The Man With the Golden Gun*.

In *The Living Daylights*, a naked woman performs gymnastic-inspired dance and floor routines all while sporting a gun, a bikini-clad woman wearing sunglasses and jewelry poses seductively, and a third woman has the Double-O-Seven logo ripple across her body as she prepares to discharge her weapon. In *Licence to Kill*, a dancing naked silhouette in the background fades to reveal a photograph of another silhouette engaged in live-action seductive gyration. Thereafter, a woman appears seductively dancing while she wears a transparent top through which the features of her breasts are clearly discernible. Nothing depicted in title sequences either preceding or following these films is as revealing.

In addition to the thematic evolution and increase in the level of sexual innuendo, particularly during the Post-Feminist Bond Woman Era, the narrative function of the title sequence changes over time. Of course, this does not always implicate the Bond Girl. In fact, several of the title sequences in films during the Golden Era of the Bond Girl serve a function other than to offer audiences an aesthetically pleasing teaser. For example, in *On Her Majesty's Secret Service*, producers intentionally sought to establish continuity in the series following the departure of Sean Connery by employing the image of a rewinding clock and clips from Bond's previous missions. In other cases, the title sequence foreshadows specific elements in the films, such as associating the belly dancer with the gypsy camp in *From Russia With Love*, the harpoon-wielding mermen and swimmers with the climactic aquatic battle in *Thunderball*, Far Eastern elements for the exotic locales in *You Only Live Twice* and *The Man With the Golden Gun*, the occult throughout *Live and Let Die*, and diamond smuggling in *Diamonds Are Forever*.

Inexplicably, a connection between the title sequence and the underlying film's plot is absent in the majority of the Post-Feminist Bond Woman Era films. In fact, the only films during this period with title sequences that remotely highlight or advance the plot are *GoldenEye* and *The World Is Not Enough*. In the former, the pre-title sequence action occurs during the Cold War, and the title sequence bridges a nine-year passage of time between the pre-title sequence and the start of the film by depicting the collapse of the Soviet Union through the tumbling of statues. In the latter, the title sequence's prominent depiction of oil rigs and oil-slicked female silhouettes forecasts the role that oil plays in Bond's mission.

The trend that begins with *GoldenEye* and *The World Is Not Enough* in the late 1990s is accentuated to a greater degree during the Revisionist

Bond Girl Era. In *Die Another Day*, the title sequence advances the plot by depicting fifteen months of torture to which Bond is subjected at the hands of the North Koreans following his capture at the conclusion of the pre-title sequence. The title sequence—together with the title song, "You Know My Name," which was performed by recording artist Chris Cornell—for *Casino Royale* introduces Daniel Craig as Double-O-Seven following the departure of Pierce Brosnan, and the title sequence for *Quantum of Solace* serves a similar purpose, establishing Craig in the role by prominently featuring his likeness. *Skyfall* will be no different, presenting images that are relevant to the mission that is about to unfold. While female silhouettes are sure to be featured in the *Skyfall* title sequence, the main focus, once again, will remain upon Bond.

* * *

There are discernible differences among the Bond films of the three eras. The preceding chapters considered the Bond Girl archetype in a comprehensive manner, deconstructing her narrative and substantive function over the course of the first eleven films. Since 1981, producers have reintroduced audiences to Bond while simultaneously bringing the franchise into two new eras in which a redesigned and reinvigorated Bond Girl archetype is prominently featured. From Bond Girl to Bond Woman, and from Bond Woman to a new kind of female lead, these post-*Moonraker* characters are modern women who, even within the Bond mythology, represent the coalescence of strength, independence, and acumen with energy, beauty, and elegance. Though they constitute the next iterations of an established archetype and are still universally classified under the umbrella term "Bond Girl," the female characters of the post-*Moonraker* films are much more, breaking free from the invisible limitations that have been attributed to that term and charting a new path.

Epilogue

In real life, a damn sight more women were tied to their apron strings than were tugging on parachute cords a la Pussy Galore.

—Susan Daly[1]

I think lip service is being paid to political correctness, but in the end they still end up in bed with Bond.

—Graham Rye[2]

It's the same with the Bond girls. All the new ones say, "Oh, I'm going to be different from the others," but before long it's always the same—"Oh, James!"

—Roger Moore[3]

Conceived in the mind of Ian Fleming during the 1950s and translated to film beginning in 1962, the Bond Girl has followed a meandering course. From the feminine ideal as an accessory under a patriarchal establishment to a reactionary archetype in response to the feminist and Women's Liberation movements of the 1960s and 1970s, the Bond Girl ultimately forged a new sense of equality within the Bond mythology by the close of the 1970s. Yet equality, of course, is not a state of being that is in any way static.

As alluded to earlier, the feminist movement has been divided into two "waves."[4] The "first-wave" of feminism that developed in the United States during the early twentieth century sought political and civil equality,[5] but it ultimately "accepted without question the sexual division"[6] inherent in a patriarchal societal structure. Only during the "second wave" of feminism that developed during the 1960s did women organize around issues such as individual freedom and choice. Gloria Steinem stated that feminism is a "'revolution and not a public relations movement.'"[7] At the same time, the feminist backlash movement suggested that the revolution was over, particularly since women were considered by some as "so equal . . . that [they] no longer need an Equal Rights Amendment."[8]

Author Susan Faludi wrote that "[a] backlash against women's rights is nothing new in American history. Indeed, it's a recurring phenomenon: it returns every time women begin to make some headway toward equality, a seemingly inevitable early frost to the culture's brief flowerings of feminism."[9] If this is true, then the progress of women's rights will always remain a process in perpetual fluctuation because "[t]he American woman is trapped on [an] asymptotic spiral, turning endlessly through the generations, drawing ever nearer to her destination without ever arriving."[10]

The journey upon which women embarked in the 1960s spawned significant changes to the social, political, and economic landscapes of the nation. Today, the number of women on college and university campuses exceeds the number of men, prompting studies and movements to encourage greater male matriculation.[11] More college-educated men identify with the Republican Party than their female counterparts, who tend to support the Democratic Party.[12] Generally speaking, Democrats tended to view the feminist and Women's Liberation movements more favorably than Republicans during the 1970s,[13] a trend that remains true today.[14]

A significant moment occurred during the 1980 presidential campaign, during which sharp lines of demarcation were set in the gender political sands. That year, the Republican Party did not endorse the ERA in its platform,[15] a move that reflected an increase in Republican skepticism over the proposed constitutional amendment between 1978 and 1980.[16] Four years later, Representative Geraldine Ferraro of New York became the first female vice presidential candidate, which prompted NOW to "abandon[] its traditional nonpartisanship and endorse[] the Democratic ticket."[17]

Women now comprise approximately 50 percent of the American workforce, with nearly 39 percent holding managerial or professional positions.[18] In 1967, the percentage of women in the American workforce hovered around 35.3 percent.[19] But equal pay remains a significant and unresolved issue, with the average American woman continuing to earn only seventy-four cents for every dollar earned by her male counterpart.[20]

Also unresolved is the issue of a woman's choice. First, there is the choice between motherhood and career. In May 2012, a so-called "Mommy War"[21] erupted after Hilary Rosen, a Democratic strategist, assailed Ann Romney, the wife of Republican presidential candidate Mitt Romney, for having "'never worked a day in her life'"[22] because she chose to stay at home and raise five children.[23] Widespread condemnation followed, particularly at the White House, which "hit warp speed in making clear that it did not endorse Rosen's comments."[24] As one writer observed, "[a]ll mothers are working mothers,"[25] and "[i]f women have learned anything over the half-century since Betty Friedan's 'The Feminine Mystique' shook the world in 1963, surely it is this: There is no single, correct way to be a mother."[26] The learning process continues, just as progress in women's rights remains ongoing.

Second, abortion has emerged as a significant election year issue in 2012 as the debate over the constitutionality of the Patient Protection and Affordable Care Act, commonly referred to as Obamacare, escalated. The Catholic Church, for example, challenged the act as running afoul of the guarantee of religious freedom, arguing that a federal mandate requiring employers to cover contraception in employee health plans is unconstitutional. Proponents of the act, however, framed the issue as an assault against contraception and a woman's right to choose, not one involving religious liberty. Ultimately, the United States Supreme Court, in June 2012, determined that the act was constitutional. Challenges based upon the act's alleged violation of religious freedom remain pending.

Speaking of the Supreme Court, President Ronald W. Reagan appointed the first female jurist, Sandra Day O'Connor, to the high court in 1981. Thirty-one years later, Ruth Bader Ginsburg, Sonia Sotomayor, and Elena Kagan—the first female dean of Harvard Law School—were nominated, confirmed, and sworn in as justices. As one writer observed, "[w]hat a difference a half century makes. By tracing the rhetoric of the four women on the Supreme Court, a positive, if slow shift is apparent: Gender no longer takes center stage."[27]

The election cycle in 1992, the so-called "Year of the Woman," witnessed the percentage of women elected to the United States Congress increase into double digits for the first time in history:[28]

> On election Tuesday 1992, American voters sent as many new women to Congress as were elected in any previous *decade*, beginning a decade of unparalleled gains for women in Congress . . . .
>
> . . . The results were unprecedented; the 24 women who won election to the U.S. House of Representatives for the first time that November comprised the largest number elected in any single election, and the women elected to the Senate tripled the number of women in that chamber.[29]

In 2006, Democrat Nancy Pelosi of California was elected the first female Speaker of the United States House Representatives. During the 2008 presidential campaign, Senator Hillary Rodham Clinton of New York fought for the Democratic Party's nomination for president, and Governor Sarah Palin of Alaska became the Republican Party's first female nominee for vice president. These significant achievements have helped, to some degree, shatter the glass ceiling and afford women greater opportunities that heretofore were unavailable or seemed virtually impossible to attain. Indeed, ninety-four women currently serve in the 112th Congress.[30]

* * *

It is difficult to contextualize the significance of these and other advancements without the benefit of understanding those circumstances American women encountered during the latter half of the twentieth century prior to the rise of "second wave" feminism. The Bond Girl offers but one lens through which to observe and appreciate the trials and tribulations of women before, during, and following the gender equality movement. Given cinematic life by Cubby Broccoli and Harry Saltzman in 1962, the Bond Girl reflects a romanticized feminine ideal that exists within a patriarchal society. Of course, "the lives of women in the first Bond movies to appear in the 1960s were markedly different from that of your average housefrau,"[31] but the underlying theme that women hold a subordinate position in the modern world is a fundamental principle that has permeated Bond's fictional parallel.

The challenge has been keeping Bond both fresh and modern. According to one writer, the Bond Girl "had always been little more than 'a life support system to a pair of breasts.'"[32] Feminists also have contended that the franchise was an "'attempt by men to keep women in their place and to ensure they still ironed their shirts.'"[33] Producer Barbara Broccoli believed otherwise, stating that "'the early women were very progressive.'"[34] Nevertheless, Broccoli acknowledged that the franchise's depiction of its female characters underwent a significant metamorphosis.[35]

The feminist and Women's Liberation movements, no doubt, left an indelible impression upon the fictional character's cinematic empire, which had been critiqued as "an increasingly tired-looking franchise."[36] But the Bond Girl's journey reveals both the extent to which the franchise remained sustainable during a time of turbulent social change and the manner in which the films reflected and responded to the social mores of that period.

That there exists a feminism of James Bond may seem contradictory, but as this work has demonstrated, it is a real phenomenon and one that can be appreciated by a diverse audience. Indeed, the gender equality movement and the Bond franchise are inextricably linked: a discussion of feminism is not complete without exploring the cultural impact of the Bond Girl, and elements of the feminist and Women's Liberation movements are ingrained in the Bond Girl's DNA. Just as feminism remains viable and the struggle for gender equality continues, so too does the most successful cinematic franchise continue to traverse new frontiers.

The female characters that have appeared in Bond films since 1979 constitute their own "second wave" of Bond Girls. Their portrayals, like their predecessors, shed significant light upon gender politics and reflect the archetype of a feminine ideal that is relevant to a new, post-feminist generation of audiences. Ultimately, they could not exist absent those characters that first made the Bond Girl a universally recognizable and celebrated cultural icon. Their stories and the journeys upon which they—as well as Miss Moneypenny and M (as portrayed by Dame Judy Dench)—embark comprise the next volume of the *Shaken & Stirred*™ series.

The Bond Girl will return in
Shaken & Stirred: The Post-Feminism of James Bond

Appendix A

Ian Fleming's James Bond Novels and Short Stories

1953	*Casino Royale*
1954	*Live and Let Die*
1955	*Moonraker*
1956	*Diamonds Are Forever*
1957	*From Russia, With Love*
1958	*Dr. No*
1959	*Goldfinger*
1960	*From A View To A Kill* (short story)
	For Your Eyes Only (short story)
	Quantum of Solace (short story)
	Risico (short story)
	The Hildebrand Rarity (short story)
1961	*Thunderball*
1962	*The Spy Who Loved Me*
	The Living Daylights (short story)
1963	*On Her Majesty's Secret Service*
	The Property of a Lady (short story)
1964	*You Only Live Twice*
1965	*The Man With the Golden Gun*
1966	*Octopussy* (short story)

Appendix B

Attributes of the Literary Bond Girl

The following summarizes numerous physical features Ian Fleming attributed to his female characters:

Novel/Short Story	Character	Eye Color Style	Hair Color/ Features/ Hands	Facial/Skin	Body Type	Chest
Casino Royale [1]	Vesper Lynd	Deep blue and wide apart	Black, cut square and low	Lightly sun-tanned; fingernails unpainted		Fine breasts
Live and Let Die [2]	Simone Latrelle (Solitaire)	Blue	Blue-black, falling to the shoulders	High cheekbones, sensual mouth, delicate jaw; fingernails short and without enamel		Deep valley between her breasts
Moonraker [3]	Gala Brand	Dark blue	Dark brown, curving inwards at the base of the neck	High cheekbones, wide mouth, full lips, black eyelashes; square-cut fingernails with natural polish		Splendid breasts, with a mole on her right breast

Diamonds Are Forever [4]	Tiffany Case	Light grey to deep grey-blue	Blonde, falling heavily to the shoulders	Lightly tanned skin, full and soft lips; unpainted fingernails		
From Russia, With Love [5]	Tatiana Romanova	Deepest blue	Fine, dark silken brown brushed straight back	Soft, pale skin with wide, full, and finely etched lips	Faultless arms, buttocks hard and flat at the sides	Faultless breasts
Dr. No [6]	Honeychile Rider	Deep blue, wide apart	Ash blonde, cut to the shoulders	Badly broken nose	Amazingly beautiful body	Beautiful, firm breasts
Goldfinger [7]	Jill Masterton	Deep blue	Pale blonde, falling to the shoulders	Sunburned skin with a bold mouth	Firm arms and legs	Thrusting breasts
	Tilly Masterton	Dark blue	Black	High cheek bones; unpainted fingernails		Fine, out-thrown breasts
	Pussy Galore	Violet or deep blue-violet	Black, in an untidy urchin cut jaw line	High check bones and beautiful	Firm, muscled thighs	
From A View To A Kill [8]	Mary Ann Russell	Blue and wide apart	Silk blonde hair	Pale, velvet skin		
For Your Eyes Only [9]	Judy Havelock	Grey	Pale gold	Wild and animal-like face with a sensuous mouth and high cheekbones	Body possessed a warm animal tang	
Risico [10]	Lisl Baum		Ash blonde	Pert nose	Burned, crème body	
The Hildebrand Rarity [11]	Elizabeth Krest	Large, clear blue	Ash-blonde, hung heavily to the base of her neck	Natural eyebrows, no lipstick; no lacquer on fingernails	Sunburned, model-like body	

Thunderball[12]	Dominetta Vitale	Dark brown with a golden flicker		Small, uptilted nose, small dimples, a gay to-hell-with-you face	Golden sunburned skin	High-riding deeply V-ed, proud breasts
The Spy Who Loved Me[13]	Vivienne Michel	Blue, clear, wide	Very dark, curvy, brown	An expanse of inquiring forehead, high cheekbones, a "too small" nose and "too big" mouth	A "good figure" until she was told her "behind stuck out too much and that [she] must wear a tighter bra"	
The Living Daylights[14]	"Trigger"		Molten gold, long, straight, and fair			
On Her Majesty's Secret Service[15]	Contessa Teresa di Vicenzo	Brilliant blue	Fair and golden			
You Only Live Twice[16]	Kissy Suzuki	Almond	Black with dark brown highlights, wavy	Hands and feet scarred and rough from work		Firm and proud breasts with coarse nipples
The Man With the Golden Gun[17]	Mary Goodnight	Wide-apart and direct blue eyes	Golden with sunburn	Pretty nose, good bones, full lips		Wears a tight frock against her bosom and hips

Appendix C

James Bond Filmography

Dr. No (1962)
Produced by Albert R. Broccoli and Harry Saltzman
Directed by Terence Young
Screenplay by Richard Maibaum, Johanna Harwood, and Berkley Mather
American theatrical release date: May 8, 1963

From Russia With Love (1963)
Produced by Albert R. Broccoli and Harry Saltzman
Directed by Terence Young
Screenplay by Richard Maibaum and Johanna Harwood
American theatrical release date: April 8, 1964

Goldfinger (1964)
Produced by Albert R. Broccoli and Harry Saltzman
Directed by Guy Hamilton
Screenplay by Richard Maibaum and Paul Dehn
American theatrical release date: December 25

Thunderball (1965)
Produced by Kevin McClory
Directed by Terence Young
Screenplay by Richard Maibaum and John Hopkins, based on the original story by Kevin McClory, Jack Whittingham, and Ian Fleming
American theatrical release date: December 21

You Only Live Twice (1967)
Produced by Albert R. Broccoli and Harry Saltzman
Directed by Lewis Gilbert
Screenplay by Roald Dahl
Additional story material by Harold Jack Bloom
American theatrical release date: June 13

On Her Majesty's Secret Service (1969)
Produced by Albert R. Broccoli and Harry Saltzman
Directed by Peter Hunt
Screenplay by Richard Maibaum
Additional Dialogue by Simon Raven
American theatrical release date: December 18

Diamonds Are Forever (1971)
Produced by Albert R. Broccoli and Harry Saltzman
Directed by Guy Hamilton
Screenplay by Richard Maibaum and Tom Mankiewicz
American theatrical release date: December 17

Live and Let Die (1973)
Produced by Albert R. Broccoli and Harry Saltzman
Directed by Guy Hamilton
Screenplay by Tom Mankiewicz
American theatrical release date: June 27

The Man With the Golden Gun (1974)
Produced by Albert R. Broccoli and Harry Saltzman
Directed by Guy Hamilton
Screenplay by Richard Maibaum and Tom Mankiewicz
American theatrical release date: December 19

The Spy Who Loved Me (1977)
Produced by Albert R. Broccoli
Directed by Lewis Gilbert
Screenplay by Christopher Wood and Richard Maibaum
American theatrical release date: July 13

Moonraker (1979)
Produced by Albert R. Broccoli
Directed by Lewis Gilbert
Screenplay by Christopher Wood
American theatrical release date: June 29

For Your Eyes Only (1981)
Produced by Albert R. Broccoli
Directed by John Glen
Screenplay by Richard Maibaum and Michael G. Wilson
American theatrical release date: June 26

Octopussy (1983)
Produced by Albert R. Broccoli
Directed by John Glen
Screenplay by George MacDonald Fraser, Richard Maibaum and Michael G. Wilson
American theatrical release date: June 10

A View To A Kill (1985)
Produced by Albert R. Broccoli and Michael G. Wilson
Directed by John Glen
Screenplay by Richard Maibaum and Michael G. Wilson
American theatrical release date: May 22

The Living Daylights (1987)
Produced by Albert R. Broccoli and Michael G. Wilson
Directed by John Glen
Screenplay by Richard Maibaum and Michael G. Wilson
American theatrical release date: July 31

Licence to Kill (1989)
Produced by Albert R. Broccoli and Michael G. Wilson
Directed by John Glen
Screenplay by Richard Maibaum and Michael G. Wilson
American theatrical release date: July 14

GoldenEye (1995)
Presented by Albert R. Broccoli
Produced by Michael G. Wilson and Barbara Broccoli
Directed by Martin Campbell
Screenplay by Jeffrey Caine and Bruce Feirstein
Story by Michael France
American theatrical release date: November 17

Tomorrow Never Dies (1997)
Produced by Michael G. Wilson and Barbara Broccoli
Directed by Roger Spottiswoode
Screenplay by Bruce Feirstein
American theatrical release date: December 19

The World Is Not Enough (1999)
Produced by Michael G. Wilson and Barbara Broccoli
Directed by Michael Apted
Screenplay by Neal Purvis, Robert Wade and Bruce Feirstein
Story by Neal Purvis and Robert Wade
American theatrical release date: November 19

Die Another Day (2002)
Produced by Barbara Broccoli, Michael G. Wilson and Anthony Waye
Directed by Lee Tamahori
Screenplay by Neal Purvis and Robert Wade
American theatrical release date: November 22

Casino Royale (2006)
Produced by Michael G. Wilson and Barbara Broccoli
Directed by Martin Campbell
Screenplay by Neal Purvis, Robert Wade and Paul Haggis
American theatrical release date: November 17

Quantum of Solace (2008)
Produced by Michael G. Wilson and Barbara Broccoli
Directed by Marc Forster
Screenplay by Joshua Zetumer, Paul Haggis, Neal Purvis and Robert Wade
Story by Michael G. Wilson
American theatrical release date: November 14

Skyfall (2012)
Produced by Michael G. Wilson and Barbara Broccoli
Directed by Sam Mendes
Screenplay by John Logan, Neal Purvis and Robert Wade
American theatrical release date: November 9 (anticipated)

Notes

Preface

[1] "25 Years of James Bond," *Playboy*, September 1987, 124+, 126.

[2] Vincent Canby, "Longevity—The Real James Bond Mystery," *New York Times*, October 16, 1983, H21.

[3] Christoph Lindner, "Introduction," in *The James Bond Phenomenon: A Critical Reader*, ed. Christoph Lindner (Manchester: Manchester University Press, 2003), 1.

[4] Tony Bennett and Janet Woollacott, *Bond and Beyond: The Political Career of a Popular Hero* (London: Palgrave Macmillan, 1987), 1.

[5] Ibid., 2.

[6] John Meagher, "Why the Ooh Has Gone Out of 007," *Irish Independent*, August 20, 2005, http://www.independent.ie/opinion/analysis/why-the-ooh-has-gone-out-of-007-245795.html.

[7] 23. "M Informs Her Spy," *GoldenEye*, special ed. DVD, directed by Martin Campbell (1995; Santa Monica, CA: MGM Home Entertainment, 1999).

[8] Virginia Blackburn, "Is There Any Good Reason Why 007 Can't Be A Woman?" *Express* (U.K.), August 18, 2005, 16.

[9] Pierce Brosnan stated that he "wasn't prepared when he got a phone call out of the blue . . . saying his tenure as 007 was done." Jeanne Wolf, "'You've Got To Be A Fighting Rooster,'" *Parade*, June 15, 2008.

[10] Meagher, "Why the Ooh Has Gone Out of 007." The six-year hiatus between 1989 and 1995 has been described as a "weary desert for millions of fans: a time of testing common to many creeds." Simon Winder, "Her Majesty's Sacred Service," *New York Times*, November 18, 2006, A17.

[11] Corie Brown and Jeff Giles, "Bond—Stirred, Not Shaken," *Newsweek*, November 22, 1999, 90.

[12] "Playboy Interview: Daniel Craig," *Playboy*, November 2008, 57+, 57.

[13] Joshua Rich, "Bond Ambition," *Entertainment Weekly*, October 28, 2005, 13.

14 Andrew Collins, "I Spy, the New 007," *Guardian* (U.K.), July 25, 1999. Vincent Canby observed: "As attractive as the character of 007 is, and as amusing as most of the films have been, this longevity is as mysterious to me as it is rare. All that one can do with any certainty is describe the phenomenon." Canby, "Longevity—The Real James Bond Mystery."

15 James Chapman, *Licence to Thrill: A Cultural History of the James Bond Films* (New York: Columbia University Press, 2000), 1.

16 Lindner, "Introduction," 9.

17 Graham Rye, *The James Bond Girls* (New York: Citadel Press, 1996), intro.

18 "The women in the films are fantastic, but so are the women in Playboy." Canby, "Longevity—The Real James Bond Mystery." The Bond-*Playboy* relationship is described in chapter 002.

19 "Bond Girls," *Playboy*, November 2008, 78+, 78.

20 Elizabeth Hurley, nar., "The World of James Bond 007," directed by Paul Hall, *GoldenEye*, special ed. DVD.

21 Maryam d'Abo and John Cork, *Bond Girls Are Forever: The Women of James Bond* (New York: Henry N. Abrams, Inc., 2003), 11.

22 Bennett and Woollacott, *Bond and Beyond*, 35.

23 Ibid.

24 The Bond Girls were "free only in the areas (bed) and respects (sexuality) that 'liberated man' required." Ibid., 241.

25 Ibid., 35.

26 Ibid., 39.

27 Ibid.

28 Ibid.

29 Ibid.

30 Ibid., 1.

31 D'Abo and Cork, *Bond Girls Are Forever*, 11.

32 Brian Dunbar, *Goldfinger* (Michigan: Longman, 2001), 31.

33 D'Abo and Cork, *Bond Girls Are Forever*, 19.

34 Ibid., 107.

35 Quoted in Bennett and Woollacott, *Bond and Beyond*, 231.

36 Emily Jenkins, "The Sensitive Bond," Salon.com, May 1, 2000, http://archive.salon.com/books/feature/2000/05/01/sensitive_bond/index.html.

37 Bennett and Woollacott, *Bond and Beyond*, 191.

38 Daniel Craig was asked to describe how the Bond Girl has developed since 1969, but he merely offered a general observation in response: "[I]n the earlier movies the girls were mostly eye candy . . . but things are more interesting now. The character is important to the plot." "Playboy Interview: Daniel Craig," 59.

39 Even James Bond, it has been written, has become a caricature of himself. Shana Alexander, "Agent 008—Where Are You?" *Life*, July 16, 1965, 27.

40 Bennett and Woollacott, *Bond and Beyond*, 173.

41 Purdue University, College of Liberal Arts, "Women's Studies," http://www.cla.purdue.edu/womens-studies/.

42 For example, only four male students at Yale University recently declared a Women's Gender and Sexual Studies major. Melissa Leon, "The Few, The Proud: Male WGSS Majors," *Yale Daily News*, April 2, 2008, http://www.yaledailynews.com/articles/view/24169.

43 West Virginia University, Center for Women's Studies, "Why Women's Studies?" http://www.as.wvu.edu/wvwmst/infohist.htm.

44 *Bond Girls Are Forever*, limited ed. DVD, directed by John Watkin (2002; Santa Monica, CA: MGM Home Entertainment, 2003).

45 Moira Walsh, "Films," *America*, January 8, 1966, 53.

46 Others embarked upon the same path in their works about Bond, albeit focusing upon different elements. For example, John Cork and Bruce Scivally commented upon the impact of a global Bondian culture:

> [W]e have tried to take the reader on a journey back through the world surrounding Bond, through the Cold War, the explosion of spymania, and the real-life espionage adventures and global changes that have occurred during the 40 years since James Bond first became a cinematic hero. This is a history of the modern world seen through a spyglass focused on the realm of a fictional character.

John Cork and Bruce Scivally, *James Bond: The Legacy* (New York: Harry N. Abrams, Inc., 2002), 9.

47 Slavoj Zizek, *Welcome to the Desert of the Real: Five Essays on September 11 and Related Dates* (New York: Verso, 2001), 39.

48 Stephen Watt, "007 and 9/11, Specters and Structures of Feeling," in *The James Bond Phenomenon*, 239.

49 Jim Leach, "'The World Has Changed': Bond in the 1990s and Beyond?" in ibid., 248.

50 Thomas Vinciguerra, "Word for Word/James Bond Scholarship; Thus Spake 007: From Ubermensch to Psychosexual Fetish Object," *New York Times*, July 13, 2003, WK5.

51 Ben Hoyle and Joanna Bale, "Goldfinger is Back: Craig is the Bond with a Midas Touch," *Times* (U.K.), November 20, 2006, 29.

52 Several essays that comprise *The James Bond Phenomenon* cite popular culture works such as Steven J. Rubin's *The Complete James Bond Movie Encyclopedia*. I have yet to discover a full-scale work that does the same.

Introduction

1 Ben Macintyre, *For Your Eyes Only: Ian Fleming + James Bond* (New York: Bloomsbury, 2008), 144.

2 "The Bond Girls: Sexpots and Psychopaths," *Playboy*, June 2000, 88.

3 Quoted in *Bond Girls Are Forever*, limited ed. DVD, directed by John Watkin (2002; Santa Monica, CA: MGM Home Entertainment, 2003).

4 John Cork and Bruce Scivally, *James Bond: The Legacy* (New York: Harry N. Abrams, Inc., 2002), 29. This introduction has also been "deemed the most memorable line of dialogue in the history of movies." Patrick Macnee, nar., "Inside Dr. No," directed by John Cork, *Dr. No*, special ed. DVD, directed by Terence Young (1962; Santa Monica, CA: MGM Home Entertainment, 2000).

5 Neal Gabler, "Male Bonding," *Modern Maturity*, January-February 2000, 52.

6 Cork and Scivally, *The Legacy, 9*.

7 Tony Bennett and Janet Woollacott, *Bond and Beyond: The Political Career of a Popular Hero* (London: Palgrave Macmillan, 1987), 11.

8 "Heroes of Our Time," *Times* (U.K.), October 27, 1966, 17.

9 Patrick Macnee, nar., "The *Thunderball* Phenomenon," directed by John Cork, *Thunderball*, special ed. DVD, directed by Terence Young (1965; Santa Monica, CA: MGM Home Entertainment, 1999).

10 See John Pearson, *James Bond: The Authorized Biography of 007* (New York: William Morrow, 1973).

11 The ice cream company Ben & Jerry's, for example, marketed a flavor called "From Russia with Buzz" for a brief period during the late 1990s and early 2000s. "Flavor Graveyard," www.benjerry.com/our_products/flavor_graveyard.

12 "James Bond Spied on By Computer," *Times* (U.K.), April 10, 1967, 10.

13 Gillian Harris, "007 Helps to Combat Car Crime," *Times* (U.K.), November 9, 1999, 13.

14 "Wasting Away," *Time*, October 12, 1970, 90.

15 Eric Fordham, "Now on to '007½' For Microfilm," *Times* (U.K.), October 2, 1978, xi.

16 Michael Evans, "Bonds of the Navy Recruit 007 Fans," *Times* (U.K.), January 7, 1998, 3.

17 Nick Nuttall, "Fitness 'Stirred' By Martini Method," *Times* (U.K.), December 17, 1999, 13.

18 In *Thunderball*, Q informs Bond that the device offers air only for brief period, "say, about four minutes." 24. "Special Spy Gear," *Thunderball*, special ed. DVD. The prop was never intended to function, though film editing gave the illusion that it did.

19 Kate Coleman, "'Pianistic Feast' with MSO," *Herald-Mail*, March 18, 2010, http://www.herald-mail.com.

20 "Ursula's 007 Bikini Sold in Auction," *BBC News*, February 15, 2001, http://news.bbc.co.uk/2/hi/europe/1170800.stm.

21 "James Bond's License To Make A Killing," *Times* (U.K.), January 1, 1994, 3.

22 Lewis Nichols, "In and Out of Books: The Bond Industry," *New York Times Book Review*, August 15, 1965, 8. One author described a "worldwide avalanche of 007 merchandise[, which] includes everything from Bond-licensed bed sheets to a complete line of what is known . . . as 'men's toiletries.' In short, the Bond image is

now so potent it even has the selling power to deodorize armpits." Shana Alexander, "Agent 008—Where Are You?" *Life*, July 16, 1965, 27. In fact, "every conceivable product" was fair game for marketing Bond, including vodka, clothing, towels, bedsheets, children's lunchboxes, playing cards, hygiene products, action figures, and other toys. Macnee, nar., "The *Thunderball* Phenomenon," *Thunderball*, special ed. DVD. Common to most of the products was the 007 logo "blazoned across them or worked into the pattern." William K. Zinsser, "The Big Bond Bonanza," *Saturday Evening Post*, July 17, 1965, 77. For example, Colgate-Palmolive's toiletries were marketed to "'make any man dangerous.'" Ibid.

23 Zinsser, "The Big Bond Bonanza."

24 Corie Brown and Jeff Giles, "Bond—Stirred, Not Shaken," *Newsweek*, November 22, 1999, 90.

25 Patrick Macnee, nar., "Ian Fleming—007's Creator," directed by John Cork, *The Living Daylights*, special ed. DVD, directed by John Glen (1987; Santa Monica, CA: MGM Home Entertainment, 2000).

26 "Bond's Creator," *New Yorker*, April 21, 1962, 32. Fleming often noted that he "had conceived Bond as 'a hero without any characteristics who was simply the blunt instrument in the hands of his government.'" "Ian Fleming, Author, 56, Dies; Created James Bond, Agent 007," *New York Times*, August 13, 1964, 29.

27 "James Bond, Ornithologist, 89; Fleming Adopted Name for 007," *New York Times*, February 17, 1989, D19.

28 Ibid.

29 Macnee, nar., "Ian Fleming—007's Creator," *The Living Daylights*, special ed. DVD.

30 Christoph Lindner, "Why Size Matters," in I*an Fleming and James Bond: The Cultural Politics of 007*, eds. Edward P. Comentale, Stephen Watt and Skip Willman (Bloomington: Indiana University Press, 2005), 223.

31 Toby Miller, "James Bond's Penis," in *The James Bond Phenomenon: A Critical Reader*, ed. Christoph Lindner (Manchester: Manchester University Press, 2003), 233-34. Bennett and Woollacott similarly discussed the "phallic code" at work in Fleming's James Bond novels.

32 Patrick Macnee, nar., "The *Goldfinger* Phenomenon," directed by John Cork, *Goldfinger*, special ed. DVD, directed by Guy Hamilton (1963; Santa Monica, CA: MGM Home Entertaiment, 1999).

33 Miller, "James Bond's Penis," 240.

34 Elisabeth Ladenson, "Pussy Galore," in *The James Bond Phenomenon*, 185.

35 Hollis Alpert, "The Ian Fleming?" *Saturday Evening Review*, May 26, 1962, 37.

36 "Espionage: 007 vs. SMERSH," *Time*, June 29, 1962, 16.

37 Michelle Orecklin, "Sisterly Bond," *Time*, October 11, 1999, 104.

38 Lycurgus Starkey, *James Bond's World of Values* (Nashville: Abingdon Press, 1966), 17.

39 Macnee, nar., "The *Thunderball* Phenomenon," *Thunderball*, special ed. DVD.

40 Annie Liebovitz and Bruce Feirstein, "Bond Girls Are Forever," *Vanity Fair*, November 1999, 247.

41 Mark Schwed, "Licensed to Still Thrill," *TV Guide*, November 13-19, 1999, 26.

42 Maryam d'Abo and John Cork, *Bond Girls Are Forever: The Women of James Bond* (New York: Henry N. Abrams, Inc., 2003), 163.

43 James Chapman, *Licence to Thrill: A Cultural History of the James Bond Films* (New York: Columbia University Press, 2000), 10.

44 Ibid.

45 Lee Pfeiffer and Dave Worrall, *The Essential Bond* (New York: Harper Paperbacks, 1999), 40. In fact, "no other vehicle in the history of entertainment so captivates the public mind" as the Aston Martin DB5. Macnee, nar., "The *Goldfinger* Phenomenon," *Goldfinger*, special ed. DVD.

46 Andrew Lycett, *Ian Fleming: The Man Behind James Bond* (Atlanta: Turner Publishing, 1995), 290.

47 Ian Fleming, "How To Write A Thriller," *Books and Bookmen*, May 1963, 14.

48 Chapman, Licence to Thrill, 1.

49 Ted Casablanca, "For His Eyes Only," *Premiere*, December 1995, 68.

50 Bosley Crowther, "The Screen: 'Dr. No,' Mystery Spoof," *New York Times*, May 30, 1963, 15.

51 Indeed, critical reaction to Ian Fleming's novels can be divided into two categories: (1) those who "warn[] against reading" and "stress[] the inferior moral or artistic qualities of the novels," and (2) those who "construe them not merely as permissibly readable but as worthwhile reading." Bennett and Woollacott, *Bond and Beyond*, 254. The James Bond novels are considered in chapter 003.

52 Miller, "James Bond's Penis," 236.

53 Quoted in Chapman, *Licence to Thrill*, 5.

54 Andrew Lycett, "Foreword" in *The James Bond Phenomenon*, viii.

55 Jeremy Black, *The Politics of James Bond: From Fleming's Novels to the Big Screen* (London: Praeger Trade, 2001), xii.

56 Matt Chapman, "Bond 23 Axes the Action, Targets an Oscar," *Total Film: The Modern Guide to Movies*, October 25, 2011, http://www.totalfilm.com/news/bond-23-axes-the-action-targets-an-oscar.

57 John Brosnan, *James Bond in the Cinema* (London: Tantivy Press, 1981), ix.

58 Bennett and Woollacott, *Bond and Beyond*, 4.

59 Black, *The Politics of James Bond*, xii.

60 Giles Coren, review of *License to Thrill: A Cultural History of the James Bond Films*, by James Chapman, *Times* (U.K.), November 18, 1999, 46.

61 Charles McGrath, "That License to Kill Is Unexpired," *New York Times*, June 1, 2008, http://www.nytimes.com.

62 Rita Delfiner, "Bond Girls in 3DD," *New York Post*, Jan. 13, 2010, 17. In April 2010, it was announced that the financial uncertainty of MGM required producers to "put the brakes" on developing and producing the next franchise installment. Claudia Eller, "Quick Takes: Bond in Tight Spot," *Los Angeles Times*, April 20, 2010, 3. Production of the next James Bond film was "cancelled altogether" as of July 2010. Stuart Heritage, "Is James Bond Past His Sell-By Date?" *Guardian*

(U.K.), July 5, 2010, www.guardian.co.uk/film/filmblog/2010/jul/05/james-bond-past-sell-by. Nearly a year later, MGM and Sony Pictures announced that "Bond 23" would open in the United States in November 2012. Ralf Ludemann, "James Bond '23' Gets U.K. Release Date," *The Hollywood Reporter*, June 2, 2011, http://www.hollywoodreporter.com/news/james-bond-23-gets-uk-194312. "Bond 23" was officially named Skyfall in October 2011. "The SkyFalls in on Latest Bond Movie," *Mirror* (U.K.), October 7, 2011, 3. The film's first trailer was released in May 2012. Simon English, "James Bond is Back to Help Loss-Making Pinewood Shepperton," *Independent* (U.K.), May 24, 2012, 62.

001
Introducing James Bond: Ian Fleming and His Feminine Mystique

1 Ben Macintyre, *For Your Eyes Only: Ian Fleming + James Bond* (New York: Bloomsbury, 2008), 147.

2 Reprinted in Andrew Lycett, *Ian Fleming: The Man Behind James Bond* (Atlanta: Turner Publishing, 1995), 199.

3 Patrick Macnee, nar., "Ian Fleming—007's Creator," directed by John Cork, *The Living Daylights*, special ed. DVD, directed by John Glen (1987; Santa Monica, CA: MGM Home Entertainment, 2000).

4 Lycett, *Ian Fleming*, 87.

5 Michael Davie, "A Vulgarian in Clubland," review of *Ian Fleming: The Man Behind James Bond*, by Andrew Lycett, *Times Literary Supplement* (U.K.), December 1, 1995, 17.

6 John Pearson, *The Life of Ian Fleming* (New York: McGraw-Hill, 1966), 8.

7 Lycett, *Ian Fleming*, 86.

8 Macnee, nar., "Ian Fleming—007's Creator," *The Living Daylights*, special ed. DVD.

9 Ibid.

10 Davie, "A Vulgarian in Clubland," 17.

11 Lycett, *Ian Fleming*, 80.

12 Henry A. Zeiger, Ian Fleming: *The Spy Who Came In With the Gold* (New York: Duell, Sloan and Pearce, 1965), 84.

13 "[M]any have said the fictional James Bond was Ian Fleming. This is certainly true up to a point." John Cork and Bruce Scivally, *James Bond: The Legacy* (New York: Harry N. Abrams, Inc., 2002), 12.

14 *James Bond*, VHS. Directed by Bill Harris. A&E Home Video, 1995.

15 Zeiger, *Ian Fleming*, 26. Recently, it has been suggested that Fleming's marriage featured both sadist and masochistic behavior:

> Their relationship thrived—thanks to their fierce physical fights. When Ann left bruises on Fleming, he would warn her that "all this damage has to be paid for some time," and so it was.

"I long for you to whip me because I love being hurt by you and kissed afterwards," Ann wrote to him. "It's very lonely not to be beaten and shouted at every five minutes." Both needed the other and were open about their unorthodox relationship.

Christopher Hudson, "The Woman Who Created 007," February 2, 2008, *Daily Mail* (U.K.), 56.

16 Macnee, nar., "Ian Fleming—007's Creator," *The Living Daylights*, special ed. DVD.

17 "Great Britain: The Man with the Golden Bond," *Time*, August 21, 1964, 22-23.

18 The libraries at Eton College maintain collections of first edition works by both Ian and Peter Fleming. "Famous Old Etonians," Eton College, http://www.etoncollege.com/default.asp.

19 Such incidents have been described as "thrash[ings] with a birch switch." Cork and Scivally, *The Legacy*, 11.

20 Macnee, nar., "Ian Fleming—007's Creator," *The Living Daylights*, special ed. DVD.

21 Cork and Scivally, *The Legacy*, 11.

22 Ibid.

23 Macintyre, *For Your Eyes Only*, 147.

24 Zeiger, *Ian Fleming*, 28.

25 Cork and Scivally, *The Legacy*, 11.

26 Lycett, *Ian Fleming*, 28. "Fleming's ruthlessness towards women may have been influenced by the gonorrhea he caught at Sandhurst." Hudson, "The Woman Who Created 007."

27 Zeiger, *Ian Fleming*, 29.

28 Pearson, *The Life of Ian Fleming*, 26.

29 Ibid., 22.

30 Ibid., 49.

31 Raymond Benson, *The James Bond Bedside Companion* (New York: Dodd, Mead & Company, 1984), 45.

32 *James Bond*, VHS.

33 Arthur Brittan, *Masculinity and Power* (Oxford: Basil Blackwell, 1989), 30-31.

34 Brian Easlea, *Fathering the Unthinkable* (London: Pluto Press, 1983), 11.

35 Joseph H. Pleck, *The Myth of Masculinity* (Cambridge, MA: MIT Press, 1981), 3.

36 Brittan, *Masculinity and Power*, 31-32.

37 Linda LeMoncheck, *Dehumanizing Women* (New Jersey: Rowman & Allanheld, 1985), 2.

38 Cork and Scivally, The Legacy, 14.

39 Ann Fleming and Mark Amory, *The Letters of Ann Fleming* (London: Collins Harvill, 1985), 37.

40 Lycett, *Ian Fleming*, 82.

41 Ibid., 151.

42 Pearson, *The Life of Ian Fleming*, 76.
43 Ibid., 83.
44 Ibid., 75, 77.
45 Ibid., 77.
46 Lycett, *Ian Fleming*, 85.
47 Pearson, *The Life of Ian Fleming*, 34.
48 Ibid., 76.
49 Godfrey Smith, "The Man Who Wasn't James Bond," *Sunday Times Magazine* (U.K.), August 13, 1989, 30+, 32.
50 Pearson, *The Life of Ian Fleming*, 80.
51 Ian Fleming, *The Man With the Golden Gun* (London: Coronet Paperbacks, 1988), 191.
52 Zeiger, *Ian Fleming*, 93.
53 Pearson, *The Life of Ian Fleming*, 78.
54 Ibid., 77.
55 LeMoncheck, *Dehumanizing Women*, 89.
56 Pearson, *The Life of Ian Fleming*, 79.
57 "Paperbacks," review of *The Life of Ian Fleming*, by John Pearson, Times (U.K.), June 1, 1968, 20.
58 Ian Fleming, *Casino Royale* (London: Coronet Paperbacks, 1988), 157.
59 Pearson, *The Life of Ian Fleming*, 35.
60 Ibid., 76, 78.
61 Zeiger, *Ian Fleming*, 82.
62 Ian Fleming, "007 in New York," reprinted in *Sunday Times Magazine* (U.K.), November 7, 1999, 54+, 57.
63 Zeiger, *Ian Fleming*, 83.
64 Ibid., 84.
65 Pearson, *The Life of Ian Fleming*, 74.
66 Ibid., 78.
67 Benson, *The James Bond Bedside Companion*, 45.
68 Fleming, "007 in New York."
69 LeMoncheck, *Dehumanizing Women*, 89.
70 Pearson, *The Life of Ian Fleming*, 75.
71 Ibid., 74.
72 Mark Amory, "In Search of the Man Who Wasn't Bond," *Times* (U.K.), June 24, 1993, 41.
73 Pearson, *The Life of Ian Fleming*, 34.
74 Andrew Lycett, "How Fleming's Friends Filled Bond's World," *Sunday Times* (U.K.), August 27, 2000, 5.
75 Davie, "A Vulgarian in Clubland."
76 Macintyre, *For Your Eyes Only*, 150.
77 Zeiger, *Ian Fleming*, 84.

78 Pearson, *The Life of Ian Fleming*, 74.

79 Ibid., 76.

80 Wright went to sleep with the window open. During the air raid, a section of masonry became dislodged and "hurtled through her open window, striking Mu in the temple and killing her at once." Macintyre, *For Your Eyes Only*, 150.

81 Lycett, *Ian Fleming*, 152.

82 Smith, "The Man Who Wasn't James Bond"; *James Bond*, VHS.

83 Lycett, *Ian Fleming*, 217.

84 Pearson, *The Life of Ian Fleming*, 74.

85 Davie, "A Vulgarian in Clubland."

002
Justifying James Bond: Taking 007 and Ian Fleming Seriously

1 "Great Britain: The Man with the Golden Bond," *Time*, August 21, 1964, 26.

2 John Brosnan, *James Bond in the Cinema* (London: Tantivy Press, 1981), ix.

3 Vincent Canby, "Film View; Longevity—The Real James Bond Mystery," *New York Times*, October 16, 1983, H21.

4 "Bond Files," *Playboy*, June 2000, 84+, 168.

5 John Pearson, "Rough Rise of a Dream Hero," *Life*, October 14, 1966, 113+, 113.

6 "Playboy Interview: Ian Fleming," *Playboy*, December 1964, 97+, 106.

7 Tim Green, "Bon Vivant and the Scourge of Smersh: The Master of Agent 007," *Life*, August 10, 1962, 47.

8 Andrew Lycett, *Ian Fleming: The Man Behind James Bond* (Atlanta: Turner Publishing, 1995), 217.

9 Geoffrey Bocca, "The Spectacular Cult of Ian Fleming," *Saturday Evening Post*, June 22, 1963, 68.

10 Godfrey Smith, "The Man Who Wasn't James Bond," *Sunday Times Magazine* (U.K.), August 13, 1989, 30+.

11 Patrick Macnee, nar., "Ian Fleming—007's Creator," directed by John Cork, *The Living Daylights*, special ed. DVD, directed by John Glen (1987; Santa Monica, CA: MGM Home Entertainment, 2000).

12 John Pearson, *The Life of Ian Fleming* (New York: McGraw-Hill, 1966), 77.

13 Ian Fleming, *Diamonds Are Forever* (New York: MJF Books, 1984), 185.

14 Pearson, *The Life of Ian Fleming*, 77.

15 Macnee, nar., "Ian Fleming—007's Creator," *The Living Daylights*, special ed. DVD.

16 Ben Macintyre, *For Your Eyes Only: Ian Fleming + James Bond*, 156.

17 Macnee, nar., "Ian Fleming—007's Creator," *The Living Daylights*, special ed. DVD.

18 Pearson, *The Life of Ian Fleming*, 70.

19 Lycett, *Ian Fleming*, 217.

[20] Ibid., 381.

[21] Macnee, nar., "Ian Fleming—007's Creator," *The Living Daylights*, special ed. DVD.

[22] Allen Dulles, "Our Spy-Boss Who Loved Bond," *Life*, August 28, 1964, 19.

[23] "Sorry to Have Troubled You," *Newsweek*, August 24, 1964, 37.

[24] Malcolm Muggeridge, "Books," *Esquire*, December 1964, 36-37.

[25] Henry A. Zeiger, *Ian Fleming: The Spy Who Came In With the Gold* (New York: Duell, Sloan and Pearce, 1965), 85.

[26] Pearson, *The Life of Ian Fleming*, 220.

[27] "Great Britain: The Man with the Golden Bond."

[28] Green, "Bon Vivant and the Scourge of Smersh."

[29] "Sorry to Have Troubled You."

[30] Dulles, "Our Spy-Boss Who Loved Bond."

[31] Macnee, nar., "Ian Fleming—007's Creator," *The Living Daylights*, special ed. DVD.

[32] Bocca, "The Spectacular Cult of Ian Fleming."

[33] "Great Britain: The Man with the Golden Bond."

[34] Pearson, *The Life of Ian Fleming*, 37.

[35] Ibid.

[36] Ibid., 200.

[37] Lycett, *Ian Fleming*, 220.

[38] "Sorry to Have Troubled You."

[39] Pearson, *The Life of Ian Fleming*, 211.

[40] Ibid., 228.

[41] Macnee, nar., "Ian Fleming—007's Creator," *The Living Daylights*, special ed. DVD.

[42] Green, "Bon Vivant and the Scourge of Smersh."

[43] Muggeridge, "Books."

[44] Macnee, nar., "Ian Fleming—007's Creator," *The Living Daylights*, special ed. DVD.

[45] Pearson, *The Life of Ian Fleming*, 211. Fleming's Bond writings were really "experiment[s] in the autobiography of dreams." Pearson, "Rough Rise of a Dream Hero," 114.

[46] Tony Bennett and Janet Woollacott, *Bond and Beyond: The Political Career of a Popular Hero* (London: Palgrave Macmillan, 1987), 4.

[47] Lietta Tornabuoni, "A Popular Phenomenon," in *The Bond Affair*, eds. Oreste del Buono and Umberto Eco (London: Macdonald, 1966), 33-34.

[48] Fleming acknowledged that "there *are* similarities" between him and Bond, but attributed any commonalities to the fact that "one writies only of what one knows, and some of the quirks and characteristics that I give Bond are ones that I know about." "Playboy Interview: Ian Fleming," 100.

[49] Pearson, *The Life of Ian Fleming*, 14.

[50] "Playboy Interview: Ian Fleming," 100.

51 Tim Rayment, "In Search of the Original James Bond," *Sunday Times* (U.K.), sec. 4, September 4, 1994, 6.

52 "Great Britain: The Man with the Golden Bond."

53 Ibid.; "Will the Real James Bond Please Stand Up?" *Sunday Times* (U.K.), September 28, 1975, 3.

54 "Enter the Real James Bond," *Sunday Times* (U.K.), October 5, 1975, 14.

55 Pearson, *The Life of Ian Fleming*, 198.

56 Ian Fleming, *Diamonds Are Forever* (New York: MJF Books, 1984), 185.

57 See John Pearson, "James Bond Alias Ian Fleming," *Life*, October 7, 1996, 102+, 109.

58 The name Leiter has been connected to then-Senator John F. Kennedy who, while ill, asked his friend Marion "Oatsie" Leiter for suggested readings. Ms. Leiter recommended a Fleming novel. Cork and Scivally, *The Legacy*, 15.

59 In an interview with *Playboy*, Fleming explained:

> [T]hough this was purely a fictional device to make Bond's particular job more interesting, the double-0 prefix is not so entirely invented as all that. I pinched the idea from the fact that, in the admiralty, at the beginning of the War, all top-secret signals had the double-0 prefix . . . . [I]t stuck in my mind and I borrowed it for Bond and he got stuck with it.

"Playboy Interview: Ian Fleming," 102.

60 Pearson, *The Life of Ian Fleming*, 193.

61 Bennett and Woollacott, *Bond and Beyond*, 47.

62 Pearson, *The Life of Ian Fleming*, 193.

63 James Chapman, *Licence to Thrill: A Cultural History of the James Bond Films* (New York: Columbia University Press, 2000), 1.

64 Ibid.

65 Kingsley Amis, *The James Bond Dossier* (New York: The New American Library, 1965), 128-29.

66 Lycett, *Ian Fleming*, 289-90.

67 Green, "Bon Vivant and the Scourge of Smersh."

68 Pearson, *The Life of Ian Fleming*, 96.

69 Cork and Scivally, *The Legacy*, 12. Fleming designed the house, which included 15-inch thick coral walls that "acted as a natural heating and cooling system, helping to keep the house at a moderate temperature." Ibid. The name GoldenEye was derived from an operation with which Fleming was involved during the war, as well as a book he had been reading. "Playboy Interview: Ian Fleming," 104. Fleming also contemplated naming his residence Shamelady after the Jamaican name for a plant that curls up when its leaves are touched. Ibid.

70 "Ian Fleming, Author, 56, Dies; Created James Bond, Agent 007," *New York Times*, August 13, 1964, 29. Any mistakes, Fleming recalled, could be corrected when the book was completed. "Playboy Interview: Ian Fleming," 104.

71 Pearson, *The Life of Ian Fleming*, 91.

72 Hollis Alpert, "The Ian Fleming?" *Saturday Evening Review*, May 26, 1962, 37.

73 Fleming himself described a typical day at GoldenEye in his *Playboy* interview. "Playboy Interview: Ian Fleming," 104.

74 Cork and Scivally, *The Legacy*, 15.

75 Lycett, *Ian Fleming*, 216.

76 Alpert, "The Ian Fleming?"

77 Amis, *The James Bond Dossier*, 128-29.

78 "Playboy Interview: Ian Fleming," 100.

79 Ibid.

80 Research and edits only occurred after Fleming completed the manuscript: "After I've finished a book I realize that I've been rather vague or thin on some topic or other, and then I go to the right man and try to get the true gen out of him and then rewrite that particular area." Ibid.

81 Pearson, *The Life of Ian Fleming*, 236; Bernard Rosenberg and David Manning White, *Mass Culture Revisited* (New York: Van Nostrand Reinhold, 1971), 347.

82 Pearson, *The Life of Ian Fleming*, 218.

83 Patrick Macnee, nar., "The *Thunderball* Phenomenon," directed by John Cork, *Thunderball*, special ed. DVD, directed by Terence Young (1965; Santa Monica, CA: MGM Home Entertainment, 1999).

84 Lycett, *Ian Fleming*, 380.

85 Reprinted in Cork and Scivally, *The Legacy*, 15.

86 *Times* (U.K.), review of *Thunderball*, March 30, 1961, 15.

87 *Times* (U.K.), review of *Live and Let Die*, April 7, 1954, 10.

88 *Times* (U.K.), review of *Goldfinger*, March 26, 1959, 15.

89 Reprinted in Cork and Scivally, *The Legacy*, 14.

90 Patrick Macnee, nar., "Inside *On Her Majesty's Secret Service*," directed by John Cork, *On Her Majesty's Secret Service*, special ed. DVD, directed by Peter R. Hunt (1969; Santa Monica, CA: MGM Home Entertainment, 2000).

91 *Times* (U.K.), review of *On Her Majesty's Secret Service*, April 4, 1963, 16.

92 *Times* (U.K.), review of *From Russia With Love*, April 11, 1957, 13.

93 Paul Johnson, "Sex, Snobbery and Sadism," *New Statesman* (U.K.), April 5, 1958, 431.

94 *Times* (U.K.), review of *The Spy Who Loved Me*, April 19, 1962, 15.

95 Anthony Boucher, "On Assignment with James Bond," *New York Times Book Review*, August 25, 1963, 4. Fleming responded to Boucher's criticism directly, stating that "he's never liked my books, and it shows what a good reviewer he is that he says so." "Playboy Interview: Ian Fleming," 106.

96 Patrick Macnee, nar., "Inside *You Only Live Twice*," directed by John Cork, *You Only Live Twice*, special ed. DVD, directed by Lewis Gilbert (1967; Santa Monica, CA: MGM Home Entertainment, 2000).

97 *Times* (U.K.), review of *You Only Live Twice*, March 19, 1964, 16.

98 "Bondomania," *Time*, June 11, 1965, 69.

99 Pearson, *The Life of Ian Fleming*, 210-11.

100 Cork and Scivally, *The Legacy*, 14.

101 Bennett and Woollacott, *Bond and Beyond*, 43.

102 Macnee, nar., "Ian Fleming—007's Creator," *The Living Daylights*, special ed. DVD.

103 "Bond Files."

104 Quoted in Cork and Scivally, *The Legacy*, 45.

105 Ibid., 14.

106 Hugh Sidey, "The President's Voracious Reading Habits," *Life*, March 17, 1961, 55+.

107 Dulles, "Our Spy-Boss Who Loved Bond."

108 Ibid.

109 Lycett, *Ian Fleming*, 383.

110 "Espionage: 007 vs. SMERSH," Time, June 29, 1962, 16.

111 Cork and Scivally, *The Legacy*, 59.

112 Ibid., 15.

113 Fred Powledge, "Clues to Oswald Traced in Books," *New York Times*, November 28, 1963, 1. In fact, Oswald borrowed four Fleming novels: *Goldfinger*, *Moonraker*, *Thunderball*, and *From Russia With Love*. Fred Powledge, "F.B.I. Studying Oswald's Stay in New Orleans," *New York Times*, November 29, 1963, 21.

114 Cork and Scivally, *The Legacy*, 15.

115 Ibid.

116 "Bond's Creator," *New Yorker*, April 21, 1962, 34. Fleming also believed that "Bond's sort of patriotic derring do was in keeping with the President's own concept of endurance and courage and grace under pressure, and so on." "Playboy Interview: Ian Fleming," 106.

117 "Playboy Interview: Ian Fleming," 106.

118 Quoted in Skip Willman, "The Kennedys, Fleming, and Cuba: Bond's Foreign Policy," in Ian Fleming and *James Bond: The Cultural Politics of 007*, eds. Edward P. Comentale, Stephen Watt and Skip Willman (Bloomington: Indiana University Press, 2005), 178.

119 Quoted in ibid., 178-79.

120 Quoted in ibid., 179.

121 Canby, "Film View; Longevity—The Real James Bond Mystery."

122 Quoted in Willman, "The Kennedys, Fleming, and Cuba: Bond's Foreign Policy," 178.

123 Willman described several efforts implemented in Cuba by the Kennedy administration and traced these endeavors to President Kennedy's fascination with James Bond. See ibid., 191-99.

124 "Great Britain: The Man with the Golden Bond."

003
The James Bond Novels: Women in Print

1 Kingsley Amis, *The James Bond Dossier* (New York: The New American Library, 1965), 132.

2 Quoted in "Images of the Week: Bond Rides Again," *Sunday Times Magazine* (U.K.), July 3, 1977, 21.

3 Emily Jenkins, "The Sensitive Bond," *Salon.com*, May 1, 2000, http://archive.salon.com/books/feature/2000/05/01/sensitive_bond/index.html.

4 Ian Fleming, "Risico," in *For Your Eyes Only* (London: Coronet Paperbacks: 1989), 121

5 Allen Dulles, "Our Spy-Boss Who Loved Bond," *Life*, August 28, 1964, 19.

6 See introduction.

7 Umberto Eco, "The Narrative Structure in Fleming," in *The Bond Affair*, ed. Oreste Del Buono and Umberto Eco, trans. R.A. Downie (London: MacDonald, 1966), 39

8 Quoted in Michael Denning, "Licensed to Look: James Bond and the Heroism of Consumption," in *The James Bond Phenomenon: A Critical Reader*, ed. Christoph Lindner (Manchester: Manchester University Press, 2003), 64.

9 Tony Bennett and Janet Woollacott, *Bond and Beyond: The Political Career of a Popular Hero* (London: Palgrave Macmillan, 1987), 70-71

10 Ibid.

11 Ibid.

12 Ibid.

13 Ibid.

14 Maryam d'Abo and John Cork, *Bond Girls Are Forever: The Women of James Bond* (New York: Henry N. Abrams, Inc., 2003), 11.

15 Eco, "The Narrative Structure in Fleming," 49.

16 Ibid.

17 Ibid.

18 B.S. McReynolds, *The 007 Dossier* (California: BS Book Publishing, 1998), 57.

19 D'Abo and Cork, *Bond Girls Are Forever*, 15.

20 Indeed, even more recent paperback editions of the James Bond novels featured prominent illustrations of women straddling weaponry. "Images of the Week: Bond Rides Again."

21 Christine Bold, "'Under the Very Skirts of Britannia': Re-Reading Women in the James Bond Novels," in *The James Bond Phenomenon*, 171.

22 Ibid.

23 Ibid.

24 Quoted in d'Abo and Cork, *Bond Girls Are Forever*, 13.

25 Ian Fleming, *Moonraker* (London: Coronet Paperbacks, 1989), 8.

26 Bold, "'Under the Very Skirts of Britannia,'" 171.

27 Ibid., 171-72.

28 Ian Fleming, "For Your Eyes Only," in *For Your Eyes Only*, 75.

29 Ibid., 73.

30 Bold, "'Under the Very Skirts of Britannia,'" 172.

31 Ibid.

32 Eco, "The Narrative Structure in Fleming," 49.

33 Ian Fleming, *Doctor No*, in *A James Bond Omnibus, Volume 1* (New York: MJF Books, 1985), 92.

34 Ian Fleming, *The Man With the Golden Gun* (London: Coronet Paperbacks, 1989), 52.

35 Ian Fleming, "From A View To A Kill," in *For Your Eyes Only*, 15.

36 William Tanner, *The Book of Bond, or Every Man His Own 007* (New York: Viking Press, 1965), 93.

37 Ian Fleming, *Live and Let Die* (London: Coronet Paperbacks, 1988), 70. She was also described as "[o]ne of the most beautiful women Bond had ever seen . . . ." Ibid., 69.

38 Ibid., 70.

39 Ian Fleming, *From Russia, With Love*, in *A James Bond Omnibus, Volume 1*, 75.

40 Fleming, *The Man With the Golden Gun*, 52.

41 Ian Fleming, *Casino Royale* (London: Coronet Paperbacks, 1988), 38-39.

42 Ibid.

43 Ian Fleming, *Diamonds Are Forever* (New York: MJF Books, 1984), 33.

44 Fleming, *Moonraker*, 118.

45 Fleming, *The Man With the Golden Gun*, 52.

46 McReynolds, *The 007 Dossier*, 53.

47 Fleming, *Moonraker*, 81.

48 Fleming, *Casino Royale*, 39.

49 Fleming, *Doctor No*, 94.

50 Ian Fleming, *Goldfinger*, in *A James Bond Omnibus, Volume 1*, 49.

51 Ian Fleming, *Thuderball*, in *A James Bond Omnibus, Volume 2* (New York: MJF Books, 1989), 118.

52 Fleming, *Live and Let Die*, 112.

53 Fleming, *From Russia, With Love*, 76.

54 Tanner, *The Book of Bond*, 94.

55 Ian Fleming, *On Her Majesty's Secret Service*, in *A James Bond Omnibus, Volume 2*, 207.

56 Ibid. (emphasis added).

57 Fleming, *From Russia, With Love*, 76.

58 Furio Columbo, "Bond's Women," in *The Bond Affair*, 101-02. In fact, the connection may be much deeper, correlating Fleming's description of the body to beauty, heterosexuality, and patriotism on the one hand and ugliness, sexual deviance, and criminality on the other. Bold, "'Under the Very Skirts of Britannia,'" 174

59 Amis, *The James Bond Dossier*, 43.

60 Lycurgus M. Starkey, Jr., *James Bond's World of Values* (New York: Abingdon Press, 1966), 17.

61 Fleming, *On Her Majesty's Secret Service*, 42.
62 Fleming, *Thuderball*, 118.
63 Ibid., 117.
64 Fleming, "For Your Eyes Only," 68.
65 Fleming, *Casino Royale*, 48.
66 Ibid., 107 (emphasis added).
67 Fleming, *From Russia, With Love*, 160-61.
68 Bold, "'Under the Very Skirts of Britannia,'" 177.
69 Ibid.
70 Ian Fleming, *The Spy Who Loved Me* (London: Coronet Paperbacks, 1989), 154-55.
71 Fleming, *Casino Royale*, 12.
72 Amis, *The James Bond Dossier*, 35.
73 Bennett and Woollacott, *Bond and Beyond*, 115.
74 D'Abo and Cork, *Bond Girls Are Forever*, 11.
75 Fleming, *Diamonds Are Forever*, 187.
76 Bennett and Woollacott, *Bond and Beyond*, 116.
77 Fleming, *Goldfinger*, in *A James Bond Omnibus, Volume 1*, 268.
78 Ladenson, "Pussy Galore," in *The James Bond Phenomenon*, 191.
79 Tilly gazed at Pussy Galore "with worshipping eyes and lips that yearned." Fleming, *Goldfinger*, 240.
80 Ibid., 263, 269. Pussy Galore dismisses Bond at a buffet, stating that she wants to "talk secrets" with Tilly. Ibid., 263. Turning to Tilly, Pussy Galore asks, "'Don't we, yummy,'' to which Tilly responds, "'Oh yes, please, Miss Galore.'" Ibid.
81 Ibid., 269.
82 Stephen Heath, *The Sexual Fit* (London: Macmillan, 1982), 96-97.
83 Bold, "'Under the Very Skirts of Britannia,'" 175. Elisabeth Ladenson explored Tilly Masterton in greater depth. See Ladenson, "Pussy Galore," 184-99.
84 Ladenson, "Pussy Galore," 195.
85 Ibid., 188-89.
86 Ibid., 198.
87 Fleming, *Goldfinger*, 317-18.
88 Ladenson, "Pussy Galore," 193.
89 Fleming, *Casino Royale*, 189.
90 28. "Double Blind," *Casino Royale*, DVD, directed by Martin Campbell (2006; Culver City, CA: Sony Pictures Home Entertainment, 2007).
91 Fleming, *Thuderball*, 116.
92 Fleming, *Casino Royale*, 40.
93 Ibid., 32, 33.
94 Henry A. Zeiger, *Ian Fleming: The Spy Who Came In With the Gold* (New York: Duell, Sloan and Pearce, 1965), 139.
95 Fleming, *Thuderball*, 117.
96 Fleming, *Casino Royale*, 105.
97 Fleming, *Diamonds Are Forever*, 190.

98 Ibid.
99 Bennett and Woollacott, *Bond and Beyond*, 123.
100 Columbo, "Bond's Women," 102.

004
Before the Bond Girl: Women on Film

1 Julie Burchill, *Girls On Film* (London: Virgin Books, 1986), 4.
2 Marjorie Rosen, *Popcorn Venus* (New York: Avon Books, 1973), 342.
3 Elizabeth Janeway, *Man's World, Woman's Place* (New York: William Morrow, 1971), 7.
4 Jan Rosenberg, *Women's Reflections: The Feminist Film Movement* (Michigan: UMI Research Press, 1983), 1.
5 Rosen, *Popcorn Venus*, 9.
6 Molly Haskell, *From Reverence to Rape* (New York: Holt, Rinehart, and Winston, 1974), 3.
7 Ibid., vii.
8 Rosen, *Popcorn Venus*, 60.
9 Burchill, *Girls On Film*, 15.
10 Rosen, *Popcorn Venus*, 60-61.
11 Pola Negri, *Memoirs of a Star* (Garden City: Doubleday, 1970), 202-03, 227.
12 Haskell, *From Reverence to Rape*, 108.
13 Josef von Sternberg, *Fun in a Chinese Laundry* (New York: Macmillan, 1965), 120.
14 Quoted in Jeanine Basinger, *A Woman's View* (New York: Knopf, 1993), 48.
15 Haskell, *From Reverence to Rape*, 108.
16 Ibid., 115.
17 Rosen, *Popcorn Venus*, 160.
18 Ibid., 160-61.
19 Verne Bradley, "Women at Work," *National Geographic*, February 1943, 101.
20 Rosen, *Popcorn Venus*, 201.
21 Susan Hartmann, *The Homefront and Beyond: American Women in the 1940s* (Boston: G.K. Hall, 1982), 180.
22 Women's Army Corps, "Women!" *New York Times Magazine*, sec. 2, September 5, 1943, 10.
23 Rosen, *Popcorn Venus*, 210.
24 Elinor M. Herrick, "What About Woman After the War?" *New York Times Magazine*, sec. 2, September 5, 1943, 7.
25 Rosen, *Popcorn Venus*, 215.
26 Brandon French, *On the Verge Of Revolt* (New York: Frederick Ungar Publishing, 1978), xviii.
27 Jeanine Basinger, *A Woman's View* (New York: Knopf, 1993), 342.
28 Rosen, *Popcorn Venus*, 282.

29 Quoted in ibid., 293.

30 Susan J. Douglas, *Where the Girls Are* (New York: Random House, 1994), 81.

31 Haskell, *From Reverence to Rape*, ix-x.

32 Gloria Steinem, "The Moral Disarmament of Betty Coed," *Esquire*, September 1962, 97.

33 Douglas, *Where the Girls Are*, 105.

34 Tony Bennett and Janet Woollacott, *Bond and Beyond: The Political Career of a Popular Hero* (London: Palgrave Macmillan, 1987), 213.

35 Ibid.

36 Maryam d'Abo and John Cork, *Bond Girls Are Forever: The Women of James Bond* (New York: Henry N. Abrams, Inc., 2003), 107.

37 John Cork and Bruce Scivally, *James Bond: The Legacy* (New York: Harry N. Abrams, Inc., 2002), 44.

005
Introducing an Archetype: *Dr. No* and *From Russia With Love*

1 James Chapman, *Licence to Thrill: A Cultural History of the James Bond Films* (New York: Columbia University Press, 2000), 51.

2 Quoted in John Brosnan, *James Bond in the Cinema* (London: Tantivy Press, 1981), 15.

3 Richard Maibaum, "My Word is His Bond: A View From the Back Room," *Esquire*, June 1965, 140-41.

4 John Pearson, *The Life of Ian Fleming* (New York: McGraw-Hill, 1966), 220.

5 Ibid., 259-60.

6 Brosnan, *James Bond in the Cinema*, 1.

7 This classic episode was included in the DVD release of the 1967 installment of *Casino Royale*. "Casino Royale (1954)," *Casino Royale*, DVD, directed by John Huston (1967; Santa Monica, CA: MGM Home Entertainment, 2002).

8 Raymond Benson, *The James Bond Bedside Companion* (New York: Dodd, Mead & Company, 1984), 11.

9 Keith Poliakoff, "License to Copyright: The Ongoing Dispute Over the Ownership of James Bond," *Cardozo Arts & Entertainment Law Journal* 18 (2000): 387, 387.

10 McClory hired Jack Whittingham to develop a movie script together. Ibid.

11 McClory's lawsuit against Fleming took approximately three years to go to trial, but settled after 10 days. William K. Zinsser, "The Big Bond Bonanza," *Saturday Evening Post*, July 17, 1965, 80. As part of the settlement, McClory, "whose work on the 'Thunderball' story wasn't credited initially, won the right to be listed as a producer on the film version as well as the right to make a remake . . . ." James Bates, "2 Bonds? Sony Says 'Never Say Never,'" *Los Angeles Times*, October 14, 1997, D10. Fleming also agreed to acknowledge McClory in future copies of the *Thunderball* novel. Zinsser, "The Big Bond Bonanza." In 1997, the Sony

Corporation acquired all or some of McClory's rights. Poliakoff, "License to Copyright," 387-88.

12 John Cork and Bruce Scivally, *James Bond: The Legacy* (New York: Harry N. Abrams, Inc., 2002), 29.

13 Ibid., 28.

14 Patrick Macnee, nar., "Inside *Dr. No,*" directed by John Cork, *Dr. No,* special ed. DVD, directed by Terence Young (1962: Santa Monica, CA: MGM Home Entertainment, 2000); Cork and Scivally, *The Legacy*, 28.

15 Chapman, *Licence to Thrill*, 54-55.

16 Cork and Scivally, *The Legacy*, 29.

17 Ibid.

18 Andrew Rissik, *The James Bond Man: The Films of Sean Connery* (London: Elm Tree Books, 1983), 25.

19 Cork & Scivally, *The Legacy*, 29.

20 Pearson, *The Life of Ian Fleming*, 333.

21 Cork and Scivally, *The Legacy*, 31.

22 Ibid.

23 Ibid.

24 Brosnan, *James Bond in the Cinema*, 9. Connery was described as a "ruggedly good-looking, dark-browned young Scotsman." Halsey Raines, "'*Dr. No*' in a Caribbean Theater of Movie Operations," *New York Times*, March 25, 1962, 125.

25 Brosnan, *James Bond in the Cinema*, 9. Cubby Broccoli agreed: "I liked the way he moved . . . . He moves extremely well." Macnee, nar., "Inside *Dr. No*," *Dr. No*, special ed. DVD.

26 Andrew Lycett, *Ian Fleming: The Man Behind James Bond* (Atlanta: Turner Publishing, 1995), 392.

27 Cork and Scivally, *The Legacy*, 36.

28 Rissik, *The James Bond Man*, 27.

29 Pearson, *The Life of Ian Fleming*, 333.

30 Macnee, nar., "Inside *Dr. No*," *Dr. No*, special ed. DVD.

31 Cork and Scivally, *The Legacy*, 36.

32 Macnee, nar., "Inside *Dr. No*," *Dr. No*, special ed. DVD.

33 Cork and Scivally, *The Legacy*, 38.

34 Steven Jay Rubin, *The Complete James Bond Movie Encyclopedia* (Chicago: Contemporary Books, 1995), 272. According to Lois Maxwell, she was offered either the part of Sylvia Trench or Miss Moneypenny. Given that the role of Sylvia Trench required her to adorn James Bond's "pajama tops," which she did not see herself wearing, she opted for Miss Moneypenny. Macnee, nar., "Inside *Dr. No*," *Dr. No*, special ed. DVD.

35 Cork and Scivally, *The Legacy*, 38.

36 Throughout the remainder of this book, dialogue from numerous Bond films is cited and discussed. Additionally, the dialogue is accompanied by descriptions of action on screen. This material is reconstructed based solely upon the author's viewing

of the films and the actions that take place. Therefore, it neither incorporates nor reflects material from the actual screenplays utilized during filming. No attempt is made to represent that the dialogue is authoritative, and the actions attributed to the characters reflect the author's subjective perspective.

37 Chapman, *Licence to Thrill*, 87.

38 Stanley Kauffman, "Films," *New Republic*, June 15, 1963, 36.

39 Cork and Scivally, *The Legacy*, 29.

40 Alan Barnes and Marcus Hearn, *Kiss Kiss Bang! Bang!* (New York: Overlook Press, 1998), 14.

41 Rissik, *The James Bond Man*, 54.

42 Quoted in Judy Klemesrud, "Where Are All the Women Who Fell for 007?" *New York Times*, June 21, 1981, D17.

43 "The Original Bond Girl," in liner notes, *Dr. No*, special ed. DVD; Rubin, *The Complete James Bond Movie Encyclopedia*, 12.

44 Macnee, nar., "Inside *Dr. No*," *Dr. No*, special ed. DVD.

45 Quoted in Klemesrud, "Where Are All the Women Who Fell for 007?"

46 Rissik, *The James Bond Man*, 54.

47 Raines, "'*Dr. No*' in a Caribbean Theatre of Movie Operations."

48 Barnes and Hearn, *Kiss Kiss Bang! Bang!*, 15. Ironically, Barbara Bach's desire to appear on set without a bra a decade later was viewed with substantial disfavor. See Tony Bennett and Janet Woollacott, *Bond and Beyond: The Political Career of a Popular Hero* (London: Palgrave Macmillan, 1987), 245; chapter 0012.

49 Macnee, nar., "Inside *Dr. No*," *Dr. No*, special ed. DVD.

50 Philip T. Hartung, "The Screen," *Commonweal*, June 21, 1963, 355.

51 Macnee, nar., "Inside *Dr. No*," *Dr. No*, special ed. DVD.

52 Ibid.

53 For a discussion of Maurice Binder's development of the gun barrel sequence, see Cork and Scivally, *The Legacy*, 46.

54 Patrick Macnee, nar., "Silhouettes: The James Bond Titles," directed by John Cork, *You Only Live Twice,* special ed. DVD. directed by Lewis Gilbert (1967; Santa Monica, CA: MGM Home Entertainment, 2000).

55 Ibid.

56 Ibid.

57 Brosnan, *James Bond in the Cinema*, 21.

58 Cork and Scivally, *The Legacy*, 48. As noted in the text, the *Dr. No* sequence is relatively undeveloped compared to subsequent title sequences, wherein "posed figures of scantily clad or naked women play the central part." Bennett and Woollacott, *Bond and Beyond*, 153.

59 1. "Logos/Main Title," *Dr. No*, special ed. DVD.

60 Cork and Scivally, *The Legacy*, 49.

61 D'Abo and Cork, *Bond Girls Are Forever*, 24.

62 Cork and Scivally, *The Legacy*, 36.

63 Chapman, *Licence to Thrill*, 74.

64 Laura Mulvey, "Visual Pleasure and Narrative Cinema," in *Popular Television and Film: A Reader*, ed. Tony Bennett (London: BFI, 1981), 214.
65 3. "'Le Cercle' of Cards," *Dr. No*, special ed. DVD.
66 Ibid.
67 Ibid.
68 Ibid.
69 Ibid.
70 5. "Sexy Golf," in ibid.
71 Ibid.
72 Ibid.
73 Bennett and Woollacott, *Bond and Beyond*, 213.
74 D'Abo and Cork, *Bond Girls Are Forever*, 27.
75 Ibid.
76 Bennett and Woollacott, *Bond and Beyond*, 228.
77 Chapman, *Licence to Thrill*, 75.
78 D'Abo and Cork, *Bond Girls Are Forever*, 132.
79 15. "Oops! Missing Files," *Dr. No*, special ed. DVD.
80 Ibid.
81 17. "Road Runner," in ibid.
82 D'Abo and Cork, *Bond Girls Are Forever*, 27.
83 18. "Stalling a Spy," *Dr. No*, special ed. DVD.
84 Rubin, *The Complete James Bond Movie Encyclopedia*, 269.
85 18. "Stalling a Spy," *Dr. No*, special ed. DVD.
86 Ibid.
87 Ibid.
88 Ibid.
89 Andy Lane and Paul Simpson, *The Bond Files* (London: Virgin, 1998), 127.
90 18. "Stalling a Spy," *Dr. No*, special ed. DVD.
91 D'Abo and Cork, *Bond Girls Are Forever*, 27.
92 Zena Marshall recalled that during filming of the bedroom scene, she was "wearing little panties. No bra, but we pinned the sheets on either side very carefully in case something would show . . . ." Ibid., 146.
93 Ibid., 27.
94 18. "Stalling a Spy," *Dr. No*, special ed. DVD.
95 D'Abo and Cork, *Bond Girls Are Forever*, 27.
96 D'Abo and Cork nonetheless disagreed, stating that "Sylvia Trench, Miss Taro and Honey Ryder were strong-willed, resourceful, and sexually independent." Ibid., 29. Certainly, this assessment is subject to debate.
97 "The Current Cinema: Yes to 'No,'" *New Yorker*, June 1, 1963, 66.
98 Benson, *The James Bond Bedside Companion*, 170.
99 "No, No, A Thousand Times No," *Time*, October 19, 1962, 63.
100 "Cinema: Hairy Marshmallow," *Time*, May 31, 1963, 80.
101 Rissik, *The James Bond Man*, 54.

[102] D'Abo and Cork, *Bond Girls Are Forever*, 27.
[103] 20. "Shell-Shocked," *Dr. No*, special ed. DVD.
[104] Ibid.
[105] Gary Giblin and Lisa Neyhouse, "James Bond and the Feminist Mistake," July 5, 2000, http://www.secretintel.com/features/feminist1.html.
[106] D'Abo and Cork, *Bond Girls Are Forever*, 29.
[107] "The Current Cinema: Yes to 'No.'"
[108] Macnee, nar., "Inside *Dr. No*," *Dr. No*, special ed. DVD.
[109] Rissik, *The James Bond Man*, 54.
[110] 21. "Wading Into Trouble," *Dr. No*, special ed. DVD.
[111] 20. "Shell-Shocked," in ibid.
[112] Ibid.
[113] Macnee, nar., "Inside *Dr. No*," in ibid.
[114] 20. "Shell-Shocked," in ibid.
[115] Giblin and Neyhouse, "James Bond and the Feminist Mistake."
[116] D'Abo and Cork, *Bond Girls Are Forever*, 29.
[117] Ibid.
[118] 26. "Dinner with the Dr.," *Dr. No*, special ed. DVD.
[119] 32. "Happily Lost At Sea," in ibid.
[120] Ibid.
[121] D'Abo and Cork, *Bond Girls Are Forever*, 29.
[122] Macnee, nar., "Inside *Dr. No*," *Dr. No*, special ed. DVD.
[123] Ben Macintyre, *For Your Eyes Only: Ian Fleming + James Bond* (New York: Bloomsbury, 2008), 144.
[124] Chapman, *Licence to Thrill*, 84.
[125] Maibaum, "My Word is His Bond: A View From the Back Room."
[126] Bennett and Woollacott, *Bond and Beyond*, 153.
[127] Producers changed Fleming's Russian counterespionage service SMERSH to the private organization SPECTRE in order to "sidestep any political issues." Patrick Macnee, nar., "Inside *From Russia With Love*," directed by John Cork, *From Russia With Love*, special ed. DVD, directed by Terence Young (1962; Santa Monica, CA: MGM Home Entertainment, 2000).
[128] 7. "Tatiana Meets Klebb," in ibid.
[129] Ibid.
[130] Ibid.
[131] Ibid.
[132] Ibid.
[133] Ibid.
[134] Ibid.
[135] Ibid.
[136] Rissik, *The James Bond Man*, 55.
[137] Hollis Alpert, "*SR* Goes to the Movies," *Saturday Review*, April 18, 1964, 29.
[138] Cork and Scivally, *The Legacy*, 50.

139 Ibid., 58. But producers did not reach a decision about the casting of Bianchi until production was about to commence. Macnee, nar. "Inside *From Russia With Love*," *From Russia With Love*, special ed. DVD.

140 Cork and Scivally, *The Legacy*, 58.

141 Ibid., 50.

142 Macnee, nar., "Inside *From Russia With Love*," *From Russia With Love*, special ed. DVD.

143 D'Abo and Cork, *Bond Girls Are Forever*, 159.

144 "Once More Unto the Breach," *Time*, April 10, 1964, 125.

145 14. "Spying On The Enemy," *From Russia With Love*, special ed. DVD.

146 D'Abo and Cork, *Bond Girls Are Forever*, 31.

147 Ibid.

148 Chapman, *Licence to Thrill*, 95.

149 D'Abo and Cork, *Bond Girls Are Forever*, 31.

150 7. "Tatiana Meets Klebb," *From Russia With Love*, special ed. DVD; Chapman, *Licence to Thrill*, 95.

151 Macnee, nar., "Inside *From Russia With Love*," *From Russia With Love*, special ed. DVD.

152 Benson, *The James Bond Bedside Companion*, 175. Daniela Bianchi noted that Lotta Lenya's casting was comical because Lenya "was a very small, very sweet woman" and Terence Young "had chosen her for the role of a tough villain," a role that was "totally different from what she was." Macnee, nar., "Inside *From Russia With Love*," *From Russia With Love*, special ed. DVD.

153 7. "Tatiana Meets Klebb," *From Russia With Love*, special ed. DVD. According to Bianchi, no one could see anything out of the thick glasses Lenya adorned for the part of Klebb. Macnee, nar., "Inside *From Russia With Love,*" in ibid.

154 7. "Tatiana Meets Klebb," in ibid.

155 Ibid.

156 "Once More Unto the Breach."

157 8. "Bond's Mission," *From Russia With Love*, special ed. DVD.

158 Ibid.

159 Ibid.

160 Ibid.

161 19. "Murder in the Mosque," in ibid.

162 Ibid.

163 D'Abo and Cork, *Bond Girls Are Forever*, 31.

164 12. "Checking for Bugs," *From Russia With Love*, special ed. DVD.

165 Ibid.

166 Ibid.

167 13. "Explosive Close Call," in ibid.

168 Ibid.

169 D'Abo and Cork, *Bond Girls Are Forever*, 31.

170 15. "The Gypsy Camp," *From Russia With Love*, special ed. DVD.

[171] Brosnan, *James Bond in the Cinema*, 56.

[172] Macnee, nar., "Inside *From Russia With Love*," *From Russia With Love*, special ed. DVD.

[173] Rubin, *The Complete James Bond Movie Encyclopedia*, 173.

[174] Macnee, nar., "Inside *From Russia With Love*," *From Russia With Love*, special ed. DVD.

[175] D'Abo and Cork, *Bond Girls Are Forever*, 23. The actresses worked with stunt arranger Peter Perkins for three weeks to perfect the choreography and rehearse. Macnee, nar., "Inside *From Russia With Love*," *From Russia With Love*, special ed. DVD.

[176] Lee Pfeiffer and Dave Worrall, *The Essential Bond* (New York: HarperCollins, 1999), 25.

[177] 15. "The Gypsy Camp," *From Russia With Love*, special ed. DVD.

[178] Ibid.

[179] Ibid.

[180] Stanley Kauffman, "Films," *New Republic*, April 25, 1964, 26.

[181] Giblin and Neyhouse, "James Bond and the Feminist Mistake."

[182] Macnee, nar., "Inside *From Russia With Love*," *From Russia With Love*, special ed. DVD.

[183] D'Abo and Cork, *Bond Girls Are Forever*, 31.

[184] Quoted in ibid., 146.

[185] 18. "Meeting Tatiana," *From Russia With Love*, special ed. DVD.

[186] Ibid.

[187] D'Abo and Cork, *Bond Girls Are Forever*, 31.

[188] Hollis Alpert, "*SR* Goes to the Movies: Think Big," *Saturday Review*, December 12, 1964, 42.

[189] 19. "Murder in the Mosque," *From Russia With Love*, special ed. DVD.

[190] Ibid.

[191] Ibid.

[192] D'Abo and Cork, *Bond Girls Are Forever*, 31.

[193] 21. "The Orient Express," *From Russia With Love*, special ed. DVD.

[194] Ibid.

[195] Ibid.

[196] Ibid.

[197] Brosnan, *James Bond in the Cinema*, 61.

[198] 21. "The Orient Express," *From Russia With Love*, special ed. DVD.

[199] Ibid.

[200] D'Abo and Cork, *Bond Girls Are Forever*, 31.

[201] 22. "A Tragic Discovery," *From Russia With Love*, special ed. DVD.

[202] D'Abo and Cork, *Bond Girls Are Forever*, 31.

[203] Maibaum, "My Word is His Bond."

[204] 26. "Escaping The Train," *From Russia With Love*, special ed. DVD.

[205] D'Abo and Cork, *Bond Girls Are Forever*, 31.

206 30. "Klebb Gets Her Kicks," *From Russia With Love*, special ed. DVD.
207 "Films: From Russia With Love," *America*, April 25, 1964, 580.
208 Shana Alexander, "Jolly Good Show by Agent 007," *Life*, April 3, 1964, 51.
209 "Films: From Russia With Love."
210 Stanley Kauffman, "Films," *New Republic*, June 15, 1963, 36.
211 Rissik, *The James Bond Man*, 54.
212 Ibid., 55.
213 D'Abo and Cork, *Bond Girls Are Forever*, 111.

006
A Mystique of Femininity: Marriage, Conformity, and a New Voice

1 Quoted in Jane Howard, "'You're a Freak if You Have a Brain,'" *Life*, November 1, 1963, 87.
2 George Sumner Albee, "Let's Put Women In Their Place," *Saturday Evening Post*, December 16, 1961, 8.
3 Vivian Gornick, "Why Women Fear Success," *New York Magazine*, December 20, 1971, 50.
4 Waverley Root, "Women are Intellectually Inferior," *The American Mercury*, October 1949, 413.
5 Ibid., 408.
6 Elaine Tyler May, *Homeward Bound: American Families in the Cold War Era* (New York: BasicBooks, 1988), 119.
7 Betty Friedan, *The Feminine Mystique* (New York: W.W. Norton, 2001), 274.
8 Dr. George Gallup and Evan Hill, "The American Woman," *Saturday Evening Post*, December 22-29, 1962, 16.
9 Rozanne M. Brooks, "Woman's Place is in the Wrong: The 'Loyal Opposition,'" in *Vital Speeches of the Day*, December 15, 1961, 151-52.
10 Friedan, *The Feminine Mystique*, 58.
11 Edna G. Rostow, "The Best of Both Worlds: Feminism and Femininity," *Yale Review*, March 1962, 384, 391.
12 Mary I. Bunting, "Our Greatest Waste of Talent is Women," *Life*, January 13, 1961, 64.
13 Editorial, "Are We Wasting Women?" *Life*, July 28, 1961, 36B.
14 May, *Homeward Bound*, 149.
15 Brooks, "Woman's Place is in the Wrong," 154.
16 Edward D. Eddy, Jr., "What's the Use of Educating Women?" *Saturday Review*, May 18, 1963, 66+.
17 Ibid., 67.
18 Ibid., 68.
19 Pauline Thompkins, "Change and Challenge for the Educated Woman," *Saturday Review*, May 18, 1963, 70.

20 Quoted in ibid., 82.

21 Editorial, "Are We Wasting Women?"

22 Gallup and Hill, "The American Woman," 18.

23 Ibid., 28.

24 Howard, "'You're a Freak if You Have a Brain,'" 88.

25 Gallup and Hill, "The American Woman," 28.

26 Ibid.

27 Simone de Beauvoir, *The Second Sex*, trans. H. M. Parshley (New York: Knopf, 1953), in *The Feminist Papers: From Adams to de Beauvoir*, ed. Alice S. Rossi (New York: Columbia University Press, 1973), 680-81, 683.

28 Kathleen C. Berkeley, *The Women's Liberation Movement in America* (Connecticut: Greenwood Press, 1999), 19.

29 Cynthia Harrison, *On Account of Sex: The Politics of Women's Issues, 1945-1968* (Berkeley: University of California Press, 1988), 76.

30 Lee Graham, "Who's In Charge Here?—Not Women!" *New York Times Magazine*, September 2, 1962, 8.

31 Patricia G. Zelman, *Women, Work, and National Policy: The Kennedy-Johnson Years* (Ann Arbor: UMI Research Press, 1982), 25.

32 "Executive Order No. 10980," *Code of Federal Regulations* Title 3, Ch.2, 138 (1961 Supp.).

33 U.S. Department of Labor, "Nomination of Esther Peterson to be Director of the Women's Bureau," http://library.dol.gov/special/daycare/peterson.htm.

34 Zelman, *Women, Work, and National Policy*, 26.

35 Berkeley, *The Women's Liberation Movement in America*, 24.

36 President's Commission on the Status of Women, *American Women: Report* (Washington, D.C.: Government Printing Office, 1967), in Zelman, *Women, Work, and National Policy*, 33.

37 In 1962, one writer noted:

> In the areas of discrimination, some of the worst examples lie in the area of employment. Although job-evaluation techniques may indicate that a woman is doing the same work as a man, surveys made by the Bureau of Labor Statistics reveal a double wage standard in every business, industry and profession.

Graham, "Who's In Charge Here?—Not Women!"

38 Harrison, *On Account of Sex*, 95-105.

39 Friedan, *The Feminine Mystique*, 517.

40 Marjorie Hunter, "U.S. Panel Urges Women to Sue for Equal Rights," *New York Times*, October 12, 1963.

41 Graham, "Who's In Charge Here?—Not Women!"

42 Ibid.

43 Friedan, *The Feminine Mystique*, 517.

44 Hannah Lees, "Women Should Not Play Dumb," *Saturday Evening Post*, January 28, 1961, 27.
45 Ibid., 68.
46 Marion K. Sanders, "A Proposition for Women," *Harper's Magazine*, September 1960, 43.
47 Mary Freeman, "The Marginal Sex," *Commonweal*, February 2, 1962, 484.
48 Bunting, "Our Greatest Waste of Talent is Women," 64.
49 Sanders, "A Proposition for Women," 44.
50 Ibid., 43.
51 C.J. McNaspy, "Three Old Ladies Shouting," *America*, March 25, 1961, 815.
52 Ibid.
53 Sanders, "A Proposition for Women," 44, 48.
54 Ibid., 41.
55 Richard H. Rovere, "Women of America, Now is the Time to Arise: Yes!" *Esquire*, July 1962, 31.
56 Ibid., 116.
57 Editorial, "Are We Wasting Women?"
58 Sanders, "A Proposition for Women," 48.
59 Rovere, "Women of America, Now is the Time to Arise: Yes!" 31.
60 Ibid., 116.
61 Jules Feiffer, "Men Really Don't Like Women," *Look*, January 11, 1966, 60.
62 Berkeley, *The Women's Liberation Movement in America*, 122.
63 Friedan, *The Feminine Mystique*, 50.
64 Betty Friedan, *It Changed My Life: Writings on the Women's Movement* (Cambridge, Mass.: Harvard University Press, 1998), vii.
65 Daniel Horowitz, *Betty Friedan and the Making of* The Feminine Mystique (Amherst: University of Massachusetts Press, 1998), 3.
66 Friedan, *The Feminine Mystique*, 237.
67 Ibid., 58.
68 Ibid., 217-18.
69 Horowitz, *Betty Friedan*, 3.
70 Friedan, *The Feminine Mystique*, 426.
71 Ibid., 167.
72 Quoted in Francine Klagsbrun, *The First Ms. Reader* (New York: Warner Paperback, 1973), 153-55.
73 Betty Friedan, *Life So Far* (New York: Simon & Schuster, 2000), 128.
74 Sigmund Freud, *The Psychology of Women* (New York: W.W. Norton, 1933), 157.
75 Ernest Jones, *The Life and Work of Sigmund Freud* (New York: Basic Books, 1961), 118.
76 Ibid.
77 Ibid.
78 Friedan, *The Feminine Mystique*, 172.
79 Friedan, *Life So Far*, 129.

80 Friedan, *The Feminine Mystique*, 184.
81 Friedan, *Life So Far*, 128.
82 Friedan, *The Feminine Mystique*, 461.
83 Ibid., 461-62.
84 Ibid., 490.
85 Howard, "'You're a Freak if You Have a Brain.'"
86 Paul Foley, "Whatever Happened to Women's Rights?" *Atlantic Monthly*, March 1964, 65.
87 Wilfrid Sheed, "The Second Sex, Etc., Etc.," *Commonweal*, March 27, 1964, 15.
88 Ibid., 16.
89 Horowitz, *Betty Friedan*, 216.
90 Sheed, "The Second Sex, Etc., Etc.," 15.
91 Horowitz, *Betty Friedan*, 218.
92 Marion K. Sanders, "The New American Feminism: Demi-Feminism Takes Over," *Harper's Magazine*, July 1965, 37+, 39.
93 Feiffer, "Men Really Don't Like Women."
94 Ibid.
95 Judith Hennessee, *Betty Friedan: Her Life* (New York: Random House, 1999), 80.
96 "The Weaker Sex?" *Newsweek*, July 1, 1963, 47.
97 Ibid.
98 Sanders, "A Proposition for Women," 48.
99 Dana Broccoli recalled that "female audiences were welcoming" the changes of the sexual revolution and the portrayal of the Bond Girl on film. Maryam d'Abo and John Cork, *Bond Girls Are Forever: The Women of James Bond* (New York: Henry N. Abrams, Inc., 2003), 111.

007
Reinforcing an Archetype: *Goldfinger* and *Thunderball*

1 Andrew Rissik, *The James Bond Man: The Films of Sean Connery* (London: Elm Tree Books, 1983), 43.
2 Quoted in Maryam d'Abo and John Cork, *Bond Girls Are Forever: The Women of James Bond* (New York: Henry N. Abrams, Inc., 2003), 38.
3 "The Bond Files; James Bond," *Playboy*, June 1, 2000, 84.
4 *Bond Girls Are Forever*, limited ed. DVD, directed by John Watkin (2002; Santa Monica, CA: MGM Home Entertainment, 2003).
5 Patrick Macnee, nar., "The *Goldfinger* Phenomenon," directed by John Cork, *Goldfinger*, special ed. DVD, directed by Guy Hamilton (1964; Santa Monica, CA: MGM Home Entertainment, 1999).
6 John Cork and Bruce Scivally, *James Bond: The Legacy* (New York: Harry N. Abrams, Inc., 2002), 63.

[7] Rissik, *The James Bond Man*, 82.

[8] James Chapman, *Licence to Thrill: A Cultural History of the James Bond Films* (New York: Columbia University Press, 2000), 99.

[9] Lee Pfeiffer and Dave Worrall, *The Essential Bond* (New York: Harper Paperbacks, 1999), 34.

[10] Rissik, *The James Bond Man*, 82.

[11] Steven Jay Rubin, *The Complete James Bond Movie Encyclopedia* (Chicago: Contemporary Books, 1995), 162. In fact, the DeMille theater in Manhattan opened for twenty-four hours on Christmas Eve in 1964, but wound up not closing until the new year. Cork and Scivally, *The Legacy*, 79.

[12] "Bondomania," *Time*, June 11, 1965, 69.

[13] Macnee, nar., "The *Goldfinger* Phenomenon," *Goldfinger*, special ed. DVD.

[14] Cork and Scivally, *The Legacy*, 81.

[15] Jeff Smith, "Creating a Bond Market: Selling John Barry's Soundtracks and Theme Songs," in *The James Bond Phenomenon: A Critical Reader*, ed. Christoph Lindner (Manchester: Manchester University Press, 2003), 128. Like with *Goldfinger*, theaters remained open for twenty-four hours to accommodate the large crowds waiting to see *Thunderball*. Patrick Macnee, nar., "The Making of *Thunderball*," directed by John Cork, *Thunderball*, special ed. DVD, directed by Terence Young (1965: Santa Monica, CA: MGM Home Entertainment, 1999).

[16] Alexis Albion, "Wanting to Be James Bond," in *Ian Fleming and James Bond: The Cultural Politics of 007*, eds. Edward P. Comentale, Stephen Watt and Skip Willman (Bloomington: Indiana University Press, 2005), 215 n. 2.

[17] Greg Hernandez, "Bond is MGM's Man with the Golden Touch," *Daily News of Los Angeles*, November 22, 2002, N1

[18] John Brosnan, *James Bond in the Cinema* (London: Tantivy Press, 1981), 75. According to Brosnan, "after *Goldfinger* there was nothing new that could be done with James Bond and his world. From then on, it was a case of the makers being forced to repeat the formula again and again, only making it more lavish each time." Ibid., 75-76.

[19] Macnee, nar., "The *Goldfinger* Phenomenon," *Goldfinger*, special ed. DVD.

[20] Philip T. Hartung, "The Screen," *Commonweal*, December 18, 1964, 422.

[21] Rubin, *The Complete James Bond Movie Encyclopedia*, 162.

[22] Macnee, nar., "The *Goldfinger* Phenomenon," *Goldfinger*, special ed. DVD (emphasis added).

[23] Hartung, "The Screen."

[24] Macnee, nar., "The *Goldfinger* Phenomenon," *Goldfinger*, special ed. DVD.

[25] Nick Foulkes and others, *Dressed To Kill*, ed. Jay McInerney (Paris: Flammarion, 1996), 23.

[26] Macnee, nar., "The *Goldfinger* Phenomenon," *Goldfinger*, special ed. DVD.

[27] "25 Years of James Bond," *Playboy*, September 1987, 124+, 131.

[28] Alan Barnes and Marcus Hearn, *Kiss Kiss Bang! Bang!* (New York: Overlook Press, 1998), 36.

29 Cork and Scivally, *The Legacy*, 63.

30 Rubin, *The Complete James Bond Movie Encyclopedia*, 45.

31 3. "Unfinished Business," *Goldfinger*, special ed. DVD.

32 Rodger Streitmatter, *Sex Sells!: The Media's Journey From Repression to Obsession* (Cambridge: Westview Press, 2004), 38-39.

33 3. "Unfinished Business," *Goldfinger*, special ed. DVD.

34 Ibid.

35 Brosnan, *James Bond in the Cinema*, 77 (emphasis added).

36 Cork and Scivally, *The Legacy*, 63.

37 3. "Unfinished Business," *Goldfinger*, special ed. DVD.

38 Brosnan, *James Bond in the Cinema*, 75.

39 Shirley Eaton, "Best of Times, Worst of Times," *Sunday Times Magazine* (U.K.), November 7, 1999, 17. Shirley Eaton was not the first Bond Girl to be painted head to toe. Ursula Andress, whose skin color was deemed too light to portray a native Caribbean seashell diver, received full-body makeup applications to darken her skin tone during the filming of *Dr. No.* Patrick Macnee, nar., "Inside *Dr. No,*" directed by John Cork, *Dr. No,* special ed. DVD, directed by Terence Young (1962: Santa Monica, CA: MGM Home Entertainment, 2000).

40 Macnee, nar., "The Goldfinger Phenomenon," *Goldfinger*, special ed. DVD; Graham Rye, *The James Bond Girls* (New York: Carol Publishing Group, 1996), 11. Margaret Nolan proclaimed that she, too, was a golden girl, which earned her "a few inches of text in the tabloids." D'Abo and Cork, *Bond Girls Are Forever*, 159.

41 Danny Biederman, liner notes, *The Best of James Bond 30th Anniversary Collection*, EMI Records USA compact disc E2-98413, 1992.

42 Leslie Bricusse, Anthony Newley, and John Barry, *Goldfinger*, Shirley Bassey perf. in ibid.

43 Ibid.

44 Ibid.

45 Richard M. Hodgens, "Brutalized Dragon-Slayer," *National Review*, February 9, 1965, 116.

46 4. "Main Title/Credit," *Goldfinger*, special ed. DVD.

47 Ibid.

48 5. "In Good Hands," in ibid.

49 6. "Pigeon Game," in ibid.

50 Eaton, "Best of Times, Worst of Times." Shirley Eaton recalled:

> I was just sitting [at the premiere of *Goldfinger*], and suddenly I heard this prissy voice coming out of my mouth, not my voice at all. God knows why my voice was dumped, I've never got the real explanation. But funnily enough they hadn't dubbed all my dialogue: I didn't have many lines—about five in all—and when I say "Not too early," that's my voice.

Ibid.

51 Rubin, *The Complete James Bond Movie Encyclopedia*, 271.
52 Pfeiffer and Worrall, *The Essential Bond*, 35.
53 7. "Spying on a Spy," *Goldfinger*, special ed. DVD.
54 Ibid.
55 Ibid.
56 Brosnan, *James Bond in the Cinema*, 79.
57 Elisabeth Ladenson, "Pussy Galore," in *The James Bond Phenomenon*, 191.
58 D'Abo and Cork, *Bond Girls Are Forever*, 35.
59 9. "Smothered in Gold," *Goldfinger*, special ed. DVD.
60 7. "Spying on a Spy," in ibid.
61 Ibid.
62 Eaton, "Best of Times, Worst of Times."
63 7. "Tatiana Meets Klebb," *From Russia With Love*, special ed. DVD, directed by Terence Young (1962; Santa Monica, CA: MGM Home Entertainment, 2000).
64 7. "Spying on a Spy," *Goldfinger*, special ed. DVD.
65 Ibid.
66 D'Abo and Cork, *Bond Girls Are Forever*, 35.
67 Eaton, "Best of Times, Worst of Times."
68 Chapman, *Licence to Thrill*, 103.
69 9. "Smothered in Gold," *Goldfinger*, special ed. DVD.
70 Cork and Scivally, *The Legacy*, 70.
71 Eaton, "Best of Times, Worst of Times."
72 "Agent 007 Takes On a Solid-Gold Cad," *Life*, November 6, 1964, 116+, 118.
73 Brosnan, *James Bond in the Cinema*, 81; "Oedipus Wrecks," *Newsweek*, December 1, 1964, 72.
74 Cork and Scivally, *The Legacy*, 70.
75 Chapman, *Licence to Thrill*, 103.
76 Pfeiffer and Worrall, *The Essential Bond*, 36.
77 D'Abo and Cork, *Bond Girls Are Forever*, 36.
78 15. "Snagging a Sniper," *Goldfinger*, special ed. DVD.
79 Ibid.
80 Ibid.
81 Landenson, "Pussy Galore," 191.
82 17. "Sisterly Revenge," *Goldfinger*, special ed. DVD.
83 Ibid.
84 Ibid.
85 Chapman, *Licence to Thrill*, 106.
86 Cork and Scivally, *The Legacy*, 70.
87 Barnes and Hearn, *Kiss Kiss Bang! Bang!*, 34.
88 Quoted in d'Abo and Cork, *Bond Girls Are Forever*, 19.
89 Arnie Kogen, "8 'James Bomb' Bomb Movies," *Mad*, March 1974, 8.
90 Cork and Scivally, *The Legacy*, 70.
91 Macnee, nar., "The Goldfinger Phenomenon.," *Goldfinger*, special ed. DVD.

92 Ibid.

93 Rye, *The James Bond Girls*, 11.

94 Rubin, *The Complete James Bond Movie Encyclopedia*, 155.

95 Cork and Scivally, *The Legacy*, 70.

96 Ibid.

97 Kogen, "8 'James Bond' Bomb Movies." *Mad* also satirized *Dr. No*, referring to the film as "Dr. No-No" and Honey Ryder as "Honey Roper" and "Miss Yes-Yes." Ibid.

98 See *Austin Powers: International Man of Mystery*, DVD, directed by Jay Roach (1997; Los Angeles, CA: New Line Home Entertainment, 2004).

99 See *Austin Powers: The Spy Who Shagged Me*, DVD, directed by Jay Roach (1999; Los Angeles, CA: New Line Home Entertainment, 2004).

100 See *Austin Powers in Goldmember*, DVD, directed by Jay Roach (2002; Los Angeles, CA: New Line Home Entertainment, 2002).

101 D'Abo and Cork, *Bond Girls Are Forever*, 35.

102 Landenson, "Pussy Galore," 197.

103 21. "Shaken Not Stirred," *Goldfinger*, special ed. DVD.

104 Ibid.

105 Ibid.

106 22. "Spy Peeping," in ibid.

107 Hollis Alpert, "*SR* Goes to the Movies: Think Big," *Saturday Review*, December 12, 1964, 42.

108 Rye, *The James Bond Girls*, 11.

109 Gary Giblin and Lisa Neyhouse, "James Bond and the Feminist Mistake," July 5, 2000, http://www.secretintel.com/features/feminist1.html.

110 28. "Mint Julip Madness," *Goldfinger*, special ed. DVD.

111 21. "Shaken Not Stirred," in ibid.

112 Ibid.

113 22. "Spy Peeping," in ibid.

114 Ibid.

115 Ibid.

116 Ibid.

117 Chapman, *Licence to Thrill*, 108.

118 22. "Spy Peeping," *Goldfinger*, special ed. DVD (emphasis added).

119 Giblin and Neyhouse, "James Bond and the Feminist Mistake."

120 25. "Spy Games," *Goldfinger*, special ed. DVD.

121 Ibid.

122 22. "Spy Peeping," in ibid.

123 Ibid.

124 Chapman, *Licence to Thrill*, 107. Chapman noted that "'the implication of lesbianism is thrown in for good measure.'" Ibid.

125 23. "Pretty Piper Pilots," *Goldfinger*, special. ed. DVD.

126 27. "Pressing Engagement," in ibid.

127 28. "Mint Julip Madness," in ibid.

128 25. "Spy Games," in ibid. As Bond later states and Goldfinger acknowledges, the gas is lethal.

129 Ibid.

130 28. "Mint Julip Madness," in ibid.

131 This observation is markedly different from the one advanced by Tony Bennett and Janet Woollacott, who suggested that Pussy Galore is "treated with respect by Goldfinger." Tony Bennett and Janet Woollacott, *Bond and Beyond: The Political Career of a Popular Hero* (London: Palgrave Macmillan, 1987), 157.

132 29. "'That's My James,'" *Goldfinger*, special ed. DVD.

133 Ibid.

134 Ibid.

135 Ibid.

136 Ibid.

137 Ibid.

138 Ibid.

139 Ibid.

140 D'Abo and Cork, *Bond Girls Are Forever*, 35.

141 "Oedipus Wrecks."

142 Chapman, *Licence to Thrill*, 106.

143 Quoted in Judy Klemesrud, "Where Are All the Women Who Fell for 007?" *New York Times*, June 21, 1981, D17

144 "An Immensely Successful Film Formula," *Times* (U.K.), September 17, 1964, 15.

145 *Bond Girls Are Forever*, limited ed. DVD.

146 They argue that no sexual repositioning of Pussy Galore occurs because she "is not required to 'submit' to Bond; rather she is required to 'choose' Bond as a sexual partner rather than the villain or anyone else." Bennett and Woollacott, *Bond and Beyond*, 163.

147 "Letters from Paris," *New Yorker*, March 25, 1965, 166.

148 Giblin and Neyhouse, "James Bond and the Feminist Mistake."

149 Bennett and Woollacott, *Bond and Beyond*, 157.

150 31. "The Man of Steel," *Goldfinger*, special ed. DVD.

151 Ibid.

152 Bennett and Woollacott, *Bond and Beyond*, 164.

153 Ibid., 157.

154 D'Abo and Cork, *Bond Girls Are Forever*, 36.

155 32. "No Time For Rescues," *Goldfinger*, special ed. DVD.

156 D'Abo and Cork, *Bond Girls Are Forever*, 36.

157 Ibid.

158 Ibid., 35.

159 Macnee, nar., "The Making of *Thunderball*," *Thunderball*, special ed. DVD.

160 Macnee, nar., "The *Thunderball* Phenomenon," in ibid.

161 Cork and Scivally, *The Legacy*, 80.

[162] Richard Schickel, "007 and a Grimy Cousin Are Out in the Cold," *Life*, January 7, 1966, 8.

[163] Philip T. Hartung, "The Screen: 007, 8, 9, etc.," *Commonweal*, February 11, 1966, 559.

[164] "Of Super Human Bondage: Thunderball," *Times* (U.K.), December 29, 1965, 10.

[165] "Subaqueous Spy," *Time*, December 24, 1965, 46.

[166] Cork and Scivally, *The Legacy*, 87.

[167] Brendan Gill, "The Current Cinema: Murder Under the Sea," *New Yorker*, January 8, 1966, 101.

[168] Louis B. Parks, "Bonded and Rated: With Films From Terrible to Terrific, 007 Guide Gives Fans a Run for Their Money," *Houston Chronicle*, November 27, 1999, 7.

[169] Cork and Scivally, *The Legacy*, 87.

[170] "Boring From Within," *Newsweek*, January 3, 1966, 56.

[171] Gill, "The Current Cinema: Murder Under the Sea."

[172] Ibid.

[173] Ibid.

[174] "Subaqueous Spy."

[175] "007 Knows What to Do," *Life*, January 7, 1966, 79.

[176] Patrick Macnee, nar., "Inside *Thunderball*," *Thunderball*, special ed. DVD.

[177] Parks, "Bonded and Rated."

[178] Macnee, nar., "The Making of *Thunderball*," *Thunderball*, special ed. DVD.

[179] 1. "Logos/Black Widow," in ibid.

[180] Ibid.

[181] Ibid.

[182] Brosnan, *James Bond in the Cinema*, 100-01.

[183] Barnes and Hearn, *Kiss Kiss Bang! Bang!*, 53. Maurice Binder has been described as "the real hero of the series" for his lavish and "dazzling" title sequences. Janet Maslin, "The Screen: James Bond," *New York Times*, May 24, 1985, C10.

[184] Rubin, *The Complete James Bond Movie Encyclopedia*, 37.

[185] Barnes and Hearn, *Kiss Kiss Bang! Bang!*, 53.

[186] Patrick Macnee, nar., "Silhouettes: The James Bond Titles," directed by John Cork, *You Only Live Twice*, special ed. DVD. directed by Lewis Gilbert (1967; Santa Monica, CA: MGM Home Entertainment, 2000).

[187] "Subaqueous Spy."

[188] "Bondomania."

[189] Initially, John Barry's "Mister Kiss Kiss Bang Bang" was conceived as the theme song for *Thunderball*, but it was ultimately abandoned. Macnee, nar., "The *Thunderball* Phenomenon," *Thunderball*, special ed. DVD.

[190] "Thunderball" was a Top 25 hit. Smith, "Creating a Bond Market: Selling John Barry's Soundtracks and Theme Songs," in *The James Bond Phenomenon*, 128.

[191] John Barry and Don Black, *Thunderball*, Tom Jones perf. *The Best of James Bond 30th Anniversary Collection.*

[192] 29. "Showing Off," *Thunderball*, special ed. DVD.

193 Ibid.
194 Macnee, nar., "The Making of *Thunderball*," in ibid.
195 Pfeiffer and Worrall, *The Essential Bond*, 47.
196 D'Abo and Cork, *Bond Girls Are Forever* 38. Cork and Scivally characterized her as a physical therapist. Ibid., 86.
197 6. "Rack & Sweat," *Thunderball*, special ed. DVD.
198 Ibid.
199 Ibid.
200 Ibid.
201 Ibid.
202 Ibid.
203 Ibid.
204 Ibid.
205 Pfeiffer and Worrall, *The Essential Bond*, 47.
206 "The Bond Files; James Bond."
207 "Boring From Within," *Newsweek*, January 3, 1966, 56.
208 6. "Rack & Sweat," *Thunderball*, special ed. DVD.
209 9. "Uncovering A Clue," in ibid.
210 Ibid.
211 14. "'Anytime, Any Place,'" in ibid.
212 D'Abo and Cork, *Bond Girls Are Forever* 38.
213 Macnee, nar., "The Making of *Thunderball*," *Thunderball*, special ed. DVD.
214 18. "Good Form!" in ibid.
215 Ibid.
216 Ibid.
217 24. "Special Spy Gear," in ibid.
218 Ibid.
219 30. "Double Date/Cross," in ibid.
220 31. "Power Failure," in ibid.
221 Rye, *The James Bond Girls*, 14.
222 Rubin, *The Complete James Bond Movie Encyclopedia*, 333.
223 Streitmatter, *Sex Sells!*, 38.
224 7. "Duty Calls A Twin," *Thunderball*, special ed. DVD.
225 Rubin, *The Complete James Bond Movie Encyclopedia*, 442.
226 7. "Duty Calls A Twin," *Thunderball*, special ed. DVD.
227 Ibid.
228 Ibid.
229 Ibid.
230 30. "Double Date/Cross," in ibid.
231 27. "Better Buckle Up!" in ibid.
232 Ibid.
233 28. "Photo/'Port Of Call,'" in ibid.
234 Ibid.

[235] Ibid.

[236] Brosnan, *James Bond in the Cinema*, 112.

[237] 33. "'Wild Things,'" *Thunderball*, special ed. DVD.

[238] D'Abo and Cork, *Bond Girls Are Forever*, 38.

[239] 33. "'Wild Things,'" *Thunderball*, special ed. DVD.

[240] Ibid.

[241] 34. "Battle of Egos," in ibid.

[242] "Killing Off Bond," *Esquire*, June 1965, 65.

[243] 34. "Battle of Egos," *Thunderball*, special ed. DVD.

[244] Ibid.

[245] 36. "'Kiss Kiss Club,'" in ibid.

[246] Ibid. (emphasis added).

[247] Brosnan, *James Bond in the Cinema*, 113-14.

[248] 36. "'Kiss Kiss Club,'" *Thunderball*, special ed. DVD.

[249] Hartung, "The Screen: 007, 8, 9, etc."

[250] Chapman, *Licence to Thrill*, 126.

[251] Ibid.

[252] Rye, *The James Bond Girls*, 14. In 1965, *Esquire* described Domino as "the plaything of the evil Largo." "Killing Off Bond."

[253] "James Bond Conquers All in *Thunderball*," *Look*, July 13, 1965, 47.

[254] D'Abo and Cork, *Bond Girls Are Forever* 128.

[255] In 1969, *Time* described the extent to which Raquel Welch captivated audiences, noting that one of her photographic poses, the "Mistress of James Bond," became a trademark:

> [She] has impeccable statistics. The skin stretches tight across her frame; one more inch, it seems, and she would burst like a succulent mango. Her measurements are 37-22-35; she bounces when she runs, she has legs that won't quit, and steam forms on the windows when she enters a room . . . . Raquel was among the top ten box-office draws.

"Sea of C Cups," *Time*, April 4, 1969, 94.

[256] Macnee, nar., "The Making of *Thunderball*," *Thunderball*, special ed. DVD.

[257] "Killing Off Bond."

[258] Rye, *The James Bond Girls* 14; "007 Knows What To Do."

[259] Macnee, nar., "The Making of *Thunderball*," *Thunderball*, special ed. DVD.

[260] "Killing Off Bond."

[261] Macnee, nar., "The Making of *Thunderball*," *Thunderball*, special ed. DVD.

[262] Cork and Scivally, *The Legacy*, 85.

[263] Ibid.

[264] 17. "Reassignment," *Thunderball*, special ed. DVD.

[265] Ibid.

266 18. "Good Form!" in ibid.
267 19. "Poolside Chat," in ibid.
268 Ibid.
269 Ibid.
270 Ibid.
271 Ibid.
272 20. "Taking A Gamble," in ibid.
273 21. "Dance Proposal," in ibid.
274 21. "Dance Proposal," in ibid.
275 Giblin and Neyhouse, "James Bond and the Feminist Mistake."
276 Rubin, *The Complete James Bond Movie Encyclopedia*, 105.
277 39. "Domino Affection," *Thunderball*, special ed. DVD.
278 Ibid.
279 Ibid.
280 Ibid.
281 Ibid.
282 Ibid.
283 42. "Caught With Spy Toys," in ibid.
284 Ibid.
285 Ibid.
286 Ibid.
287 Ibid.
288 Ibid.
289 Macnee, nar., "The *Goldfinger* Phenomenon," *Goldfinger*, special ed. DVD.
290 Macnee, nar., "The Making of *Thunderball*," *Thunderball*, special ed. DVD.
291 "James Bond Conquers All in *Thunderball*."
292 "Killing Off Bond."

008
Shaken & Stirred: The Feminist and Women's Liberation Movements in America

1 Reprinted in Robin Morgan, ed., *Sisterhood Is Powerful: An Anthology of Writings From the Women's Liberation Movement* (New York: Random House, 1970), 533.
2 Eleanor Perenyi, "Women of America, Now is the Time to Arise: 'Maybe(?)'" *Esquire*, July 1962, 37.
3 Ruth Brine, "Women's Lib: Beyond Sexual Politics," *Time*, July 26, 1971, 37.
4 Susan J. Douglas, *Where the Girls Are* (New York: Random House, 1994), 123.
5 Kathleen C. Berkeley, *The Women's Liberation Movement in America* (Connecticut: Greenwood Press, 1999) 27.
6 Brine, "Women's Lib: Beyond Sexual Politics."
7 Brigid Brophy, "Women are Prisoners of their Sex," *Saturday Evening Post*, November 2, 1963, 10.

8 Marjorie Carpenter, "Women, the Problem or the Answer?" in *Vital Speeches of the Day*, January 1, 1964, 185.

9 Hannah Lees, "Women Should Not Play Dumb," *Saturday Evening Post*, January 28, 1961, 27.

10 Paul Foley, "Whatever Happened to Women's Rights?" *Atlantic Monthly*, March 1964, 65.

11 Ibid.

12 Stephen's College, "About Stephens—Mission," http://www.stephens.edu/stephens/mission/.

13 Carpenter, "Women, the Problem or the Answer?"

14 Ibid., 185-86.

15 Elaine Kendall, "Why Do They Treat Women Like Guinea Pigs?" *Saturday Evening Post*, July 16, 1966, 166.

16 Quoted in Patricia G. Zelman, *Women, Work, and National Policy: The Kennedy-Johnson Years* (Ann Arbor: UMI Research Press, 1982), 45.

17 Ibid., 55.

18 42 U.S.C. § 2000e-2(a)(1)-(2) (2006).

19 Berkeley, *The Women's Liberation Movement in America*, 28.

20 *Meritor Sav. Bank, FSB v. Vinson*, 477 U.S. 57, 63 (1986) (citing 100 Cong. Rec. 2577-2584 (1964)).

21 Quoted in Zelman, *Women, Work, and National Policy*, 62.

22 Berkeley, *The Women's Liberation Movement in America*, 29.

23 Cynthia Harrison, *On Account of Sex: The Politics of Women's Issues, 1945-1968* (Berkeley: University of California Press, 1988), 191.

24 Christopher Lasch, "Feminist Ideology," *Commentary*, April 1966, 104.

25 John Herbers, "For Instance Can She Pitch for the Mets?" *New York Times*, August 20, 1965, 1.

26 "De-sexing the Job Market," *New York Times*, August 21, 1965, 20.

27 Ibid.

28 Harrison, *On Account of Sex*, 191.

29 Betty Friedan, *It Changed My Life: Writings on the Women's Movement* (New York: Random House, 1976), 82.

30 Cheryl Gibbons Bartholomew, *Gender-Sensitive Therapy: Principles and Practices* (Long Grove, Illinois: Waveland Press, 1992), 20; Janet Saltzman Chafetz, *Masculine, Feminine or Human?: An Overview of the Sociology of the Gender Roles* (Itasca, Illinois: F.E. Peacock, 1972), 106.

31 Betty Friedan, *Life So Far* (New York: Simon & Schuster, 2000), 174.

32 Judith Hole and Ellen Levine, *Rebirth of Feminism* (New York: Quadrangle, 1971), 82.

33 Judith Hennessee, *Betty Friedan: Her Life* (New York: Random House, 1999), 107.

34 Friedan, *Life So Far*, 176.

35 Ibid.

36 Excerpted from "NOW Statement of Purpose dated October 29, 1966," in Carolyn Johnston, *Sexual Power: Feminism and the Family in America* (Tuscaloosa: University of Alabama Press, 1992), 249.

37 Ibid.

38 Susan Edmiston, "How to Write Your Own Marriage Contract," *New York Magazine*, December 20, 1971, 66+, 66.

39 Ibid., 71.

40 "National Organization for Women Bill of Rights, 1968," reprinted in Hole and Levine, *Rebirth of Feminism*, 441. The bill of rights was adopted at NOW's first national conference in Washington the previous year.

41 Ibid.

42 Ibid.

43 Ibid., 442.

44 Ibid., 87.

45 Hennessee, *Betty Friedan: Her Life*, 105.

46 Kendall, "Why Do They Treat Women Like Guinea Pigs?"

47 "We Wonder What Will Happen," *America*, December 24-31, 1966, 822.

48 Ibid.

49 Ibid.

50 Daniel Horowitz, *Betty Friedan and the Making of* The Feminine Mystique (Amherst: University of Massachusetts Press, 1998), 228.

51 Douglas, *Where the Girls Are*, 144.

52 Hole and Levine, *Rebirth of Feminism*, 247.

53 Helen Dudar, "Women's Lib: The War on 'Sexism,'" *Newsweek*, March 23, 1970, 71.

54 Douglas, *Where the Girls Are*, 135-36.

55 Ibid., 27.

56 Hole and Levine, *Rebirth of Feminism*, 251.

57 "Who's Come a Long Way, Baby?" *Time*, August 31, 1970, 17.

58 Ibid.

59 Johnston, *Sexual Power*, 252.

60 Myra Marx Ferree and Beth B. Hess, *Controversy and Coalition: The New Feminist Movement* (Boston: Twayne, 1984), 224.

61 James Stuart Olson, ed., *Historical Dictionary of the 1960s* (Westport, Connecticut: Greenwood, 1999), 477-78.

62 One author explained: "[I]t remains both relevant and interesting that Obama is 'friendly' with an unrepentant terrorist who was involved in a movement that killed innocent people, and that he even accepted donations from him to his campaign." David Freddoso, *The Case Against Barack Obama: The Unlikely Rise and Unexamined Agenda of the Media's Favorite Candidate* (Washington, DC: Regnery Press, 2008), 126.

63 Irwin Unger and Debi Unger, eds., *The Times Were A Changin': The Sixties Reader* (New York: Three Rivers Press, 1998), 85; see also Olson, *Historical Dictionary of the 1960s*, 477.

64 "Who's Come a Long Way, Baby?"

65 Ibid.

66 Susan Brownmiller, *In Our Time: Memoir of a Revolution* (New York: Random House, 1999), 8.

67 Michael E. Adelstein and Jean G. Pival, eds. *Women's Liberation: Perspectives* (New York: St. Martin's Press, 1972), 21.

68 Hole and Levine, *Rebirth of Feminism*, 123.

69 Douglas, *Where the Girls Are*, 140.

70 Hole and Levine, *Rebirth of Feminism*, 123.

71 Douglas, *Where the Girls Are*, 156.

72 Brownmiller, *In Our Time*, 37.

73 Betty Rollin, "They're a Bunch of Frustrated Hags," *Look*, March 9, 1971, 16.

74 Hole and Levine, *Rebirth of Feminism*, 269.

75 Dudar, "Women's Lib: The War on 'Sexism.'"

76 "Who's Come a Long Way, Baby?"

77 Dudar, "Women's Lib: The War on 'Sexism.'"

78 "This Ad Contains A Pack of Truths," *New York Magazine*, December 20, 1971.

79 "Who's Come a Long Way, Baby?"

80 Sookie Stambler, *Women's Liberation* (New York: Ace Books, 1970), 31.

81 Women's International Terrorist Conspiracy From Hell, "Confront the Whoremakers at the Bridal Fair," in Berkeley, *The Women's Liberation Movement in America*, 164-65.

82 "Who's Come a Long Way, Baby?"

83 SCUM Manifesto, in Morgan, ed., *Sisterhood Is Powerful*, 514-15.

84 Hole and Levine, *Rebirth of Feminism*, 414.

85 Ibid., 420.

86 Edward Glynn, "How to Unnerve Male Chauvinists," *America*, September 12, 1970, 146.

87 Ibid.

88 "Ladies' Day," *Newsweek*, August 24, 1970, 16.

89 Dudar, "Women's Lib: The War on 'Sexism.'"

90 Ibid.

91 Hennessee, *Betty Friedan: Her Life*, 107.

92 Brownmiller, *In Our Time*, 8.

93 "Feminist Yearbook," *Newsweek*, November 16, 1970, 113+, 114.

94 Ibid., 113.

95 Johnston, *Sexual Power*, 255.

009
Perpetuating an Archetype: *You Only Live Twice* and *On Her Majesty's Secret Service*

1 Alan Barnes and Marcus Hearn, *Kiss Kiss Bang! Bang!* (New York: Overlook Press, 1998), 75.

2 Lee Pfeiffer and Philip Lisa, *The Incredible World of 007* (New York: Carol Publishing Group, 1995), 56.

3 Quoted in John Cork and Bruce Scivally. *James Bond: The Legacy* (New York: Harry N. Abrams, Inc., 2002), 316.

4 James Chapman, *Licence to Thrill: A Cultural History of the James Bond Films* (New York: Columbia University Press, 2000), 117.

5 "What Has Happened to the Bond Girls?" *Telegraph Sunday Magazine* (U.K.), September 17, 1978, 10.

6 Maryam d'Abo and John Cork, *Bond Girls Are Forever: The Women of James Bond* (New York: Henry N. Abrams, Inc., 2003), 107.

7 Stanley Marwick, *The Sixties: Cultural Revolution in Britain, France, Italy, and the United States* (Oxford: Oxford University Press, 1998), 680.

8 Raymond Benson, *The James Bond Bedside Companion* (New York: Dodd, Mead & Company, 1984), 188.

9 Ibid., 126.

10 Patrick Macnee, nar., "Inside *You Only Live Twice,*" directed by John Cork, *You Only Live Twice,* special ed. DVD, directed by Lewis Gilbert (1967: Santa Monica, CA: MGM Home Entertainment, 2000).

11 Cork and Scivally, *The Legacy*, 100.

12 Steven Jay Rubin, *The Complete James Bond Movie Encyclopedia* (Chicago: Contemporary Books, 1995), 97.

13 Cork and Scivally, *The Legacy*, 100.

14 D'Abo and Cork, *Bond Girls Are Forever*, 41.

15 Ibid. *Playboy* also noted that each Bond adventure featured four recognizable types: "the Angel With a Wing Down, the Naïve Beauty, the Comrade in Arms and the Villainous Vixen." "The Bond Files; James Bond," *Playboy*, June 1, 2000, 84.

16 Roald Dahl, "007's Oriental Eyefuls," *Playboy*, June 1967, 86+, 87.

17 Ibid.

18 Ibid.

19 Christopher Hitchens, "Bottoms Up: Ian Fleming, the Man Behind James Bond, Was a Sadist, a Narcissist, and an All-Around Repressed Pervert. But He Also Saw Past the Confines of the Cold War," *Atlantic Monthly*, April 1, 2006, 100+.

20 Tony Bennett and Janet Woollacott, *Bond and Beyond: The Political Career of a Popular Hero* (London: Palgrave Macmillan, 1987), 158.

21 "006 ¾," *Time*, June 30, 1967, 83.

22 Penelope Gilliatt, "The Current Cinema: Nether Villainy," *New Yorker*, June 24, 1967, 74.

23 Charles K. Feldman, who obtained the rights to *Casino Royale*, unsuccessfully sought to jointly produce the film with Broccoli and Saltzman. Cork and Scivally, *The Legacy*, 93.

24 Ibid., 97.

25 Reproduced in ibid., 108.

26 "Killing Off Bond Again," *Esquire*, March 1967, 74.

27 "A Superlatively Well Produced Film," *Times* (U.K.), June 15, 1967, 8.

28 Despite the apparent rivalry between the two films, *Casino Royale* could not compete with *You Only Live Twice*. One critic described *Casino Royale* as a "bit of a mess" that was worth foregoing because it was "not for the most part really funny (though it tries), really sexy (though it tries even harder) or, considering the fortune which was spent on it, really lavish." John Russell Taylor, "Many Hands Make Light Weight," *Times* (London), April 14, 1967, 8.

29 Macnee, nar., "Inside *You Only Live Twice*," *You Only Live Twice*, special ed. DVD.

30 Cork and Scivally, *The Legacy*, 99.

31 Macnee, nar., "Inside *You Only Live Twice*," *You Only Live Twice*, special ed. DVD.

32 Ibid.

33 Graham Rye, *The James Bond Girls* (New York: Carol Publishing Group, 1996), 19.

34 Ibid.; Dahl, "007's Oriental Eyefuls." 86.

35 "Killing Off Bond Again."

36 Dahl, "007's Oriental Eyefuls," 91.

37 Macnee, nar., "Inside *You Only Live Twice*," *You Only Live Twice*, special ed. DVD; Cork and Scivally, *The Legacy*, 99.

38 Cork and Scivally, *The Legacy*, 99.

39 Macnee, nar., "Inside *You Only Live Twice*," *You Only Live Twice*, special ed. DVD.

40 Dahl, "007's Oriental Eyefuls," 87.

41 Macnee, nar., "Inside *You Only Live Twice*," *You Only Live Twice*, special ed. DVD.

42 D'Abo and Cork, *Bond Girls Are Forever*, 146.

43 21. "Becoming Japanese," *You Only Live Twice*, special ed. DVD.

44 Ibid.

45 Ibid.

46 Gilliatt, "The Current Cinema: Nether Villainy."

47 Barnes and Hearn, *Kiss Kiss Bang! Bang!* 79.

48 Rubin, *The Complete James Bond Movie Encyclopedia*, 117.

49 2. "Dead On The Job," *You Only Live Twice*, special ed. DVD.

50 Ibid.

51 Jennifer Tung, "View; Asian 'It' Girls Say So Long to the Dragon Lady," *New York Times*, May 21, 2000, ST1+, 4.

52 2. "Dead On The Job," *You Only Live Twice*, special ed. DVD.

53 5. "Pure Guesswork," in ibid.

54 Howard Thompson, "Critics' Choices; Broadcast TV," *New York Times*, March 31, 1985, G2.

55 "A Superlatively Well Produced Film."

56 11. "Japanese Customs," *You Only Live Twice*, special ed. DVD.
57 Ibid.
58 Ibid.
59 "Killing Off Bond Again."
60 11. "Japanese Customs," *You Only Live Twice*, special ed. DVD.
61 6. "Sumo Pick-Up," in ibid.
62 "Killing Off Bond Again."
63 D'Abo and Cork, *Bond Girls Are Forever*, 42.
64 Dahl, "007's Oriental Eyefuls," 91.
65 9. "Welcome to Japan," *You Only Live Twice*, special ed. DVD.
66 Ibid.
67 Ibid.
68 11. "Japanese Customs," in ibid.
69 D'Abo and Cork, *Bond Girls Are Forever*, 42.
70 Ibid.
71 John Cork and Collin Stutz, *James Bond Encyclopedia* (London: DK Adult, 2007), 100.
72 "13. A Drop In The Ocean," *You Only Live Twice*, special ed. DVD.
73 Gary Giblin and Lisa Neyhouse, "James Bond and the Feminist Mistake," July 5, 2000, http://www.secretintel.com/features/feminist1.html.
74 16. "Little Nelly," *You Only Live Twice*, special ed. DVD.
75 Ibid.
76 21. "Becoming Japanese," in ibid.
77 Cork and Scivally, *The Legacy*, 97.
78 22. "Sweet Taste Of Death," *You Only Live Twice*, special ed. DVD.
79 "The Bond Files; James Bond."
80 Gilliatt, "The Current Cinema: Nether Villainy."
81 Brosnan, *James Bond in the Cinema*, 141.
82 Giblin and Neyhouse, "James Bond and the Feminist Mistake."
83 D'Abo and Cork, *Bond Girls Are Forever*, 42.
84 Dahl, "007's Oriental Eyefuls," 87.
85 Pfeiffer and Worrall, *The Essential Bond*, 60.
86 Cork and Stutz, *James Bond Encyclopedia*, 42.
87 "Killing Off Bond Again."
88 12. "Spicy Dealings," *You Only Live Twice*, special ed. DVD.
89 Brosnan, *James Bond in the Cinema*, 135.
90 15. "For England . . ." *You Only Live Twice*, special ed. DVD.
91 Ibid.
92 Ibid.
93 Ibid.
94 Dahl, "007's Oriental Eyefuls," 87.
95 15. "For England . . ." *You Only Live Twice*, special ed. DVD.
96 Ibid.

97 Brosnan, *James Bond in the Cinema*, 135.
98 15. "For England . . ." *You Only Live Twice*, special ed. DVD.
99 19. "The Strickest Orders," in ibid.
100 Gilliatt, "The Current Cinema: Nether Villainy."
101 "Killing Off Bond Again."
102 D'Abo and Cork, *Bond Girls Are Forever*, 42.
103 Giblin and Neyhouse, "James Bond and the Feminist Mistake."
104 D'Abo and Cork, *Bond Girls Are Forever*, 42.
105 "Killing Off Bond Again."
106 23. "Mrs. Bond," *You Only Live Twice*, special ed. DVD.
107 Brosnan, *James Bond in the Cinema*, 142.
108 24. "Strictly Business," *You Only Live Twice*, special ed. DVD.
109 25. "'Honeymoon's Over,'" in ibid.
110 26. "A Fly On The Wall," in ibid.
111 Ibid.
112 Giblin and Neyhouse, "James Bond and the Feminist Mistake."
113 Ibid.
114 31. "Imminent Destruction," *You Only Live Twice*, special ed. DVD.
115 Giblin and Neyhouse, "James Bond and the Feminist Mistake."
116 D'Abo and Cork, *Bond Girls Are Forever*, 42.
117 Bosley Crowther, "Screen: Sayonara, 007: Connery Is at It Again as Whatshisname," *New York Times*, June 14, 1967, 40.
118 Gilliatt, "The Current Cinema: Nether Villainy."
119 Pauline Kael, "Movies: Consumer Guidance," *New Republic*, July 15, 1967, 27.
120 "006 ¾."
121 Crowther, "Screen: Sayonara, 007." Connery, was not "that sleek, greasy-lipped dummy of the earlier films[.]" Kael, "Movies: Consumer Guidance."
122 Paul D. Zimmerman, "Unredeemed Bond," *Newsweek*, June 26, 1967, 73. A *New Yorker* review described as Connery as "deflated. Once dashing in himself, he has become the instrument of dashing production ideas." Gilliatt, "The Current Cinema: Nether Villainy."
123 Richard Corliss, "Bond Keeps Up His Silver Streak After 25 Years, the 007 Formula Remains Stirring But Not Shaken," *Time*, August 10, 1987, 54+.
124 Simon Winder, "Her Majesty's Sacred Service," *New York Times*, November 18, 2006, A17. Yet *You Only Live Twice*, "for all its brilliance and ritualized fun, lack[ed] that sense of absurd surprise that gave the early pictures such punch." Paul D. Zimmerman, "Unredeemed Bond," *Newsweek*, June 26, 1967, 73.
125 Patrick Macnee, nar., "Inside *On Her Majesty's Secret Service,*" directed by John Cork, *On Her Majesty's Secret Service,* special ed. DVD, directed by Peter R. Hunt (1969; Santa Monica, CA: MGM Home Entertainment, 2000).
126 Brosnan, *James Bond in the Cinema*, 152-53.
127 Cork and Scivally, *The Legacy*, 115.

128 Macnee, nar., "Inside *On Her Majesty's Secret Service*—An Original Documentary," *On Her Majesty's Secret Service*, special ed. DVD. According to one critic, "Connery's sense of timing [wa]s as right as Bond's. It's time to quit." Paul D. Zimmerman, "Unredeemed Bond."

129 Cork and Scivally, *The Legacy*, 111.

130 Ibid., 118.

131 Macnee, nar., "Inside *On Her Majesty's Secret Service*—An Original Documentary," *On Her Majesty's Secret Service*, special ed. DVD.

132 Cork and Scivally, *The Legacy*, 115.

133 Brosnan, *James Bond in the Cinema*, 151-52.

134 Macnee, nar., "Inside *On Her Majesty's Secret Service*—An Original Documentary," *On Her Majesty's Secret Service*, special ed. DVD.

135 Brosnan, *James Bond in the Cinema*, 152.

136 Cork and Scivally, *The Legacy*, 118.

137 Kael, "Movies: Consumer Guidance."

138 Andrew Rissik, "James Bond: From Action Man to a Slapstick Puppet Hero," *Times* (U.K.), February 2, 1980, 12.

139 Quoted in Cork and Scivally, *The Legacy*, 122.

140 Brosnan, *James Bond in the Cinema*, 152.

141 "On Her Majesty's Secret Service," *Times* (U.K.), December 18, 1969, 13.

142 Jay Cocks, "Looney Tune," *Time*, January 10, 1972, 50.

143 "New 007 Film Top Money Maker in Britain," *Times* (U.K.), December 7, 1970, 3.

144 Peter Davalle, ed., "Broadcasting Guide: Personal Choice," *Times* (U.K.), September 4, 1978, 23.

145 D'Abo and Cork, *Bond Girls Are Forever*, 45.

146 "On Her Majesty's Secret Service."

147 A.H. Weiler, "Screen: New James Bond," *New York Times*, December 19, 1969, 68.

148 Judy Klemesrud, "Where Are All the Women Who Fell for 007?" *New York Times*, June 21, 1981, D17; Barnes and Hearn, *Kiss Kiss Bang! Bang!*, 83.

149 Tony Bennett and Janet Woollacott, *Bond and Beyond: The Political Career of a Popular Hero* (London: Palgrave Macmillan, 1987), 197.

150 Rubin, *The Complete James Bond Movie Encyclopedia*, 349.

151 Rye, *The James Bond Girls*, 23.

152 "On Her Majesty's Secret Service."

153 Vincent Canby, "The Ten Worst Films of 1969," *New York Times*, January 4, 1970, 81.

154 11. "Break-In," *On Her Majesty's Secret Service*, special ed. DVD.

155 D'Abo and Cork, *Bond Girls Are Forever*, 47.

156 19. "A Madman's Plan," *On Her Majesty's Secret Service*, special ed. DVD.

157 15. "The Alpine Room," in ibid.

158 Chapman, *Licence to Thrill*, 143.

159 Angela Scoular, who had suffered from alcoholism, depression, and had battled bowel cancer, "ended her life by drinking drain cleaner and pouring it over herself."

"Death By Drinking Drain Cleaner 'Was Not Suicide,'" *Herald* (Scotland), July 21, 2011, at 5. In addition to her role as Ruby Bartlett, Scoular portrayed Buttercup in the 1967 version of *Casino Royale*. Tom Pettifor, "Leslie Phillips' Wife in 'Cancer Suicide,'" *Mirror* (U.K.), April 13, 2011, at 25.

[160] 17. "Playtime," *On Her Majesty's Secret Service*, special ed. DVD.

[161] Ibid.

[162] D'Abo and Cork, *Bond Girls Are Forever*, 47.

[163] 27. "Help Wanted," *On Her Majesty's Secret Service*, special ed. DVD.

[164] 32. "End Credits," in ibid.

[165] Ibid.

[166] 19. "A Madman's Plan," in ibid.

[167] Ibid.

[168] Quoted in d'Abo and Cork, *Bond Girls Are Forever*, 45.

[169] Ibid.

[170] Cork and Scivally, *The Legacy*, 119.

[171] Brosnan, *James Bond in the Cinema*, 153.

[172] Ibid.

[173] *The Awakening*, which was condemned by Kate Chopin's contemporaries, Joyce Carol Oates, ed., *The Oxford Book of American Short Stories* (New York: Oxford University Press, 1992), 129, has become "a favorite text in women's studies and women's history classes" that is recognized today as an important work in the history of women's rights. Deborah G. Felder, *A Bookshelf of Our Own: Must-Reads For Women* (New York: Citadel, 2006), 79.

[174] Brosnan, *James Bond in the Cinema*, 153.

[175] 2. "Beach Rescue," *On Her Majesty's Secret Service*, special ed. DVD.

[176] Ibid. Apparently, producers "felt it necessary to refer to and attempt to 'send up' the Connery performance." Bennett and Woollacott, *Bond and Beyond*, 159.

[177] Barnes and Hearn, *Kiss Kiss Bang! Bang!*, 93.

[178] Patrick Macnee, nar., "Silhouettes: The James Bond Titles," *You Only Live Twice* special ed. DVD. The same theme is repeated when Bond, cleaning out his desk, discovers various relics from his previous missions. The appropriate soundtracks from the previous five films are heard in the background depending upon the item Bond examines.

[179] D'Abo and Cork, *Bond Girls Are Forever*, 45.

[180] 4. "Queen of Hearts," *On Her Majesty's Secret Service*, special ed. DVD.

[181] Ibid.

[182] 6. "Full of Surprises," in ibid.

[183] Brosnan, *James Bond in the Cinema*, 156.

[184] 6. "Full of Surprises," *On Her Majesty's Secret Service*, special ed. DVD.

[185] Ibid.

[186] Ibid.

[187] Ibid.

[188] Ibid.

189 Ibid.
190 7. "Draco's Proposal," in ibid.
191 Ibid.
192 Ibid.
193 Ibid.
194 Ibid.
195 Brosnan, *James Bond in the Cinema*, 156.
196 D'Abo and Cork, *Bond Girls Are Forever*, 45.
197 7. "Draco's Proposal," *On Her Majesty's Secret Service*, special ed. DVD.
198 Ibid.
199 Chapman, *Licence to Thrill*, 141.
200 Ibid.
201 Ibid.
202 Ibid.
203 Ibid.
204 Ibid.
205 Brosnan, *James Bond in the Cinema*, 158.
206 D'Abo and Cork, *Bond Girls Are Forever*, 45.
207 Zimmerman, "Unredeemed Bond."
208 D'Abo and Cork, *Bond Girls Are Forever*, 47.
209 24. "Love To The Rescue," *On Her Majesty's Secret Service*, special ed. DVD.
210 11. "Break-In," in ibid.
211 25. "Wedding Plans," in ibid.
212 Ibid.
213 Giblin and Neyhouse, "James Bond and the Feminist Mistake."
214 Ibid.
215 31. "Mrs. James Bond," *On Her Majesty's Secret Service*, special ed. DVD.
216 Ibid.
217 Brosnan, *James Bond in the Cinema*, 176.
218 Barnes and Hearn, *Kiss Kiss Bang! Bang!*, 91.
219 Chapman, *Licence to Thrill*, 143.
220 Giblin and Neyhouse, "James Bond and the Feminist Mistake."
221 Quoted in d'Abo and Cork, *Bond Girls Are Forever*, 45.
222 Jack E. White, "Why We Now Can't Dig Shaft: A Black Knight Errant is Transformed into a Thug," *Time*, June 26, 2000, 72.
223 Melissa August, et al., "The 100 Worst Ideas of the Century," *Time*, June 14, 1999, 37.
224 Canby, "The Ten Worst Films of 1969."
225 Tony Nourmand, *James Bond Movie Posters: The Official 007 Collection* (San Francisco: Chronicle Books, 2003), 68.

0010
Shaken, Stirred, and Undeterred: The Antifeminism Movement and Backlash Across America

1 Robert Boyers, review of *The New Chastity and Other Arguments Against Women's Liberation*, by Midge Decter, *The New Republic*, November 25, 1972, 30.

2 Robert Orben, *2100 Laughs For All Occasions* (New York: Doubleday & Co., Inc. 1986), 218.

3 Quoted in Robin Morgan, ed., *Sisterhood Is Powerful: An Anthology of Writings From the Women's Liberation Movement* (New York: Random House, 1970), 35.

4 Feminist Yearbook," *Newsweek*, November 16, 1970, 113+.

5 "Women's Liberation Revisited," *Time*, March 20, 1972, 29.

6 Christopher Lasch, review of *The Better Half: The Emancipation of the American Woman*, by Andrew Sinclair, *Commentary*, April 1966, 104.

7 Gloria Steinem, *Moving Beyond Words* (New York: Simon & Schuster, 1994), 121.

8 Helen Dudar, "Women's Lib: The War on 'Sexism,'" *Newsweek*, March 23, 1970, 71. Of course, critics focused upon what they perceived as the absurdity of these karate workshops:

> The karate experts would like us to believe that physical differences between the sexes are merely a matter of different lifestyles . . . . But there has never been a culture of women that was as tall or strong as men. Either these women haven't read their biology or they discredit it because it doesn't fit their arguments.

Ibid., 75 (quoting Morton Hunt, whom the author described as "perhaps the most knowledgeable lay writer on sex roles").

9 Gloria Steinem, "What It Would Be Like If Women Win," *Time*, August 31, 1970, 23.

10 Steinem, *Moving Beyond Words*, 19.

11 Ibid.

12 "Liberating Magazines," *Newsweek*, February 8, 1971, 101-02.

13 "Women's Lit," *Newsweek*, April 26, 1971, 65.

14 Ibid.

15 "Liberating Magazines." Indeed, according to one editor of *Good Housekeeping*, the magazine's new fiction demonstrated that "when a woman has to choose between a career or marriage to find true happiness, sometimes the career wins but often it's home and family." Ibid.

16 "Women's Liberation Revisited."

17 "Women's Lit."

18 Ibid.

19 "Who's Come a Long Way, Baby?" *Time*, August 31, 1970, 17.

20 “Ah, Sweet Ms-ery,” *Time*, March 1972, 55.
21 Kate Miller and Casey Swift, “De-Sexing the Language,” *New York Magazine*, December 20, 1971, 103.
22 Elizabeth Peer, “Dirty Words,” *Newsweek*, February 4, 1974, 78.
23 Ibid.
24 Ibid.
25 “Ah, Sweet Ms-ery.”
26 Miller and Swift, “De-Sexing the Language.”
27 “Ah, Sweet Ms-ery.”
28 Ibid.
29 Judith Hole and Ellen Levine, *Rebirth of Feminism* (New York: Quadrangle, 1971), 226.
30 Michael Korda, “Liberation, U.S.A.,” *Newsweek*, July 16, 1973, 17.
31 Susan J. Douglas, *Where the Girls Are* (New York: Random House, 1994), 193.
32 “Ah, Sweet Ms-ery.”
33 Ibid.
34 Stefan Kanfer, “Sispeak: A Msguided Attempt to Change Herstory,” *Time*, October 23, 1972, 79.
35 Shana Alexander, “No Person’s Land,” *Newsweek*, March 18, 1974, 43.
36 “302 Women Who Are Cute When They’re Mad,” *Esquire*, July 1973, 82-83.
37 Ibid.
38 Hole and Levine, *Rebirth of Feminism*, 229.
39 Douglas, *Where the Girls Are*, 194-95.
40 Peter N. Carroll, *It Seemed Like Nothing Happened* (New Brunswick: Rutgers University Press, 1990), 271.
41 Douglas, *Where the Girls Are*, 203; “Big Bea,” *Time*, October 1, 1973, 66.
42 Susan Faludi, *Backlash: The Undeclared War Against American Women* (New York: Three Rivers Press, 2006), 161.
43 Douglas, *Where the Girls Are*, 211.
44 “TV’s Super Women,” *Time*, November 22, 1976, 69.
45 Douglas, *Where the Girls Are*, 213.
46 Ibid., 214.
47 Betty Rollin, “They’re A Bunch of Frustrated Hags,” *Look*, March 9, 1971, 15-16.
48 Ibid.
49 “Behavior,” *Time*, December 14, 1970, 50.
50 Rollin, “They’re A Bunch of Frustrated Hags.”
51 Robert Boyers, “Don’t Run Down the Sisterhood,” *New Republic*, November 25, 1972, 32.
52 Annette K. Baxter, “Is Gloria Steinem Dead?” *Newsweek*, September 2, 1974, 11.
53 Rollin, “They’re A Bunch of Frustrated Hags.”
54 “302 Women Who Are Cute When They’re Mad.”
55 Rollin, “They’re A Bunch of Frustrated Hags.”
56 Carroll, *It Seemed Like Nothing Happened*, 27.

57 Korda, "Liberation, U.S.A."
58 Joseph Adelson, "Is Women's Lib A Passing Fad?" *New York Times Magazine*, March 19, 1972, 26-27.
59 Rollin, "They're A Bunch of Frustrated Hags."
60 Linda Wolfe, "Free and Nervous," *Saturday Review*, October 21, 1972, 73.
61 Korda, "Liberation, U.S.A."
62 Adelson, "Is Women's Lib A Passing Fad?"
63 "Who's Come a Long Way, Baby?"
64 Ibid.
65 Wolfe, "Free and Nervous."
66 Ibid.
67 Rollin, "They're A Bunch of Frustrated Hags."
68 Ibid.
69 Ibid.
70 Jean Curtis, "When Sisterhood Turns Sour," *New York Times Magazine*, May 30, 1976, 15.
71 Joreen, "Trashing: The Dark Side of Sisterhood," *Ms.*, April 1976, 49.
72 Curtis, "When Sisterhood Turns Sour."
73 Rollin, "They're A Bunch of Frustrated Hags."
74 Judith Hennessee, *Betty Friedan: Her Life* (New York: Random House, 1999), 228.
75 Baxter, "Is Gloria Steinem Dead?"
76 Adelson, "Is Women's Lib A Passing Fad?"
77 Baxter, "Is Gloria Steinem Dead?"
78 Douglas, *Where the Girls Are*, 232.
79 "The Senate: Woman Power," *Newsweek*, April 3, 1972, 28.
80 Ann Scott, "The ERA: What's in it for you?" *Ms.*, July 1972, 82-83.
81 "Chronology of the Equal Rights Amendment, 1923-1996," http://www.now.org/issues/economic/cea/history.html.
82 National Counsel of Women's Organizations, "The History Behind the Equal Rights Amendment," by Roberta W. Francis, http://www.equalrightsamendment.org/era.htm.
83 Scott, "The ERA: What's in it for you?"
84 Phyllis Schlafly, *The Power of the Positive Woman* (New York: Arlington House, 1977), 11.
85 Carolyn Johnston, *Sexual Power: Feminism and the Family in America* (Tuscaloosa: University of Alabama Press, 1992), 277.
86 "Is Equal Rights Amendment Dead?" *U.S. News & World Report*, December 1, 1975, 39.
87 Joseph Lelyveld, "Should Women Be Nicer Than Men?" *New York Times Magazine*, April 17, 1977, 126.
88 Carol Felsenthal, *The Sweetheart of the Silent Majority: The Biography of Phyllis Schlafly* (New York: Doubleday, 1981), 235-39.

89 Douglas, *Where the Girls Are*, 235; Carroll, *It Seemed Like Nothing Happened*, 268.

90 "Chronology of the Equal Rights Amendment, 1923-1996."

91 Carroll, *It Seemed Like Nothing Happened*, 271.

92 Baxter, "Is Gloria Steinem Dead?"

93 Ibid.

94 Adelson, "Is Women's Lib A Passing Fad?"

95 Margaret Walters, *Feminism: A Very Short Introduction* (New York: Oxford University Press, 2006), 137.

96 Faludi, *Backlash*, 464.

97 Betty W. Taylor, Sharon Rush and Robert John Munro, *Feminist Jurisprudence, Women and the Law: Critical Essays, Research Agenda, and Bibliography* (Littleton, CO: Fred B. Rothman & Co., 1998), 180.

98 Jessica Valenti, *Full Frontal Feminism: A Young Women's Guide to Why Feminism Matters* (Emeryvilly, CA: Seal Press, 2007), 3.

99 Christina Hoff Sommers, *Who Stole Feminism?: How Women Have Betrayed Women* (New York: Simon & Schuster, 1995), 17.

100 Estelle Freedman, *No Turning Back: The History of Feminism and the Future of Women* (New York: Ballantine Books, 2003), xi.

101 Robin Morgan, ed., *Sisterhood Is Forever: The Women's Anthology For a New Millennium* (New York: Washington Square Press, 2003), lv.

0011
Refining an Archetype: *Diamonds Are Forever*, *Live and Let Die*, and *The Man With the Golden Gun*

1 Alexander Walker, *National Heroes: British Cinema in the Seventies and Eighties* (London: Harrap, 1986), 58.

2 John Brosnan, *James Bond in the Cinema* (London: Tantivy Press, 1981), 206.

3 Quoted in *Bond Girls Are Forever*, limited ed. DVD, directed by John Watkin (2002; Santa Monica, CA: MGM Home Entertainment, 2003).

4 Ibid.

5 Paul D. Zimmerman, "Bottled in Bond," *Newsweek*, December 27, 1971, 61.

6 Andrew Rissik, *The James Bond Man: The Films of Sean Connery* (London: Elm Tree Books, 1983), 85.

7 The film actually performed quite well, but it took approximately two years after its release to break even at the box office. Brosnan, *James Bond in the Cinema*, 179.

8 John Cork and Bruce Scivally, *James Bond: The Legacy* (New York: Harry N. Abrams, Inc., 2002), 126.

9 Patrick Macnee, nar., "Inside *Diamonds Are Forever*: An Original Documentary," directed by John Cork, *Diamonds Are Forever,* special ed. DVD, directed by Guy Hamilton (1971; Santa Monica, CA: MGM Home Entertainment, 2000).

10 Ibid.

11 Cork and Scivally, *The Legacy*, 128; Macnee, nar., "Inside *Diamonds Are Forever*: An Original Documentary," *Diamonds Are Forever*, special ed. DVD. According to director Guy Hamilton, Reynolds possessed "all the right elements for Bond." Patrick Macnee, nar., "Inside *Live and Let Die*," directed by John Cork, *Live and Let Die*, special ed. DVD, directed by Guy Hamilton (1973; Santa Monica, CA: MGM Home Entertainment, 1999).

12 Brosnan, *James Bond in the Cinema*, 204.

13 Macnee, nar., "Inside *Diamonds Are Forever*: An Original Documentary," *Diamonds Are Forever*, special ed. DVD.

14 Cork and Scivally, *The Legacy*, 131; Macnee, nar., "Inside *Diamonds Are Forever*: An Original Documentary," *Diamonds Are Forever*, special ed. DVD.

15 Peter Waymark, "Mr Connery Explains Lure of 007," *Times* (U.K.), April 12, 1971, 3.

16 Cork and Scivally, *The Legacy*, 140-41.

17 Brosnan, *James Bond in the Cinema*, 204.

18 "The New Face of 007," *Time*, January 8, 1973, 60.

19 John Russell Taylor, "The Birth of a Private Woman," *Times* (U.K.), July 6, 1973, 11.

20 Jay Cocks, "Water Pistols," *Time*, January 13, 1975, 5.

21 Paul D. Zimmerman, "Thunderbore," *Newsweek*, December 30, 1974, 56.

22 Cork and Scivally, *The Legacy*, 144.

23 Rissik, *The James Bond Man*, 55.

24 James Chapman, *Licence to Thrill: A Cultural History of the James Bond Films* (New York: Columbia University Press, 2000), 149.

25 Brosnan, *James Bond in the Cinema*, 180.

26 Maryam d'Abo and John Cork, *Bond Girls Are Forever: The Women of James Bond* (New York: Henry N. Abrams, Inc., 2003), 53.

27 Ibid.

28 Roger Greenspun, "The Tried and True Gets Tried Again," *New York Times*, August 19, 1973, 107.

29 Zimmerman, "Bottled in Bond."

30 John Russell Taylor, "1971: A Vintage Year for the Cinema," *Times* (U.K.), December 31, 1971, 7.

31 David Brudnoy, "Film," *National Review*, February 18, 1972, 172-73.

32 Gary Giblin and Lisa Neyhouse, "James Bond and the Feminist Mistake," July 5, 2000, http://www.secretintel.com/features/feminist1.html.

33 Zimmerman, "Bottled in Bond."

34 "007 Beats 'The Godfather,'" *Times* (U.K.), December 27, 1972, 2.

35 Zimmerman, "Bottled in Bond."

36 Waymark, "Mr Connery Explains Lure of 007."

37 Walker, *National Heroes*, 57.

38 Sean Connery was supposedly plagued by a "spreading pauch." Brudnoy, "Film."

39 Waymark, "Mr Connery Explains Lure of 007."

40 Quoted in Cork and Scivally, *The Legacy*, 137.

41 Brosnan, *James Bond in the Cinema*, 181.

42 John Cork and Collin Stutz, *James Bond Encyclopedia* (London: DK Adult, 2007), 119.

43 1. "Logo/Where Is Blofeld?" *Diamonds Are Forever*, special ed. DVD.

44 Ibid.

45 Ibid.

46 As one example of Bond's ineffectiveness, he is unable to distinguish (and understandably so) between the two Blofelds. One is Blofeld himself, while the other is a decoy. Bond decides to kick Blofeld's cat toward one of the two Blofelds and, in the process, actually kills the decoy. "Right idea, Mister Bond," the real Blofeld quips as a second white cat adorned in a diamond collar appears. 20. "Double Jeopardy," in ibid. "Wrong pussy," Bond acknowledges. Ibid.

47 "Film Review: Monday August 11th; Sean Still Sparkles," *Daily Record* (U.K.), August 9, 2003, 23. James Chapman characterized *Diamonds Are Forever* as the "most camp" of the films in the franchise. Chapman, *Licence to Thrill*, 159. Following closely behind is *A View To A Kill*, which has been described as replete with "camp and preposterousness." Craig D. Lindsey, "Bond Begins Anew," *News & Observer* (NC), November 17, 2006, 22. This view with regard to *A View To A Kill* is not unique. See Rich Copley, "To 'Die' For, *Lexington Herald Leader* (KY), November 22, 2002, 16.

48 Quoted in Andy Medhurst, "Batman, Deviance and Camp," in *The Many Lives of the Batman: Critical Approaches to a Superhero and His Media*, eds. Roberta E. Pearson and William Uricchio (London: British Film Institute, 1991), 115.

49 Luke Freeman, "Sean Connery's Hairpiece," http://commanderbond.net/article/1043.

50 Graham Dwyer, "Shaken, Not Stired: 40 Years of 007," *Daily Yomiuri* (Japan), March 6, 2003, 17.

51 Alan Barnes and Marcus Hearn, *Kiss Kiss Bang! Bang!* (New York: Overlook Press, 1998), 102.

52 Dennis W. Allen, "Alimentary, Dr. Leiter: Anal Anxiety in *Diamonds Are Forever*," in *Ian Fleming and James Bond: The Cultural Politics of 007*, eds. Edward P. Comentale, Stephen Watt and Skip Willman (Bloomington: Indiana University Press, 2005), 27.

53 Brosnan, *James Bond in the Cinema*, 200.

54 Graham Dwyer, "Sacred Agent 007: James Bond and His Entourage of Heinous Villains Are Cultural and Cinenatic Icons," *Daily Yomiuri* (Japan), February 3, 2000, 7.

55 Raymond Benson, *The James Bond Bedside Companion* (New York: Dodd, Mead & Company, 1984), 204.

56 Ibid., 205.

57 At the same time, *You Only Live Twice* was criticized for under-utilizing Donald Pleasance in the role of Blofeld. Moira Walsh, "Films," *America*, June 24, 1967, 81.

58 Allen, "Alimentary, Dr. Leiter: Anal Anxiety in *Diamonds Are Forever*," 27. At one point, Bond conceals himself from Franks by wrapping his hands around himself

in order to simulate kissing someone. This act, too, suggests that appearance is detached from reality. 7. "Killing Bond," *Diamonds Are Forever*, special ed. DVD.

59 28. "Cleaning Up The World," *Diamonds Are Forever*, special ed. DVD.

60 It is Q who initially informs Bond that Franks "has escaped—killed one of the guards on the way up to London." 6. "Proper Identification," in ibid.

61 7. "Killing Bond," in ibid.

62 Ibid.

63 Chapman, *Licence to Thrill*, 158.

64 13. "What A Circus," *Diamonds Are Forever*, special ed. DVD.

65 Ibid.

66 19. "The Trip Upstairs," in ibid. (emphasis added).

67 Brosnan, *James Bond in the Cinema*, 200-01.

68 "[A]ny similarity between Willard Whyte and Howard Hughes [wa]s purely coincidental," ibid., 188, but it is apparent that Hughes was an inspiration for the character. See Cork and Scivally, *The Legacy*, 126-28.

69 24. "Wild Kingdom," *Diamonds Are Forever*, special ed. DVD.

70 "Weird Aura of Howard Hughes Attracts Guests at $2,500 a Night," *Peterborough Examiner* (Canada), June 28, 2003, C3.

71 Allen, "Alimentary, Dr. Leiter: Anal Anxiety in *Diamonds Are Forever*," 24.

72 Cork and Scivally, *The Legacy*, 133.

73 Macnee, nar., "Inside *Diamonds Are Forever*: An Original Documentary," *Diamonds Are Forever*, special ed. DVD.

74 Ibid.

75 Anthony Horowitz, "Why Bond Does the Best Baddies," *Daily Mail* (U.K.), August 10, 2007, 15.

76 Steven Jay Rubin, *The Complete James Bond Movie Encyclopedia* (Chicago: Contemporary Books, 1995), 457.

77 Melanie Rickey, "A Diamond Geezer," *Times* (U.K.), November 6, 2002, 13.

78 Dwyer, "Sacred Agent 007."

79 Allen, "Alimentary, Dr. Leiter: Anal Anxiety in *Diamonds Are Forever*," 28.

80 Ibid., 29.

81 Benson, *The James Bond Bedside Companion*, 205.

82 Allen, "Alimentary, Dr. Leiter: Anal Anxiety in *Diamonds Are Forever*," 31.

83 31. "Bombe Surprise," *Diamonds Are Forever*, special ed. DVD.

84 Allen, "Alimentary, Dr. Leiter: Anal Anxiety in *Diamonds Are Forever*," 31.

85 Ibid.

86 John Stanley, "Daniel Mangin's 'Psycho Killers and Twisted Sisters': Gay Stereotypes in the Movies," *San Francisco Chronicle*, October 13, 1991, 32.

87 Paul Clark, "Spree for Two: More Assassin Teams," *Cincinnati Enquirer*, January 28, 2007, 7D.

88 Brosnan, *James Bond in the Cinema*, 200.

89 Allen, "Alimentary, Dr. Leiter: Anal Anxiety in *Diamonds Are Forever*," 41 n. 11.

90 Ibid., 32.

91 31. "Bombe Surprise," *Diamonds Are Forever*, special ed. DVD.

92 John Barry and Don Black, *Diamonds Are Forever*, Shirley Bassey perf. *The Best of James Bond 30th Anniversary Collection*, EMI Records USA compact disc E2-98413, 1992.

93 Ibid.

94 Ibid.

95 Benson, *The James Bond Bedside Companion*, 206.

96 Mark Edwards, "Waxing Lyrical," *Sunday Times* (U.K.), August 10, 2008, 30.

97 Chris Hastings, "Actually, Bond Girls Are Feminist Icons," *Sunday Telegraph* (U.K.), September 21, 2008, 3.

98 Jill St. John was the first American actress to portray a primary Bond Girl in the franchise. Graham Rye, *The James Bond Girls* (New York: Citadel Press, 1996), 27.

99 Macnee, nar., "Inside *Diamonds Are Forever*: An Original Documentary," *Diamonds Are Forever*, special ed. DVD.

100 Cork and Scivally, *The Legacy*, 128.

101 Ibid.

102 *Bond Girls Are Forever*, limited ed. DVD.

103 Thomas Berger, "Films," *Esquire*, June 1972, 61.

104 Zimmerman, "Bottled in Bond."

105 Ibid.

106 D'Abo and Cork, *Bond Girls Are Forever*, 126; Barnes and Hearn, *Kiss Kiss Bang! Bang!*, 99.

107 Cubby Broccoli and Harry Saltzman reportedly saw the pictorial and "immediately offered [Wood] a sexpot role" in *Diamonds Are Forever*. "Vegas Comes Up 007," *Playboy*, December 1971, 180, 183. Years later, *Playboy* again noted that Wood "came to producers' attention via our pages." "25 Years of James Bond," *Playboy*, September 1987, 124+, 125.

108 Jay Cocks, "Looney Tune," *Time*, January 10, 1972, 50.

109 Lola Larson, an Olympic gymnast, was cast as Bambi, although stuntwoman Donna Garrett had originally signed on for the part. Macnee, nar., "Inside *Diamonds Are Forever*: An Original Documentary," *Diamonds Are Forever*, special ed. DVD.

110 Thomas Berger, "Films," *Esquire*, June 1972, 61.

111 Zimmerman, "Bottled in Bond."

112 Quoted in Chapman, *Licence to Thrill*, 161.

113 Colin L. Westerbeck, Jr., "The Screen," *Commonweal*, January 7, 1972, 325.

114 Rubin, *The Complete James Bond Movie Encyclopedia*, 330.

115 Cork and Scivally, *The Legacy*, 306.

116 D'Abo and Cork, *Bond Girls Are Forever*, 53.

117 "The Bond Girls," *Playboy*, June 2000, 88.

118 11. "Plenty of Help," *Diamonds Are Forever*, special ed. DVD.

119 Ibid.

120 Ibid.

121 Ibid.

122 Ibid.

123 "Dinner With Plenty," in ibid.

124 Ibid.

125 Ibid.

126 Ibid.

127 12. "Breakfast With Tiffany," in ibid.

128 Ibid.

129 Ibid.

130 Ibid.

131 Ibid.

132 Berger, "Films."

133 Benson, *The James Bond Bedside Companion*, 205.

134 Ibid.

135 Ibid.

136 Brosnan, *James Bond in the Cinema*, 190.

137 Richard Corliss, "Bond Keeps Up His Silver Streak After 25 Years, the 007 Formula Remains Stirring But Not Shaken," *Time*, August 10, 1987, 54+.

138 Giblin and Neyhouse, "James Bond and the Feminist Mistake."

139 11. "Plenty of Help," *Diamonds Are Forever*, special ed. DVD.

140 Chapman, *Licence to Thrill*, 158.

141 Ralph Gardner, Jr., "No Aston Martin, But a Limo Will Do," *New York Times*, May 3, 2007, G2.

142 Cocks, "Looney Tune."

143 Westerbeck, Jr., "The Screen."

144 Benson, *The James Bond Bedside Companion*, 205.

145 Pauline Kael, "The Current Cinema: Saint Cop," *New Yorker*, January 15, 1972, 82.

146 Chapman, *Licence to Thrill*, 163.

147 Gloria Steinem remarked that "'[a] woman reading *Playboy* feels a bit like a Jew reading a Nazi manual.'" Quoted in "Cupcake v. Sweet Tooth," *Time*, March 20, 1972, 63. Thus, depicting the so-called feminist female characters in the film would have simply been anathematic.

148 Vincent Canby, "A Benign Bond," *New York Times*, December 18, 1971, 34.

149 Cocks, "Looney Tune."

150 "Women's Lib: A Second Look," *Time*, December 14, 1970, 68.

151 "Women's Liberation Revisited," *Time*, March 20, 1972, 39.

152 *Time* noted the extent to which lesbianism caused substantial damage: "Says one N.O.W. official: 'I have heard a woman called Communist, radical, bitchy, everything—and she can take it. But if anyone so much as breathes the word lesbian at her, she goes to pieces' . . . . [L]esbianism has been called the lavender herring of Women's Liberation." Ibid.

153 One critic would disagree with this observation, having described Bambi and Thumper as "a couple of scantily clad knockout bodyguards." Anne-Marie O'Connor, "Keeping His Eye On Earth and Sky," *Los Angeles Times*, July 13, 2008, F1, 6. O'Connor's characterization, however, entirely ignored Bambi.

154 Cork and Stutz, *James Bond Encyclopedia*, 39. Willard Whyte, however, suggests that Bambi and Thumper work for him. Regardless, Bambi and Thumper are not their own independent women and answer to a male superior.

155 Ibid.

156 24. "Wild Kingdom," *Diamonds Are Forever*, special ed. DVD.

157 Ibid.

158 Ibid.

159 Ibid.

160 Brosnan, *James Bond in the Cinema*, 195.

161 Greg Goldin, "Outside the Box: A Major Exhibit at the Hammer Museum Reestablishes—Once Again—the Reputation of Architect John Lautner," *Los Angeles Magazine*, August 1, 2008, 80+, 88.

162 Craig Kellogg, "Diamonds Are Forever: And so is John Lautner's Legacy—if the Hammer Museum, Los Angeles, Has Anything to Do With It," *Interior Design*, June 1, 2008, 178.

163 At least six people are "more or less drowned" in *Diamonds Are Forever*. Westerbeck, Jr., "The Screen."

164 Benson, *The James Bond Bedside Companion*, 205.

165 Giblin and Neyhouse, "James Bond and the Feminist Mistake."

166 *Bond Girls Are Forever*, limited ed. DVD.

167 Taylor, "1971: A Vintage Year for the Cinema."

168 Giblin and Neyhouse, "James Bond and the Feminist Mistake."

169 *Bond Girls Are Forever*, limited ed. DVD.

170 6. "Proper Identification," *Diamonds Are Forever*, special ed. DVD.

171 Ibid.

172 Ibid.

173 Lee Pfeiffer and Dave Worrall, *The Essential Bond* (New York: Harper Paperbacks, 1999), 78.

174 6. "Proper Identification," *Diamonds Are Forever*, special ed. DVD.

175 Ibid.

176 Ibid.

177 12. "Breakfast With Tiffany," in ibid.

178 6. "Proper Identification," in ibid.

179 Ibid.

180 Pfeiffer and Worrall, *The Essential Bond*, 78.

181 12. "Breakfast With Tiffany," *Diamonds Are Forever*, special ed. DVD.

182 Ibid. (emphasis added).

183 Ibid.

184 14. "The Next Link," in ibid.

185 7. "Killing Bond," in ibid. (emphasis added).
186 14. "The Next Link," in ibid.
187 18. "A Tight Squeeze," in ibid.
188 Ibid.
189 Ibid.
190 19. "The Trip Upstairs," in ibid.
191 25. "Blofeld's Escape," in I id.
192 Ibid.
193 29. "Any Sensible Animal," in ibid.
194 Ibid.
195 Ibid.
196 Ibid.
197 30. "'Stupid Fools,'" in ibid.
198 Quoted in Susan Daly, "Feminist Icons or Spy Candy?" *Irish Independent*, September 27, 2008, 14+, 14.
199 Vincent Canby, "The Bad Guys Are Black," *New York Times*, July 15, 1973, 101.
200 Macnee, nar., "Inside *Diamonds Are Forever*: An Original Documentary," *Diamonds Are Forever*, special ed. DVD.
201 Brudnoy, "Film."
202 Giblin and Neyhouse, "James Bond and the Feminist Mistake."
203 Macnee, nar., "Inside *Live and Let Die*," *Live and Let Die*, special ed. DVD.
204 Greenspun, "The Trued and True Gets Tried Again."
205 Taylor, "The Birth of a Private Woman."
206 Ibid.
207 Richard Schieckel, "Dirty Trick," *Time*, July 9, 1973, 40.
208 Ibid.
209 Brosnan, *James Bond in the Cinema*, 207.
210 Benson, *The James Bond Bedside Companion*, 207. *Live and Let Die* was Fleming's second novel and [was] written at a time when he was at the peak of his enthusiasm for both Bond as a character and the whole enterprise of being a thriller writer (late it would become a chore), and as a result it has a pace and zest that none of the other books can match. Brosnan, *James Bond in the Cinema*, 207.
211 Stanley Kauffmann, "Stanley Kauffmann on Films: Oil and Troubled Waters," *New Republic*, July 28, 1973, 35.
212 Schieckel, "Dirty Trick." John Cork and Bruce Scivally, however, noted that "[t]here were few raves for Moore's performance, but nor were there many pans." Cork and Scivally, *The Legacy*, 149.
213 Chapman, *Licence to Thrill*, 163.
214 Walsh, "Films."
215 Roger Greenspun, "The Screen: 'Live and Let Die' Opens," *New York Times*, June 28, 1973, 56. With the exception of a "few token black good guys, the film is white against black." Kauffman, "Stanley Kauffmann on Films."

[216] Canby, "The Bad Guys Are Black." "Fleming's treatment of the blacks in the novel is embarrassingly patronizing," and that "the film version of *Live and Let Die* . . . went out of its way to reflect the changes that occurred in American Black consciousness during the years since the novel was written." Brosnan, *James Bond in the Cinema*, 207-08. Instead, the film portrayed African Americans who were "*proud* blacks[,] and there's not a hint of patronization in the way they're presented." Ibid., 208.

[217] Rubin, *The Complete James Bond Movie Encyclopedia*, 242.

[218] Penelope Gilliatt, "The Current Cinema: The Wits vs. the Nitwits," *New Yorker*, July 9, 1973, 56.

[219] Schieckel, "Dirty Trick."

[220] Gilliatt, "The Current Cinema."

[221] Taylor, "The Birth of a Private Woman."

[222] Paul McCartney and Linda McCartney, *Live and Let Die*, Paul McCartney and Wings perf. *The Best of James Bond 30th Anniversary Collection.*

[223] Brosnan, *James Bond in the Cinema*, 211.

[224] Ibid.

[225] 48. "End Credits," *Live and Let Die*, special ed. DVD.

[226] Brosnan, *James Bond in the Cinema*, 211.

[227] 5. "Magnetic Closet Case," *Live and Let Die*, special ed. DVD.

[228] Ibid.

[229] Ibid.

[230] Achieving the special effect was a logistical challenge: "Amusingly, this scene required the services of an assistant director who, on his hands and knees and out of camera range, had to pull on a wire inside Ms. Smith's dress, and the costume designer, also on her hands and knees, who had to help pull the dress down." Brosnan, *James Bond in the Cinema*, 211.

[231] Benson, *The James Bond Bedside Companion*, 207.

[232] D'Abo and Cork, *Bond Girls Are Forever*, 54. Gloria Hendry's status as a Bunny has been emphasized in *Playboy*. See "Sainted Bond," *Playboy*, July 1973, 147+, 147.

[233] Brosnan, *James Bond in the Cinema*, 213.

[234] 15. "*Mrs.* Bond?" *Live and Let Die*, special ed. DVD.

[235] Ibid.

[236] Ibid. Bond's remark, which is another double entendre, also refers to Rosie's wig, which flies off her head after Bond tosses her onto the bed.

[237] Ibid.

[238] Ibid.

[239] Ibid.

[240] Ibid.

[241] Cork and Scivally, *The Legacy*, 146.

[242] 15. "*Mrs.* Bond?" *Live and Let Die*, special ed. DVD.

[243] Ibid.

[244] Ibid.

[245] 16. "Morning Fishing," in ibid.
[246] 17. "Future Teller," in ibid.
[247] 16. "Morning Fishing," in ibid.
[248] 18. "Double Agent," in ibid.
[249] Ibid.
[250] Ibid.
[251] The use of "sir" also has significant racial implications that are beyond the scope of this work but warrant consideration and discussion.
[252] The interracial overtones were controversial at the time, with United Artists expressing reservations about Bond engaging in sexual relations with an African American woman. Cork and Scivally, *The Legacy*, 146. Publicity photos featuring Roger Moore with Gloria Hendry adorned in a wedding gown also caused a stir. Ibid.
[253] 18. "Double Agent," *Live and Let Die*, special ed. DVD.
[254] Brosnan, *James Bond in the Cinema*, 213.
[255] Rosie is "shot by a voodoo scarecrow in the jungle while fleeing" from Bond. Benson, *The James Bond Bedside Companion*, 210.
[256] 19. "'Where is Bond Now?'" *Live and Let Die*, special ed. DVD.
[257] Benson, *The James Bond Bedside Companion*, 208.
[258] 17. "Future Teller," *Live and Let Die*, special ed. DVD.
[259] 19. "'Where is Bond Now?'" in ibid.
[260] Benson, *The James Bond Bedside Companion*, 208.
[261] Giblin and Neyhouse, "James Bond and the Feminist Mistake."
[262] Macnee, nar., "Inside *Live and Let Die*," *Live and Let Die*, special ed. DVD; Cork and Scivally, *The Legacy*, 146.
[263] Macnee, nar., "Inside *Live and Let Die*," *Live and Let Die*, special ed. DVD.
[264] Cork and Scivally, *The Legacy*, 144.
[265] Macnee, nar., "Inside *Live and Let Die*," *Live and Let Die*, special ed. DVD.
[266] Rubin, *The Complete James Bond Movie Encyclopedia*, 384.
[267] Greenspun, "The Screen."
[268] Brosnan, *James Bond in the Cinema*, 212.
[269] Benson, *The James Bond Bedside Companion*, 208. It is also possible that Solitaire is the victim of a "poor script." Ibid., 209.
[270] "Sainted Bond," 147.
[271] Brosnan, *James Bond in the Cinema*, 212.
[272] 19. "'Where is Bond Now?'" *Live and Let Die*, special ed. DVD.
[273] Greenspun, "The Screen."
[274] 11. "It's In The Cards," *Live and Let Die*, special ed. DVD.
[275] D'Abo and Cork, *Bond Girls Are Forever*, 54.
[276] 11. "It's In The Cards," *Live and Let Die*, special ed. DVD.
[277] Greenspun, "The Screen."
[278] 21. "Blasphemous Bond," *Live and Let Die*, special ed. DVD.
[279] Ibid.

280 Ibid.
281 Ibid.
282 D'Abo and Cork, *Bond Girls Are Forever* 54.
283 Benson, *The James Bond Bedside Companion*, 209.
284 22. "Out of Sight," *Live and Let Die*, special ed. DVD.
285 Ibid.
286 Ibid.
287 Ibid.
288 47. "Disarming Guest," in ibid.
289 16. "Morning Fishing," in ibid.
290 17. "Future Teller," in ibid.
291 19. "'Where Is Bond Now?'" in ibid.
292 25. "'Valuable Piece,'" in ibid.
293 Ibid.
294 26. "Cab Capture," in ibid.
295 30. "Unmasked Man & Plan," in ibid.
296 31. "Solitaire/Death Card," in ibid.
297 Ibid.
298 Ibid.
299 46. "Romantic Train Ride," in ibid.
300 Ibid.
301 D'Abo and Cork, *Bond Girls Are Forever* 54.
302 Ibid.
303 Ibid.
304 Giblin and Neyhouse, "James Bond and the Feminist Mistake."
305 Schieckel, "Dirty Trick."
306 Gilliatt, "The Current Cinema."
307 James Chapman, "Bond and Britishness," in *The Cultural Politics of 007*, 139.
308 Cork and Scivally, *The Legacy*, 149.
309 Benson, *The James Bond Bedside Companion*, 211.
310 Nora Sayre, "Film: James Bond and Energy Crisis," *New York Times*, December 19, 1974, 60.
311 Ibid. Raymond Benson opined that *The Man With the Golden Gun* was Fleming's "weakest" novel. Benson, *The James Bond Bedside Companion*, 211.
312 Gary Arnold, "The Latest From 007," *Washington Post*, December 18, 1974, C1.
313 Paul D. Zimmerman, "Thunderbore," *Newsweek*, December 30, 1974, 56.
314 Cocks, "Water Pistols."
315 Sayre, "Film: James Bond and Energy Crisis."
316 Benson, *The James Bond Bedside Companion*, 213.
317 David Denby, "Escapist Movie," *New York*, July 9-16, 1979, 91.
318 Chapman, "Bond and Britishness," 139. *The Man With the Golden Gun* did not perform as well at the box office as Roger Moore's debut film. Ibid. Together, *The Man With the Golden Gun* and *Live and Let Die* underperformed Sean Connery's

last film, *Diamonds Are Forever*, by $10.3 million and $3.8 million, respectively. Ibid.

319 Cocks, "Water Pistols."

320 Zimmerman, "Thunderbore."

321 John Barry and Don Black, *The Man With the Golden Gun*, Lulu perf. *The Best of James Bond 30th Anniversary Collection.* The theme song, which was composed by John Barry, was not very successful on the charts. Jeff Smith, "Creating a Bond Market: Selling John Barry's Soundtracks and Theme Songs," in *The James Bond Phenomenon: A Critical Reader*, ed. Christoph Lindner (Manchester: Manchester University Press, 2003), 118. The song was described as "singularly uninspiring." Brosnan, *James Bond in the Cinema*, 223.

322 Barry and Black, *The Man With the Golden Gun*, Lulu perf. *The Best of James Bond 30th Anniversary Collection.*

323 Ibid.

324 Indeed, the plot of the film demonstrates that The Man With the Golden Gun hunts for sport. Matthew Tedesco, "The Moreal Status of the Double-O Agent: Thinking About the License to Kill," in *James Bond and Philosophy*, ed. James B. South & Jacob M. Held (Chicago: Open Court, 2006), 113.

325 D'Abo and Cork, *Bond Girls Are Forever*, 57.

326 Barnes and Hearn, *Kiss Kiss Bang! Bang!*, 119.

327 The female characters, it has been suggested, were weakened by a deliberate attempt to mock Bond's sexual adventures. D'Abo and Cork, *Bond Girls Are Forever*, 57. However, it is apparent that the Bond Girls in *The Man With the Golden Gun* succumb to their own weaknesses and not anything that is directly attributable to Bond.

328 Arnold, "The Latest From 007."

329 Brosnan, *James Bond in the Cinema*, 224.

330 Arnold, "The Latest From 007."

331 Gary Arnold, "'Tis the Season to See Movies," *Washington Post*, December 8, 1974, E3.

332 D'Abo and Cork, *Bond Girls Are Forever*, 57.

333 *Bond Girls Are Forever*, limited ed. DVD.

334 8. "A Water Pistol?" *The Man With the Golden Gun*, special ed. DVD, directed by Guy Hamilton (1974; Santa Monica, CA: MGM Home Entertainment, 2000).

335 D'Abo and Cork, *Bond Girls Are Forever*, 57.

336 Brosnan, *James Bond in the Cinema*, 224.

337 D'Abo and Cork, *Bond Girls Are Forever*, 57.

338 Zimmerman, "Thunderbore." "The script allows Bond to beat up a woman . . . ." Gilliatt, "The Current Cinema."

339 D'Abo and Cork, *Bond Girls Are Forever*, 57.

340 Benson, *The James Bond Bedside Companion*, 213.

341 Maud Adams watched the scene with Maryam d'Abo during her *Bond Girls Are Forever* documentary interview. Of Bond's physical violence toward Andrea,

Adams remarked, "[Y]ou couldn't do that today." *Bond Girls Are Forever*, limited ed. DVD.

342 8. "A Water Pistol?" *The Man With the Golden Gun*, special ed. DVD.

343 Ibid.

344 19. "Man in the Middle," in ibid; Brosnan, *James Bond in the Cinema*, 224. This plot twist, however, is curious, particularly since Scaramanga displays a wax replica of Bond in his residence at which he discharges his weapon in the film's pre-title sequence.

345 D'Abo and Cork, *Bond Girls Are Forever*, 57.

346 Barnes and Hearn, *Kiss Kiss Bang! Bang!*, 120.

347 19. "Man in the Middle," *The Man With the Golden Gun*, special ed. DVD.

348 Ibid.

349 Ibid.

350 Brosnan, *James Bond in the Cinema*, 224.

351 *Bond Girls Are Forever*, limited ed. DVD.

352 20. "An Eye For An Eye," *The Man With the Golden Gun*, special ed. DVD (emphasis added).

353 Benson, *The James Bond Bedside Companion*, 214.

354 Cork and Scivally, *The Legacy*, 151; Patrick Macnee, nar., "Inside *The Man With the Golden Gun*," directed by John Cork, *The Man With the Golden Gun*, special ed. DVD.

355 Rye, *The James Bond Girls*, 35.

356 D'Abo and Cork, *Bond Girls Are Forever*, 166.

357 Cork and Scivally, *The Legacy*, 151.

358 Arnold, "The Latest From 007."

359 David Robinson, "A Trip Back to the Forest of Dean," *Times* (U.K.), December 20, 1974, 7.

360 Pfeiffer and Worrall, *The Essential Bond*, 98.

361 Brosnan, *James Bond in the Cinema*, 226.

362 Yet, the field experience that Goodnight possesses is trivial.

363 Chapman, *Licence to Thrill*, 175.

364 D'Abo and Cork, *Bond Girls Are Forever*, 57.

365 Brosnan, *James Bond in the Cinema*, 226.

366 D'Abo and Cork, *Bond Girls Are Forever*, 57.

367 Benson, *The James Bond Bedside Companion*, 214 (emphasis added).

368 7. "Lady Killer," *The Man With the Golden Gun*, special ed. DVD.

369 Ibid.

370 13. "Hungry to Bed," in ibid.

371 D'Abo and Cork, *Bond Girls Are Forever*, 57.

372 18. "This Moment," *The Man With the Golden Gun*, special ed. DVD.

373 Ibid.

374 D'Abo and Cork, *Bond Girls Are Forever*, 57.

375 19. "Man In The Middle," *The Man With the Golden Gun*, special ed. DVD.

376 Ibid.
377 D'Abo and Cork, *Bond Girls Are Forever*, 57.
378 19. "Man In The Middle," *The Man With the Golden Gun*, special ed. DVD.
379 Ibid.
380 Benson, *The James Bond Bedside Companion*, 214.
381 Brosnan, *James Bond in the Cinema*, 227.
382 D'Abo and Cork, *Bond Girls Are Forever*, 57.
383 Brosnan, *James Bond in the Cinema*, 229.
384 29. "Island Escape," *The Man With the Golden Gun*, special ed. DVD.
385 Ibid.
386 Brosnan, *James Bond in the Cinema*, 230.
387 29. "Island Escape," *The Man With the Golden Gun*, special ed. DVD.
388 Ibid.
389 Ibid.
390 Ibid.
391 D'Abo and Cork, *Bond Girls Are Forever*, 57.
392 7. "Lady Killer," *The Man With the Golden Gun*, special ed. DVD.
393 Ibid.
394 Benson, *The James Bond Bedside Companion*, 214.
395 26. "A Killer Lunch," *The Man With the Golden Gun*, special ed. DVD.
396 Harry Saltzman had pledged his stock in EON Productions as a guarantee on his loans. Patrick Macnee, nar., "Inside *The Spy Who Loved Me,*" directed by John Cork, *The Spy Who Loved Me,* special ed. DVD, directed by Lewis Gilbert (1977; Santa Monica, CA: MGM Home Entertainment, 2000).
397 See Giblin and Neyhouse, "James Bond and the Feminist Mistake." Producers endeavored to balance "the humour the films needed and strong roles for the leading females." D'Abo and Cork, *Bond Girls Are Forever*, 57.
398 D'Abo and Cork, *Bond Girls Are Forever*, 57.

0012
Reconsidering an Archetype: *The Spy Who Loved Me* and *Moonraker*

1 Quoted in James Chapman, *Licence to Thrill: A Cultural History of the James Bond Films* (New York: Columbia University Press, 2000), 188.
2 Quoted in Maryam d'Abo and John Cork, *Bond Girls Are Forever: The Women of James Bond* (New York: Henry N. Abrams, Inc., 2003), 166.
3 Ben Macintyre, *For Your Eyes Only: Ian Fleming + James Bond* (New York: Bloomsbury, 2008), 144.
4 Raymond Benson, *The James Bond Bedside Companion* (New York: Dodd, Mead & Company, 1984), 215.
5 Dinitia Smith, "Albert Broccoli, Film Producer, Dies at 87," *New York Times*, June 29, 1996, 26.

6 Jack Kroll, "Down to 001," *Newsweek*, June 29, 1981, 72. Cubby Broccoli enlisted the assistance of his stepson, Michael G. Wilson, who has remained an important asset to the franchise. Benson, *The James Bond Bedside Companion*, 215.

7 Chapman, *Licence to Thrill*, 188.

8 John Cork and Bruce Scivally, *James Bond: The Legacy* (New York: Harry N. Abrams, Inc., 2002), 186.

9 "Image of the Week: Bond Rides Again," *Sunday Times* (U.K.), July 3, 1977, 21.

10 Steven Jay Rubin, *The Complete James Bond Movie Encyclopedia* (Chicago: Contemporary Books, 1995), 25.

11 Ibid.

12 Christopher Porterfield, "Giggles, Wiggles, Bubbles and Bond," *Time*, August 8, 1977, 58.

13 "Bond Strikes Again," *Sunday Times* (U.K.), September 4, 1977, 55.

14 Benson, *The James Bond Bedside Companion*, 216.

15 John Brosnan, *James Bond in the Cinema* (London: Tantivy Press, 1981), 256.

16 See id.

17 Cork and Scivally, *The Legacy*, 174.

18 James Chapman, "Bond and Britishness," in *Ian Fleming and James Bond: The Cultural Politics of 007*, eds. Edward P. Comentale, Stephen Watt and Skip Willman (Bloomington: Indiana University Press, 2005), 137. Raymond Benson enumerated thirteen of forty-six similarities between *The Spy Who Loved Me* and *You Only Live Twice* that had been identified by Saul Fischer. Benson, *The James Bond Bedside Companion*, 216-17.

19 Benson, *The James Bond Bedside Companion*, 215.

20 D'Abo and Cork, *Bond Girls Are Forever*, 59.

21 Equal Pay Act of 1963, Pub. L. No. 88-38, 77 Stat. 56 (codified at 29 U.S.C. § 206(d) (2006)).

22 D'Abo and Cork, *Bond Girls Are Forever*, 59.

23 Janet Woollacott, "The James Bond Films: Conditions of Production," in *The James Bond Phenomenon: A Critical Reader*, ed. Christoph Lindner (Manchester: Manchester University Press, 2003), 113.

24 Patrick Macnee, nar., "Inside *The Spy Who Loved Me,*" directed by John Cork, *The Spy Who Loved Me,* special ed. DVD, directed by Lewis Gilbert (1977; Santa Monica, CA: MGM Home Entertainment, 2000).

25 Benson, *The James Bond Bedside Companion*, 240.

26 2. "Deep Sea Hijacking," *The Spy Who Loved Me*, special ed. DVD.

27 Ibid.

28 Charles Taliaferro and Michel Le Gall, "Bond as Chivalric, Comic Hero," in *James Bond and Philosophy*, ed. James B. South & Jacob M. Held (Chicago: Open Court, 2006), 107.

29 2. "Deep Sea Hijacking," *The Spy Who Loved Me*, special ed. DVD.

30 Graham Rye, *The James Bond Girls* (New York: Citadel Press, 1996), 39.

31 Brosnan, *James Bond in the Cinema*, 239.

32 Marvin Hamlisch and Carole Bayer Sager, *The Spy Who Loved Me*, Carly Simon perf. *The Best of James Bond 30th Anniversary Collection*, EMI Records USA compact disc E2-98413, 1992.

33 Ibid.

34 4. "Main Titles," *The Spy Who Loved Me*, special ed. DVD.

35 Cork and Scivally, *The Legacy*, 175.

36 Lee Pfeiffer and Dave Worrall, *The Essential Bond* (New York: Harper Paperbacks, 1999), 112.

37 Patrick Macnee, nar., "Silhouettes: The James Bond Titles," directed by John Cork, *You Only Live Twice*, special ed. DVD, directed by Lewis Gilbert (1967; Santa Monica, CA: MGM Home Entertainment, 2000).

38 Ibid.

39 Ibid.

40 Cork and Scivally, *The Legacy*, 173.

41 Rubin, *The Complete James Bond Movie Encyclopedia*, 295. Naomi was described as a "stunningly beautiful assistant pilot." Pfeiffer and Worrall, *The Essential Bond*, 108.

42 Benson, *The James Bond Bedside Companion*, 220.

43 Macnee, nar., "Inside *The Spy Who Loved Me*," *The Spy Who Loved Me*, special ed. DVD; D'Abo and Cork, *Bond Girls Are Forever*, 163.

44 D'Abo and Cork, *Bond Girls Are Forever*, 172.

45 Pfeiffer and Worrall, *The Essential Bond*, 108.

46 18. "Arrival In Sardinia," *The Spy Who Loved Me*, special ed. DVD.

47 See Benson, *The James Bond Bedside Companion*, 220.

48 Rubin, *The Complete James Bond Movie Encyclopedia*, 295.

49 Brosnan, *James Bond in the Cinema*, 246.

50 D'Abo and Cork, *Bond Girls Are Forever*, 59.

51 Benson, *The James Bond Bedside Companion*, 220.

52 Brosnan, *James Bond in the Cinema*, 246.

53 D'Abo and Cork, *Bond Girls Are Forever*, 59. When a scantily clad harem woman presents herself in a subservient manner to Bond, he is immediately persuaded to remain overnight, justifying his decision as follows: "When one is in Egypt, one should delve deeply into its treasures." 8. "Desert Trek," *The Spy Who Loved Me*, special ed. DVD.

54 Steve Rubin, "The 007 'Girls': Are They In Bondage Forever?" *Los Angeles Times*, June 24, 1979, N45.

55 Macnee, nar., "Inside *The Spy Who Loved Me*," *The Spy Who Loved Me*, special ed. DVD.

56 Bruce Williamson, "Bonded Barbara," *Playboy*, June 1977, 106, 218.

57 Rubin, *The Complete James Bond Movie Encyclopedia*, 25.

58 Woollacott, "The James Bond Films: Conditions of Production," 112.

59 Rye, *The James Bond Girls*, 39.

60 Cork and Scivally, *The Legacy*, 310.

61 Macnee, nar., "Inside *The Spy Who Loved Me*," *The Spy Who Loved Me*, special ed. DVD.

62 Tony Bennett and Janet Woollacott, *Bond and Beyond: The Political Career of a Popular Hero* (London: Palgrave Macmillan, 1987), 195.

63 "Polyglotez-vous?" *Times Higher Education Supplement* (U.K.), July 29, 1977, 5. Janet Woollacott noted that this became a contentious issue:

> You have the traditional Bond girl image, which involves having the girl photographed in a bikini, in a bathing suit. This was something that took a certain amount of hassling with Barbara at the beginning. But it was something that was absolutely required because a Bond girl must . . . be seen within the Bond mold.

Woollacott, "The James Bond Films: Conditions of Production," 113 (quoting a 1976 interview with Saul Cooper at the Open University).

64 Woollacott, "The James Bond Films: Conditions of Production," 113.

65 Brosnan, *James Bond in the Cinema*, 240.

66 Quoted in Bennett and Woollacott, *Bond and Beyond*, 245.

67 Ibid., 198.

68 Susan Daly, "Feminist Icons or Spy Candy?" *Irish Independent*, September 27, 2008, 14+, 14.

69 1. "Logos," *The Spy Who Loved Me*, special ed. DVD.

70 Ibid.

71 Ibid.

72 Rye, *The James Bond Girls*, 39.

73 Woollacott, "The James Bond Films: Conditions of Production," 111.

74 Brosnan, *James Bond in the Cinema*, 240. Indeed, "Anya was constructed to be both the Russian and female equivalent to Bond . . . ." Bennett and Woollacott, *Bond and Beyond*, 196.

75 Woollacott, "The James Bond Films: Conditions of Production," 111.

76 Rubin, *The Complete James Bond Movie Encyclopedia*, 280.

77 11. "The Mujamba Club," *The Spy Who Loved Me*, special ed. DVD.

78 Ibid.

79 Ibid.

80 Ibid.

81 Ibid.

82 Rubin, *The Complete James Bond Movie Encyclopedia*, 194.

83 11. "The Mujamba Club," *The Spy Who Loved Me*, special ed. DVD.

84 Ibid.

85 12. "On Jaws' Trail," in ibid.

86 Ibid.

87 Alan Brien, "Custard-Pie World of James Bond," *Sunday Times* (U.K.), July 10, 1977, 37.

88 15. "Pyramid Headquarters," *The Spy Who Loved Me*, special ed. DVD.
89 Ibid.
90 16. "Q's Laboratory," in ibid.
91 Ibid.
92 Ibid.
93 Ibid.
94 21. "Underwater Attack," in ibid.
95 18. "Arrival in Sardinia," in ibid.
96 21. "Underwater Attack," in ibid.
97 22. "Aboard The *USS Wayne*," in ibid.
98 Christopher Porterfield, "Giggles, Wiggles, Bubbles and Bond," *Time*, August 8, 1977, 58.
99 26. "The Revolt," *The Spy Who Loved Me*, special ed. DVD.
100 22. "Aboard The *USS Wayne*," in ibid.
101 D'Abo and Cork, *Bond Girls Are Forever*, 59.
102 Janet Maslin, "'Spy Who Loved' A Bit Long on Bond," *New York Times*, July 28, 1977, 59.
103 Brosnan, *James Bond in the Cinema*, 255.
104 31. "Escape From Atlantis," *The Spy Who Loved Me*, special ed. DVD.
105 Brosnan, *James Bond in the Cinema*, 255.
106 Woollacott, "The James Bond Films: Conditions of Production," 112.
107 Arthur Knight, "*SR* Goes to the Movies: Getting Away with Murder," *Saturday Review*, January 1, 1972, 22.
108 Gary Arnold, "Bond Meets Barbie," *Washington Post*, July 13, 1977, C9.
109 Brosnan, *James Bond in the Cinema*, 256.
110 D'Abo and Cork, *Bond Girls Are Forever*, 59.
111 Pfeiffer and Worrall, *The Essential Bond*, 107.
112 Tony Chiu, "An Old James Bond Hand Produces No. 0011," *New York Times*, July 1, 1979, D17.
113 Benson, *The James Bond Bedside Companion*, 224.
114 Patrick Macnee, nar., "Inside *Moonraker*," directed by John Cork, *Moonraker*, special ed. DVD, directed by Lewis Gilbert (1979; Santa Monica, CA: MGM Home Entertainment, 2000). *The Spy Who Loved Me* was the most successful film since *Thunderball*. Rubin, "The 007 'Girls': Are They In Bondage Forever?"
115 Brosnan, *James Bond in the Cinema*, 259.
116 Cork and Scivally, *The Legacy*, 177.
117 Chiu, "An Old James Bond Hand Produces No. 0011."
118 Brosnan, *James Bond in the Cinema*, 222.
119 D'Abo and Cork, *Bond Girls Are Forever*, 61.
120 Gary Arnold, "Durable Bond," *Washington Post*, June 29, 1979, C1.
121 Cork and Scivally, *The Legacy*, 181. The film grossed $10 million within four days and, within another six days, had receipts exceeding $20 million. Ibid. *Moonraker*, in short, "made sack-loads of money," ibid., 183, and was the franchise's largest grossing film at the time. Benson, *The James Bond Bedside Companion*, 222.

122 Brosnan, *James Bond in the Cinema*, 257.
123 Vincent Canby, "Screen: 'Moonraker' Puts Bond in Orbit," *New York Times*, June 29, 1979, C3.
124 Jack Kroll, "An Energy Crisis For James Bond," *Newsweek*, July 2, 1979, 68.
125 David Ansen, "The End of Summer," *Newsweek*, September 10, 1979, 76.
126 Pfeiffer and Worrall, *The Essential Bond*, 116.
127 D'Abo and Cork, *Bond Girls Are Forever*, 123.
128 Macnee, nar., "Inside *Moonraker*," *Moonraker*, special ed. DVD.
129 D'Abo and Cork, *Bond Girls Are Forever*, 123.
130 Macnee, nar., "Inside *Moonraker*," *Moonraker*, special ed. DVD.
131 *Bond Girls Are Forever*, limited ed. DVD, directed by John Watkin (2002; Santa Monica, CA: MGM Home Entertainment, 2003).
132 Brosnan, *James Bond in the Cinema*, 264.
133 Vincent Canby, "Screen: 'Moonraker' Puts Bond in Orbit," *New York Times*, June 29, 1979, C3.
134 Judith Martin, "'Moonraker' Is Unsuited To Its Genre," *Washington Post*, June 29, 1979, 23.
135 Kroll, "An Energy Crisis For James Bond."
136 Rubin, *The Complete James Bond Movie Encyclopedia*, 285.
137 Charles Champlin, "James Bond Goes to Space," *Los Angeles Times*, June 29, 1979, C1.
138 Gary Giblin and Lisa Neyhouse, "James Bond and the Feminist Mistake," July 5, 2000, http://www.secretintel.com/features/feminist1.html.
139 Frank Rich, "Agent 007 Goes into Orbit," *Time*, July 2, 1979, 72.
140 Kroll, "An Energy Crisis For James Bond."
141 D'Abo and Cork, *Bond Girls Are Forever*, 172.
142 Susan Lardner, "The Current Cinema: Extravagance and Thrift," *New Yorker*, July 9, 1979, 75.
143 John Simon, "Tremendous Trivia," *National Review*, August 17, 1979, 1048.
144 Tom Hutchinson, "Bond Beset," *Sunday Telegraph* (U.K.), July 1, 1979, 14.
145 Kroll, "An Energy Crisis For James Bond."
146 Giblin and Neyhouse, "James Bond and the Feminist Mistake."
147 4. "The Drax Estate," *Moonraker*, special ed. DVD.
148 6. "Dufour-play," in ibid.
149 Ibid.
150 Benson, *The James Bond Bedside Companion*, 224-25.
151 D'Abo and Cork, *Bond Girls Are Forever*, 61.
152 6. "Dufour-play," *Moonraker*, special ed. DVD.
153 Ibid.
154 Benson, *The James Bond Bedside Companion*, 225.
155 Brosnan, *James Bond in the Cinema*, 267.
156 Benson, *The James Bond Bedside Companion*, 225.
157 Brosnan, *James Bond in the Cinema*, 267.

[158] D'Abo and Cork, *Bond Girls Are Forever*, 61.

[159] 6. "Dufour-play," *Moonraker*, special ed. DVD.

[160] Manuela has been likened to Paula in *Thunderball*, Rosie in *Live and Let Die*, and Goodnight in *The Man With the Golden Gun*. Benson, *The James Bond Bedside Companion*, 225. She is, in fact, most akin to Paula. Unlike Rosie, Manuela is not a double-agent.

[161] Rubin, *The Complete James Bond Movie Encyclopedia*, 43.

[162] Pfeiffer and Worrall, *The Essential Bond*, 117.

[163] 15. "Revelry In Rio," *Moonraker*, special ed. DVD.

[164] D'Abo and Cork, *Bond Girls Are Forever*, 61.

[165] Ibid.

[166] Pfeiffer and Worrall, *The Essential Bond*, 117.

[167] Jeremy Martin, "'Quantum' Mechanics," *San Antonio Current*, November 19, 2008, 35.

[168] Macnee, nar., "Inside *Moonraker*," *Moonraker*, special ed. DVD.

[169] Ricard Corliss, "Bond Keeps Up His Silver Streak: After 25 Years, the 007 Formula Remains Stirring But Not Shaken," *Time*, August 10, 1987, 54.

[170] The name Holly Goodhead "doesn't fit the character at all." Benson, *The James Bond Bedside Companion*, 224.

[171] Rubin, *The Complete James Bond Movie Encyclopedia*, 169.

[172] Rye, *The James Bond Girls*, 43.

[173] Karen Hershenson, "Female Bonding Bikini-Clad Beauties Behind the Film Legend Evolved into High-IQ Commandos," *Contra Costa Times*, November 17, 1995, 4.

[174] A. Francesca Jenkins, "The Status of Latinas at the Five Sisters," *Hispanic Outlook in Higher Education*, February 23, 2009, 18.

[175] Vassar College, "History," http://admissions.vassar.edu/about_first.html; Joanne V. Creighton, "Why We Need Women's Colleges," *Boston Globe*, May 21, 2009, 9A.

[176] David Abel, "Women's Colleges Face New Gender Issues For Some, Coed Status Becoming A Necessity," *Boston Globe*, October 10, 2000, B1.

[177] Vassar College, "History."

[178] Benson, *The James Bond Bedside Companion*, 224.

[179] Chapman, *Licence to Thrill*, 195.

[180] 4. "The Drax Estate," *Moonraker*, special ed. DVD.

[181] Ibid.

[182] Ibid.

[183] Ibid.

[184] 5. "Centrifugal," in ibid.

[185] 10. "Trailing Dr. Goodhead," in ibid.

[186] Ibid.

[187] D'Abo and Cork, *Bond Girls Are Forever*, 61.

[188] Chapman, *Licence to Thrill*, 195.

[189] 14. "Disarming Dr. Goodhead," *Moonraker*, special ed. DVD.

190 Ibid. This comment reflects the extent to which the CIA's "fall from public grace is now being reflected even in Bond's fantasy world." Brosnan, *James Bond in the Cinema*, 267. The CIA's reputation was greatly maligned during the Watergate scandal earlier in the decade and by the Church and Pike Committees in the United States Congress, as well as the President's Commission on CIA Activities Within the United States, also referred to as the Rockefeller Commission.

191 14. "Disarming Dr. Goodhead," *Moonraker*, special ed. DVD.

192 Ibid.

193 Ibid.

194 D'Abo and Cork, *Bond Girls Are Forever*, 61.

195 Brosnan, *James Bond in the Cinema*, 265.

196 16. "A Toothy Clown," *Moonraker*, special ed. DVD.

197 Ibid.

198 Ibid.

199 Giblin and Neyhouse, "James Bond and the Feminist Mistake."

200 *Bond Girls Are Forever*, limited ed. DVD.

201 31. "Globe Tracking/Re-Entry," *Moonraker*, special ed. DVD.

202 Hutchinson, "Bond Beset."

203 D'Abo and Cork, *Bond Girls Are Forever*, 61.

204 Brosnan, *James Bond in the Cinema*, 265.

205 David Ansen, "Nobody Does It Longer," *Newsweek*, June 13, 1983, 77.

0013
Reconciling an Archetype: *A Quantum of Solace* for the Next Generation

1 Ben Macintyre, *For Your Eyes Only: Ian Fleming + James Bond* (New York: Bloomsbury, 2008), 160.

2 Quoted in John Cork and Bruce Scivally, *James Bond: The Legacy* (New York: Harry N. Abrams, Inc., 2002), 317.

3 "Playboy Interview: Daniel Craig," *Playboy*, November 2008, 57+, 58.

4 Raymond Benson, *The James Bond Bedside Companion* (New York: Dodd, Mead & Company, 1984), 226.

6 Graham Rye, *The James Bond Girls* (New York: Citadel Press, 1996), 43.

7 *Bond Girls Are Forever*, limited ed. DVD, directed by John Watkin (2002; Santa Monica, CA: MGM Home Entertainment, 2003).

8 It appears that a female hoists a weapon in the title sequence for *Diamonds Are Forever*, but the image is brief and does not feature the entire figure of the woman.

9 Steven Jay Rubin, *The Complete James Bond Movie Encyclopedia* (Chicago: Contemporary Books, 1995), 123.

10 Jay Scott, "Plenty Moore of the Same; 007 Has Lost A Few Steps But Is Still in the Running," *Globe and Mail* (Canada), June 10, 1983, E1.

11 "Octopussy," *People Weekly*, June 20, 1983, 10.

Epilogue

1 Susan Daly, "Feminist Icons or Spy Candy?" *Irish Independent*, September 27, 2008, 14+, 14.

2 Quoted in Chris Hastings, "Actually, Bond Girls Are Feminist Icons," *Sunday Telegraph* (U.K.), September 21, 2008, 3.

3 Quoted in Bryony Gordon, "'I'm the Worst Bond, They Say,'" *Daily Telegraph* (U.K.), September 24, 2008, 23.

4 Harry M. Benshoff and Sean Griffin, *America on Film: Representing Race, Class, Gender, and Sexuality at the Movies* (Oxford: Wiley-Blackwell, 2004), 272.

5 Margaret Walters, *Feminism: A Very Short Introduction* (New York: Oxford University Press, 2005), 137.

6 Olive Banks, *Becoming A Feminist: The Social Origins of 'First Wave' Feminism* (Upper Saddle River, NJ: Prentice Hall, 1986), 81.

7 Quoted in Ginia Bellafante, "Feminism: It's All About Me!" *Time*, June 29, 1998, 54+.

8 Susan Faludi, *Backlash: The Undeclared War Against American Women* (New York: Three Rivers Press, 2006), 1.

9 Ibid., 61.

10 Ibid.

11 Jose Cardenas, "Where Are the College Guys?" *St. Petersburg Times*, February 5, 2007, 1B.

12 James A. Fussell, "National Polls Show That the Gender Gap is Widening," *Tribune* (San Luis Obispo, CA), October 31, 2004, H1.

13 Kira Sanbonmatsu, *Democrats, Republicans, and the Politics of Women's Place* (Ann Arbor, MI: University of Michigan Press, 2004), 64.

14 Ibid., 63.

15 The 1980 Republican Party platform advanced

> support [for] equal rights and equal opportunities for women, without taking away traditional rights of women such as exemption from the military draft. We support the enforcement of all equal opportunity laws and urge the elimination of discrimination against women. We oppose any move which would give the federal government more power over families.
>
> Ratification of the Equal Rights Amendment is now in the hands of state legislatures . . . . At the direction of the White House, federal departments launched pressure against states which refused to ratify ERA. Regardless of one's position on ERA, we demand that this practice cease.

The American Presidency Project, "Republican Party Platform of 1980," http://www.presidency.ucsb.edu/platforms.php.

16 Sanbonmatsu, *Democrats, Republicans, and the Politics of Women's Place*, 67. Republican support for the ERA apparently increased after the election. Ibid.

17 Christina Wolbrecht, *The Politics of Women's Rights: Parties, Positions, and Change* (Princeton, NJ: Princeton University Press, 2000), 3.

18 Barbara Letvin, "Women Band Together," *St. Petersburg Times*, February 7, 2010, 1F.

19 Janice Min, "Confessions of an Alpha Wife," *New York Post*, February 4, 2010, 39.

20 Victor Volland, "Women Mark Equal Pay Day, Releasing Figures on Disparity," *St. Louis Post-Dispatch*, April 4, 1998, 18.

21 Paul Begala, "End the Mommy Wars!" *Newsweek*, May 14, 2012, 18.

22 Laura Green, "Breach in Equal Pay," *Palm Beach Post*, May 21, 2012, 1A. Democratic political consultant Paul Begala described the comment as a "10-megaton explosion in the Mommy Wars." Begala, "End the Mommy Wars!"

23 Green, "Breach in Equal Pay."

24 John Holleman, "Rich or Poor, Mothers Deserve Our Gratitude Deck," *St. Louis Post-Dispatch*, May 13, 2012, U3.

25 Margaret Sullivan, "How Moms Make It Work," *Buffalo News* (NY), May 13, 2012, G1.

26 Ibid.

27 Nichola D. Gutgold, "Ginsburg Should Remain on Supreme Court," *Allentown Morning Call* (PA), May 29, 2012, A10.

28 Garance Franke-Ruta, "The Palin Effect? GOP Women Run in Record Numbers," *The Star-Ledger* (Newark, NJ), May 2, 2010, 7.

29 Women in Congress, "Assembling, Amplifying, and Ascending: The Decade of Women, 1992-2002," http://womenincongress.house.gov/historical-essays/essay.html.

30 "Women in Congress," available at http://womenincongress.house.gov/historical-data/representatives-senators-by-congress.html?congress=112. Representative Gabrielle Giffords of Arizona resigned in 2012, reducing the number to ninety-four. Ibid.

31 Daly, "Feminist Icons or Spy Candy?"

32 Chris Hastings, "Actually, Bond Girls Are Feminist Icons," *Sunday Telegraph* (U.K.), September 21, 2008, 3.

33 Quoted in ibid.

34 Ibid.

35 Ibid.

36 Daly, "Feminist Icons or Spy Candy?"

Appendix B

1 Ian Fleming, *Casino Royale* (London: Coronet Paperbacks, 1988), 38-39.

2 —, *Live and Let Die* (London: Coronet Paperbacks, 1988), 70-71.

3 —, *Moonraker* (London: Coronet Paperbacks, 1989), 78, 81-82.

4 —, *Diamonds Are Forever* (New York: MJF Books, 1984), 33, 35, 71.

5 —, *From Russia With Love*, in *A James Bond Omnibus, Volume 1* (New York: MJF Books, 1985), 75-76.

6 —, *Doctor No*, in ibid., 92, 94, 96.

7 —, *Goldfinger*, in ibid., 48-49, 179-81, 240, 317-18.

8 —, "From A View To A Kill," in *For Your Eyes Only* (London: Coronet Paperbacks: 1989), 15-16.

9 —, "For Your Eyes Only," in ibid., 68, 82-83.

10 —, "Risico," in ibid., 121, 130.

11 —, "The Hildebrand Rarity," in ibid., 159, 161-62.

12 —, *Thuderball*, in *A James Bond Omnibus, Volume 2* (New York: MJF Books, 1989), 117-18, 200.

13 —, *The Spy Who Loved Me* (London: Coronet Paperbacks, 1989), 19, 21.

14 —, "The Living Daylights," in *Octopussy & The Living Daylights* (London: Coronet Paperbacks, 1989), 113.

15 —, *On Her Majesty's Secret Service*, in *A James Bond Omnibus, Volume 2*, 42, 193.

16 —, *You Only Live Twice*, in ibid., 165, 174.

17 —, *The Man With the Golden Gun* (London: Coronet Paperbacks, 1988), 52, 55, 189.

Index

B

N

Q

R

S

V

W

X

Y

Z

Lightning Source UK Ltd.
Milton Keynes UK
UKOW05f0616060417
298487UK00018B/658/P

9 780985 99610